Ascension

St Helena

SOUTH ATLANTIC
OCEAN

Walvis Bay
Luderitz

Cape Town

Tristan da Cunha

Gough

S.W.A

Augrabies Falls
Roman's Drift

CAPE PROVINCE

Saldanha
Bay

Robben
Island

Simonstown

Cape Town

Matjiesfontein

KAROO

Knysna

Port
Elizabeth

0   50   100   150   200 miles
0   100   200   300 km

CW00706215

THE BEST OF
LAWRENCE
GREEN

THE BEST OF
LAWRENCE
GREEN

EDITED BY MAUREEN BARNES

TIMMINS PUBLISHERS
CAPE TOWN

This book is copyright under the Berne Convention. No portion may be reproduced by any process without written permission. Inquiries should be made to the Publisher.

First published by Timmins Publishers, 1985

ISBN 0 86978 279 7

Cover design and illustrations by René Hermans

Printed in South Africa by
Mills Litho (Pty) Limited
11th Avenue, Maitland

Set in 10 point Times Roman

Contents

Lawrence Green

To come upon Lawrence Green's work for the first time in the Eighties is to discover an Africa that has all but disappeared; an Africa gone so recently that we can still hear the faint echo of its fading heartbeat.

He was not a great writer (his journalistic background showed itself too clearly in his style), but he had the rare gift of being able to recreate an atmosphere. A Capetonian told me that at the time Green wrote of Cape Town and called it "Land of the Afternoon", that's exactly what it was.

"When I was young," he said, "Cape Town was a small, sleepy and peaceful place. There was no stress, no rush, no violence. It was always summer. And it was always afternoon."

Green's love of Southern Africa, its peoples, its oceans, its flora and its fauna, shines through to give warmth and humanity to his work.

He did not always personally recall the events of which he writes, but he made it his business to seek out people who did. He was an indefatigable traveller and, according to those who knew him, a great listener. Thus it is that in the thirty-three books he wrote over forty years, we frequently get glimpses of Africa as it was well over a century ago.

Green seemed always to have a sense of time running out, of an Africa which was changing before his eyes. What others took for granted, he recognised as fleeting, and recorded it for posterity. By the time he died in 1972, aged seventy-two, he had a devoted following of armchair adventurers to regret his passing.

These stories, the selection of which was wholly subjective, were chosen to give as broad a view as possible of Green's Africa.

Maureen Barnes 1985

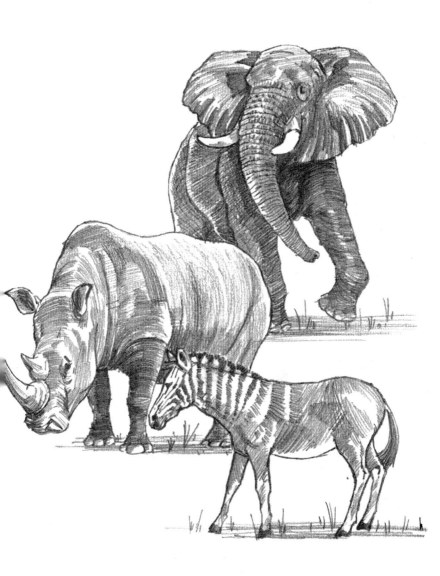

Animals

Since Lawrence Green wrote these tales of animals, much has changed in Africa and most of it for the worse where fauna are concerned.

When Green wrote in 1935 of the diminishing herd of Knysna elephants, about a dozen existed. These have now almost disappeared.

And the rumour that a herd of quaggas had been positively identified proved false. This gentle and defenceless creature, once prolific, is, alas, as dead as the dodo – about which Green also has something interesting to say. All that remains of the quagga are some pathetic remnants – the mounted skin of a foal can be seen in the South African Museum in Cape Town.

The passing years since these stories were written have improved the prospects for some species. The bongo and the okapi have thus far survived the ravages of time and man. And, happily, Green was wrong in his prediction that the white rhino – so rare in the Thirties that there was not a single one in captivity – was doomed. The species has since recovered. Instead, it is the black rhino which is now threatened.

To read Green's account of the springbok migrations, gleaned both from first-hand accounts and from local lore, is to feel the terror and excitement that was Africa.

The poignant message in Green's animal stories is even more relevant today.

Giants of the Jungle

1935

Strange creatures still remain to be found in Africa. How can we scoff at legends of mystery animals with the evidence before us of spoors, photographs, the reports of trustworthy hunters – yes, and even living specimens of hitherto unknown animals?

Remember please that the okapi was nothing more than a rumour until Sir Harry Johnston discovered it in 1900. An okapi is now flourishing on bananas and vegetables in the Antwerp Zoo. The bongo, regarded as a myth for years, was recently captured in North Kenya by Colonel Percy Smith. This rare antelope, with its long horns and brilliant chestnut body with white stripes, was shipped alive to London. Its home is in the Ituri forests, where dwell a race of pygmies who were themselves unknown for years after the Belgian colonisation of the Congo.

Then there is the quagga, a charming animal resembling the okapi in some ways and the zebra in others. Naturalists believed that the last quagga was shot half a century ago. The other day news came that a small herd has been definitely identified in a remote corner of South West Africa.

The Union government is taking steps to protect the quaggas from those ruthless modern hunters who set out in motor cars to kill every wild animal which has a market value. Dead or alive, a quagga would be worth a large sum – thousands of pounds alive, I should say – to any large zoo or museum. In the whole of South Africa, where thousands of quaggas roamed within living memory, there is now only one museum specimen. Boer hunters shot them mercilessly for their hides, and by 1870 there was hardly a quagga to be seen on the vast plains south of the Vaal River.

"Qua-ha-ha!" That is the cry of the quagga and the reason for the strange name. It most closely resembles the mountain zebra, but it is akin to the horse and the ass, too. The specimen in the Cape Town Museum is a light-brown foal; but full-grown quaggas usually have reddish brown heads and necks, with the under-body, legs and tail nearly white. High crests and standing manes give the quagga a handsome appearance.

The rediscovery of the quagga was made by a mine manager with long experience of the wildlife of Africa. He realised when he first sighted the quagga that when he reported his find the naturalists would say that he had confused the quagga with Burchell's zebra, with which it is often confused. So he remained silent until he could arrange a trip to the same spot with several friends. It was in a lonely, mountainous area of the Namib Desert, more than sixty miles from the railway line, and far from any farm.

On the second occasion he saw a herd of fourteen quagga at close range, and pointed out their distinguishing marks to his friends. The quagga were lighter in colour than zebras; and most important of all, they were striped only to the shoulders. Zebras are striped all over; and a herd of zebras in the vicinity made comparison easy and certain. The quaggas, it was noted, grazed apart from the zebras.

Many stories of the quagga having been seen in distant and unsettled parts of Southern Africa reach the museum authorities. Investigation usually proves that they are mountain zebras. The mine manager, however, could hardly have been mistaken; he anticipated criticism and made a careful study of the herd.

A living quagga was presented to the London Zoo by Sir George Grey in 1858. Quaggas were easily tamed, and made delightful and useful pets. They could be interbred with the horse; indeed two beautiful horse-quaggas were often seen drawing a phaeton in Hyde Park in 1826 – a queer sight which was recorded in the newspapers of the day. Long before that a tame quagga was kept at Windsor.

Tanned quagga skins, soft as silk, may still be seen with the hair scraped off in a few South African farmhouses. The flesh is delicious. On the old Market Square at Bloemfontein the wagons of the hunters used to stand loaded with quagga biltong, which was bartered for ammunition and provisions.

Some of Africa's lost animals are known only by their bones. It was only in 1932 that the first South African variety of kangaroo was identified. Dr W. Beetz, a geologist, at work on the famous diamond terrace at Kleinzee, Namaqualand, made the discovery of the fragments.

The importance of these remains of a creature no larger than a rat lies in the fact that marsupials are found living today only in Australia and South America – countries so far apart that naturalists cannot explain the migration. But with this new knowledge the theory that there was once a land-bridge between the continents – Lemuria some call it – is greatly strengthened. It is not too much to hope that a living specimen of the South African kangaroo may still be found in Namaqualand; for corners of this great territory of drought and diamonds are seldom visited by white men, and then only by prospectors. An animal the size of a rat, with long incisor teeth and a pouch, might easily escape the observation of such casual travellers.

Mr F. Grobler, a well-known South African hunter, brought such a queer tale to Cape Town in July 1932, that he would probably never have told it without a photograph to support him. This was the story of the weird monster known among the natives of the Dilolo swamps in Angola as *chepekwe.*

"I think it is a member of the dinosaur family," Mr Grobler told me. "Its weight would be about four tons, and it attacks rhino, hippo and elephants. Hunters have heard the *chepekwe* devouring a dead rhino – crunching the bones and tearing out huge lumps of meat. It has the head and tail of a lizard. A German scientist has photographed it. I went to the swamps in search of it; but the natives told me it was extremely rare, and I could not locate the monster. Nevertheless I am convinced the *chepekwe* does exist. Here is the photograph."

It was not a clear picture – photography in the primaeval jungles of Africa is always difficult – but it revealed something new to science. Certainly it was not a crocodile. The *Cape Argus* published the photograph, and most of the experts who joined in the subsequent controversy admitted that a few relics of prehistoric times might still linger in the remote swamps of the tropics.

That Africa was indeed a playground for giants of the animal world has been proved up to the hilt. A British Museum expedition

15

in Tanganyika excavated a dinosaur graveyard a few years ago. Many of the giant skeletons were perfectly preserved, and the bones were so numerous that the scientists were able to send specimens to a number of museums. More than one type was found; there were some that must have walked on all fours and others that held their enormous bodies erect, supported by the tail. It is possible, indeed, that some of these fossils were once flying lizards. Once again Africa's reputation as the land of surprises was demonstrated.

The dwarf elephants of the Congo were regarded as a myth until an expedition stumbled across one – a tiny female, not five feet high, but fully grown, tusks weighing two pounds.

Officers of the Victoria Nyanza steamers have described a long-necked prehistoric beast seen in the lake. The Barotses of the Zambezi declare they have encountered a monster which they call the Great One; and some white hunters who went in search of it returned with a report of a footprint seen in wet mud – a footprint five feet long. We know the. brontosaurus lived in swamps; and there are still swamps along the lonely reaches of the Zambezi which no white explorer has ever penetrated.

A hunting leopard of a new species was captured in Rhodesia only a few years ago. Possibly a "Nandi bear" will be trapped or shot one of these days. Selous, perhaps the greatest of all African hunters, believed in this ferocious beast. Reports of its crimes crop up persistently in several East African territories. Thus, when a native child is missing, the Nandi bear is blamed. When a native strolling in the forest suddenly finds that his scalp has been taken off by an animal in a tree, he runs back to the village shouting curses on the Nandi bear. All agree that the mysterious animal can climb trees. As a rule the Nandi bear leaves human beings alone, feeding voraciously on such pigs, goats or antelopes as it encounters. It comes out only at night.

While most of the evidence regarding the Nandi bear comes from native sources, there are a few more reliable descriptions. Major Braithwaite and Mr Kenneth Archer, well-known British hunters, saw a mysterious creature shambling away from them like a bear – a creature with dark brown hair. And Mr R. Hauser of Uganda once set poison for hyenas near Lake Alberta, and found an animal three times the size of the ordinary spotted hyena lying dead near the trap.

The head resembled a bear and the skin was yellow brown. An old witch doctor declared it was not a hyena, though he did not know the name of it. Mr Hauser took a photograph of the strange beast; but he lost both his camera and his elephant gun while crossing a river shortly afterwards. Fame still awaits the first man to bring in a Nandi bear, alive or dead.

Africa is saying farewell to giant animals which once crashed through the forests in enormous herds. The white rhinoceros is passing. Soon, when old hunters meet at the "Place of the Winds", they will speak of this great beast as a friend who has gone for ever "into the blue".

Only two fast-diminishing herds of these grotesque creatures of the dawn world now remain – one in the Sudan, the other in Zululand. Both are protected by the governments of those territories. But in the valley of the Umfolosi, in Zululand, some of the white rhinos – there were not more than a score all told – have died of starvation, following on a long drought.

In daylight the white rhino is almost as dark as the common black rhinoceros. You have to see a family of white rhino – bull, cow and one or two calves – at night to realise why they are called white. The skin has some peculiar quality which gives it a white appearance under the South African moon. A weird sight – this glimpse of the rarest land mammal in the world feeding on grass in the tropical bush country.

White rhinos are seldom seen while the sun is up – that is why so few photographs of them have ever been taken. They rest and sleep in the impenetrable bush all day, and go trotting off to water at sundown. It is said that white rhino are never found more than forty miles from a river.

Unmolested, the white rhino is a mild fellow. He lives in a dim world, with his clear sight limited to about twenty-five yards. Nature compensates him with almost incredible powers of smell. The hunter who approaches down wind is detected half a mile away. His hearing is acute, too, as baffled cinema men have discovered; the whirring of a camera is enough to send the white rhino galloping off beyond range.

No zoo in the world possesses a white rhino. In the past a few young ones have been captured, but they were too sensitive to live long in captivity. It would be impossible to capture a fully grown white rhino alive. When attacked by human beings they are infuriated to madness, and charge the first large object in sight. They have been known to dash into trees, burying their great horns in the wood.

The presence of a white rhino is often revealed by tick birds and egrets, which hover over the broad back or rest on it. The tick birds are the white rhino's danger signal – they set up a shrill chatter of alarm when human beings, or lions, are near. It is not known whether lions attack the white rhino; but the fact that the rhino walks with its head down and long horn thrust forward suggests an attitude of defence. The throat is a vulnerable spot.

Such are the doomed, mysterious survivors of this once-great species. The largest of them are about fourteen feet long, twelve feet in circumference, and more than six feet in height. They breed slowly – not more than once in four years. The world will not see their like again.

*

Elephants take us back to the dawn of the world. Other creatures of the darkness of prehistoric times are now known only by their bones. The elephant crashes trumpeting into our day as a surviving mammoth, the real king of all the animals, wise and brave and strong.

There are still wild elephants close to the southern tip of Africa – the famous dwarf elephants of the Addo Bush and the giants of the Knysna forests, only three hundred miles from Cape Town, the last herd of great tuskers south of the Zambezi.

Few people, even in South Africa, know the Knysna herd. You may spend all your life in the town of Knysna with never a glimpse of them. Yet they are there, in the cool green shelter of the remote forest; descendants of the legions that made their home among the tall stinkwood trees when the world was young. Out of all those untold thousands only eleven, perhaps thirteen elephants remain. Some of this last herd, no doubt, saw the first white men arrive with their muzzle-loaders. Long before that they escaped the poisoned arrows and pits of Bushman hunters. How long will they resist the advance of the woodcutters and the gradual destruction of their forest stronghold?

In the forest, seven miles from Knysna, I met a timber foreman – one of the handful of men who know the elephants. "They were rooting up the ferns in a kloof when I last saw them," he said. "Talking to each other with voices like turkey cocks, rolling in the mudholes, tobogganing down the muddy slopes with their feet together like great dogs. I was not more than three hundred yards away, but they could not get my scent – the wind was in my direction. For ten minutes I watched them at play; then I shouted. They all went swaying off blindly into the undergrowth, gaining speed like battering rams, the old ones urging the calves along, until they disappeared, still trumpeting and breaking down the young trees in their path."

On rainy days, sometimes, the herd leaves the forest to rove the open veld. Elephants detest heat, and the blind flies that worry them in the open on hot days. Also, they seem to know that they are less likely to encounter human beings in wet weather.

The foreman once found an elephant skeleton, with one tusk in the ground, broken, and the other missing – stolen by some poacher. Years ago there was a daring band of Knysna woodcutters who used to prey on the elephant herds. The ivory was smuggled away under loads of timber in ox wagons fitted with false bottoms. Elephant hunting was still permitted in the Northern Transvaal in those days; and there the poachers sold their tusks.

Major Pretorius, the well-known South African hunter, was recently allowed to shoot two of the Knysna herd for museum specimens. He found the herd in a patch of forest, sent beaters and dogs to a rise in the ground above the elephants, and waited with his huge express elephant gun. The dogs drove the maddened herd into the open, and Major Pretorius selected a magnificent old bull. The eighth shot brought it down. You can see this bull in the Cape Town Museum – a record specimen measuring twenty-two feet three inches long and twelve feet six inches high. Six more shots killed a smaller bull.

In Knysna men still talk of the Duke of Edinburgh's hunt in 1864. Old engravings in many homes illustrate that famous scene – the Duke, firing at an enormous tusker at a range of eighteen yards while his frenzied horse bolts. The Duke took two fine heads and skins back to England with him.

A fully grown African elephant is twice the size of the Asiatic species; and there is some foundation for the statement of the Knysna people that their elephants are the largest in the world.

So much mystery still surrounds the life story and habits of the elephant that it is not remarkable that the Knysna herd provides riddles for the people of the forests. There is a government station in the forest at Deepwalls. Year after year, sometimes on the same night each year, the whole herd crosses the road at the thirteenth milestone near Deepwalls. They remain in a lonely, burnt-out clearing for two days; then they return to their favourite abode at a place called Oubrand. No one can say what strange instinct moves them to make this regular pilgrimage.

·Even this small herd does tremendous damage in the plantations. They pull up the young trees in search of tasty roots, tear off branches, chew off leaves at the top, and sometimes make a combined attack on larger trees which one elephant cannot break down alone. A fire belt of young blackwood trees valued at two hundred pounds was recently destroyed in this way.

They seem to hate any man-made thing. They hurl wagons off the road, trample down loose stone beacons placed by surveyors, and carry off farm gates.

It is thirty years since the Knysna herd killed a man. He had foolishly pitched his camp on the elephant trail; and while he slept that night his dog attacked an elephant. Furiously the elephant charged the dog and crushed the sleeping man.

The woodcutters fear the elephants. When they are felling timber near Oubrand they always lash a rope ladder to a huge tree. Only a year ago the value of this precaution was proved; for a party of woodcutters were "treed" for two days. Of course there are many false alarms, and a famous practical joke is played by the woodcutters. One of the party creeps away from the camp at night, rolls a log down towards his companions, and blows into a paraffin tin. This reproduces exactly the terrifying noise of a charging elephant. The camp clears out, and the humorist is able to jeer at the men in the tree tops.

It is said that the Knysna elephants, at intervals of many years, go pounding across country for a hundred miles to visit their small cousins in the Addo Bush. There are between thirty and forty in the Addo herd. Scientists believe that they were once giants, like the

Knysna elephants, and that in the course of thousands of years they have become dwarfs to fit in with the low scrub bush which hides them. Most of them have lost their tusks during this process. At the beginning of the century the Addo herd was hundreds strong, and devastated many a farm. It was found impossible to keep the elephants within their reserve, forty miles long and twenty miles wide, and so the thunder of guns was heard in the bush and the elephants were thinned out. These attacks made the survivors more alert and irritable, certainly more dangerous than ever before. He is a bold man who goes hunting in the fastnesses of this dying race.

One of the most daring Addo hunters was a strange character named Crick – a man who lived in the bush for weeks on end for the sheer love of being alone in the wild. Crick once accompanied a farmer named Attrell on an attempt to capture a calf elephant. Attrell was caught by a cow elephant and crushed to death before Crick could get in the deadly brain shot. Crick never recovered from this experience. He disappeared into the bush and was found dead weeks afterwards, with a revolver beneath his body – one chamber empty.

Chains of fire have been used in recent years to prevent the Addo elephants from wandering out of their reserve. In hot, dry weather they become restless; nothing but fire will keep them away from the neighbouring farms. Occasionally they succeed in breaking through the flaming bush, and then they run amok on cultivated land, causing enormous damage. One cow elephant crossed the boundary early this year, wrecked the fence round a homestead and stamped the garden flat. Within an hour the elephant created a scene reminiscent of a cyclone.

Major Pretorius, the hunter mentioned earlier, shot eighty of the Addo elephants just after the Great War at the request of the authorities. The order was given reluctantly, for the value of this last herd of dwarf elephants as a sight for tourists was fully realised. Farming near the reserve, however, had become almost impossible owing to the frequent raids of the herd. Dams had been ruined, fences uprooted, irrigation canals destroyed. In the circumstances, the plan of thinning out the herd was justified. It was a nerveracking task, as one incident alone will prove.

Major Pretorius was accompanied on the hunt by a Brigadier-

General Ravenshaw, a distinguished officer of whose courage there could be no doubt. The general set out by himself one day in pursuit of a leopard, and the chase led him deep into the wilderness of the Addo Bush. Suddenly he found himself in the midst of the elephants. His beaters fled. General Ravenshaw was found dead – untouched. Heart failure had caused his tragic end; for there is no more terrifying experience in the world than to be alone, without an elephant gun, among an infuriated herd.

Mr F.W. Fitzsimons, the South African naturalist, who has studied these elephants for many years, believes that the thirty to forty survivors will perish unless they are provided with a proper water supply. It is when the wells of the reserve dry up that they go crashing over the farms to slake their great thirst.

Every farmer in the territory has stories to tell of chance encounters with the Addo elephants. One farmer, taking a load of forage to the nearest town by wagon at night, heard the elephants trumpeting along the road. They smelt the forage and began cautiously to approach the wagon. But the farmer was a man of resource. He seized a bundle of hay, set fire to it and dropped it on the road. The elephants stood back until the light they feared had died away. By firing more and more hay, the farmer reached safety – but he had little forage to sell when he arrived.

Another farmer named Pienaar was not so fortunate. He was out driving cattle when a lone bull elephant – one of the "rogues" of the herd – charged and killed him. If there were no rogues there would be little danger in the Addo Bush. Often a rogue will charge immediately it gets wind of a human being. The experienced hunter waits until this terrifying mass of deadly elephant comes thundering to within twenty or thirty yards before he fires. He has one shot only, and only a miracle will save him if he misses then.

It is said that the Addo elephants have a system of signals which they use when they are being hunted. Often, a herd of elephants makes more noise than an express train passing through a station. Their trumpeting could be heard easily above the roar of a liner's siren. But approach the Addo elephants when they are feeding, let the sentinel get wind of you – and lo! a shrill call goes out which puts every elephant on guard. They may stampede with the noise of an earthquake; or they may vanish silently into the bush with only a bough cracking here and there to show which way they have gone.

Stray elephants from Portuguese East Africa are seen occasionally in the Northern Transvaal; but the elephants of Knysna and Addo are the very last herds in South Africa. It is remarkable that even these small herds survive, for organised elephant hunting such as F.C. Selous knew was at an end in South Africa nearly half a century ago.

Before very long we may have to write the drama of the last great tusker's death in the South African forests.

*

In the Kaffrarian Museum at King William's Town there stands a hippopotamus which gave South Africa thrill after thrill for more than two years. For this enormous stuffed hide was once Huberta the Hippo – the famous roving hippo which was looked upon by white South Africans as a friend, and by natives as the reincarnation of a great chief.

Flags were flown at half-mast in Durban on the tragic day when the "assassination" of Huberta became known. Four farmers convicted of the deed were each fined twenty-five pounds or three months' hard labour. A wave of protest swept through the country, and a museum director wrote: "I have entirely despaired of human nature. There are some people who cannot see an interesting specimen without itching to take a pot shot at it."

How did Huberta the Hippo capture the affection of the whole of South Africa? It is a fascinating story. To realise the sensation caused everywhere by the appearance of Huberta, it must be understood that South Africa – apart from a few game reserves – is no longer a wonderland of big game. Thousands of people living in the cities have never seen the wild game of the country except in captivity. So when a full-grown hippopotamus strolled into the village of New Guelderland, fifty miles from Durban, the event received large headlines in all the newspapers.

Indians and natives working in the fields of sugar cane were the first to raise the alarm. They heard a snorting and a bellowing, and they ran for safety. The hippo remained until hundreds of people were staring wide-eyed with astonishment; then retreated into the thicket.

Undoubtedly this adventurous hippo had wandered from the Umfolosi sanctuary, near Lake St. Lucia, Zululand – the last-known breeding place of the hippo within the borders of the Union. At first she was named Billy by the special correspondents who rushed to the spot; but it was as Hubert the Hippo that she became a national character. It was not until after her death that the mistake about her sex was discovered, and she was renamed Huberta.

From the day of her first appearance until her death Huberta was a marked hippo. After she had startled the plantation workers at Guelderland she very quickly achieved notoriety. An enterprising press photographer went out among the sugar cane. But when he levelled his camera Huberta charged him.

Curious crowds flocked to see her. As they grew bigger they annoyed Huberta more and more and finally she moved off. From that moment began her journeyings which were to last two years and make her the most famous hippo that ever lived.

She moved first in the direction of Durban. As she approached the city she passed through areas which grew more and more thickly populated with every mile. Naturally the sensation she caused was enormous.

Yet she showed extraordinary cunning, for no one in the district ever caught more than a glimpse of her huge body. She travelled chiefly by night and spent the day wallowing submerged in the little rivers of the countryside. But farmers used to hear snortings at night and sometimes they found fences which looked as though a tank had charged them. Sometimes, too, they saw her and then the newspapers used to publish bulletins describing her latest movements.

As she approached Durban, which is one of the largest cities in South Africa, the excitement grew. "Hubert On His Way" stated the headlines (they thought she was a bull then) and people waited eagerly to see where she would make her next appearance. Of course, had it been necessary, an organised hunt could have put an end to her career then and there. But by this time Huberta was a public character. She had roused the amusement, even the affection, of the entire population. It had been proved that she was quite harmless. Occasionally she charged people who were too inquisitive. She had done a little damage to the farms across which she made her way. But nobody really minded this. It is no exaggeration to say that all South Africa was chuckling over the newspaper descriptions of her adventures.

Her greatest escapade followed. She called at an hotel just outside Durban one night, appeared suddenly and gave some of the habitués a severe nervous shock. After this, however, she decided that she was coming too closely into contact with civilisation. She made a wide detour and was not heard of again until she reached the coast, twenty miles south of Durban. Journeying on, she came to the mouth of the Umzimvubu River, near Port St. Johns. There she settled down for a time and lived happily on the river. But again her fatal curiosity got the better of her, and one night she visited the village of Port St. Johns. A town councillor, so it is said, was crossing the square to a meeting. He flashed his electric torch in front of him and saw the yawning mouth of a hippo. He did not attend the meeting!

Huberta sat down in the square and soon the entire population of the village turned out to see her. It was the most exciting thing that ever happened in Port St. Johns, or is ever likely to happen there. Huberta bore the shouting of men and women and the barking of dogs for half an hour. Then she left Port St. Johns, never to return. Her wanderings had begun again.

Huberta's odyssey now became a less pleasant one. The Bloemfontein Zoo had sent a party out to capture her alive. They were hard upon her trail. But Huberta by this time had lived upon the fringes of civilisation for nearly two years. She had developed amazing cunning. She passed through areas inhabited by natives and they saw not the least sign of her. Often she travelled extremely fast. She would be reported at one point and be fully thirty miles away next morning. She was still travelling south. She had crossed the border and entered the Cape Province, skirted East London and then plunged into the Keiskama River. This was the perfect home for the hippo, though no hippo had lived there for more than fifty years. However, it looked as though Huberta would settle there, and while she did her pursuers had little hope of catching her.

Then one day a farmer reported to the magistrate at Peddie near King William's Town that he had seen a dead hippo in the river. They went to the spot and with eighteen oxen and chains hauled out the body. It was Huberta with bullet holes above her eyes. She was a full-grown cow hippo nine feet two inches in length and with a girth of eight feet one inch. She must have weighed nearly four tons.

Every paper in South Africa published an obituary. Museums quarrelled for the right to preserve her hide. There was a popular outcry against the unknown marksmen who had shot her. Eventually four men made voluntary confessions. They were charged under the game laws and fined twenty-five pounds each.

Huberta will always be remembered with affection in South Africa. To the natives the stuffed carcass will remain an object of awe for generations. While she lived they quickly surrounded her with legends. To many of them she was the reincarnation of one of the great chiefs of the past who had come back to earth to lead the Bantu nation to the greatness that once was theirs. So strong was this feeling that the expedition from Bloemfontein which set out to capture the hippo was handicapped because its Basuto boys became infected with the local superstition and believed there was a spirit in Huberta and that they dared not lay hands upon her.

In the South African parliament a member asked the minister of justice what steps were being taken to bring the culprits who had killed the hippo to book. Everyone, he said, had been distressed to hear of the death of this famous national character (laughter). The Minister solemnly replied that he had ordered the police to investigate.

No hippo ever had as much publicity as Huberta. She might have had a more honoured death but perhaps it was as well she died. For she lived as hippos were never meant to live, a lonely beast wandering southward searching for the mate she would never find. Had she lived she must inevitably have been captured for a zoo. That was a fate her free and roving nature could never have endured.

GREAT AFRICAN MYSTERIES

The Springbok Migrations
1955

Those vast springbok migrations which devastated the karoo districts of South Africa almost up to the end of last century must have formed the most dramatic scenes in the whole world of mammals.

One cannot see everything, but I am sorry these cavalcades of fur and flesh occurred before my time. There was a *trekboer* once, a natural artist as a storyteller, whose tale gave me the human side of it; one of those tales which carried the ring of personal experience in every vivid detail.

This man had left the Transvaal with his family in the 1870s as a boy of ten. They were members of the first Thirstland Trek, a group of people impelled by real or imaginary grievances, and certainly by a restless spirit, to seek a new country. Many died in the desert. Some reached Angola. But this family of Van der Merwes broke away from the ill-fated wagons and headed south. They spent their lives trekking with their sheep and cattle in search of grass. When the old people died, the son Gert went on living the only life he knew; sometimes in Bechuanaland, in the Kalahari and often in the North West Cape. By the time he was twenty-one he had a wife and three children, two coloured shepherds and a Bushman *touleier* to lead the oxen and find the way from one water hole or vlei to the next.

One morning Gert van der Merwe's wagon was plodding along the dry, hard bed of the Molopo River where it forms the southern border of the Bechuanaland Protectorate. Gert noticed that the Bushman seemed worried about something. In the middle of the morning the Bushman left his oxen suddenly and ran off into the bush on the high northern bank of the river. At noon Gert stopped for the usual outspan and meal. His wife had just settled down to the cooking when the Bushman raced into camp and urged the party to inspan and follow him immediately. "The *trekbokke* are coming," the Bushman declared. "It will be death to stay in the river bed."

Gert packed up, wondering whether the alarm was justified, but remembering that he had his family with him. The Bushman led the wagon out of the river bed, up the north bank to a hill. Van der Merwe drove the wagon up the hill as far as the oxen would pull it. Then they went to the summit of the hill and the Bushman pointed.

At first Gert could see nothing unusual, but later he observed a faint cloud of dust along the horizon. It was miles away and did not suggest any great danger to him. However, the Bushman persuaded him to cut and pile thorn bushes as a barrier round the wagon and cattle. The Bushman explained that if the running springbok came over the hill instead of round it they would trample every living thing in their path to death. However, he hoped the thorn bush and the wagon would make them swerve.

After protecting his wagon and stock, Gert climbed the hill again. By now the dust was only a few miles away, rising high in the air and spread over a wide front. Gert's hill appeared to be in the centre of the oncoming game. Now, for the first time, he felt a little nervous, for he realised that anything could happen if such a stampede passed through the camp. So he ordered his wife and children into the wagon and made the dogs fast under the wagon tent. With the aid of the two coloured men and the Bushman he gathered heaps of dry wood and placed them in front of the wagon. By throwing green stuff on top of each pile he hoped to send up enough smoke to startle the buck and cause them to swing aside.

Gert waited on the hill summit. The buck were still hidden in their dust screen, but hares and jackals and other small animals were racing past the hill and taking no notice of the human beings. Snakes were out in the open, too, moving fast and seeking cover under the rocks on the hill. Gert and his men threw stones at the snakes that came too close, but the snakes seemed to be dominated by a greater fear. Meerkat families and field mice also appeared in large numbers.

At last came a faint drumming. No doubt the Bushman had sensed this drumming hours before, with his ear to the ground. Only now could Gert hear it. The cloud of dust was dense and enormous, and the front rank of the springbok, running faster than galloping horses, could be seen. They were in such numbers that Gert found the sight frightening. He could see a front line of buck at least three miles long, but he could not estimate the depth. Ahead of the main body were swift *voorlopers,* moving along as though they were leading the army.

When the buck came within a mile of the hill the Bushman ran to the wagon and climbed in despite the growling of the dogs. He was taking no chances. Gert and the coloured men then moved back, pausing only to light the fires. They remained with the cattle, which had sensed the danger and were milling round and lowing nervously. Gert's wife wanted him inside the wagon; but he was gripped by the vast spectacle and climbed on to the hood for a better view.

The first solid groups of buck swept past on both sides of the hill. After that the streams of springbok were continuous, making for the river and the open country beyond. Then the pressure increased, the buck became more crowded. No longer was it possible for them to swerve aside when they reached the fires and the wagon. Gert said he could have flicked the horde with his whip from where he sat on the wagon tent. Some crashed into the wagon and were jammed in the wheels, injured and trampled upon. The wagon became the centre of a mass of dead and dying buck; and Gert saw more biltong than he could have secured in a year's expensive shooting. But the thorn barrier had broken, and the buck were among the cattle. Before long the terrified, bellowing cattle stampeded and vanished into the dust in the direction of the river. Gert had to let them go. There was only death for anyone who ventured after them among the horns and hooves of the buck.

At the height of the rush, said Gert, the noise was overwhelming. Countless hooves powdered the surface to fine dust, and everyone found it hard to breathe. Gert's wife, who had been watching the rush with frightened interest, had to draw the blankets over herself and the children. The dust had almost smothered them. Everything in the wagon was an inch deep in pale yellow dust, and the coloured men had also turned yellow.

Within an hour the main body of springbok had passed, but that was not the end of the spectacle. Until long after sunset, hundreds upon hundreds of stragglers followed the great herd. Some were exhausted, some crippled, some bleeding. Gert wondered what had happened to the hares and jackals, and the snakes which had not taken cover in time. Next day he found the answer.

All night lone buck passed the wagon. The air cleared, but dust rose again when there was any movement in the camp. At daybreak Gert climbed the hill to see whether he could find his cattle. He had food, and there was a water-hole not far away in the dry river bed; but without the oxen he was stranded.

The morning air was so clear, the day so bright, that Gert felt for a moment as though the events of the previous day had a nightmare quality. Then he saw that the landscape, which had been covered with trees of fair sizes, green with food for his cattle, were gaunt stumps and bare branches. The buck had brushed off all herbage in their passing, and splintered the young trees so that they would never grow again.

Far in the distance Gert thought he could see a few of his oxen. After breakfast he set off with his men to recover them. Every donga leading into the river, every little gully was filled with buck. It seemed that the first buck had paused on the brink, considering the prospects of leaping across. Before they could decide, the ruthless mass was upon them. Buck after buck was pushed into the donga, until the hollow was filled and the irresistible horde went on over the bodies.

Other sights reminded Gert of the fate he and his family had escaped by accepting the Bushman's warning. Small animals were lying dead everywhere – tortoises crushed almost to pulp, fragments of fur that had been hares. A tree, pointing in the direction of the advancing buck, had become a deadly spike on which two springbok were impaled.

For a fortnight Gert camped on that hill beside the Molopo, searching for his cattle. He found half of them. The fate of the others remained a mystery. They might have been borne along by the impetus of the stampede until they fell and were trampled to death; or they might have escaped from the living trap far away from the wagon. Gert inspanned the survivors thankfully and the wagon rolled on, away from the scene of destruction. When he told the tale, it was clear that he regarded it as the most memorable episode in a life which he regarded as the finest on earth. *"Ons lewe lekker. Dit is vir ons heeltemal goed genoeg,"* declared Gert at the end of his story. "We live well. It is absolutely good enough for us."

*

Such was the experience which came unbidden to farmers and their families, usually in lonely places, though nowadays it is hard to find anyone who watched the stampede. There are legends which men heard from their fathers and grandfathers. I am never satisfied with a legend when I can find the living memory, so I sought more survivors, men in their seventies and eighties. Two of them were over ninety, and they had seen a lot; but they spoke to me in wonder of the *trekbokke*.

I know that the mighty elephants set out on slow migrations, sometimes in large herds. The great treks of the North American bison, the caribou moving northwards, were marvellous sights. The little lemmings of Norway, descending from their mountain homes in millions to lay waste the countryside, have been studied and discussed for hundreds of years. But the springbok also moved resolutely over wide areas in millions. They, too, were drowned in thousands when they came to rivers or the sea.

I once met a man who kept a store on the banks of the Orange River late last century. He saw the springbok form a living bridge over the river as they raced towards the Kalahari – "to reach better pastures," so he said. Many perished so that the main body might cross with dry hooves on their backs.

Then there was an ex-trooper of the old Cape Police named Cochran who had to patrol the south bank of the Orange River in 1897, along a fence put up in the hope of keeping the rinderpest out of the Cape Colony. Cochran saw the migrating springbok charge the fence along a front of five hundred yards and bring it down. The leading springbok fell and were trampled and crushed; and the stench was so revolting that a gang of Hottentots had to be employed digging trenches and burying the buck. "I collected two pairs of enormous springbok horns from the dead at the fence," Cochran told me. "They were so large that everyone wanted to buy them. Some of the young troopers with me flogged their souvenirs in the Upington bars for a few bottles of lager. I got six pounds for mine, but I should have taken them to England and given them to a museum. They were record horns."

That year, too, Cochran watched thousands of springbok trekking through Kenhardt village. Everyone in the place seemed to be shooting from his stoep. It was probably the most devastating migration within living memory. Police gave the alarm and distributed ammunition to farmers at half-price. The damage was tremendous, but it might have been worse. For the invasion ceased suddenly. The springbok horde turned and raced back to the Kalahari. It was said that rain had fallen behind them, and the north wind had brought them, over hundreds of miles, the irresistible smell of damp earth and young grass.

A farmer in the Calvinia district pointed out to me a plateau which rose gradually from the plain but ended in a precipice. Long ago, he said, the Bushmen saw thousands of springbok feeding there during a migration. They drove them cleverly towards the precipice, and then shot an arrow at one buck near the edge. As they expected, the panic-stricken wounded buck jumped over the precipice, and the herd instinct impelled thousands of buck to follow. Thus the Bushmen secured the greatest feast of last century. They sent word far and wide to the clans, they gorged and they danced. For years the bones of the springbok lay in deep depressions at the foot of the precipice.

Trained naturalists seem to have missed the springbok migrations. Thus the scientific picture can be built up only from hearsay and the scanty records left by farmers, hunters and travellers. John Millais painted the buck, but very few cameras were turned on the massed herds. Descriptions are vivid enough and tally extremely well until you come to the point where the observers try to explain the migrations.

The migratory springbok belonged mainly to the old Cape Colony. They were common in the Orange Free State and Transvaal, but the enormous herds were found in the Kalahari and the Karoo. Van Riebeeck and his men never saw a springbok. It was less than two centuries ago that the English gardener, Francis Masson of Kew, gave the earliest description of this antelope. Masson accompanied Dr Thunberg into a country called "Koud Bocke Veld" or "cold country of antelopes, so named from a species called springbok". Masson declared: "This animal when hunted, instead of running, avails itself of surprising springs or leaps."

During a later journey, Masson reported that since the Cold Bokkeveld had been settled by white people the springbok were no longer so plentiful. Once in seven or eight years, however, the springbok came in flocks of many hundreds of thousands from the interior, spreading over the whole country and not leaving a blade of grass or a shrub. Peasants were obliged to guard their cornfields night and day, or the springbok would cause a famine wherever they passed.

Masson remarked that the migrating springbok were always followed by lions. "It is observed, where a lion is, there is a large open space," he wrote. (A later observer declared that a lion borne onward by the avalanche of buck was crushed to death, though it left much evidence of its wrath.) Masson himself admitted that he never saw more than twenty springbok in a herd; but he met a party of Dutchmen who had been pursuing Bushmen, and they informed him that they had seen great flocks of springbok to the north.

Then comes the first of many theories. Masson thought the springbok were forced southwards by dry seasons. When rain fell they returned to the interior.

Thomas Pringle the poet formed the same opinion about half a century later, when he saw the face of the country near the Little Fish River speckled with springbok as far as the eye could reach. "We calculated we had sometimes within view not less than twenty-thousand of these beautiful animals," Pringle recorded. "They were probably part of one of the great migratory swarms which, after long-continued droughts, sometimes inundate the colony from the northern wastes."

Landdrost (afterwards Sir Andries) Stockenstroom of Graaff-Reinet wrote to the colonial secretary about the springbok in 1821, a great drought year. "They have come from the parched desert in such droves that all numerical description must appear exaggerated," he reported. "An eye witness can only believe the fact that farms have been left on account of the exhausted state to which they have been reduced by these animals, which rendered the support of cattle on the same farms impossible."

Stockenstroom also wrote to Pringle on the subject. "It is scarcely

33

possible for a person admiring the springbok thinly scattered over the plains to figure to himself that these ornaments of the desert can often become as destructive as locusts," he wrote. "The incredible numbers which sometimes pour in from the north during protracted droughts, distress the farmer inconceivably."

When the springbok approached (said Stockenstroom) the farmers surrounded their fields with heaps of dry manure, the fuel of the Sneeuberg, and set fire to it in the hope that the hordes would turn aside from the smoke. This seldom proved effective. Often the buck carried flocks of sheep along with them in the mad stampede, and the owners never saw them again.

Stockenstroom gave much thought to the mystery and stated boldly that although the farmers were baffled, he had solved the migration problem. The springbok, he pointed out, multiplied in the deserts to the south of the Orange River. There the herds were undisturbed save by an occasional Bushman hunter. Finally the desert swarmed with buck. Then a drought would leave the water holes empty and the soil parched. Thirst drove the springbok out of the desert, and they returned only when rain had fallen on their secluded plains.

That was Stockenstroom's view. Not long afterwards the hunter, Major Cornwallis Harris, saw the Griqualand West area "literally white with springbucks, myriads of which covered the plains." He summed up: "On the failure during drought of the stagnant pools on which the springbucks rely, they pour down like the devastating curse of Egypt from their native plains in the interior."

Sir John Fraser, whose father was the Dutch Reformed Church minister at Beaufort West in 1849, left a memorable impression of the springbok invasion of the village in that year. A *smous* drove into the village one day looking bewildered, and told the people that countless buck were on the way, leaving the veld bare. This report was not taken seriously. Soon afterwards the people of Beaufort West were awoken one morning by the trampling of all kinds of game. Springbok filled the streets and gardens, and they were accompanied by wildebeest, blesbok, quagga and eland. For three full days the *trekbokke* passed the village, and they left the veld looking as though it had been consumed by fire.

Some observers have stated that a migration usually started with small herds of springbok becoming restless and seeking their own kind. They gathered in larger and larger herds, moving as inevitably as the tides. Sometimes the *trekbokke* sauntered along their instinctive paths. The kids travelled in a sort of migrating nursery on one side of the main body of buck; and at intervals the ewes would visit them and suckle their young. Suddenly huge groups of buck would take fright and begin *pronking,* with backs arched, in twenty-foot leaps. Then came the stampede, all dashing along faster than horses and even more gracefully. They grazed hungrily but hastily and passed on leaving only torn earth. On the farms they broke through any wire fencing they encountered; though it was only towards the end of last century that they met this obstruction. Fearlessly they surged between homesteads and outbuildings. They filled the dams and trampled their drowning and their dead ruthlessly in the mud.

David Livingstone watched a small migration in 1875, and formed his own opinion. He discovered that the springbok often left their northern areas at a time when grass and water were plentiful. "The cause of the migration seems to be their preference for places where they can watch the approach of a foe," suggested Livingstone. "Oxen are often terrified in high grass. The springbok possesses this feeling in an intense degree and becomes uneasy as the Kalahari grass grows tall. Vegetation being scantier in the more arid south, the herds turn in that direction. As they advance and increase in numbers the pasturage gets so scarce that they are obliged to cross the Orange and become a pest of the sheep farmer in a country which contains little of their favourite food."

I found confirmation of Livingstone's theory in the more recent observations of G.W. Penrice, a naturalist who studied the springbok herds in the coastal belt of Angola. "At certain seasons they congregate in one vast herd and trek to some other veld where they again disperse into smaller troops," Penrice wrote. "One never finds springbok in country where there is high grass; they seem to like to be able to see all round. During one year of exceptionally heavy rain on the coast the grass grew very long, which resulted in all the buck trekking farther south to a more sandy veld."

The author and poet, William Charles Scully, was magistrate of Springbokfontein in Namaqualand when the last springbok migrations came that way. He, too, had a theory. He said that although the motive seemed to have puzzled hunters and naturalists from time immemorial, the explanation was really simple and obvious. Rain fell in Bushmanland in summer, but the winter was rainless. Bushmanland was bounded on the west by granite mountains rising from the sandy plain. "Here no summer rains fall, but in early winter the south-west wind brings soaking showers, and the sandy plains lying among the mountains become clothed for a few weeks with rich, succulent vegetation," Scully went on. "This occurs at the season when the springbuck fawns are born, and when, consequently, the does require green food. Hence the westward 'trek', which is, I believe, of hoar-ancient origin."

Scully described the most sensational of all recorded springbok migrations (in 1892) which ended in the South Atlantic. "The springbucks as a rule live without drinking," he pointed out. "Sometimes, however – perhaps once in ten years – they develop a raging thirst and rush madly forward until they find water. It is not many years ago since millions of them crossed the mountain range and made for the sea. They dashed into the waves, drank the salt water, and died. Their bodies lay in one continuous pile along the shore for over thirty miles, and the stench drove the *trekboers* who were camped near the coast far inland."

Some farmers in the track of the *trekbokke* believed that the movement was due to disease, such as *brandsiekte* (scab) or rinderpest. There is evidence that the rinderpest years of 1896-97 left the springbok untouched, though *brandsiekte* was certainly present in some of those shot. But the theory of illness is complicated by clear evidence that while the *trekbokke* looked emaciated in certain years, during other treks they were obviously sleek and healthy.

Mr S.C. Cronwright-Schreiner (Olive Schreiner's husband) made a determined attempt to solve the mystery during the 1896 migration, the last of the great cavalcades of *trekbokke* ever seen. Travelling by Cape cart in the wake of the migration, he found every homestead festooned with biltong. It was estimated that hundreds of thousands of buck had been shot in the Prieska district alone that year, and nearly as many wounded. Motherless springbok kids were dying by the thousand. Yet the migration went on – in millions.

It baffled Cronwright-Schreiner. He studied the works of Darwin and Lloyd Morgan on migration, investigated all the South African opinions on the subject, and finally declared: "I do not think they afford sufficient evidence to justify any hard-and-fast conclusion. It is a fact that there are not sufficient, carefully collected, intelligently considered and rigorously tested facts to enable us to come to any definite conclusion as to the whole 'mentality' of these treks. Shall we now ever obtain such facts?"

No one plotted the springbok migration routes accurately, so that significant evidence on that point has been lost. It is believed that they never went back on their tracks, but travelled a huge square or oval. No one knows how long a trek lasted, though it has been stated that the *trekbokke* were always back in their original haunts within six months to a year. The speed of a migrating horde varied considerably. One hundred miles may have been an ordinary day's trek. The buck were capable of covering much greater distances.

Karoo farmers last century firmly believed in two varieties of springbok – the lean *trekbok* and the fatter *houbok* (about fifteen pounds heavier), which remained in one area. Such a reliable observer as Scully mentioned shooting a *houbok* in the Richtersveld which was nearly twice as large as the springbok of the desert. The adult springbok ram weighs from seventy to eighty pounds and seldom more than ninety. Only one species of springbok is found in South Africa, known to scientists as *Antidorcas marsupialis marsupialis;* and it has been established that differences in weight are simply due to age and condition. In South West Africa, however, the springbok is of a heavier sub-species.

While farmers and *trekboers* did not always welcome the springbok invasions, they were able to profit or at least balance their losses by taking heavy toll of the herds. Convoys of wagons, carrying whole families, intercepted the *trekbokke,* muzzle-loaders went into action, and one bullet often killed more than one buck.

This was hunting on a gigantic scale, and nowhere else in the world has such slaughter been known. Each group of hunters would form an old-fashioned laager with the Cape carts and wagons outspanned in the shape of a large horseshoe. Men and boys would ride out to prey on the fringe of the migration. The women would help with the skinning and cutting of the biltong.

For decades last century each springbok skin fetched sixpence at the store. (The thin leather was used for bookbinding.) Biltong was threepence a pound, and it was a lean springbok indeed which did not provide eight pounds of dried biltong. Backhouse, in 1839, recorded that in the market at Cradock fresh springbok fetched thirteen pence apiece. There were long periods when a fat springbok could be bought in the karoo villages for one shilling and sixpence.

Were there really millions of buck in these migrations? Some naturalists have doubted whether the springbok could ever have existed in the numbers which staggered the early travellers. Descriptions of the *trekbokke,* however, are at least unanimous on this point. One of the finest accounts was given a century ago by that picturesque hunter Gordon Cumming, old Etonian, cavalry officer, red-bearded and kilted Scot. He travelled by ox wagon and shot mercilessly for five years, at a time when South Africa was indeed a hunter's paradise and no one seemed to realise that some of the animals would one day be exterminated. His bag was far larger than those of later, and more selective hunters such as Selous.

One night Gordon Cumming lay awake in his wagon for two hours before the dawn, listening to the springbok grunting and realising that a large herd was feeding near the camp. When he rose, he found that it was no mere herd, but a dense, living mass of springbok marching slowly and steadily.

They were coming through a gap in the western hills, pouring through like a floor, and disappearing over a ridge. "I stood upon the fore-chest of my wagon for nearly two hours, lost in wonder at the scene," recorded Gordon Cumming. "I had some difficulty in convincing myself that it was reality which I beheld, and not the wild picture of a hunter's dream. During this time the vast legions continued streaming through the neck in the hills in one unbroken compact phalanx.

"At length I saddled up and riding into the middle of them with my rifle and after-riders, fired into their ranks until fourteen had fallen, when I cried 'Enough'. We then retraced our steps to secure from the ever voracious vultures the venison which lay strewed along my track."

Gordon Cumming confessed that he could form no idea of the number of antelopes he beheld that day; but he has no hesitation in saying that "some hundreds of thousands were within the compass of my vision".

One of the boers in the area told Gordon Cumming: "You this morning beheld only one flat covered with springboks, but I have ridden a long day's journey over a succession of flats covered with them as far as I could see, and as thick as sheep in a fold."

Scully was lost when it came to counting the springbok he saw in the 1892 migration. "In dealing with myriads, numbers cease to have any significance," he declared. "One might as well endeavour to describe the mass of a mile-long sand dune by expressing the sum of its grains in cyphers as to attempt to give the numbers of antelopes forming the living wave that surged across the desert and broke like foam against the western granite ridge."

Mr T.B. Davie of Prieska recorded his impressions of four great springbok migrations between 1887 and 1896. "The whole country seemed to move, not in any hurry or rush, but a steady, plodding march, just like *voetganger* locusts," he declared. Mr Davie saw the springbok in one continuous stream from Prieska to Draghoender (forty-seven miles), plodding on, and just moving aside far enough to avoid the wheels of his cart.

A family on the farm Witvlei had to sit round the well – their last water supply after the springbok had filled the dam – keeping the buck off with bullets and stones. In the end the thirsty springbok beat down the defence, and soon the well was packed with dead and dying buck.

That year the springbok poured through the main street of Prieska, and the magistrate sat on the steps on his courthouse and picked off a few good specimens with his rifle. Prieska was always in the path of the migration.

During the 1888 trek, Mr Davie and his friend Dr Gibbons made a deliberate attempt to estimate the numbers of *trekbokke*. They were on the farm Nels Poortje in the Prieska district when the sea of antelopes overwhelmed the district. In front of them was a kraal which, the farmer told them, held fiften hundred sheep.

"Well," said Dr Gibbons, "if fifteen hundred can stand there, then about ten thousand can stand on an acre, and I can see in front of me ten thousand acres covered with buck. That means at least one hundred million buck. Then what about the miles upon miles around on all sides as far as the eye can reach covered with them."

They gave it up. No wonder men spoke of myriads of buck.

During the 1896 trek, Cronwright-Schreiner and two other farmers (all accustomed to counting small stock) surveyed the springbok on a vast, open plain and tried to form an accurate estimate with the aid of field glasses. They counted section after section, and agreed that there were half a million springbok in sight at that moment. But the whole trek covered an area of one hundred and forty miles by fifteen miles. "When one says they were in millions, it is the literal truth," declared Cronwright-Schreiner.

Millais, in his life of Selous, dealt with the wholesale destruction of game after the breech-loading rifle arrived in South Africa in the 1870s. He met a trader who kept accurate records of the skins he handled; and between 1878 and 1880 this man exported nearly two million skins, mainly springbok.

Yes, there were millions of springbok on the move, millions of buck followed by lions and leopards, hyenas and jackals, and vultures to pick out the eyes of those that fell. When the *trekbokke* raced through a narrow poort, it meant death for any human being in their path. At the time of the Great Trek a frontier farmer found his three young sons and his Hottentot shepherd trampled to death on the veld after the buck had passed.

Nearly seventy years ago there was a Kalahari trader named Albert Jackson. He was still living in Port Elizabeth in recent years, and he told me one personal experience of the springbok migration which helped to bring the scene to life for me.

"I slept on the veld during the 1896 migration," Jackson recalled. "Often I put my ear to the ground, and even at night, when the buck were resting, it felt like an earth tremor."

No longer is the springbok seen in millions. Yet the national emblem of South Africa, the only gazelle in the country, is in no danger of extinction. As recently as May 1954 large herds of springbok, possibly fifteen thousand buck, streamed out of the Kalahari and into the Gordonia district like the migratory swarms of last century. Farmers complained urgently that their fences were being broken and their grazing destroyed. The magistrate and a police officer flew over the invasion area and decided that there was no need to lift the ban on all hunting in force for three years in that district. Farmers would be allowed to fire their rifles to frighten the buck away – but only under police supervision.

Venison has a market value. In districts where shooting is allowed, farmers preserve their springbok herds carefully, and the guest who disobeys the rules at a springbok shoot will never be asked again. Only the rams and the old ewes are killed.

Seldom now will you see fifty springbok shot on one farm in a day; yet in the Nineties of last century one hunting party would bring in a thousand, twelve hundred buck between dawn and sunset. The migrations and the massacres have ended but the mystery remains.

KAROO

The Dodo Egg

1956

I am always fascinated by rarities, and it was an extreme rarity which Miss M. Courtenay Latimer lifted gently from her safe at my request. Miss Courtenay Latimer is the Director of the East London Museum, and the first coelacanth netted in South African waters bears her name *(Latimera chalumnae);* for she realised the scientific value of the brilliant steel-blue fish and brought Professor Smith on the scene. However, the dodo egg which Miss Latimer showed me is probably worth more than any fish.

Some oologists, as the egg experts call themselves, regard this large cream-coloured egg as the most important survival in the whole egg world. It must be worth hundreds of pounds; more than the pale greenish egg of the great auk; or the foot-long, ivory-coloured fossil egg of Madagascar's *Aepyornis titan,* largest bird in the ancient world. In fact, the only egg which might rival the dodo egg would be a perfect moa egg. Fragments of these eggs have been found in New Zealand caves, and have fetched high prices, but a complete moa egg has never been found.

Both the moa and the dodo became extinct at about the same time, late in the seventeenth century. The home of the dodo, the grey dodo with the massive beak, was Mauritius. Similar birds were found on the neighbouring islands of Reunion, where there was a white dodo, and Rodriguez, where an unsociable, long-legged dodo was rightly named the solitaire. Obviously the islands were once a single land mass, and the birds must have developed their local differences in isolation.

A plump bird was the dodo, as large as a goose, but in reality a gigantic ground pigeon. (The late Dr Robert Broom, the scientist, regarded Delalande's green pigeon of South Africa as a living link.) On islands where the birds have no natural enemies and no need to use their wings they tend to become flightless. Then man arrives and the birds are doomed.

The dodo ought to have survived longer than it did, for the Dutch cooks in the ship that took possession of Mauritius could do nothing with such a tough and unpalatable bird. Unfortunately later ships landed pigs, which smashed the eggs, and cats and dogs which ate the dodos, young and old. Some seamen were so eager to taste fresh food that they joined in the massacre.

Sir Thomas Herbert, an early English visitor, said of the dodo: "Her body is round and fat, which occasions the slow pace; and so great that few of them weigh less than fifty pounds; meat it is with some, but better to the eye than to the stomach, such as only a strong appetite can vanquish. It is of a melancholy visage, as sensible of Nature's injury in framing so massive a body to be directed by wings, such indeed as are unable to hoist her from the ground. Her stomach is fiery so that she can easily digest stones, in that and shape not a little resembling the ostrich."

Naturalists have studied the descriptions written by those who saw the living dodo without gleaning much scientific information. Its habits and diet remain a mystery, though it is known that the dodo nested on the ground and laid one egg at a time. François Cauche, a French visitor in the seventeenth century, said the egg was the same size as that of the Cape pelican. I once saw pelicans nesting on an island in False Bay, but it did not occur to me to study their eggs. In the same account Cauche said the egg was the size of a halfpenny bread roll, though I suspect the translator of turning the centimes into English currency. Nowhere else could I find any details of the eggs, and Cauche's evidence is vague and slender.

The story of Miss Courtenay Latimer's egg is a romance of the sea. This dodo egg is an heirloom, and it has been in the possession of her family for more than a century. Back in the 1840s, a Mr L. O. Bean of Port Elizabeth was pursuing his hobbies of zoology and botany. He introduced a number of plants into South Africa, and he was aided in his activities by Captain van Syker, owner and skipper of a sailing vessel trading among the Indian Ocean islands.

Mr Bean's daughter Lavinia collected birds' eggs. One day in

1846 Captain van Syker told Lavinia that he was calling at Mauritius and promised to bring her an egg from there. He returned on January 15, 1847 and handed the delighted girl a large egg. He had secured it from a shipwrecked sailor who had settled on the island. This man owned two of the eggs, and he was unwilling to sell them. However, he owed Captain van Syker money and he parted with one egg in settlement of the debt. The sailor told the captain that it was the egg of a bird which had been exterminated by Dutch sailors.

The last of the dodos were still waddling about the more remote parts of Mauritius in 1681, but there is evidence to show that by 1693 the whole species had been exterminated. While I was travelling about this large island some years ago I heard a remarkable creole legend to the effect that the dodo still lived in the remote forests high in the mountains of the interior. But I fear that the dodo will not be rediscovered in the sensational manner of the New Zealand huia. The dodo has been dead for two and a half centuries.

Lavinia Bean was Miss Latimer's great aunt. Before she died in 1935 at the age of ninety-eight she gave the egg to Miss Latimer; probably the only dodo's egg in the world.

Of course there have been doubts about the egg, difficult to refute because of the absence of other dodo eggs for comparison. In the scanty literature on the dodo, old authors mentioned a reputed dodo egg in a Bordeaux collection, and two more owned by a Russian naturalist. These three eggs appear to have vanished long ago. Miss Latimer has made inquiries in every possible direction without even hearing a rumour of another dodo egg.

Some of the scientists who gathered in East London in 1945 for the South African museums conference thought the egg might be an abnormal ostrich egg. Miss Latimer then set to work to defend the good name of her heirloom. If you put an egg under a magnifying glass you can study the "pitting pattern", which comes up as clearly as a human thumbprint. She found that the dodo egg displayed a "pitting pattern" similar to that of the pigeon egg, as Dr Broom had suggested. Moreover, it was shaped and coloured more like the pigeon egg than the ostrich egg. (The dodo, you will remember, was an ungainly member of the pigeon family.) Miss Latimer found that the pitting on her dodo egg was coarse, close and reddish in colour, whereas all the ostrich eggs she examined were pitted sparsely with fine greyish pit holes. She examined one hundred and twenty-five abnormal ostrich eggs from a farm, and another thirty odd abnormal eggs from the Port Elizabeth Museum. Her dodo egg remained unique in its pitting pattern, texture, shape, form and colour.

So I agree heartily with Miss Courtenay Latimer when she sums up: "In the light of the evidence supplied and of the history of this egg, I am satisfied that it is a dodo egg." The history is convincing. There have been practical jokes in the world of science, but there was no reason at all why Captain van Syker should have brought an ostrich egg from the island of the dodo for the daughter of his friend in Port Elizabeth. And if he had, the magnifying glass would have revealed the fake.

Bones of the dodo are not so rare as the eggs, though they must rank among the most valuable bones known to science. I believe the only complete, authentic dodo skeleton is one which I gazed upon with awe in the museum at Port Louis, Mauritius. Towards the end of last century a number of dodo bones were recovered from a swamp and sent to London. Experts under Sir Edward Newton at the British Museum then restored and mounted two skeletons, one perfect example for the island museum and another almost perfect skeleton for themselves.

A stuffed dodo, which had been decaying for years in the Ashmolean Museum, Oxford, was thrown on a bonfire two centuries ago. Someone saved the head and a foot, precious relics today. There are realistic pictures of the dodo, however, for living dodos were taken to Europe in the seventeenth century and painted by Roelandt Savery in Holland and other artists in England.

Miss Latimer recently acquired a life-size dodo effigy from the British Museum for the East London Museum. In the Durban Museum there is a fairly complete dodo skeleton. It was in 1919 that Mr Chubb, the curator, heard of this skeleton in private hands in Mauritius. He managed to buy it for the ridiculous sum of forty pounds. Between the wars, dodo bones amounting to about one-third of a skeleton were sold in London for two hundred and fifty pounds. The Durban skeleton includes the complete tail bones, the last rib, and the bones of the tiny wings. It has been valued at more than a thousand pounds. Interest in the dodo is proved by the thousands of postcards of the bird which the museum has sold.

Visitors recall the pictures in "Alice in Wonderland" when they see the enormous hooked beak.

This beak, incidentally, is of great scientific importance, for nothing else like it exists in the bird kingdom. It must have evolved as a result of a diet which demanded strong crushing power. As a whole, the dodo presents a picture of laziness and stupidity, and a notice in the British Museum points the moral: "The dodo is illustrated here as illustrating quite a serious principle: that in wild nature the creature which finds itself in easy surroundings and allows its powers to fall into disuse is likely to be exterminated when faced with new and more exacting conditions." No wonder the scientific name for the dodo is *Didus ineptus*.

Madagascar was another island where the birds lived too easily. I have already mentioned the *Aepyornis titan,* a bird so large that an ostrich would have been dwarfed beside it. Sinbad's story of the fabulous roc, which carried off elephants to feed its young, may have been based on the *Aepyornis.* Strange to say, the *Aepyornis* was still alive in the twelfth century, A.D., and was probably exterminated by Indonesian invaders about that time. Several nearly complete skeletons and many fragments have been found.

This monstrous, wingless bird stood over twelve feet high on its massive legs. The hunters who killed it may have been brave men; or perhaps it was a brainless bird without the deadly kick of the ostrich. Certainly it laid the largest egg known to science, equal to one hundred and fifty hens' eggs.

Shortly before World War II an American collector secured an *Aepyornis* egg at a price which he would not disclose. The modern story of that egg went back to 1912, when a savage herdsman in the Tandroy area of Madagascar saw a white object drifting along a flooded river. He reached out for it, saw that it was an egg, and remembered the tribal story of the mighty bird that had once roamed the land.

Scientists who examined the scene decided that after a thousand years the egg must have been washed out of a protecting alluvial deposit by the heavy rains. The finder had given the egg to his chief, who had taken it to a white trader in the nearest town and received five head of cattle in exchange. That immense egg, a foot long, ten inches across, pockmarked by sand and insects, went from hand to hand. Finally a missionary took it to San Francisco in the hope of raising funds for his church. He was successful. And the collector had gained one of the finest specimens of the *Aepyornis* egg. But there are twenty-five other known specimens in the museums of the world. It is not unique, like the dodo egg. Since that discovery French district administrators in Madagascar have been offering the natives a reward of ten thousand francs for every *Aepyornis* egg they bring in. I believe one happy man handed over a perfect fossil egg not long ago and claimed the reward.

Cape Town has an *Aepyornis titan* egg. It reposed in the museum cellar for many years, until a palaeontologist recognised the value of it and placed it in a showcase. Museums do not always realise what they have got. I know a wise old taxidermist who was serving his apprenticeship in Scotland when a woman whose husband was a sailor offered him the skin of a strange bird for a few shillings. He refused it, and the skin was thrown away. That bird lingered in his mind. Years afterwards he realised that it was a great auk. The woman had called it a hawk, and he was not interested in hawks.

No doubt he would have dealt with a dodo egg in the same way in his youth. But relics of the queer, extinct birds of the Indian Ocean islands turn up once in a lifetime. Fame and fortune await the man who goes to Mauritius and discovers a dodo egg.

THERE'S A SECRET HID AWAY

A Mysterious Traveller
1972

Of all the birds that have slaked their little thirsts at the old fountain in the Cape Town public gardens, the rarest and most mysterious was one that dipped its red and yellow bill into the water on May 15, 1893. It was the size of a partridge with glossy black plumage, a flat red comb on the head, long red and yellow legs. The wings were so short that it could not fly but it walked with the gait of a penguin and it could run very fast. This creature was described by one scientist in recent years as "the strangest bird in the world".

Someone caught the strangest bird and took it to the South African Museum. How long it lived there is not recorded but it was identified as a rail or coot from the Tristan da Cunha group of islands. Seventy years later Professor J.M. Winterbottom the ornithologist was going through the bird skins at the museum when he came across this specimen. It aroused his interest to such an extent that he tried to discover further details. He searched the shipping records for a clue but found nothing helpful. Yet it was obvious that a flightless land bird could only have crossed fifteen hundred miles of open ocean on board some ship.

The professor had reopened an old mystery with wide scientific angles, a mystery that touches me deeply for several reasons. It carried me back half a century to a scene of my youth; the triangle of islands that make up the Tristan group, with Gough Island as an outlier to the south. I saw the peak of the great island again; the mountain torrents and gulches and rocky beaches; the huge black mass of Inaccessible looming up with a cloud like the smoke of a volcano;

48

little Nightingale with its huge sea bird colonies and rare land birds. I remembered the cottages of volcanic stone thatched with the reeds the people called tussick, homes boarded inside with timber from lost ships. I saw the ox carts loaded with juniper trees for firewood or kelp for manure; the huts filled with potatoes, the lamb houses and pigsties. I could almost taste the "island tea" made from herbs and the dish of mollymauk, an albatross the size of a goose, set before me by Mrs Repetto; and wild, sweet, red berries made into a pie. Bob Glass, my host during two visits to Tristan, gave me mollymauk eggs for breakfast. I recalled the bird skins used by the Tristaners for bartering when ships called; skins that I carried away as souvenirs. I though of the collection of skins my host Bob Glass had shown me. But I was a young reporter, not an ornithologist. What rarities had I handled during those nights in the island cottage?

Tristan islanders looked upon me as a strange visitor from the "Houtside Warl". They talked of the small world they knew; of pennerwins and goneys, a thrush they called starchy, of island cocks and island hens. They knew their own birds, past and present, and they talked as people who lived on birds and their eggs – not as scientists.

Flightless birds have a great fascination for ornithologists, not only from the evolutionary point of view but also because of the geological aspect. Did the birds fly to these lonely islands and then lose the power of flight? Or was there once a land-bridge to explain their presence? Five species of land birds are found in the Tristan group and two of these are flightless. The man who made the first known ascent of the Tristan peak (six thousand seven hundred feet high) discovered the first of these flightless birds. He was Captain Dugald Carmichael, an army officer with a scientific bent, and he accompanied the military detachment that occupied Tristan in 1816. Early in the following year Carmichael made the steep ascent, forced his way through the dense brushwood, grass and fern and gained a table land after three hours' climbing. He went on to a swamp where there were "myriads of petrel burrows" and finally reached the volcanic crater with its pool of water. On the way down Carmichael noted four species of albatross breeding. He said that hogs secreted themselves in the deepest recesses of the woods; there they lived on wild celery and were safe from hunters. Goats lived on the highest ridges. He saw a thrush, a bunting and a moorhen; these

birds were found all over the island and he collected specimens.*
The flightless moorhen hid in the woods and was run down occasionally by dogs. The other birds were caught by the soldiers in nets.

Seven years later came a talented young Englishman named Augustus Earle, later to become famous as the artist who accompanied the *Beagle* expedition and as a friend of Charles Darwin. He had landed on Tristan as a visitor but his ship was driven off by heavy weather and he was marooned for seven months before another ship picked him up. Earle said the moorhen was known to the settlers as the island cock. It stood erect, armed with sharp spurs for defence and also to assist it in climbing rocks. Its only call was a sound like the repetition of the word cock. The flesh was plump, fat and excellent eating. Earle recorded the fact that the garrison had brought cats with them; and these cats, with the mammals Carmichael mentioned, have a bearing on the fate of the tasty island cock.

Tales of this interesting bird reached the scientific world from time to time but it was not until Sir George Grey's period as governor at the Cape that live specimens were secured. Grey instructed a former employee, who was visiting Tristan, to bring back birds. Thus five island cocks were landed at Cape Town. Grey sent them on to the London Zoo and one bird reached Regent's Park alive.† It was examined by members of the Royal Zoological Society and the species was named *Gallinula nesiotis*. They found that the colour was similar to the common moorhen but darker, with head and body dull black. The bird had a red garter round the base of the thigh and stout legs. It could flutter a little but it used its legs, not wings, to escape from enemies. Sir Wyville Thomson, the naturalist, pointed out that the wing feathers were too soft and short for flight. The breastbone was weak but the bones of the lower extremity were large and powerful and the muscles were strong.

* Carmichael's birds from Tristan were sold to private collectors in London. All vanished except one *(Nesospiza acunhae)* which was identified in the Berlin Museum many years later. It was extinct on Tristan in 1873, when H.M.S. *Challenger* called, but is still found on Inaccessible, with a smaller form on Nightingale.

† Sir George Grey also sent a collection of South African animals to the London Zoo on this occasion. It included a female kudu, the first to reach Europe alive; the first live steenbok and the second live blesbok; a grysbok, blaauwbok, zebra with peculiar markings, a Stanley crane, wattled crane, dassies and snakes.

Members of the H.M.S. *Challenger* expedition visited the Tristan group in 1873 and climbed to the domain of the great South Atlantic oceanic birds on the peak. The redoubtable H.N. Moseley, the naturalist, saw a black albatross on a nest of earth a foot high; and the mollymauk was also nesting there, a handsome bird with grey wings. Moseley had hoped to secure specimens of the island cock but in this he was disappointed. The *Challenger* reports stated that the Tristan island cock, renamed *Porphyriornis nesiotis,* had been almost exterminated. As time went on the island cock was regarded as extinct.*

However, there was a surprise in store for the scientific world. American sealers from the schooner *Francis Alleyn* spent four months on Gough Island in 1888 and 1889 and George Comer, the second mate, collected birds for the American Museum of Natural History. Among the specimens he carried back to Connecticut were two live gallinules and a number of skins. These birds appeared to be identical with the Tristan island cock. Gough Island lies two hundred miles to the south of the main islands. It is now of special interest to South Africa owing to the weather station maintained there by the government. But this little-known outpost is a grim place that claimed the lives of sealers in the old days and South African meteorologists in recent years. Portuguese navigators discovered the island in 1501 and named it Diego Alvarez; and Captain Charles Gough R.N., put it on the chart two centuries later and gave it his name. It remained almost unknown until 1955, when a Cambridge University expedition spent six months there. Even now some of the mysteries remain unsolved. Gough is mountainous, with an area of forty square miles; it has a plateau and a three thousand foot peak. From the sea parts of the island resemble the Twelve Apostles range in the Cape Peninsula. It is covered with thick and treacherous bush in which the men lost their way and were frozen to death. South African scientists have described it as a wet

* In fact the island cock lingered on until the early years of this century. An adventurous character I knew as an old man, Mr. P.C. Keytel, built a house on Tristan and lived there form 1907 to 1909, trying to open up trade in sheep with the Cape. He chartered the schooner *Greyhound* for the purpose. Once he set out for Gough Island with Bob Glass as pilot but returned to Tristan without sighting the island. Keytel collected natural history specimens for the South African Museum and he secured one mature specimen of the island cock and one juvenile of the species.

island, soft underfoot, reminiscent of the Knysna forests with such dense undergrowth that objects only a few feet away are often hidden. Apart from the sealers of last century, Gough Island was never occupied for long until the South African weather station was established there. Gough was for many years an unexplored zoological mystery.

Members of the Scottish Antarctic Expedition who landed there from the *Scotia* early this century were the first scientists to set foot on the island. One of these visitors, Mr R.N. Rudmore Brown, summed up as follows: "Looked at from an impartial standpoint Gough Island is but a relatively insignificant rock in mid-ocean, but its very isolation makes it of great interest. It may throw light on some former continuity of land in the Southern Hemisphere and it cannot fail to elucidate various problems of biological distribution when its flora and fauna have been thoroughly investigated."

Mr W. Eagle Clarke, the expedition's ornithologist, was impressed by the beauty of Gough Island rising abruptly from the ocean with sheer precipices several hundred feet high, green slopes, moss-covered cliffs and rushing waterfalls shooting out into the sea. The scientists landed on the eastern side where a ravine gave access to the interior. At the seaward end there were a few acres of level ground with grass, ferns and wild celery. A narrow beach one hundred yards long was strewn with boulders. Up to one thousand feet the island was thickly covered with tussock grass and buckthorn trees. The *Scotia* had waited for three days before it was possible to land the scientists and they were only able to spend three hours on shore. During that brief visit they obseved nineteen species of birds and added twelve species to the known list of island birds. Among the birds collected were three land species, the flightless gallinule Comer had discovered and two buntings. Comer's gallinule had been given the scientific name of *Porphyriornis comeri*. Clarke secured five specimens. He said these birds were abundant in the dense undergrowth along the sides of the stream in the glen where they landed. When the birds tried to hide they were betrayed by the brilliant colours of the bill and feet.

Scientists from the *Scotia* were reluctant to leave this paradise for naturalists, almost untrodden by foot of man. Clarke pointed out that the land birds found on Gough belonged to genera unknown elsewhere except on the Tristan group; thus Gough must be regarded as an outlier of that group. Yet the relationship was remote as the buntings of Gough and Inaccessible were quite distinct. In summer Gough was a breeding station for petrels. The other birds found in great numbers were *tubinares:* shearwaters, albatrosses and mollymauks.

At first it was thought that Comer had discovered a new species of gallinule. When the Tristan island cock was compared with the Gough Island bird, however, only small differences were found; the Tristan species had scarcely any white on the outer edge of the wing and the colour of the feet was slightly darker. Nevertheless, the two birds are almost indistinguishable and *Porphyriornis comeri* can only be regarded as a sub-species. Colonel H.F.I. Elliott declared not long ago that they were both obviously moorhens, races of one species. He said that the name coot, used in labelling London Zoo specimens, was inept for a bird that seldom entered the water. Comparisons were difficult as there were few specimens of the extinct Tristan bird available.

When the *Francis Alleyn* landed her sealers in the summer of 1888 the skipper relied on a chart made by Captain Peter Heywood R.N. of H.M.S. *Nereus* in 1811, and this gave no idea of the interior. Before long a storm blew up and the *Francis Alleyn* vanished over the horizon. Comer and his shipmates made a hut out of turf with an upturned dinghy as roof. They lived on fish, seals, the young of the albatross and they collected thousands of penguin eggs. A seaman named José Gomez broke through the bush to a plateau and returned with half a sack of potatoes. Obviously the potatoes had been planted by an earlier shore party from a sealing vessel and the potato patch had been walled in with stones. Gomez led his companions to the spot later. They were all caught in a blizzard, Gomez was lost and perished in the snow.

Comer sailed round to the north coast of Gough in a dinghy in search of seals. There to his astonishment he found two bearded Americans living in a cave. They had been there for two years, Robinson Crusoes who had been left there by a sealing vessel to extract oil from rockhopper penguins. They were using the snow-bound mountain caves as deep-freeze chambers; there they had buried thousands of penguins. Comer, a keen amateur naturalist and collector, also noted a bird he had never seen before; a small bird with glossy black plumage. The two Crusoes told him that these birds were useless for commercial purposes but they often ate them. Comer had seen flightless birds in New Zealand and he knew that he had made an important discovery. He called it the mountain cock, and described it as a little larger than a quail. "They are generally black though occasionally one is nearly brown," he wrote. "They could not get on to a table three feet high. Bushes grow on the island up to two thousand feet and the birds are found as far as the bushes grow. I don't know how many eggs they lay. They can be caught by hand. When alarmed their note is a shrill whistle. They eat the eggs of other birds and also follow the tide down to feed on small *crustacae,* but are careful never to enter the water. Salt water is fatal to them but they splash in fresh water."

Comer's men killed about three hundred fur seals, not enough to show a profit on the expedition. They also killed three hundred skua gulls for the feathers. When the *Francis Alleyn* returned Comer caught a number of the flightless birds and took them with him; all but two fell into the sea on the way to the ship and died. The two survivors improved in health and grew fat. They loved raw meat and killed and ate live mice that were placed in their cage. On board ship the birds were fed on hard tack and dry canary seed. They fought in the cage. They had a peculiar habit in the wild state and in captivity of hopping over obstacles instead of going round or under. In Connecticut, the schooner's home port, they were tethered by rope yarns to the legs but both escaped and were never seen again.

Besides the flightless bird that bears his name Comer also discovered an albatross new to science. He described a single grove of flowering trees on Gough that have since proved of great interest to botanists; trees known as *sophora* and resembling an orchard. Botanists have stated that the nearest relatives to these trees are in Chile, Reunion Island in the Indian Ocean and New Zealand. The seeds float in sea water and appear to have been dispersed by ocean currents. The valley where the trees were found has been marked on the map as Comerdale.

Gough Island was without visitors for years until 1919, when a diamond prospecting expedition spent some months there. The little *Quest* put in three years later, after Shackleton's death, and her ornithologist, Captain G.H. Wilkins, discovered a new bunting the size of a thrush which he named *Rowettia* in honour of the man who financed the expedition. Previous visitors had been confused by differences in plumage between the young birds of this species and the green-coloured adult. Apart from the whaling research ship *William Scoresby* in 1927 and a Norwegian vessel in 1934, lonely Gough remained in the great hush until 1955, when the only important expedition ever to land there made a careful survey. This consisted of eight Cambridge University scientists led by Dr Martin Holdgate. They selected Gough because it was the last remaining sub-Antarctic island that had never been investigated. During six months' work they filled in some of the gaps in scientific knowledge; yet when they departed many riddles had still to be solved. Like previous visitors they were hampered by the canopy of branches and ferns that made progress at the rate of a quarter of a mile an hour a fast pace. They had to cut their way through the jungle. Branches were so intertwined that it was impossible to walk round or under the trees; the scientists had to crawl through or over the obstructions and use axes. Their clothes were often torn to ribbons.

Holdgate's party did not find Comer's flightless landrail friendly. It was secretive, running away at the slightest noise and darting into the high tussock grass at the unexpected sight of man. They heard the shrill call in all parts of the island. Fur seals, almost exterminated by the Americans last century, had multiplied and there was a colony about thirteen thousand strong; more than half the world population of this rare species of fur seal. Millions of prions and petrels filled the sky. The only land mammals they found were mice, which must have come on shore with the sealers long ago. Fortunately they were too small to prey on the birds. Rats would have wiped out the flightless birds as the rats from the wreck of the *Henry B. Paul* had done at Tristan. (Those rats not only exterminated *Porphyriornis nesiotis* but also made life difficult for the human population.) After six months the Cambridge scientists departed, still wondering how many millions of years had passed since the peak called Gough had risen above the ocean from the long Atlantic submarine ridge. What were the "continental affinities" of Gough? Did it provide evidence of the continuity of land in the southern hemisphere? The scientists marvelled at the journeys of plants and animals across the ocean to this little speck in the Roaring Forties. Holdgate and his colleague J.B. Heaney pointed out that after arrival many forms of life were cut off from interbreeding with stocks from the outside world. "Over the years, two stocks tend to diverge," these scientists wrote. "Thus the island acquires peculiar species found nowhere else in the world. Study of such endemic species is of great interest."

Most important of all the flightless birds of the Tristan group is the rail now known as *Atlantisia rogersi*, now found only on Inaccessible Island. This island lies twenty miles to the east of Tristan, six square miles of beaches, high cliffs, and a plateau covered with tussock. The islanders sail over there twice a year to see whether any timber has drifted on to the beaches, and they also collect sea birds and eggs. It is a hazardous voyage in open, canvas boats. Rumours of the flightless rail drifted out to the world of science many years before the first specimens were secured. The islanders observed it last century and called it the island hen because it was much smaller than the Tristan island cock. They described it as a small black bird the size of a day-old chick with a long, slender black beak, small head, wings short and soft and useless. The bird ran like a partridge in the long grass and fed on seeds and insects.

The first scientists to hear of this bird were Moseley and his colleagues on board H.M.S. *Challenger*. The ship called at Inaccessible; and there they met two Germans, the Stoltenhoff brothers, who had settled on the island. The brothers knew the bird well for they had often eaten it. "It is one of my few regrets that we found it impossible to get a specimen," wrote Sir Wyville Thomson. Lord Crawford's yacht *Valhalla* visited Inaccessible a year later but the ornithologist searched in vain for the elusive bird. Seventeen years passed and the *Quest* arrived; but Wilkins had no better luck than those who had gone before. Wilkins left a preserving outfit with the Reverend H.M. Rogers, the Tristan missionary, and asked him to secure specimens. Rogers sailed over to Inaccessible on the next collecting trip (in 1923) and the islanders caught five island hens for him. Rogers sent one specimen to the South African Museum in Cape Town and three skins and a bottled specimen to the British Museum in London. The ornithologists were delighted. They declared that the island hen was unique, entirely different from the Tristan island cock or the Gough Island bird. Here was the smallest flightless rail in the world. It was named *Atlantisia rogersi* in honour of the clergyman. My friend Rogers died not long after he returned to England, for three years of hardship and food shortages had undermined his health. His name lives on in the annals of ornithology.

Dr Percy Lower of the British Museum staff examined the first specimens and declared that *Atlantisia rogersi* was a true rail and was not even generically allied to the moorhen-like gallinules of Tristan and Gough. "Nothing like it is known to science, though certain Pacific Island rails may have sprung from the original stock," Lower wrote.[*] "Inaccessible is one of the least man-spoilt islands known, a sanctuary practically intact for oceanic sea birds. It is noteworthy that the other islands of the group have no such rail as *Atlantisia*. This is the most interesting rail now living. In a bird that has been marooned on one of the most isolated scraps of land in the world for hundreds of thousands or even millions of years, one would expect patent signs of degeneration or even complete atrophy. Nothing of the sort has happened. There has been no general increase of size, as with other flightless birds."

Naturalists have been concerned about the future of *Atlantisia,* for Inaccessible was partially ravaged by fire years ago and there are wild pigs on the island. The eggs of *Atlantisia* (described by Lord Rothschild F.R.S., as greyish milk-white and very large for the size of the bird) would fetch high prices if they came on the market. Collectors would also compete for skins. Specimens have been sent to many museums in recent years. One ornithologist wrote: "It is sincerely to be hoped that the bird will not be exterminated by any evil-disposed person for the sake of money."

Dr Erling Christophersen of the Norwegian expedition that visited Tristan in 1937 transported specimens of *Atlantisia* from Inaccessible to the main island, but a diet of condensed milk proved unsuitable and the birds died. Christophersen noted the deep-set fiery eyes of the birds and the way they used their voices to keep together in the dark tunnels of tussock grass. He said *Atlantisia*

---

[*] New Zealand has an extremely rare flightless rail that was thought to be extinct – the *takahe,* discovered as a fossil in 1847. The live bird has been sighted about four times since then and was last seen in 1948 near Lake Te Anan. It is heavily built, about the size of a hen, with scarlet legs and beak.

nested in November and laid two eggs. They were safe from human interference, he thought, because they lived in an underworld of vegetation closed to man. Sea hens might menace them; he found a whole *Atlantisia* in the stomach of a sea hen. If rats ever reached Inaccessible the *Atlantisia* species would be doomed; like the fairy tale birds of bygone days they would vanish into the mists of the past.

Colonel H.F.I. Elliott visited all the islands of the Tristan group in the 1950s and found that *Atlantisia* was not so shy or hard to locate as he had expected. In the Salt Beach area of Inaccessible it could always be watched or caught without difficulty. Its normal cry was "chunk chunk" but when alarmed it scuttled off with a "pseep". Elliott said that previous observers had underestimated the *Atlantisia* population. It had been put as low as twelve hundred but Elliott heard the birds all over the island from sea level to the highest point and he though there were ten to twenty thousand pairs. At present the species had no serious enemies apart from the skua gull. Permits were issued sparingly by the British government; the fee was five shillings a skin or clutch of eggs. Elliott found that *Atlantisia* travelled well in a small cask with the top netted. The birds could jump two feet vertically, fluttering their useless wings. They could be kept in a wire enclosure and fed on worms and insects and Tristan cranberries. One bird left outside the enclosure died after digging a burrow a foot deep. Some ornithologists have seen in *Atlantisia* a distant relative of the ostrich and the kiwi. They were unable to explain the presence of this smallest rail on Inaccessible.

The discovery of flightless birds always excited the old seafarers. Such a one was Peter Mundy of Cornwall who landed on uninhabited Ascension three centuries ago and saw "a strange kind of fowle, colour grey or dappled, white and black feathers intermixed, eyes red like rubies, wings very imperfect wherewith they cannot raise themselves from the ground. They were taken running, in which they are exceeding swift, helping themselves a little with their wings. They can neither fly nor swim. It was more than ordinary dainty meat, relishing like a roasting pig."

Mundy wondered how they had come to this lonely island, "three leagues from the coast of Guinea". Were they created on the island from the beginning? Did the earth produce them like mice, serpents, worms and insects? Peter Mundy declared that he would leave the problem to more learned men. He was an accurate observer, however, and though no one else reported this flightless bird, scientists think that Mundy saw a rail that is now extinct. Bones of a large flightless rail have been identified on St Helena. Many islands in the Indian Ocean had flightless rails but they were exterminated by cats and rats and the last survivor is the Aldabra rail. This bird is a plump, tame creature, innocent as a dodo.

Dr Bernard Stonehouse, leader of a scientific expedition to Ascension, declared that the Ascension and Tristan flightless birds were possibly descendants of birds that had wandered from the normal migration routes, found the islands habitable, and became flightless after many generations. Stonehouse said that it could happen again, for his party found a moorhen on Ascension exhausted after its long flight from South America or South Africa. Men who had lived for years on Ascension informed him that they had seen others.

This is the theory held by most ornithologists. Dr Martin Holdgate pointed out that the flying ancestors of the flightless birds were afraid of being blown into the sea. They did not appear from nowhere. The rails must have reached Gough Island airborne ages ago and changed during thousands of years. Stonehouse recalled that a related species, the American purple gallinule, was an occasional visitor to Tristan at the present time, proving that such birds were capable of crossing the ocean.

Another school of thought holds that there was once a land-bridge from the continents to the islands and that flightless birds originated from flightless ancestors. Dr Erling Christophersen drew attention to the ostrich species of South America, Africa and Australia. Many scientists believed that these birds had degenerated, each on its own continent. But ostriches harboured lice, a peculiar, isolated group of lice. One species of lice was found on South American and African ostriches; another species on the South American and Australian ostriches. So the ostriches must have brought the lice with them as lice could not fly the oceans or exist away from the bodies of their hosts. Thus the birds must have found land connections between South America, Africa and Australia.

Dr Lowe of the British Museum retained an open mind on the origin of *Atlantisia*. He could find no evidence that the Tristan group had once formed part of a continuous land mass. However, there were forty species of flowering plants, three were possibly South American in affinity and two might be related to South African forms; but the Tristan group had a temperate oceanic flora with no strong link with any continent. Lowe thought that birds marooned on these isolated scraps of land for hundreds of thousands or millions of years might undergo a gradual loss of flight and radical changes in structural details. He was not in a position to decide. "One would have expected to find signs of degeneration – but there is nothing of the sort," Lowe remarked. Lowe had previously made a special study of the ostrich and had come to the conclusion that these flightless birds were not descendants of birds that once flew but that they represented a stage between reptilian ancestors and the present flying birds. He found nothing in the structure of the ostriches to suggest that their ancestors used their wings for flight. It was a debatable subject, said Lowe, but he could not lose sight of the fact that ostriches were very reptilian. Some ornithologists held that loss of the power of flight came very easily and quoted the steamer duck, great auk, dodo and many other examples; these birds, they said, had become flightless in comparatively recent times. The same fate may have overtaken the early ancestors of the ostriches, but Lowe preferred to await the verdict of the future.

Holdgate declared that the volcanic Tristan group arose by eruption in mid-ocean and had never been linked to any continent by land. The fauna and flora reached the islands by migration. Study of the various species threw light on plant and animal distribution. Then the migrants were cut off effectively and evolution took a peculiar course, leading to endemic species that occurred nowhere else in the world. Hence their interest for the biologist.

Yngvar Hagen, ornithologist of the Norwegian expedition, declared that there was no doubt that the ancestors of *Atlantisia* were real flying birds. The flightless *Atlantisia* still used its wings as brakes when jumping downwards. When one of these birds was held in the hand it flapped eagerly with its wings in the effort to escape, soft and soundless as a bat yet without power.

Dr Austin Rand, curator of birds at the Chicago Natural History

Museum, remarked that the remoteness and small size of the Tristan islands, and the presence of five species of resident endemic land birds, formed an extreme case of colonisation of far, isolated oceanic isles by land birds. However, the mystery could be explained by the large numbers of stragglers that reached the islands. The prevailing winds blew from South America to South Africa. To postulate an ancient land mass or bridge to explain the distribution of a single species seemed to involve mighty changes for a small result. Rand mentioned the continental drift theory, the breaking apart of Africa and South America. He summed up in favour of the widely accepted theory of overseas colonisation. The land birds of the Tristan group were entirely of American origin; accidental wanderers aided by the westerly wind. The purple gallinule from America was the ancestor of the Tristan island cock, *Porphyriornis nesiotis* and the Gough Island mountain cock, *Porphyriornis comeri.* The great modification in skeleton and feathers of *Atlantisia* indicated that this flightless rail might be the oldest of the Tristan endemics and it was impossible to suggest the original stock.

Rand found it almost incredible that the birds that colonised one of the Tristan islands from South America should not have covered the intervening ten or twenty miles of water to the other islands. Yet only two of the five endemic species were recorded from all three islands; the small-billed sparrow and the thrush. Rand surmised that the flightless gallinule of Gough might not be directly related to the Tristan form. Each might be descended from different individuals of the same parent stock, some of which colonised each island independently. Similar appearance might be the result of similar change under similar severe ecological conditions. Rand could trace no African relationships as no African land birds had been found in the Tristan group. Although the group was less than forty miles across, in 1952 six species of land birds, including two gallinules, arrived there as strays over two thousand miles of water.

Elliott pointed out that Rand had overlooked the fact that no two islands in the Tristan group shared a completely identical bird; the smaller bunting of Inaccessible being the only apparent exception. During thousands of years there had been no tendency for resident land birds to wander or to be carried by storms from island to island;

even those as close as Inaccessible and Nightingale. This urge to remain in its native locality is found among other species of birds, however, and is known to scientists as philopatry.

Dr J.C. Greenway, an American authority on extinct and vanishing birds, favours the South American origin of the Tristan birds. He pointed out, however, that we must presume that the stock from which they sprang had become extinct on the mainland or that evolution and mutation had obscured the characters their ancestors once possessed. Both in Africa and South America there were gallinules similar to the island forms. Greenway said that the Tristan thrush, *Nesochicla eremita,* was in danger of going the same way as the Tristan island cock. Indeed, the islanders were under the impression that it had become extinct; their ancestors had told them that it had nested on Tristan but they had not seen it on the main island for years; only on Inaccessible. It was rather like a blackbird and it clung to the scrub on the slopes near the Tristan summit. Members of the Christophersen expedition rediscovered the bird. This thrush is now the only land bird on the main island, the thrush known to the islanders as starchy.

Then there is *Nesopiza wilkinsi,* a giant-billed bunting found only on Nightingale, though it may have existed on Tristan before the rats arrived. It resembles a canary with a huge beak and yellow-green feathers. Few men have seen it alive since it was first reported in 1873 by *Challenger* scientists. Wilkins of the *Quest* shot one in 1922, the one bunting seen in the trees during the four hours he spent on shore. It was not photographed alive until 1948, when a Cape Town expedition in the *Pequena* carried out a fisheries survey of the whole group. This large, stout-billed form occurs side by side with the small, typical bunting on Nightingale. The Christophersen party watched three of the large buntings cracking nuts in the trees. They shot three. The bird needs protection, for there are probably no more than thirty pairs left in the world, all on this tiny oceanic island.

A last glance at little *Atlantisia.* Greenway thought that *Atlantisia* may have occurred on Tristan long ago. It may have been extirpated by the bellicose island cock, which may have been a much later immigrant. There were no fossil remains and it was only possible to speculate. Greenway was completely baffled by two problems: first, why *Atlantisia* did not occur on Nightingale; and secondly, why the flightless gallinule was confined to Tristan and Gough and was never recorded on Inaccessible and Nightingale. "These problems are inherent in the study of insular faunas and there is seldom an answer," remarked Greenway.

Greenway was pessimistic regarding the future of the Tristan birds. Portuguese explorers had left pigs and goats on shore. Dogs had been trained to locate nesting burrows. Within living memory one Tristan islander had brought in one thousand chicks of the great-winged petrel to be stored for food. Fat of sea birds was used for cooking. Two species of albatross, probably confined to the Tristan group, were now extremely rare and it was doubtful whether they would survive for long.

The man who first spoke to me about the rare birds of Tristan and Gough was Robert Franklin Glass, grandson of "Governor" William Glass, founder of the world's most remote colony. Glass collected bird skins and eggs as I have said. I must bring Bob Glass into the picture because I think he may have played an important part in the mystery of the *Porphyriornis comeri* caught that day in 1893 at the drinking fountain in the Cape Town Public Gardens. Unlike most of the Tristaners of his day, Glass was a well-travelled man. I spent five nights as his guest in his island cottage and he told me his life story. He had been a sailor, a soldier during the South African War, a diamond digger, a factory worker in Cape Town. After many adventurous years of roaming the world Bob Glass returned to his island home during a depression in 1908 and remained there for the rest of his life. He was a tall man with a persuasive voice; clever by island standards but unscrupulous. I liked his sense of humour but I could see that he was unpopular on the island. He tried to pass himself off as headman when a ship called but no one listened to his orders. I often wish that I had been an ornithologist when Bob Glass brought out his bird skins for my benefit, for there may have been great rarities in that amateur collection, badly preserved with salt. The skins Glass gave me in exchange for a slab of chocolate and a pair of trousers had been sewn into a mat; a handsome mat of rockhopper penguin feathers. He informed me that my pillows and mattress were stuffed with the same feathers. (I only wish he had killed the fleas.) Glass had spent months on Gough Island as a sealer and he had known Comer, discoverer of the mountain cock. This meeting occurred during the years Bob Glass spent at sea, first in the whaling schooner *Swallow* and later in the Cape Town sealing schooner *Wild Rose*. The sealers gathered to swap yarns of their experiences at Gough Island and other lonely places. Glass also visited England and the United States during his voyages.

Why should Glass have brought one or more specimens of *Porphyriornis comeri* to Cape Town? Colonel Elliott noted in one of his scientific papers the strong demand for Tristan specimens, especially in America. "The gift to a non-islander of a rare bird or egg has long been a gambit, and the islander expects something in return," Elliott wrote. Glass was an opportunist. He took diamondiferous gravel back to Tristan with him from the river diggings and claimed that he had found diamonds on Gough Island – a trick that deceived the manager of a Cape Town firm and caused enormous trouble and expense.* Such a man as Glass would not have missed a chance of collecting rare birds on Gough Island. Glass landed on Gough with others from the *Wild Rose* in 1891 and was picked up in 1892 after spending eleven months there. He and his companions had built huts in the glen near the landing place; and they were so pleased to see the *Wild Rose* that they set fire to everything before they left.

When Professor Winterbottom investigated the mystery of "the strangest bird in the world" he had before him the record of Comer's discovery. Comer left Gough Island in the *Francis Alleyn* in 1889 and sailed for the United States with his birds without calling at Table Bay. The professor appealed for information about ships calling at Gough in 1892 or 1893 but received no replies. Long afterwards I discovered the details of the *Wild Rose* expedition. Obviously the bird found in the Cape Town public gardens arrived in the *Wild Rose* in 1892, and after a period in captivity it was released. It provided a mystery for the naturalists of 1893 and for Professor Winterbottom seventy years later. I cannot prove that Bob Glass was the culprit but those who knew that peculiar old character will agree with me that my guess is shrewd and logical; that for reasons best known to himself he got rid of his Gough Island rail by leaving it at the fountain.

WHEN THE JOURNEY'S OVER

* A full account of this expedition appears in "Eight Bells at Salamander" (Timmins 1960).

Peoples

The somewhat anachronistic style of Green's earlier works should be read in the context of the time in which they were written. Talk of class, race and social standing does not disguise the kindly and sympathetic eye with which he viewed his fellow man, as these often tragic stories will illustrate.

Although the selection of tales are of men of vastly different backgrounds, the qualities they reveal serve to emphasise how much the various races have in common, rather than their differences. Woodsmen in the Knysna forest, Boers trekking across the Kalahari, Bushmen, Hottentots and Ovambos fighting for their lives – all show the same human mixture of courage and foolhardiness, ignorance and endurance, cruelty and kindness.

"People of the Forests", written in 1936, is a good example of the value of Green's record-keeping, and the long period of time his work spans. He recalls speaking to Mr C.W. Thesen, then resident of Knysna, whose descendents are still prominent in the town. Mr Thesen told Green how, in 1869, he sailed from Norway to settle in South Africa. So often in Green's stories we get first-hand accounts from over a century ago.

Last of the Bushmen

1933

Outside the ranks of the scientists, there are few men in South Africa with a wider knowledge of that fast-vanishing race, the Bushmen, than Donald Bain. Son of a former magistrate of Bushmanland and grandson of Andrew Bain, the South African explorer and geologist, Donald Bain has spent years of his life leading expeditions into the more remote corners of the sub-continent in search of these *wilde bosmannetjies,* as the farmers call them.

The most successful journey of all took Bain, with Dr Grant John, Dr Cadle and Mr Frederick Goodwin, into the Kaokoveld. There they gathered round them the dregs of a nation which for many centuries occupied alone and unchallenged the whole of Southern Africa.

Unconscious of all the upheavals which had swept over the peoples of the Northern hemisphere, undisturbed by the economic necessity which had forced our ancestors along the path, from the cave to the palace and from the stone-headed club to the rifle, the Bushmen have advanced but slowly. The incentive which compelled our ancestors to seek a surer weapon than the club and to select from the grasses of the field those most suited to his digestive organs, had in this case been missing. Their possessions were vast. Countless thousands of antelope roamed the country, fruits, berries and nuts grew in great profusion, and all was theirs. Separated from all intercourse with the slowly evolving civilisations of the north by the impenetrable barrier of tropical Africa, they had remained in ignorance of the existence of any people but themselves.

Then came the terrible awakening. Savage men, taller and stronger than the Bushmen, descended upon them from the north.

Organised hordes, with strange animals and deadly weapons, took possession of their favourite hunting grounds and despoiled them of their women. Futile were their efforts at retaliation and gradually but surely they were driven to seek refuge among the inaccessible mountains or out upon the desolate and unwanted wastes.

Reduced in numbers and carrying on for centuries a hopeless warfare against the intruders, they struggled and fought for their very existence. But the great catastrophe was still to come. Hard as was their lot, it was still possible to find a refuge on the great arid plains, and here, during certain seasons at least, the game herds collected and food was plentiful. Life, it is true, was precarious. When for months at a time the game trekked into the territory of their invaders, it became necessary to eat lizards, locusts, snakes – any living thing. Driven by the dreadful pangs of hunger they descended upon their enemies and drove away their cattle. To be caught was certain death, but it was a sporting chance and they took it without hesitation. Then at the southern extremity of the great African continent appeared the white man.

Centuries earlier the ancestors of these two races had met in the Northern Hemisphere and a war of annihilation had begun. It may have, and probably did last for many generations; but it could have only one ending – the extermination of the pygmy. But for those who escaped into Africa, the student of anthropology would know the pygmy only as an extinct human race, whose remains, thousands of years old, are found buried in the caves of Southern Europe. In those dark ages they had fought as man to man, armed only with battle-axe of wood or stone, the only advantage possessed by the one being a longer reach and greater physical endurance. Now at their second meeting the handicap was greater, overwhelmingly in favour of the white man, who mercilessly drove all before him.

Surrounded on all sides, with no hope of retreat, giving and asking no quarter, the Bushman fought desperately – fought with the courage of a wild animal at bay. The white man's terms were death or bondage.

As incapable of accepting the drudgery of bondage as is the freedom-loving antelope of becoming a draught animal, to the Bushman the terms meant death. Armed only with his puny poisoned arrow he made a valiant stand, but his doom was certain.

Retreating always before the advance guard of civilisation, he was driven from his strongholds in the mountains out upon the desert plains. Accustomed only to obey the demands of nature, acknowledging no chief or leader, he was incapable of even the most primitive organisation. His mode of living made it impossible to collect in large communities; singly or in scattered families they followed the ever-diminishing herds of game. Remorseless, the white man followed, destroying all before him; and many authentic accounts are on record of the heartless persecution and cold-blooded butchery of little bands of this tragic race.

It is now nearly a century since the Bushmen disappeared from the habitable portions of South Africa. A few lingered awhile among the inaccessible mountains of Basutoland and along the lower reaches of the Orange River, but these have long since disappeared. A few scattered remnants found their way into the Kalahari, a waterless land ordinarily described as uninhabitable by man; and it is here and in the Kaokoveld that the descendants of those refugees are found today. In the vast unwanted territories he found safety and refuge from his enemies.

Driven first from a land of running streams and shady trees into one of stunted bush and isolated springs, he was afterwards hounded from these to open sandy plains, where he was obliged to suck from the sand the alkaline moisture it contained. Again he was driven still further into the waterless sand dunes of the desert, where a merciful Providence had provided a melon from which it was possible for mortals, in dire distress, to obtain sufficient moisture to live. But for the existence of this melon, the Bushman would by now have been as extinct as the quagga. Of the suffering and hardships of these tortured refugees we have no record.

Any other race faced with the prospect of having to obtain their water supply from the juice of the melon and their food from the roots and berries of the desert shrubs would probably have lain down and died. Many of the Bushmen doubtless did die, their spirit broken at last; but there were those who determined to live, and live they did. Donald Bain told me the story of the expedition which found and studied some of the descendants of these tenacious fugitives.

Although the expedition into the Kaokoveld was arranged in

71

detail in Cape Town, it was at Outjo, in South West Africa, that Bain made the final preparations and replenished his stores. On leaving Outjo he travelled for eighty miles without seeing a human being, and arrived at Okaukuejo, the most northerly station in the South West African territory. Here he found two policemen; and to them – they pass months at a stretch without sight of a white man – the coming of the expediton was an event. The desperate isolation of such a station is a very real hardship.

Another dozen miles and there opened up before the explorers one of the wonders of the world, the Etosha Pan. They halted and for minutes gazed spellbound, as must every man who for the first time beholds this picture. An ocean, it seemed, lay before them. An ocean apparently as vast as the Atlantic, but studded with fantastic islands, and upon the surface of the water moved weird and monstrous animals.

In reality they beheld the bed of a one-time inland sea which had covered an area of four thousand five hundred square miles. For reasons which cannot be definitely stated, the rivers which once emptied into this sea have been diverted into other channels and now flow into the ocean. The wonderful mirage effect is but a mockery of its bygone glory. The camera, more truthful than the human eye, records no islands; and the huge sea monsters are wildebeest and zebra licking, from the alkaline deposit on the surface of the pan, the salt which their systems demand.

Far beyond the horizon in the north and east lay the border of the pan; no human being has ever crossed it, no man ever will. For a mile or more along the shore the surface will bear the weight of man and beast, but beyond that all is black and saline slime. The gently sloping beach is now a grass-covered plain. Here once roared the mighty waves, but now the silence is broken only by the bark of the zebra, the cry of the jackal or the roar of the lion. Beyond the beach lay the forest, and in the forest all that they had come to seek.

They pushed on. Of a road there was no sign, but they clung to the beach and skirted the forest. Innumerable game paths crossed at right angles in the direction they were travelling, and made the going rough and slow. Great herds of wildebeest stampeded across the path, raising blinding clouds of dust.

The zebra, most inquisitive of all game, raced in droves not away from but towards them, standing gazing for a while and then perhaps following for a mile or more. Springbok, startled at the sound of the motor, raced towards the bush. Follow-my-leader is a rule which the springbok never fails to obey, and once the leaders had crossed the path the remainder of the herd made desperate attempts to do likewise. It never occurred to them that they could slow down for a moment and join their companions behind the car. They were obeying some instinct, developed through the countless centuries of their evolution, which demanded that they should follow in the direction taken by their leaders at whatever cost to themselves.

The party camped that night on the edge of a small crater, in the centre of which was a reed-covered marsh with pools of good clear water on the outskirts. Here in the daytime drank wildebeest and zebra, and after dark the more timid antelope, the wily jackal, the slinking leopard and loud-voiced hyena, all of whom fled in silence and terror at the approach of the lord of the forest. They were undisturbed by lion, but at the same spot only a few days before a traveller found one of his donkeys badly mauled before dark only about thirty yards from his wagon. Another donkey had been attacked and killed by a zebra stallion, and what few bones the hyena had left lay scattered round the camp.

An early start, and they were on the way again. Of the game which had been so plentiful the day before there was not a sign. Not a living thing could be seen on the miles of flat country ahead. As soon as the cool of the evening set in the game strike into the forest, and would stay there during the day but for the merciless blindfly which, with the warmth of the morning, become deadly active and attack man and beast alike, driving them in desperation from the shelter of the trees to seek refuge on the open plains. As the morning advanced they observed herds dashing from the forest into the open as though all the terrors of hell were behind them; and by eleven o'clock they were once more threading their way through a living mass.

The beach narrowed until finally the forest met the edge of the pan, and it became necessary to grope through the timber. Suddenly and without warning the forest opened, and they beheld in the distance, not a bunch of lions, a herd of elephants, or a lonely bull rhino, but – a castle! Anything more incongruous it would be difficult to imagine. They had arrived at Namutoni. Here the Germans during their occupation of that territory had maintained a large garrison as a protection against a sudden raid from the warlike Ovambo tribes in the north. With Teutonic thoroughness they had erected massive fortifications impregnable against attack from any savage nation. Although the country to the northward was nominally under their protection, no official ventured to disturb the privacy of the chiefs whose despotic rule was no less absolute than that of the Zulu chiefs of the last century.

Since South Africa received the mandate for this land the fort has been abandoned, and is now fast falling into ruins. The dreaded Ovambos are governed by one or two officials, and are at peace with the world. Herds of game of every description take shelter under the shadow of the castle walls and drink from the spring and water troughs to which, but a few years ago, were led the chargers of the German cavalry regiment.

Here Bain and his companions met Captain Nelson, game warden, and although not officially so called, Bushman commissioner. He is the only white man in a territory as large as the British Isles. He has a comfortable little cottage some distance from the castle, and he welcomed the party with that spontaneous hospitality which stamps the pioneer, and is of that quality which sweeps aside conventionality and all such city-bred trivialities. To the man of the veld, money, education and position are as naught, and man is judged, not by the condition of his fingernails or the colour of his socks, but by his ability to keep smiling – in other words, his manliness.

Below the castle is a splendid swimming bath hidden in a cluster of large, shady trees; and through it flows a crystal clear stream of beautiful spring water. This, too, is a relic, though well preserved, of the German occupation. Bain camped within reach of the swimming bath and prepared for the great work of the expedition – studying the Bushman. The administration had procured one of the few coloured men in the country who could serve as an interpreter. He was a wily and indolent fellow, and Bain could not always be certain that his questions or replies were correctly interpreted; but he certainly had an intimate knowledge of the country and its primitive inhabitants, together with all that was undesirable of the habits of the Europeans.

Captain Nelson had spent several years in the neighbourhood and his untiring efforts to secure the confidence of the Bushmen had met with considerable success. During the German occupation, and for some time afterwards, it was impossible to approach a Bushman settlement; or, if one did, it was only to find that the occupants had fled. Too often had the dreaded appearance of the white man meant slaughter, and generations of persecution had developed an instinct to hide. With the lion, the Bushman hid in the thicket, and with the snake he crawled on his belly through the stones. He feared them both, but he feared them less than the white man. Gradually, however, he began to realise that a change had come to pass, and, although still distrustful of strangers, he is now comparatively easy to approach.

On the following morning Captain Nelson and Bain set out with the tame half-breed Bushman interpreter as guide, and at the end of a few hours arrived at a Bushman encampment. The camp consisted of half a dozen huts, and the occupants were seven men, nine women and a dozen children. The women had that moment returned with their meagre collection of roots and bulbs, and the men were away on the chase. They had been away for three days, and it had been many days, so the women said, since they had tasted meat.

Once sure that the visitors were friends, the women crowded round and were delighted with presents of sweets and tobacco. With childlike simplicity they offered in return a tortoise shell full of berries, some of which Bain ate, and found not at all unpleasant. Soon the men of the camp arrived, and approached without hesitation, having recognised the familiar figure of Captain Nelson. The party consisted of six men and a boy, all armed with bows and quivers full of poisoned arrows. They said they had not succeeded in killing anything, but had found a lion kill, and had seized the remains. The interpreter, a voracious feeder, expressed his desire for food, and immediately the boy ran off, returning in a few minutes with a long, narrow strip of half-cooked meat, which was eagerly devoured.

Bain informed the Bushmen of the object of his visit, and requested them to shift their camp to a more accessible place. As an inducement, he promised them plenty of food and a ration of tobacco and sugar. They eagerly agreed, and promised, furthermore, to send word to a neighbouring camp some twenty miles to the south. These two *werfs* combined made up about thirty-five souls, and Bain decided to pitch his camp with theirs, and thus keep their movements under hourly observation.

He broke camp, said a reluctant farewell to the bath, and left for the water hole, where he expected to find the Bushmen encamped. At the sound of the engine men, women and children ran out to meet the visitors; but an accidental touch on the hooter sent them scampering off into the bush, or down into the long grass, where they lay like a covey of partridges. It was obvious at once that a far greater number had collected than Bain had anticipated – a hundred and thirty altogether. Word had gone forth, and passed along in that mysterious manner which has so often puzzled travellers in Africa, that food in plenty was to be obtained, and, like the vulture, they had gathered from far and wide. One family, with a baby of a few weeks old and two children hardly able to walk, had travelled eighty miles across country infested with lions, dependent for their food on the berries and roots they could find on the way.

Bain had brought a supply of mealie meal, sufficient to feed thirty adults on a normal ration for at least a fortnight; but here were a hundred more than he had bargained for, and most of them were half-starved and capable of eating five men's rations at a single sitting. There was nothing for it but a trip of a hundred and fifty miles for supplementary supplies; but the need was temporarily met by Captain Nelson, who lent the entire contents of his private store.

Surrounded by the entire population, the visitors off-loaded their lorry and prepared to make themselves comfortable. During the preceding two months they had been on the move all the time, with only an occasional break of two or three days, and they were eagerly looking forward to the weeks ahead and the luxury of real camp life. With a few green mopani branches and great bundles of dry grass, collected on the spot, the Bushmen soon constructed a separate hut for each member of the party. In design they were much alike, and similar to their own, one of which usually accommodates the entire family; but, try as he would, Bain found it impossible to shelter his six feet four within the allotted space. More grass and boughs were brought, and a kind of verandah added, but even then his feet were either in the sun or out in the rain.

The camp in order, Bain collected the mob and measured to each man, woman and child a liberal ration of mealie meal sufficient for the day only. It would have been easier to have issued rations for a week at a time than to have done so every day, a business which occupied a full hour every morning; but a Bushman only stops eating when there is nothing left to eat. They would have finished their week's supply in the first twenty-four hours, and have starved for the rest.

As soon as the camp had settled down and the Bushmen recovered from the first excitement of the arrival, the party paid a visit to their huts, which stood about fifty yards away. They had been erected in a rough, irregular circle, with the openings or doorways so arranged that their neighbours on either side were unable to view the interior of the hut. No effort was made to close the aperture either day or night, and the arrangement of the openings was the only attempt at domestic privacy. Constructed as they were of a few boughs, and covered with grass to keep out the sun, they would more rightly be called screens than huts. In diameter they were about five feet and were nearly five feet high.

In the centre a small fire is kept going all night, round which the family huddle together. In some cases a raw hide mat serves as bed and mattress, but the sleepers never have any covering. No attempt is made to tan and preserve the skins of the many wild animals upon which they live.

Within the circle formed by the huts are a number of fires, kept going continually, and used haphazardly by the occupants. The raw hide mat, one or two tortoise shells, a bladder containing water, and perhaps an old tin can or rough clay pot comprise their household goods and kitchen utensils.

Food is seldom boiled. Roots and berries are eaten raw. Their meat is cut into long, narrow strips, thrown on the coals and eaten while still decidedly underdone – a revolting habit. Catching hold of one end of the strip, which may be eighteen inches to two feet long, they cut off a piece about an inch from the lips. This is swallowed without much preliminary chewing, and very soon the strip disappears, to be followed immediately by another until their stomachs become grotesquely distended.

During six weeks in camp with the Bushmen, Bain never saw one who refused food or stopped eating while there was any more to be had; and yet he declares it would be unfair to call them gluttons. On the whole they eat a good deal less than the average white man; but the only storehouse they possess is the stomach, and this has adapted itself in a wonderful manner to the requirements of its owner. If the average man were to fill himself at one sitting with the same amount of food he would probably die – certainly he would be unable to move for days. This makes not the slightest difference to the Bushman, who, with stomach frightfully distended, will dance all night or show the greatest activity in the hunt next day.

The first night in the Bushman camp was a memorable one. The visitors had shed much of their bulky junk on the way up, including camp stretchers, and had merely thrown their blankets on the ground, often too tired even to shake them out. They had reached the point of absolute indifference as to where or how they slept, wishing only to be undisturbed. When a herd of elephants stampeded among the trees fifty yards away, or a lonely bull came marching round the camp, there was little to choose between the trumpeting of the beasts and the snores of the men.

Bain had a dog, old Ugly, his companion for several years, and he had come to rely entirely upon his judgment. When he barked, and he barked to some purpose, Bain sat up and took notice, though strangely enough he was not even wakened by the yapping of the rest of the pack.

Here, however, the visitors met something against which the dogs were no protection, and even Ugly was scared. No sooner had they settled round the fire than the scorpions began to arrive. Big ones, small ones, fat ones and lean, they came from all directions. They tired of killing them, for they were apparently without number.

Lions, too, were numerous. If they slept at any distance from the fires it meant taking a chance with the lions; if they slept near them it was a hundred to one on being stung by a scorpion. In the end they decided they preferred the lions and spend a very uncomfortable night well beyond the range of the firelight. Sunrise found them cutting poles, and next night every man slept upon a structure of his own manufacture, which, though somewhat resembling an ancient four-poster, had little to recommend it beyond the fact that it was scorpion proof.

Notwithstanding the liberal ration of mealie meal issued the day before, the guests still had a hungry look. Captain Nelson declared that a good feed of meat was required before they could be of any service, so Bain climbed on board the lorry and made for the edge of the pan. From the thousands around, he selected a particularly fat zebra and an old bull wildebeest, and was soon back in camp with a carload of meat. The entire population turned out to watch the carcasses off-loaded. As soon as permission had been given they set to, with every imaginable kind of knife, and within a quarter of an hour every man, woman and child was sitting at the end of a strip of flesh.

By the evening not a particle of meat was left. A well-fed atmosphere pervaded the camp and soon after dark was heard the weird chanting of the women, preceding an all-night dance. Answering calls not unlike the hunting cry of the jackal came from different quarters of the camp; and before long the whole mob had collected in a clearing just beyond the circle of huts. The women ranged themselves in a group, chanting and clapping in weird monotony, and without any effort to clear the ground the men fell into step behind one another, forming a circle of about fifty feet in diameter. The dance had started and would continue with scarcely a break until the early hours of the morning.

The endless circle went round and round, stepping in very good time to the clapping of the orchestra. Then there was a change in the formation. One man had worked his way forward and with one hand held a pair of sharp sticks above his head to represent the horns of the gemsbok. Bunched behind, but following him, were a group of four or five, and then followed the remainder. Round they went in this formation, perhaps a dozen times. Then one of the foremost group, who were pretending to be dogs, dashed forward and barked at the "gemsbok", who took one look round and leapt forward. Another circle or two, and again the dogs dashed forward, barking fiercely. The gemsbok slashed sideways and appeared to be growing uneasy. At shorter intervals now the dogs would approach, bark, yelp and tear at the buck, who replied by slashing right and left.

The hindmost group, representing the hunters, had, up to this time, patiently followed in the rear; but now they grew more excited, uttering wild shouts of encouragement to the dogs and brandishing their weapons in the air. The dogs become bolder, the buck visibly wearied. Panting and heaving, slashing and leaping, the gemsbok struggled on. Again and again the dogs rushed in and sprang aside as the horns whipped round. Louder and fiercer came the shouts from the hunters. At length the "buck" turned, bayed at last, dogs and hunters mingled, and the din was fearful. Down went the buck, fighting to the last, dogs and hunters closed in, and the dance was over.

Only a day or two before Bain and his companions had watched this very scene, with a real buck and dogs, when a wounded gemsbok had turned upon a pack of mongrels. Time after time had the dogs attacked, only to be scattered in all directions by those fearsome four-foot needle-pointed horns. One dog, a fraction of a second too late, was tossed a dozen yards or more, then stretched himself out and died.

A few moments later and the orchestra was again in full swing. One by one the men rose and joined in the monotonous circle. A legend exists among the Bushmen that once upon a time they were in possession of slaves, and this was the origin of the slave dance now to be performed. Round and round danced the ever-growing circle until every male, from the octogenarian to the smallest boy, had joined the band. Gradually four men worked their way to the front. They carried bundles and looked sick and weary.

On they danced, now ranging themselves abreast and a yard or two in front of the advancing horde. Wearily they dragged their footsteps, furtive glances were cast behind them, but on pressed the mob. Their feet began to drag, wild looks were cast to right and left as though in contemplation of a sudden dash for liberty. Threatening shouts from the rear startled them into greater activity and for a few moments they carried themselves erect, soon, however, to drag their tired feet once more.

Bent double, gasping, groaning, eyes dilated with fear, they shuffled on before their relentless masters. Struggling forward a few paces they would throw down their bundles and, with their digging sticks, endeavour to loosen a bulb or a root, anything to relieve the pangs of hunger. Each attempt brought a yell from the mob, and the sticks of the nearest fell on the shoulders of the slaves. Slower and slower, gradually weakening under the blows of their masters, until dropping finally, and unable to rise, they were "beaten to death" by the mob.

Well after sunrise the next morning Bain took a stroll through the camp and found the entire population still fast asleep. The dogs – and there were many of them – stood up, but made no sound beyond an occasional growl.

The Bushman dog is the only domesticated animal he has ever possessed. His origin, like that of his master, is unknown. Faithful and uncomplaining, dog has followed man in his wanderings through the African continent, and did not even desert him when, hunted from the arid plains of the great Karoo, he was forced into the waterless sands of the desert. Nondescript in colour, he stands about fourteen inches at the shoulder with a length of body seemingly out of proportion to his height. A broad forehead, sharp muzzle, upright ears and long drooping tail, give him the appearance of a mongrel; but he is possibly the oldest and certainly the most cunning breed of dog in the world.

A fugitive with his master, he has learned the value of silence. Rowdy, senseless barking may be all very well for a civilised dog, but, indulged in by him, would immediately betray his master's hiding place. He has learned to slink behind the hunter, taking advantage of every patch of shade, reserving his energy for the moment when he is called upon to distract the quarry's attention and enable his master to approach unseen and deal the death blow. Sensing danger, he will whine round his master; but a Bushman dog never barks save when lions are round the camp.

Polygamy is common among the Bushmen, and would no doubt be the rule, but for the fact that the husband finds himself fully occupied in finding food for one wife, without adding to his troubles by the addition of a second. They have no marriage ceremony. The consent of the parents having been obtained the couple move into a hut of their own, and thenceforth they are man and wife.

Infant mortality is great, and only a very small percentage of the children survive. The child is entirely dependent upon its mother for its sustenance until such time as its stomach is able to cope with an irregular diet of roots, tubers and underdone flesh. That diet can hardly be calculated to induce a normal or abundant milk secretion, and it is hardly to be wondered at that few children survive.

Should another arrive while the previous one is still dependent upon its mother, it is the custom to destroy the second one immediately after birth. It is a custom born of absolute necessity, like that of burying a helpless infant with the mother in the event of her death while nursing her offspring. There are no facilities in a Bushman camp – in fact it is impossible – to raise an infant should the mother die. Theirs is an endless struggle for existence, and only the fittest survive.

The children are given a great deal of liberty, and punishment is almost unknown. Those who are old enough accompany the women in their search for roots and berries. The smaller ones are hidden in or near the *werf* and, like the animals among which they live, these children will lie in absolute silence and almost without moving until their mothers return.

The boys, as soon as they are reckoned strong enough to pull a bow, accompany the men on the hunt. Every male child, even to the baby in arms, carries his bow and arrows; it is his only toy and very early in life he has acquired remarkable skill. They spend the greater part of the day stalking and shooting mice, doves or other small birds. Bain has often laughed at the sight of a wee mite toddling up to his mother for a drink and, when he has finished, throwing himself prone upon the ground and, taking advantage of the available cover, wriggling in the direction of some real or imaginary bird, with his tiny bow and bunch of grass arrows clasped firmly in his hands.

With such a huge family to feed, it was not long before it became imperative to start on the long journey for fresh supplies. Great was the rejoicing in camp when the lorry returned and double rations were issued. The greater part of the day was spent in feasting and sleeping, to be followed, as usual, by an all-night dance.

Bain noted several new dances, including the vulture dance, a most realistic imitation of a flock of vultures round a dead carcass; the wolf and jackal dance; the snake dance; the baboon dance and kudu dance. The three latter are danced by the women only. After each dance, into which the women put every bit as much vigour and action as the men, they would sit down, remove the small tortoise shell which hung suspended from the neck, extract from it a small puff of jackal skin, dab into the contents and proceed to powder themselves! The powder is ground from the dried leaves of a certain shrub and has quite a pleasant perfume until overwhelmed by the odour of sweat and rancid grease.

Around her waist the Bushman woman wears a rawhide belt from which is suspended in front a soft leather apron or fringe about four inches wide and fifteen inches long, and, behind, the roughly tanned skin of one of the smaller antelope. A string or two of glass, wooden or ostrich eggshell beads are worn round the neck, but the chief ornament consists of narrow circles or bracelets of skin, cut from the forehead of the zebra or antelope, and worn from the wrist to the elbow. A few short strings of beads, bone buttons or ostrich eggshell discs are occasionally strung into the hair, but generally speaking the women make little or no effort to adorn themselves.

In addition to the small tortoise-shell powder box, already described, they carry a small leather bag, about six inches by six, which contains pipe, tobacco, possibly a flint and steel, or other small and prized articles. Women while nursing their babies wear, in addition, a coarse leather mantle tied round the waist and over the shoulder. In this the baby will ride uncomplaining for hours at a time.

The men's apparel differs but little from that of the women, except that, instead of the fringe, they wear in front a small apron made from the stomach of the gemsbok. The apron behind is smaller or is frequently discarded altogether. Both men and women wear sandals, cleverly cut in one piece from the raw hide of either the gemsbok or zebra.

In manner they are gentle, pleasant and extremely good-natured. A quarrelsome or disagreeable disposition is not tolerated, the culprit being regarded as mentally deficient. In all the weeks during which this large gathering of Bushmen were under daily and hourly observation, Bain never observed a single unfriendly act nor once heard a voice raised, even for a moment, in anger.

A pleasing trait in the character of the Bushmen is their generosity and hospitality to one another. A handful of sweets or other much-loved trifle such as coffee, sugar, or tobacco, presented to one in compensation for some special service, will immediately and quite naturally be distributed among as many as happen to be standing round. No hungry Bushman ever presents himself at the hut of another without sharing in whatever his more fortunate brother may possess, be it roots, berries or good fat flesh.

Relieved of the daily necessity of hunting or digging for food, the Bushmen settled down, probably for the first time in their experience, to a life of leisure. They were, however, by no means idle. Bows were being prepared by the laborious process of paring and whittling down long selected saplings with a piece of sharpened iron not unlike a short, broad chisel. The process was a slow one, and infinite pains were taken to get the exact proportions.

Arrow shafts were prepared in the same way, and fitted with four feathers, cut from the quill of the vulture, and neatly bound to the shaft with threads of sinew. The arrowhead, cut from an old piece of scrap iron, beaten and flattened, was an immense undertaking. A few tools and an anvil would enable a man to make sufficient arrowheads in a single day to meet his requirements for a dozen years, but the Bushmen have no tools worthy of the name, and the task involves much labour and infinite patience.

The poison with which their arrows are tipped is obtained from a large bulb found in particular localities only. To obtain this poison it is often necessary for the Bushmen to make a journey of forty or fifty miles. The bulbs are cut into small pieces, placed in an old clay pot, and set on a slow fire. As the mass heats it exudes a sticky liquid which is allowed to simmer slowly until it has reached the consistency of putty. It is then cooled off, after which it is ready for use. It requires twenty-five pounds of the raw material to produce an ounce of poison, but this would be sufficient to tip at least a dozen arrows. The Bushmen are particularly careful never to handle or touch the poison with their fingers.

In addition to the bulb, which belongs to the same family as the belladonna, they use also the milk of the euphorbia; but the poison most favoured, and regarded as by far the most effective, is that obtained from the larva of a grub which, at certain seasons of the year, is to be found hanging in large numbers, like dried leaves, on the branches of a tree. Snake venom is never or very rarely used owing to the slowness of its action and the difficulty in obtaining sufficient quantities.

Following on a spell of sultry, thundery weather, came the

insects. Centipedes – hundreds of them – as thick as a sausage and quite a foot long, prowled round the kitchen, eating anything from potato peelings to carefully preserved trophies.

Moths, in all sizes, from almost nothing to the size of bats, made life hideous anywhere within ten yards of a lantern. Huge armies of spiders and beetles arrived from nowhere, and ate one another indiscriminately. The snakes, enlivened by the heat of approaching summer, uncoiled themselves and issued forth, hungry and lean after months of fasting.

The Bushmen have no antidote for snake poison, neither have they any for the poison of their own manufacture. The children are inoculated in the chest with the flesh of a certain lizard, and this, it is said, gives them a measure of immunity, but judging by the fear displayed at the sight of a snake, it is obvious that they can have little faith in its effectiveness.

By this time a very marked improvement in the condition of our Bushmen became clearly visible. The digestive organs of these emaciated men and women were apparently able to deal comfortably with the enormous quantities of food which they consumed daily. The wrinkles and loose folds of skin, which were so noticeable at first, were rapidly disappearing. Even the vermin with which they are normally covered, and which find suitable cover in these same wrinkles and folds had, for a time at least, departed.

About this time a party of Ovambos arrived from the north. They had with them a quantity of tobacco, dagga, and a few knives of their own manufacture, and these they proceeded to trade for sinew, beads and ostrich eggshell. The tobacco, from its smell and general appearance, might have been anything but what it was represented to be, but the Bushmen eagerly parted with their stocks of sinew and shell in return for a very small portion of this much desired leaf, declaring that it was infinitely superior to anything Bain had to offer.

Bain had noticed one woman, on the day of his arrival, as differing from the remainder of the crowd. Tall, wonderfully graceful and with beautiful limbs, she formed a marked contrast to the stunted, pot-bellied objects who constituted the female population of the camp. She was certainly not a Bushman woman, but all inquiries as to her origin met with evasive replies or obvious fabrications, making it clear that some mystery surrounded her presence among these people. She formed a favourite theme for speculation among the party; but the answer to the riddle is doubtless to be found in the fact that, until quite recently, the Bushmen were at perpetual war with the Ovambos. This tribe occupies the territory bordering on the Kunene River and, when the copper mines were opened in the Protectorate, a certain amount of labour was recruited among them. This necessitated a three-hundred-mile walk, accompanied often by their women, through country inhabited by Bushmen, and it frequently happened that the entire party walked into a cleverly concealed ambush, and were annihilated.

Why, in this particular case, the life of one was spared, will never be known. She certainly had no recollection of the event, nor had her larger stature and physical perfection prevented her from mating with a particularly repulsive pygmy, and adapting herself to the life of his people.

As the weeks passed the visitors began to wish that they had pitched camp a little further from that of the Bushmen. The flies became a horror. With the dawn they arrived and followed everyone, in one huge swarm, until bedtime. They poisoned the smallest scratch and worried it until it became a festering sore. Every time a pot was opened a couple of dozen would commit suicide in the contents. Life became altogether unbearable, and Bain decided to leave as soon as possible.

Before leaving, he presented every man with a shirt, and all the women with bright coloured cloths and sufficient material for a dress. The men immediately donned their shirts and gathered round in evident regret at the departure.

The rubbish had been placed in a large heap near their abandoned huts, and as Bain drew away there was a wild rush for that heap. Old men and young, women and children jostled one another in one glorious scramble for coloured paper, old rags, rusty nails or bits of string; in fact the entire contents of the rubbish pile had disappeared before the visitors were out of sight!

Perhaps the most memorable event of the whole trip was the arrival at Namutoni and the supper which followed. For many weeks the three-course menu had never varied beyond bread and jam, mealie meal porridge and venison. They had been cooking in petrol tins without lids. Captain Nelson's invitation to supper was eagerly accepted, and they sat down for the first time for nearly four months at a real table covered with a real cloth, and awaited the arrival of the dish, the delicious odour of which pervaded the cottage.

The day before a camel patrol had arrived from the south on its way through to Ovamboland, and had thoughtfully, as is the way with men in lonely places, procured a few small cabbages which they had carried in their saddlebags and presented to Captain Nelson.

Bain says he has eaten most things calculated to tickle the palate, but never has he tasted anything quite so good as that heaped-up plateful of boiled cabbage, or eaten anything with quite so much relish.

There are living today a far greater number of Bushmen than is generally supposed. They occupy the uninhabited territory around the Etosha Pan, and extend through the Kalahari to Bechuanaland. They may be said to occupy the entire Kalahari from the Okavango to the Orange River. No census, of course, has ever been taken, and it is impossible even to estimate the number; but, guessing, Bain says that there are not less than five thousand.

Life would be less precarious certainly if the Bushman built himself a four-roomed cottage and settled down to keep pigs and grow potatoes, but the reason he is prevented from so doing is the same that prevents a jackal from curling up on the hearthrug or a seagull from sleeping on a hen roost.

They are divided into clans or tribes, and are known under distinctive names; and each clan, although acknowledging no chief or tribal organisation, occupies well-defined and recognised areas. Trespassers from one clan into the territory of another are at first politely warned, and should the warning pass unheeded the guilty ones are ambushed, a few silent arrows carry death to the lawbreakers, the vultures gather round and the episode is at an end.

Each clan has adapted itself to the locality in which it dwells, and the customs vary somewhat, and are governed by the conditions under which the Bushmen live. In the north, where game is plentiful, they are hunters first and last. In the south, where game is comparatively scarce, they subsist almost entirely on t'sama, a small desert watermelon which springs up after the first thunderstorms of summer.

Without these melons the desert would be uninhabitable; and the Bushmen have learned to extract the moisture from the t'sama, which constitutes their only water supply. The residue or pulp is eaten, the seeds are cracked open and the kernels ground, between stones, into meal. The seeds, too, are roasted, and a beverage brewed, faintly resembling coffee.

The t'sama is most prolific, growing in patches covering many acres, and producing millions of melons. These are unaffected by exposure for many months, and buried in the dry sand, as they are sometimes stored by the Bushmen, they will remain in good condition for a very considerable period. It was without question the existence of this melon which enabled the Bushman to escape complete destruction.

Gradually but surely – unconscious of his fate – the Bushman is entering upon the last phase of his sorrowful history. Even now a small army of surveyors are looking through those three-legged weapons and planting those tiny white flags, which, as the Bushman already has learned, will be followed soon by the invasion of the white man, the destruction of the game, and his banishment for ever.

Belonging to some unknown prehistoric age, physically inferior and in mental development some thousands of years behind the rest of mankind, the Bushman would have been more kindly served if fate had dealt the final death blow when his forefathers perished at the hands of our cave-dwelling ancestors.

He who has chafed at the confinement of the city with all its petty conventions, and has yearned for the freedom of the veld, will sympathise in some degree with the feelings of these little men. Their fate is sealed, already the advance upon their desert home has begun. Not only ignorant, but incapable of organised effort, they are defenceless; hopeless and dumb, they retire before these insatiable intruders.

The original invaders of their country, the savage tribes from the north, have in their turn been conquered by the white man. To them, however, has been allocated fertile territory in which they are allowed to govern themselves, and from which the white man is excluded. The antelope – even the lion, the wolf, and the jackal – have sanctuaries jealously guarded by the laws of the white man into which they may retire and live their lives undisturbed and in safety.

But of all the vast territory which once belonged to the Bushmen, not one corner remains today. Hemmed in on all sides they can but retreat into the heart of the desert, and there, among the burning, waterless sands, be slowly forced out of existence.

THE COAST OF TREASURE

People of the Forests
1936

Deep in the green silence of the Knysna forests you will find a race of white people more isolated than any other human beings in South Africa. Grown men and women who have never seen a village; children who know only the faces of their parents and their too numerous brothers and sisters. Truly a race apart, these half-wild woodcutters and their families – strange folk indeed.

Years ago these People of the Forests dressed in skins and lived in *skerms* with only three walls. Even today the old men, with their long beards, are like Rip van Winkles in our modern world. Progress has hardly touched these exiles. There are some, of course, who have made the great trek to the timber mills of Knysna, returning with marvellous tales which were, no doubt, heard politely and disbelieved. A few adventurous spirits have gone out into the world boldly, learnt other trades, and forgotten the sunless life of the backwoods. Many of the present-day woodcutters have been to school. A few have money in the bank. Some of their homes are clean and well furnished.

But there still remains that tragic race apart – the people living so far from civilisation that they have had no chance of rising above their environment. A friendly, generous people struggling for their mere food in one of the hardest trades in the world. But so primitive that it has been found almost impossible to help them.

Of English, Scottish and Dutch descent are these men of the axe. For more than a century they have brought the enormous stinkwood and yellowwood trees crashing down; felling, squaring, sawing in those hot, moist forests where elephants roam. They have always been paid by results, and they show themselves no mercy as they hack out their livelihood from the ancient trees. Seldom are they well-nourished; yet they are capable of terrific labour.

For them the call of the woods is irresistible. They go out first as little boys, carrying water for the working parties, robbing wild hives, shooting bush doves, making fires for the coffee. Small wonder that they cannot be kept at school long. As soon as they have reached their teens they are ready to sweat over the huge, felled tree trunks with axe and saw. The woodcutter can see no further than the dense wall of his forests, no other future for his children. Year after year the number of trees allotted to woodcutters in the government reserves is being reduced. But in the mind of the woodcutter there is no threat to his existence, no plain warning.

An old woodcutter enters the magistrate's office with some long and intricate grievance.

"This is a matter for the conservator of forests," says the patient magistrate at last.

"Yes, but the magistrate is our father, and he must tell us what to do," mumbles the old man.

"Well, how many children have you?"

The woodcutter sets down his axe and counts on his fingers. "Piet and Jan – they are working for me, and Koos is in the Industrial School at Knysna."

"That's good. Any others?"

"Well, there is Hendrik. He has passed Standard Six, which is as much as a man can learn. And two more little ones."

"What will they do?"

"Go and work in the bush."

"One day there will be no more bush. I tell you, oupa, you're afraid to cross over that old mountain – you think the devil will catch you on the other side."

And the old man laughs uneasily, and goes away mumbling. For the woodcutters there is no world beyond the Knysna forests.

The foreman on a private forest estate told me that he once took a middle-aged woodcutter with him on a hunting expedition to the open veld near George, fifty miles away. They travelled by motor car, and the woodcutter was astounded. "I never thought Africa was so large," he exclaimed.

There is a pathetic story, too, of a woodcutter who went mad, ran amok with his axe, and killed a coloured boy. He was sent to an asylum in Cape Town. At the end of three years, during a period of sanity, he escaped and trudged back towards his beloved forests. He had no map, no knowledge of the road, nothing but a strong, sure instinct, like a homing pigeon. Fearing detection, he tramped along at night, avoiding villages, taking a route that lay along mountain slopes. For more than three hundred miles he stumbled on, coming at last to the lonely shack where dwelt his wife and children. One night he spent with them – then he was found and taken back. "Sentence me to years of imprisonment if you like," was his plea, "but let me know that one day I can come home."

Such is the spell of the forests. Men bred in cities feel as though they are facing a sinister and mysterious presence when they step out of the sunlight into that maze of creepers, ferns and trees. They would lose themselves in five minutes after leaving a path. The woodcutters find their way by sun and stars, and never lose their keen sense of direction. But twenty years ago a woodcutter's child disappeared in the forests. There was a great search, and undoubtedly the child would have been found but for the sudden rain that washed away all track and trace of the poor, frightened thing. All trace obliterated for ever – except a hat, which they took back to the mother . . .

The talk when woodcutters gather is all of accidents. There was the man whose legs were pinned down by the tree he had just felled – the only miscalculation of that kind on record. When found, he had worn his fingers almost to the bone in his efforts to dig away the earth beneath him. Sometimes a woodcutter grows careless and chops himself; but as a rule their high standard of skill never fails. One expert used to give demonstrations outside the bars in Knysna, placing half a crown between his toes and splitting it with a stroke of the axe. This trick brought him so many drinks one evening that he became over-confident and sliced off a toe!

Planks arrive at the Knysna factories, sometimes looking as though they had been planed by machinery; twenty feet long, without a deviation of one-thirty-second of an inch, all done by axe and saw. Yet most of these old craftsmen earn little – from twenty-four pounds to sixty pounds a year. It is possible for a woodcutter in a private forest, with the help of two young sons, to make eighteen shillings a day clear profit. But such earnings cannot be maintained for long. Rain and illness – usually through over-exertion – bring the average income down to a small figure.

The little body of men licensed to fell trees in the government forests numbers about three hundred at the present time. No new names have been added to the roll of registered woodcutters for many years, so that one old type is dying out.

Each year the trees to be sold are numbered by forest department officials, the woodcutters inspect them, draw lots for the trees, and gather at different forest stations for the allotment. They have to pay for the trees, of course, and there is an element of chance in the business which appeals mightily to the old men. If all their trees are perfect, then they can obtain good prices. But there is always the risk of rot, bad heart and poor colour; and sometimes it is difficult to persuade the forester that a tree is defective enough to justify a refund of the purchase price.

Old woodcutters, however, claim that they can look at a stinkwood tree and tell at once whether the wood will have that dark colour which is so desirable. It is a pity that stinkwood has only come to be valued as a wood for furniture in recent years. Thousands of tons of it went in wagons; and today supplies are limited.

Many of the woodcutters cannot read, write or count; but they know to the nearest penny how much is due to them for their work. Like the alluvial diamond diggers, their output is often pledged far in advance to their storekeepers. They are improvident, but they dislike being in debt. It is a tribute to their honesty, as a class, that they are allowed to buy necessities for months on end when, through illness, they are unable to pay. One man owed a hundred pounds at the end of a long illness. He paid back every penny within a year, and still had thirty pounds over; though Heaven alone knows how much sawdust and sweat went towards the repayment of that debt.

They could improve their economic position by growing some of their own food; but as I have said, the woodcutters are a race apart, never content to till the soil for long. During slack times some of them work as wagoners or farm labourers. Then, just at a time when they are most needed, they dash back to the forest life.

There are far too many boy and girl marriages in the forests.

Youths of twenty, who have saved enough money to buy axes, consider that they are established for life. Another crazy shack of poles, boards and galvanised iron appears on someone else's land. The young man takes a girl of fourteen or fifteen as wife. Another huge family – each baby a fresh problem for the local authorities – is raised.

With all their faults and follies, the woodcutters are, in the main, sober and law-abiding. The police have stopped the brewing of bee wine – a devastating spirit made from wild honey and yeast. At New Year, the chief festival of the forests, the woodcutters send for barrels of wine and play their guitars and concertinas.

Meat is a luxury to be enjoyed, at most, once a week. I visited one of their stores in the main forest and saw displayed the simple things they buy. Meal, coffee, sugar and tobacco – those are the most important items in the woodcutter's daily life. Sardines, salmon and bully beef are not bought every day. Old Dutch medicines were there, of course, for emergencies. And rows of field boots and blankets and tools – expensive articles to be gazed at wistfully and purchased only after long consideration.

It is good to know that the firms which cut down trees at Knysna also grow new trees. One day I went out to the forests and plantations with Mr C.W. Thesen, who sailed out from Norway to South Africa with his family in a little tops'l schooner in 1869. "There are more trees here today than when we came," he told me. "Not indigenous trees, of course – they are too slow. It is estimated that the South African yellowwood tree takes two thousand years to grow. But the blackwood tree we imported from Tasmania is said to grow twenty times faster than in its mother country. Plant all you can, I tell everyone. If only I had started planting in 1870, I would be reaping the harvest now."

There are still many tall yellowwood trees in that rich Knysna belt; enough, perhaps, to last out the lives of those old, bearded woodcutters whose names appear on the register. They are men of another century, like the trees. And who knows what strange monsters brushed their wings against the great tree trunks we see today in the Knysna forests!

*

Snakes flashed across the narrow road as I motored up into the Outeniquas, away from the main road, into country which, half a century ago, was marked "unexplored virgin forest" on surveyors' maps.

I was bound for the Bergplaas settlement – a new town which has been created by the Union forestry department with the idea of giving useful and profitable work to the poorest class of white man in South Africa. "No tourist ever goes to Bergplaas," the forestry officer in George had told me. "It is remote – but full of interest."

So I climbed and twisted along those lonely roads, bordered by that great green tangle of bush and trees where, only a few years ago, the bellowing and crashing of elephants was heard. I passed men like Voortrekkers, resting beside old wagons, with a smell of coffee and woodsmoke, the very breath of romance, hanging over their outspans. It is good for city-dwelling South Africans to enter this green world of the forests and step back into an age when life on the veld was an adventure.

Suddenly an enormous amphitheatre in the foothills appeared, and I saw the hundred tin-roofed cottages of Bergplaas among the pines. As I ran down towards the thatched house of the forester, I noticed that the place was alive with children; healthy, bare-footed children showing well-nourished faces such as one does not see in the back streets of our cities.

The forester was a strong, sun-tanned man in khaki, with a pipe, and a rifle resting beside his desk; one of those essentially outdoor men who always seem out of place in an office. He was the ruler of an area of twenty-five thousand acres, the guardian of timber worth many thousands – a character such as Zane Grey or Jack London might have taken for their books. From his windows I could see many square miles of his domain; mysterious contours of untouched forest; huge, steep patches of ground freshly planted; and, close to the settlement, the vegetable gardens of the settlers.

From all parts of South Africa come men and their families to work at Bergplaas. Married men only. "Poor whites" they are called – the class which, in the past, has been so difficult to help because they have not shown much sturdy self-reliance or desire to help themselves. These settlers of Bergplaas are really men of all types and trades; miners, small farmers, road makers, woodcutters.

There they receive a fresh start in life. They work harder than they have ever worked before. Some succeed, save money, or buy motor cars. Others drift back to the cities again, for in every scheme there must be a percentage of failures.

One thing is certain – the work of clearing this mountainous country for plantations ranks among the most exacting occupations in South Africa. The settlement was started seven years ago. Since then, six thousand acres have been cleared and planted. Those who believe that the poor white is incapable of strenuous labour over long periods should examine the results achieved at Bergplaas and similar settlements.

"As a matter of fact, they work too hard if you put them on piecework," a forestry official told me. "They work themselves to death. We have had to limit the amount of piecework for that very reason. Men were leaving their cottages at three o'clock in the morning, day after day, and clearing the ground by the light of fires, to earn more money. Some men were making twenty-five pounds a month – a large sum in their minds – and they would have broken down under the strain."

The ordinary pay is six shillings and fourpence a day, with free medical attendance, free education for their children, and a comfortable cottage at a rent of ten shillings a month. Living expenses are small, for most families keep poultry, several own cows and goats, and nearly all grow their own vegetables. There is a recreation hall, where dances and debates are held. A welfare officer, appointed by the labour department, lives at Bergplaas. Two private stores and two butchers' shops have been established.

Against these advantages must be set the weary daily routine in the distant plantations. The men must leave home at five, and sometimes at four in the morning to reach the spot which is being cleared in time for the day's work. This means climbing in the darkness, and often in drenching rain, up the rough mountainside, through muddy forests and stony slopes. They may work wet to the skin until half-past four in the afternoon, when they return exhausted over the long trail to the settlement. But very few of them care to miss a day's work. Six shillings and fourpence! In the George district the top pay for a white labourer is five shillings a day. The men of Bergplaas have learnt how to work, and there is a danger that they will injure themselves by working too hard. Still, some of them have been there years now; and they may see the completion of the scheme in fifteen years' time. It is something for a labourer to have a practical certainty of regular work for that period. Forestry is a sound investment. Some of the pines which have been planted at Bergplaas will be cut and sold – to thin the plantations – within the next eight years. During the following twenty years they will become much more valuable. The demand for timber in South Africa is so great that even the huge forests of George and Knysna can only supply a small part of it.

Fire is the only risk. The forester pointed to a small wooden box with a handle in his office – a sailor's foghorn, used here to sound the warning. "They can hear it on the mountain peaks, but not in the valleys," he said. His eyes were always roving the green carpet of the tree tops for signs of smoke – the threat of disaster. The forester's office is eleven hundred feet above the sea; and miles away, far higher, is a foreman's cottage, linked by telephone. One of the forester's prayers, I suppose, is that the bell may never ring to announce a forest fire.

Odd characters drift into Bergplaas as settlers. Among recent arrivals was the man who played with snakes. He walked into the forester's office one day with a tree snake, six feet long, over his shoulder. This man lacked entirely the sense of horror which most of us experience at the mere sight of a snake. He would see a snake in the forest, creep up and grip it just behind the head. Professional snake catchers use a forked stick in this dangerous form of hunting – this man used his bare hands.

He had been bitten twenty times, and had not a mark on his hands. Once the forester saw a snake strike out at the man and plant the poison in his hand. "You'll be dead tonight if you don't go to the doctor," he said. The man laughed, and survived.

But when I was at Bergplaas the man who played with snakes was in the hospital. A berg adder, one of the deadly snakes of the Outeniquas, had bitten into a vein. He was making a slow recovery, and he will never play with snakes so carelessly again.

These people of the forests live close to nature. They see the game and the wild creatures that have been driven back from the new roads and the farms into remote mountain sanctuaries. Here grysbok roam, and the bushbuck that will turn at bay and charge the hunter. Partridges are seen in large coveys. Leopards and tiger cats prowl in search of food. And, of course, there are the cunning baboons which tear up the young trees and have to be scared away with bullets.

No one likes shooting baboons; they show too many human qualities, and will even sacrifice their lives during a hunt by trying to protect their females and babies.

Baboons are almost fearless in the presence of a woman – unless she carries a rifle. A whole pack will retreat at the sight of a man. The forester at Bergplaas told me that it was never necessary to organise an attack on the baboons. "If you kill a few of them on a plantation, they will keep away from that spot for years," he said.

The sun was tipping the rocks of the mountain summits with gold as I left the people of the forests in their lonely settlement. That night I was down at the coast, drinking French wine with a shaded light on my white tablecloth, and listening to discreet electric music. The day had given me as strange a contrast in the lives of men in South Africa as any I had experienced. From "unexplored virgin forest" to the terrace of a modern hotel is a long journey.

SECRET AFRICA

Hereros, Hottentots, Berg Damaras

1953

Not since the early years of the century have the Hereros appeared so prominently in the world's news. Once they were a powerful race, about eighty thousand strong. They owned so many cattle that at the unaccustomed sound of a rifle shot the vast herds stampeded in all directions and the earth quivered as they thundered over the veld.

Seldom in the world's history has a whole race been sentenced to death. That was the fate of the Herero people when they rebelled against German rule early this century. Even today, with a rising birth rate, there are only about thirty-three thousand of them in the whole territory.

Hereros are tall people, especially the men. Bristling moustaches are common. Features are almost European, with well-shaped noses, high foreheads and oval faces. Babies are almost white at birth, though they soon take on the light brown or chocolate colour of the race. The Hereros admire fatness, probably because most of them are lean to the point of undernourishment.

Herero women are even more impressive than the men. In remote places, such as the Kaokoveld, they still wear the three-pronged *ekoris,* the cowhide headpieces which bear a strong resemblance to the ancient Viking headdress. When the white missionaries arrived with their wives, however, the Herero women copied the short bodices, tight waists and sweeping dresses. They retain these Victorian styles to this day, and contrive to look stately in clothes in which other natives would appear ridiculous.

The dominant characteristic of the Herero is pride. They have a deep contempt for other native races, while their attitude towards white people is one of distrust. Unlike other Bantu races, the Hereros pamper their women. Inheritance is through the mother's side of the family. Women exert unusual influence in everyday affairs. "By my mother's tears," swears a Herero when he takes an oath in court.

Origins of all the native races of South West Africa are mysterious and controversial. There is a legend among the Herero people that they were once known as the Mbandu, living in a distant land of reeds where water was abundant. About four centuries ago they migrated to South West Africa. Pastor Meinhof, a German linguist, found similarities between the languages of the Hereros and certain Nile tribes. *Ganda* means "town" along the Nile, and the Hereros say *onganda* to denote a large settlement. The V-shaped filing of the upper front teeth is observed among the Hereros and also on the Nile. Other authorities think the Hereros came from Lake Tanganyika, Northern Rhodesia, or Northern Angola.

Dr Hans Schinz, the early German traveller, declared that the name Herero came from the sound of assegais hurled in battle. The missionary Dannert pointed out that *herera* meant "to rejoice", so that the Hereros were "the joyful people". But there is another word *erero* (the past), and the Hereros describe themselves as "the ancient people". All these theories have been rejected by Dr Heinrich Vedder, the modern authority, in favour of the *okuhererera* legend. The Hereros say that they gained their present name only after they had finally decided to remain in South West Africa. *Okuhererera* means "to have made up one's mind".

Old books refer to the Hereros as Damaras, but this is entirely wrong. The pioneer traders heard the Hottentots talking of the Hereros as *Buri-Daman* (cattle people). They corrupted the *Daman* to Damaras, and called the Herero country Damaraland.

Hereros believe in a mystic spirit they call the Great Magician, and pray to their ancestors to intercede for them. Their cult of ancestor worship still influences their daily lives. In the beginning, they say, the Great Magician caused men and women to emerge in pairs from the trunk of a huge *omumborombonga* tree. First came Mukuru (the "old one") and his wife Kamungurunga, father and mother of the Herero race. Other human couples followed, and many of the animals also in pairs. Berg Damaras, goats and baboons (classed together and despised by the Hereros) entered the world from a rock. It was dark when life was created, and no one knew where to go. Then a stupid Berg Damara lit a fire and frightened the lions and all the other wild animals away. That is why they have remained wild to this day.

The Great Magician sent light and the people started to share out the domestic animals. When the Herero ancestors took the bull and the cow a violent argument arose, and soon everyone realised that different languages were being spoken. The human beings split up, and went their way with such cattle as they could seize. Away, too, roamed the original Hereros, taking their chosen cattle in triumph. Ever since then their descendants have loved cattle and regarded the herding of cattle as their sole destiny.

Mukuru's first act on leaving the *omumborombonga* tree was to light the holy fire and instruct Kamungurunga to tend it. Their children carried the holy fire wherever they settled; and they dared not allow it to burn out, for that would have meant the extinction of the tribe. In far corners the Herero priestesses still keep the holy fires alight and blow them into great blazes on festive occasions.

Hereros revere their ancestors and pass down the positions of old graves so that descendants may go there and pray. In this way missionaries have been able to compile Herero family trees going back more than four centuries. I doubt whether there is another native race in Africa offering such possibilities for patient research. Apart from the graves, the Hereros prefer to name the years rather than use numerals. Wars and weather and other events were impressed on their memories; so that Dr Heinrich Vedder and others have been able to compile long lists of dates with considerable accuracy. The year of floods, of false rumours, the year of the rushing sound, the berries, the climbing of the mountain, the smallpox, the hail, the comet, the year of the camel (brought by the Germans in 1889) – all these fit neatly into the story of the Herero nation.

Early white explorers in South West Africa heard rumours of the cattle-owning Hereros living in the fine pasturelands of the interior. Charles John Andersson, the Swede, gave the first accurate description of them about a hundred years ago. He said they were not a truthful people. They had great faith in witchcraft. At one time they lived in the Kaokoveld, but this country became too small for them and so they spread out into Damaraland. They enslaved many of the primitive Berg Damaras and drove the rest into the mountains. At first they pressed the Hottentots south; but these were formidable enemies, and when the Hottentots counter-attacked the Hereros had to give way. Andersson found the Hereros scattered and cowed.

In time, however, a brown Napoleon arose among the Hereros. He was Maharero, and his crafty father sent him to serve as a soldier under Jonker Afrikaner, the dreaded Hottentot leader. There young Maharero learnt the use of firearms; so that when he became chief he was able to defeat the Hottentots completely.

Maharero was also a clever politician. He realised the danger of German annexation and sought the protection of the Cape government. Unfortunately the British stopped at Walvis Bay and the Hereros soon found themselves under the German flag. They found themselves regarded as trespassers on their own grazing lands.

More and more land was confiscated, and traders robbed the Hereros of their cattle. Affairs reached the breaking point when the Germans took the old burial place of the Herero chiefs at Okahandja, cut down the sacred trees, and turned the place into a vegetable garden. In 1904 the Hereros decided to fight.

Before taking up arms, however, the Herero chief, Samuel Maharero, issued written instructions to his followers: "My people shall not lay hands on the following, namely: women and children, Englishmen, Boers, Bastards, Berg Damaras or Hottentots. I have taken an oath that their property will not be regarded as enemy property, neither that of the missionaries. Enough!"

Maharero's order was not carried out by all his men. One night in January, 1904, one hundred and twenty-three Germans (including three women and children) were taken by surprise by the Hereros and murdered.

German troops poured into the country, armed with modern rifles, maxims, quick-firing Krupp guns. Towards the end of 1904 the Hereros had been defeated in the field, thousands had been captured, while the remainder had taken refuge in the Waterberg mountains and the bushveld north of Gobabis. Yet the war dragged on. Governor Leutwein, regarded as too lenient, was superseded by the merciless General von Trotha. One of Von Trotha's first acts was to issue his notorious extermination order. Here is a translation of the text:

"I ask you, where is the Herero nation? Where is their headman Samuel Maharero today, who was in possession of thousands of cattle? He has fled like a wild animal over the English border, he has become as poor as the poorest veld-Herero.

"You must come with a white flag with all your followers and nothing will happen to you. If anyone thinks that after this order there will be any leniency shown to him he had better leave the country, *because if he is again seen in German territory he will be shot, and thus will all rebels be exterminated.*"

Peace envoys came in from the Hereros to discuss terms. That evening they were shot. "I wished to ensure that never again would there be a Herero rebellion," remarked Von Trotha lightly.

In the final drive, six German divisions were flung in a great arc against the retreating Hereros to prevent them from escaping into the Bechuanaland Protectorate with their cattle. One night the German troops, marching with their ox teams and wagons, sighted the fires of the huge Herero camp. But in the morning the pursuing Germans saw only skins and pots, and in the distance a pillar of dust. The Hereros, abandoning everything, had fled into the desert. They made grass fires to delay the chase. Here and there German patrols followed the line of flight. (Long afterwards a Bechuanaland Protectorate police sergeant who was sent out to the unmapped western frontier saw German names carved on a huge baobab tree, the names of troopers who had off-saddled there, and then turned back to their own territory.) Several German patrols ventured too far and died of thirst.

Among the Hereros the desert exacted a heavy toll. The gaunt survivors found a route along an old watercourse; they dug up a few moist roots and sucked the t'sama melons where they came upon them; but there was never enough water for that broken legion, and men, women and children dropped by the score day after day. How many came at last to the sanctuary of the Ngami water holes it is impossible to say. There were no white officials in Ngamiland at that time. Those who reached Lake Ngami with the last of the Herero cattle soon regained their strength and founded a colony in which the tribal conditions and customs remained unchanged. On that far shore the tall Hereros still worship their ancestors and keep their holy fires blazing. The hunting is good, they have their beehive huts, their milk and grain, horses and guns. Small in numbers among the teeming Batawanas, these Hereros with their memories of old conquests have secured a dominant position. The best cattle and the finest land are theirs. Magnificent crops of mealies, corn, tobacco and cotton are grown in the old lake area in spite of the lack of surface water. Round the shore, where waves thrown up by storms once pounded, there live several distinct races of people who found refuge there from wars and oppression. The most prosperous are the cattle-owning Hereros, five thousand exiles with their principal village at Sehitwa.

Von Trotha boasted that his army had killed sixty-five thousand Hereros during the war of extermination. Leutwein put it in a different way. "At a cost of several hundred millions of marks and several thousand German soldiers," he wrote, "we have, of the three business assets of the Protectorate – mining, farming and native labour – destroyed the second entirely and two-thirds of the last."

Leutwein was right. According to official German figures, only about fifteen thousand starving and resentful Hereros remained in South West Africa at the end of the struggle. Von Trotha was recalled, and his successor Governor von Lindequist was more humane. He revoked the extermination order and persuaded the surviving Hereros to come in from the mountains. But even then the horrors did not end. The prisoners were put to work on railway and harbour construction; and many more died from ill-treatment and disease in the concentration camp at Shark Island, Luderitz.

Professor Bonn, a realistic German scientist, summed it all up in a lecture in these words: "We solved the native problem by smashing tribal life and by creating a scarcity of labour. We tried to assume to ourselves the functions of Providence, and we tried to exterminate a native race whom our lack of wisdom had goaded into rebellion. We succeeded in breaking up the native tribes, but we have not yet succeeded in creating a new Germany."

A queer sequel to the Herero war was the pledge of the Herero women never again to bear children while Germany ruled their country. They kept the oath rigidly until South African troops occupied the territory seven years later.

Mr R.S. Cope, the South African native commissioner responsible for settling the Hereros in reserves after World War I, told me how he travelled with the chiefs in search of suitable country. At first the Hereros were difficult, he said, and their idea was to leave South West Africa in a body and join their people in Bechuanaland. Nevertheless, he persuaded them to settle in the reserves they now occupy at Epukiro, Aminius and Waterberg. Boreholes were provided, for without water the land of red dunes and *kameeldoring* trees, on the Kalahari edge (where the Epukiro and Aminius reserves are situated) is uninhabitable. Waterberg, as the name implies, is finer country, envied by many white farmers.

At the time of the settlement, Mr Cope assured me, the areas granted to the Hereros were ample for their cattle. He thinks, however, that the Union government might have shown more vision and allowed space for a people whose birth rate rose after the Germans had departed. Today the Hereros feel cramped in their reserves. So do the white farmers in a land where many are landless.

Any happiness the sullen Herero enjoys is found in his cattle. Only since the Union occupation has the Herero become a cattle-owner again. Next in his affections come his horse and his gun. He is a polygamist when he can afford such luxuries.

Every year, just after the full moon in August, the Hereros gather at Okahandja. They march to the graves of their old chiefs, wearing scraps of military uniform or even tartan kilts. Every year the old heathen ceremonies are revived. The graves of the chiefs are in the centre of Okahandja, under the huge trees where once the royal kraal stood. Now there is only the tombstone with its inscription in English, German and the Herero language:

THE HERERO CHIEFS
TJAMUAHA, DIED 1859, AND HIS SON MAHARERO, DIED OCTOBER 5, 1890; SAMUEL MAHARERO, BORN 1856, DIED MARCH 14, 1923.
HERE LIE THREE CHIEFS AT REST. THEY RULED THE COUNTRY FOR THE GOOD OF THE HERERO PEOPLE, BUT NOW THEY ARE DEAD. THEY WERE CHIEFS INDEED.

Samuel Maharero died as an exile in Bechuanaland, and his body was brought here for burial beside his father and grandfather. Once the Hereros hoped that the tribal glory would return; but now they have lost all hope, for the last chief of the royal blood, Traugott Maharero, was buried at Okahandja in 1945. The line is extinct and the people of yesterday have ceased to pray for a tomorrow.

*

Hottentot is a weird name for a race, and no one has been able to give a convincing explanation of it. South West Africa is now the last country in which you will find pure Hottentots living with a semblance of the old tribal organisation. They call themselves Khoi-Khoi (men of men) or the "red people", though they are not an outstanding native race like the Zulus and it takes imagination to detect a reddish appearance. Many of them, with narrow eyes and yellow skins, look distinctly Chinese. There are about thirty-one thousand of them in the territory.

The superior Hottentot dislikes the name, regarding it (not without reason) as a term of contempt. Some say it arose from the clicking, stuttering speech with which the Hottentots greeted the first white men they met. Other investigations declare that the early Hottentots shouted a welcome which sounded like "Hautitou". Scientists prefer the word Nama for the race and language.

Very often the layman finds it impossible to distinguish between Hottentot and Bushman; and that some relationship exists is obvious. As a rule, the Hottentot is taller, with a longer and narrower head. Cheekbones and eyes are similar. Hottentot women display steatopygia (the elongated buttocks) to an even more marked degree than the Bushman women. It is now generally accepted that the Bushmen migrating southwards through Africa, met and mingled with a race of Hamitic invaders. Somewhere in the area of the Greak Lakes there arose a mixed people – the Hottentots. No doubt the Hamites provided the cattle and certain peculiarities of language which stamp the Nama tongue as different from the Bushman dialects.

According to Hottentot tradition, they came from the north-east, over the high plateau of Africa, their faces always turned to the setting sun until they reached the "great waters" of the South Atlantic. Then they turned south at last. Some tribes remained in South West Africa, others migrated all the way to the Cape. They brought long-horned cattle with them, larger than the Herero cattle, and also fat-tailed sheep. Unlike the Hereros, they enjoy eating meat not only at funeral feasts but whenever they can afford to slaughter an ox.

Thus the Hottentots may claim a material culture superior to the Bushmen. Milk is their main food. In recent years some have taken to agriculture. They possess the art of smelting iron, but they were never painters. Their tribes are far larger than the Bushman clans. In the recent past, their organisation in time of war was most formidable.

Hottentots use *matjieshuisies* as dwellings, mat huts of beehive shape and far more comfortable than the Bushman *skerms*. A doctor who lived in a Hottentot area for years declared that he found enough skill in their medical remedies to cause the scoffer to cease scoffing. "Here lies the root and origin of modern medicine," summed up the doctor.

For headaches the Hottentots take dagga or shave the head in furrows and massage the nape of the neck. The juice of aloes is served as a warm broth after excesses of eating and drinking. Fat is rubbed into the body to cure many internal pains. They can reduce dislocations and apply splints to broken limbs. In the old days they amputated limbs; and there is skeletal evidence proving that the patients recovered. They knew all about bleeding and cupping with ox horns for colics.

Like the Bushmen, the Hottentots have their snake-bite remedies. Dried cobra venom is taken daily to give immunity. Roots are used to draw out poisons, the leaves of the *kougoed* plant are chewed for toothache, and the same leaves are administered as a narcotic. Rare mountain varieties of buchu are prized as medicines, and some are so hard to locate that a thimbleful is exchanged for a sheep. Wild olives, taken as a draught, produce sweating, and there is an aromatic bush which alleviates convulsions.

Two groups of Hottentots are found in South West Africa – the pure and primitive Nama tribes which settled there about six centuries ago during the migration; and the so-called Orlams who left these tribes behind and went on far to the south of the Orange River. They returned during the eighteenth and early nineteenth centuries as a result of the pressure of white settlement. Orlams appears to be a Cape Malay word variously translated as "the foreigners", "intelligent", or "cunning". Certainly the Orlams were more advanced than the pure Namas, for when they returned they had learnt Cape Dutch and they owned horses and rifles. Most of them had come under missionary influence, and a very few were educated men of great ability with a little white blood in their ancestry.

The old Nama tribes were the Bondelswarts of the Warmbad area, the Fransman Hottentots of Gochas, the Red Nation of Hoachanas, the Veldschoendragers who lived on the edge of the Kalahari, and the Topnaars of the north. Most powerful of the newcomers were the Afrikaners and the Witboois. Other groups of Orlams settled at Gobabis, Berseba and Bethanie.

At first the Namas resisted this immigration from the south, but they soon found they were no match for the well-armed Orlams. War after war established the Orlams as the rulers, with Jager Afrikaner and his son Jonker as great and ruthless leaders. Girls and cattle were the prizes.

Jager Afrikaner had fought a war for the Cape government against the Bushmen towards the end of the eighteenth century. This little victory went to his head, and he turned into a more dangerous raider than any Bushman. He used an island in the Orange River as his base, recruited an army of Hottentots and half-castes, and terrorised the northern border. Those pioneer missionaries, the Albrechts brothers, had to ride for their lives from Warmbad in 1811 while Afrikaner wrecked the mission. This bandit, further emboldened, raided the Cape districts as far south as Stellenbosch; and he made forays to the north and robbed the Hottentots of South West Africa.

Although he was a small man with one arm partially disabled as a result of a bullet wound, Jager Afrikaner was a daring hunter. He could swim out to a rock in the Orange River at night with his gun on his head and wait for the hippo to rise. He killed his hippo at point-blank range, firing down the throat. Once, in a guerrilla fight, he raced for miles on foot after twenty armed enemies, retreating only when his gun was shot to pieces in his hands.

That great missionary, the Reverend Robert Moffat, reopened the Warmbad mission in 1818 and set about converting Jager Afrikaner. Frontier farmers predicted tragedy, and Moffat wrote:

"One said he would set me up as a mark for his boys to shoot at and another, that he would strip off my skin and make a drum of it to dance to. Another most consoling prediction was that he would make a drinking cup of my skull."

Moffat was not deterred. He speedily converted Jager Afrikaner and took him to Cape Town (disguised as his servant) to meet Lord Charles Somerset, the governor. A rumour had gone round that Moffat had been murdered by Afrikaner. "My testimony as to the entire reformation of Afrikaner's character and his conversion was discarded as the effusion of a frenzied brain," Moffat recorded. Lord Charles Somerset was so pleasantly surprised that he presented Afrikaner with a wagon.

Jager Afrikaner died peacefully in 1823, but by that time his son Jonker had crossed the Orange River and was playing havoc with the Hottentot tribes in the north. Halfway through the century he was ruling Windhoek, and it was not until Andersson rallied the Hereros that the Hottentots under Jonker Afrikaner were defeated.

Greatest of all Hottentot leaders, one of the most remarkable natives Africa has produced, was Kaptein Hendrik Witbooi. He too had come up from the Cape Colony in the 1860s as a young man, the son of a chief. Hendrik had received a sound education. Olpp, a German missionary at Gibeon, trained him as an evangelist, and finally Hendrik Witbooi learnt to write Dutch with a power no other Hottentot had ever possessed.

Hendrik was a stunted Hottentot (nicknamed The Short One) with a serious face. He had lost his right thumb in a fight with the Hereros, but he could write clearly with the pen held between the index and middle fingers. Some of the white pioneers came to know him well, and in fairly recent years I heard stories of Witbooi at first hand.

Religious teaching had an unfortunate effect on Hendrik Witbooi, for he heard voices and saw himself as a "yellow Messiah" appointed to save his race from defeat. Thanks to Olpp's influence, he avoided clashes with white people for a long time; but he fought cruel campaigns against Hottentot chiefs who refused to acknowledge his leadership. He also raided the Herero cattle so that Maharero never felt safe. Before long Witbooi was signing his letters "King of Great Namaqualand".

Witbooi alone of all the native chiefs realised what the German protectorate in South West Africa meant, and at the start he decided to resist. His stronghold was in the Naukluft mountains on the edge of the Namib desert; from there he made forays and terrorized the land. "I shall go on making war until God gives me a sign that I must make peace," wrote Witbooi to the *kaptein* of the Rehoboth Basters.

Von François, the first German military officer, saw that there would be no peace in the land unless a settlement with Witbooi was reached. He offered him protection.

"What is protection, from what are we to be protected, and from what danger and difficulty and need is one chief protected against another?" wrote Witbooi in his letter of refusal.

Von François then attacked Witbooi's stronghold without declaration of war. The surprise attack was so successful that Hendrik Witbooi had a cup of coffee in his hand when the firing started. But the old Hottentot warrior extricated his fighting men and escaped. He tried to stir up his old enemies, the Hereros, against the Germans but failed. Walvis Bay traders refused to supply him with ammunition. The invincible Witbooi had to negotiate an armistice and agree to live quietly at Gibeon. He never forgave Von François for attacking him without warning.

Witbooi became friendly with Governor Leutwein and Captain von Burgsdorff, the German district chief at Gibeon. He lived pleasantly after years of warfare, driving about in a magnificent carriage drawn by four grey horses. In time the Germans came to regard Witbooi as their most valuable ally, and Witbooi assisted them loyally in six native wars.

But the ageing kaptein was still a proud mystic. One day Leutwein showed him two new field guns, and remarked: "Look, my Emperor has thousand of these guns."

"I know your Emperor is stronger than I am – but don't always be reminding me," replied Witbooi.

One of the Afrikaner pioneers of South West Africa explained to me why Witbooi's fighting men always wore white bands round their wide-brimmed hats. "The Hereros were afraid of Witbooi, and he knew it," said my informant. "When the Witboois went into battle the sight of their white hatbands struck terror into the hearts of their enemies. And in the bush they would use their hats as decoys – stick them up to be fired at while they lay under cover."

Witbooi was on such good terms with the Germans during his later years that Governor Leutwein often invited him into the officers' mess and drank a bottle of wine with him. No other native leader enjoyed such a privilege. Yet in the end Hendrik Witbooi turned on his German friends. He was over eighty, and his men were helping the Germans in the north against the Hereros in the 1904 campaign. It is said that word reached Witbooi that his Hottentots were being badly treated, and that some had been deported to the Cameroons. About this time, too, Witbooi had come under the influence of a man named Stuurman, a "priest" of the Ethiopian Church, who urged him to take up arms agains the Germans.

Thus, after a decade of friendship, old Witbooi fought the Germans again. He fought so vigorously that the farmers raced for Keetmanshoop to find sanctuary. Von Trotha offered a reward of a thousand pounds for him, dead or alive. Von Burgsdorff rode out in search of Witbooi with the idea of reasoning with him. Near Mariental he encountered a band of Witbooi's fighters. They asked Von Burgsdorff whether Hendrik Witbooi's declaration of war had been received. Von Burgsdorff assented. He was shot dead on the spot.

Not far from this scene Hendrik Witbooi led an attack on a German military wagon. Witbooi was shot in the ankle, and though he escaped the wound proved fatal. He was buried on the farm now known as Witbooisende. German troops were approaching, but the Hottentots held them back while Witbooi's son and others hastily dug a grave. While bullets whistled over them they removed all traces of digging and then retreated.

"A born leader and ruler, that Witbooi was," wrote Leutwein shortly afterwards. "He was a man who might have become world famous had it not been his fate to be born to a small African throne. His life was forfeit. Therefore the German bullet which killed him was a release for him and for us. It brought to him the honourable death of a soldier and it saved us from a serious dilemma. The little chief had, however, immortalised his name in the history of the country. First his obstinate resistance to the mighty power of the German Empire; then his loyal support of our cause for ten years; and eventually the rebellion. To me he is still the little chief who so loyally stood by my side. He was the last national hero of a dying race."

Further south the Bondelswart Hottentots were in revolt. Before the death of Witbooi they had shot Lieutenant Jobst, the German officer at Warmbad. Their own leader, Kaptein William Christian, had been killed; but the Bondels had besieged the Warmbad fort where all the white people had taken refuge. The alarm signal was given rapidly over the heliograph line to Windhoek, and reinforcements poured into the south. Nevertheless, the war against the cunning Hottentot guerrillas dragged on for years. Even when the Bondelswarts surrendered, the rifles were handed in reluctantly. Muzzle-loaders were given up while breech-loaders were hidden. The leaders, Morris and Marengo, were hunted over the Cape border with prices on their heads.

Marengo was a half-breed with a grudge against all white people because of a flogging he had received from a farmer. He escaped from internment in the Cape and raised the Bondelswarts again. This time the Cape government felt some responsibility in the matter and agreed to co-operate with the Germans if Marengo crossed the border again.

The end of Marengo was a drama typical of the frontier. It was described to me by a police sergeant who took part in the operations. "Marengo crossed the Orange River with four hundred men and a signaller on a distant kopje warned us he was coming," said the sergeant. "When Marengo saw the troop of sixty Cape Mounted Police he started firing; from the whine of the bullets we could tell the Hottentots were using Martini and Mauser rifles captured from the Germans. Our officer gave the order to charge and we rushed them on horseback, firing as we went. Three men rose suddenly in front of me, and one was Marengo. I recognised him in a flash by his powerful build, wide-brimmed hat, brown riding breeches and leggings. A trooper shot at him and missed. Then the officer shot him right between the eyes. Almost immediately the rest of the Hottentots threw down their arms and surrendered."

Thus ended a campaign which cost Germany thirty million pounds and two thousand of her troops. Major Elliott and his officers received the Kaiser's decorations. Broken rifles, ration tins, water bottles and skeletons in lonely mountain passes and valleys still tell the story of the guerrilla war. Under the mimosas at the water holes you will find graves of the German dead.

*

South West Africa's most mysterious people are the Berg Damaras, a negroid race of unknown origin. They have even lost their own language, and all they can tell you is that they were the first nation to occupy the territory. No one is in a position to contradict them on that point.

Berg Damaras are short, thickset people without excess fat on their bodies. They dread water, for according to their firm belief, washing renders the hunter powerless in the chase. Thus the true negro black of the Berg Damara's skin is seldom visible, though the negro features, receding foreheads and flat noses, are distinct enough.

Haukhoin (real men), the Berg Damaras call themselves. The Herero name for them, Ovazorotua, is not so flattering, for it means "black slaves". There are about thirty-seven thousand of them in South West Africa today. A German census taken in 1911 showed only about twelve thousand, eight hundred Berg Damaras, but there were many at that time living beyond the law.

Some scientists agree with the statement that the Berg Damaras are the oldest of the present inhabitants of South West Africa, older even than the Bushmen. The early Dutch explorers from the Cape discovered them in the mountains; and they were probably the last of all the native races of Africa to come under missionary influence.

The Reverend C. Hugo Hahn was fascinated by the problem of the Berg Damaras a century ago. He trekked by ox wagon to their headquarters at Okombahe on the Omaruru River within sight of the Brandberg. Hahn noted that the language was an "insoluble riddle", for they spoke only Nama, the Hottentot tongue. Obviously they had been enslaved by the Hottentots so long ago that even the Berg Damaras living as free men in the most inaccessible mountain strongholds revealed no trace of a language of their own. Later research by Dr Heinrich Vedder, however, has revealed certain expressions which are not of Nama origin. Some of the loan words appear to be derived from Sudanese languages. But the ancestral home of the Berg Damaras has never been fixed. It is possible that they were negroes who migrated down the coast from West Africa.

Hahn formed a favourable impression of the Berg Damaras, for they brought him little presents and did not beg. "This was a pleasant change from the Namaqua and Herero *werfts,* where travellers and missionaries are pestered by the begging of the people," he recorded. He thought that the Berg Damaras were braver than other native races. Their great aim was to possess firearms. They worked hard, conserved their resources, and made loyal servants.

Among the people Hahn met were Berg Damaras who had only recently left their hiding places in the Erongo Mountains. While living in the remote places they had revenged themselves on the Hottentots by raiding their cattle. "These men revealed in their bearing that they had always been free," Hahn recorded. "Some had found refuge in the Brandberg, but the rest had settled at Okombahe, where they live unmolested."

Daniel Cloete, a coloured missionary, had settled at Okombahe at the time of Hahn's visit, and he had taught the children to sing German hymns. "They have a great talent for vocal music, and an excellent memory for it," Hahn said. "They surpass the Hottentots, who are good singers. Otherwise they are intellectually below the other races, though this is possibly an effect of the oppression they have suffered for so long."

In the Omatako area in 1870 Hahn found a number of Berg Damaras and at one kraal they entertained him by drumming on the hollow stem of a tree covered with hide. They also played the kudu horn and one-stringed bow. They lived in cone-shaped bush huts and made clay pots and wooden bowls.

Palgrave in 1875 found the Berg Damaras growing mealies, pumpkins, calabashes and tobacco at Okombahe. Previously they had sown wheat along a mile of river bed, harvested three hundred muids and sold the crop at two pounds a muid. "For people recently reclaimed from savagery their progress is astonishing," Palgrave reported. He described them as provident people, becoming rich in cattle and goats, but without the Herero love of cattle. Originally, he thought, they were an agricultural people like the Ovambos. Nevertheless, they were probably the finest cattle masters in the world. They worked harder than the Hereros and made good servants. At the time of his journey, Palgrave estimated that four-fifths of the Berg Damara race were either living the Bushman life in isolated places or were slaves of the Hereros and Hottentots. He recommended that if the Cape government decided to annex South West Africa the Berg Damaras should be given their freedom. "The Berg Damara is the hewer of wood and drawer of water, and he rather likes it," summed up Palgrave. "The fates have willed it."

A missionary, the Reverend C.G. Buttner, pointed out that the Berg Damaras had no tribal organisation. They were enslaved, robbed and murdered on all sides, but as a nation they never defended themselves. At the most, a Berg Damara family group might attempt to resist when attacked. In wars between the Hereros and Hottentots the Berg Damaras simply served their masters on both sides.

Once the Berg Damaras were all slaves, for only a nation in total subjection could lose its language so completely. Last century, however, they formed three main groups – the serfs, the valley people and the Ou-Khoin (the people of the mountain tops). The bulk of the race are now working for white farmers or living in reserves. They deserted the gorges of the Brandberg range early this century, when their water holes failed; but families may still be found in the fastnesses of Erongo and Waterberg and the lonely country round Franzfontein. The bow-and-arrow Berg Damaras have not yet died out.

Hottentots will tell you dark tales of the Berg Damaras as sorcerers and credit them with great skill in treating pains in any part of the body. Scientific enquiry, however, has revealed that the Berg Damaras are poor herbalists compared with the Bushmen and Hottentots. They treat most ailments by making shallow incisions or burning the afflicted part. Old people are often covered with scars as a result of this treatment.

The diet of the Berg Damaras is equally simple. They rejoice when the locust plague appears, and make a porridge of roasted locusts. Honey is a luxury, and even the Bushmen cannot surpass them in observing the line of flight of the bees or seeking the honey bird's aid. *Veldkos* plays such a vital part in the lives of the primitive Berg Damaras that their calendar starts each year in April, when the *uintjies* are ripe. These wild onions, about the size of a pea, are dug up with sharp sticks. The strong juice makes their cheeks swell, but they suffer this inconvenience gladly. Berries, lizards, caterpillars and mice are other Berg Damara delicacies.

Women and children are allowed to eat hares if they bury the fur. The men will not touch this meat for fear that they will not return to life after death. This superstition is based, of course, on the old hare and moon fable, related by many other African races. Several authorities have laid down that the Berg Damaras had no religious views of their own before they came under missionary influence. Members of the race spoke vaguely of a large black rock in the north, known to them as their great-grandfather, from which all living things emerged. Vedder, however, discovered an old religion – different from Hottentot and Herero beliefs – among the isolated Berg Damaras of the Otavi highlands and elsewhere.

The original Berg Damaras, it seems, handed down a tradition of a supreme divinity called Gamab, god of thunder and water. Gamab did not create the world, but they looked to him for the annual revival of the larders of nature. Gamab, the Berg Damaras admit, is a cannibal. He sits round the fire with his elders in his village beyond the stars eating human flesh. When the supply runs short, Gamab directs an arrow towards a selected victim on earth, and the feast goes on.

Primitive though they are, the Berg Damaras possessed one art which the superior Hereros lacked, that of working in iron and copper. As slaves they made weapons for the Hereros, and later repaired their guns. Hereros and Hottentots called the Berg Damaras baboons because they lived in the rocks and dug for roots. Certainly the Berg Damaras can climb like baboons; they have inherited hard feet, and they are among the finest mountaineers in Africa. And in spite of their low mentality, they are not without their poets, their proverbs and their fables.

When the Union forces occupied South West Africa a fresh survey was made of the Berg Damara people. They had become scattered during the German colonisation scheme, and many had shared the fate of the Hereros during the native wars simply because the soldiers were unable to distinguish between harmless Berg Damara and hostile Herero.

Chief Judas Goraseb of Okombahe told Union officials: "We

were the very first people in this land. My people were here long before the Hottentots and Hereros came. The Hereros drove us away from the old chief's village of Okanjande in the Kaokoveld to settle in Windhoek." Goraseb was able to give the names of fifteen Berg Damara chiefs who had ruled before him, going back for centuries. Yet the great riddle of the Berg Damaras remains. Here are negroes with the hunting methods of the Bushman, the language of the Hottentot and some of the Herero customs.

Along the Orange River and in other parts of South Africa there are relics of a vanished people called the Kattea. It may be that the small, pitch-black Vaalpens tribe of the Northern Transvaal are the modern Kattea people. The Berg Damaras, according to some theorists, are a branch of the Kattea. In ancient times, some Berg Damaras will tell you, they lived by a great river that flowed all the year round. That may have been the Niger or the Congo, the Nile or the Orange. The missionary Irle put forward the dramatic theory that the Phoenicians and the Berg Damaras intermarried and produced the light-skinned Hottentots. Such theories make one thoughtful, but the Berg Damaras remain a mystery.

Today the Berg Damaras are scattered over the face of the land. There is only one native race in South West Africa which still holds every inch of its ancestral domain. This is the Ovambo people, with their degenerate cousins the Okavango tribes. If you love Old Africa and the last outposts there is another long, hard trek before you.

LORDS OF THE LAST FRONTIER

South West Afrikaners

1953

Mankind has been moving over the face of Africa for untold centuries, but the strangest migration of white people within living memory was that disastrous episode known as the Thirstland Trek. It brought the first organised body of farmers to South West Africa, and the price they paid in terms of suffering was high.

I have been gripped by this trek ever since I heard the drama related many years ago by a few of the original trekkers. They had survived an ordeal which some regard as the most painful chapter in the whole story of the Afrikaner race. Theirs was an achievement which ranks with the Great Trek; for although it was carried out on a small scale the dangers were greater and the casualties relatively much higher. Like the Voortrekkers of 1836, the Thirstland trekkers were true pioneers depending on their ox wagons, their guns and their Bibles. I followed the tracks of the Thirstland wagons, camped at the same water holes, stood beside the great trees in lonely places and the rivers where they buried their dead. Now I can visualise the whole tortuous progress of the trek . . . last of all Afrikaner treks to freedom.

Trek! There is no more powerful word in the Afrikaans language. For that reason, no doubt, it has been taken over by English dictionaries. But in Afrikaans there is also the word *trekgees* – trek fever, the restless spirit that drives all wandering men to find out for themselves what lies over the horizon.

Trekgees impelled the Voortrekkers to load their wagons and face dangers known and unknown on the long journey that carried the frontiers of civilised South Africa north to the Limpopo. Forty years later a few Voortrekker patriarchs, and their sons and grandsons, felt the mysterious urge again, and planned the Thirstland Trek.

It was in the Transvaal Republic, during the rule of President Thomas Burgers, that this almost inexplicable movement arose. Burgers was regarded by some as a despot and heretic; politics were bitter and times were hard. In this atmosphere certain bold spirits decided that a better land awaited them in the west. Burgers, however, was only one factor in the movement. As a Thirstland veteran summed up long afterwards: "A drifting spirit was in our hearts, and we ourselves could not understand it. We just sold our farms and set out north-westwards to find a new home."

Gert Alberts, a born leader, took charge of the first Thirstland Trek. He had as adviser Johannes van der Merwe, eighty-two years of age, a Voortrekker who found himself impelled to trek again. No clearer example of the *trekgees* is needed. Van der Merwe was a wealthy man with a pleasant farm near Pretoria called Rusfontein; but he could not rest. However, he travelled in great comfort, in a special wagon built more like a modern caravan, and with an excellent native cook named Paadjie Rol. The venerable Van der Merwe came out of the long journey in perfect health and lived to the age of ninety-two.

South West Africa, then known as Damaraland, was regarded as the destination. The trekkers little knew that many of them would trek much farther on, to Angola, and remain there for half a century. Nor could one of them have imagined that those who followed would leave their dead in hundreds along the trail.

A year passed in preparation. Then, early in 1875, the convoy of wagons crept up to the Crocodile River. Only three families turned back at that point. All the rest faced the Kalahari desert crossing without flinching.

Trek! Ten families with sixteen wagons moved westwards. They had about fourteen hundred cattle, and wisely Commandant Alberts split the column into three groups, travelling at intervals of two days, so that the rare water holes along the route would not be overcrowded. In this way they reached Lake Ngami safely – the "land of many vleis" as they called it – losing only a few cattle on one waterless stretch of three days. The first trek was a small family affair, cleverly planned and carried out.

They waited beside the water while Alberts and a companion

named Kruger went forward to interview Lambert, the Hottentot *kaptein* of Gobabis, with the idea of securing permission to live in his territory. Lambert suggested a temporary settlement at Rietfontein and promised to talk to other chiefs about a permanent abode. I happen to know Rietfontein, though few South Westers have seen this far corner. Rietfontein is a tiny oasis in that dramatic right-angle turn which the frontier of South West Africa makes with Bechuanaland. The spring at Rietfontein never dries up, and I camped there under the trees and found it pleasant after the dunes and spare bush of the desert. Bushmen were evidently watching me. I came upon the remains of a tortoise they had been eating, the shell still hot from the fire; but never a Bushman did I see at that place.

For almost a year the first trek rested at Rietfontein. I found a grave there with a stone bearing the name of Alletta van der Merwe, born 1817, died 1877; and three other unmarked graves. But the main event during this period was the call for help which came from the second party of Thirstland trekkers led by Jan Greyling.

Greyling was a hunter who had been in the Kalahari before, and he was elected leader for that reason. A more unfortunate choice could hardly have been made; though the ordeal of the desert might have broken more resourceful men. Greyling's party was too large – nearly five hundred men, women and children in one hundred and twenty-eight wagons; more than seven thousand oxen and cows, five hundred horses, a thousand sheep and goats, two hundred dogs, hundreds of fowls, ducks and geese.

It was realised that such a large party could not be controlled without discipline. A meeting was held, councillors elected, laws passed and a criminal court appointed. Provision was made for marriages by trek officials, wills, estates, and fines for assault, bribery, slander and other crimes. "All murderers shall be hanged," one article read. There was to be no hunting on Sundays, and no wasteful shooting.

Here was an exodus indeed, and the desert could not support such numbers. On the third day the cattle became difficult to handle. The water hole where they had expected to find refreshment only yielded water by the spoonful. The trekkers had to push on hurriedly, night and day, for two more days to reach the next water hole at Haakdoorn Pan. By this time the frantic cattle were out of control. They stormed into the shallow water of the pan and transformed it into a mud bath. Hundreds of oxen sank into the mud and died there. Herds broke away after slaking their thirst and headed back for the Transvaal.

So there was only the foul, moist mud for the people in the wagons. They had to pack the mud in their shirts and wring out the water drop by drop. Fathers cried as they watched the distress of their wives and children. They opened the stomachs of dead oxen and drank the blood of sheep. Some tried to quench their thirst with neat brandy and vinegar.

One of the patriarchs who saw all this as a boy told me of a queer sight that lingered in his memory. "The cattle were mad with thirst," he recalled. "They made for anything bright, such as the metal tyres of the wagons, and licked them. Some oxen even dashed into our camp fires and tried to drink the flames. After that a great many went blind. It was pitiful to hear the weird lowing of the cattle in agony. When the oxen reached a good water hole after seven days of thirst they could not drink at all. They just stood with their noses in the water."

Wagon after wagon struggled through the sand, with thirst as the deadly menace every second of the day and night. Sacks of mealies, potatoes and other provisions had to be thrown away so that the weak oxen could go on hauling the wagons. Treasured furniture was left in the desert. Many wagons had to be abandoned, and these were plundered by Bushmen. Occasionally the Bushmen would bring ostrich eggs filled with water, and they could ask what they liked for them. Never was there enough water. A British missionary, the Reverend J.D. Hepburn, who had been visiting Khama in Bechuanaland, heard of the plight of the trekkers and sent his wagon loaded with barrels of water. The trek went on, the ordeal was repeated until the wagons reached Ngami. By this time there were not enough oxen left to bring the wagons into South West Africa. It was at this desperate stage that Greyling's urgent message reached Van der Merwe and Alberts at Rietfontein. Alberts went to the rescue with nearly two hundred oxen and saved the situation – for a time.

Greyling had lost the confidence of his followers, and returned to the Transvaal. Others gave up hope of a Land of Canaan, and went cautiously back on their tracks in small parties, their wagons loaded with water. Ten families joined the Rietfontein camp. A number of others moved off into the north along the Okavango River.

Strange to say, the second trek had come through the Kalahari without the loss of a single human life as a result of thirst. They were no longer wealthy cattle owners, but they had survived the desert. Along the Okavango, however, malaria took a heavy toll. Some of the letters written by these trekkers have been preserved.

"We are in great distress," one wrote. "Fever is raging. Our cattle and sheep are almost all dead. The worst is the sore famine. God save us from this wilderness of hunger, care and sorrow."

Axel Eriksson, the trader, came upon this party in the midst of their suffering. He was so moved that he decided to appeal to sympathisers at the Cape for money to enable the survivors to settle in healthy territory. I found his description of the scene in a letter published in a Cape Town newspaper. "It is a bitter and heartrending story," he wrote. "It is hard to see them now, poor and sick and dying, in distress. Many have neither dog nor fowl left. Many children, driven by hunger, eat earth and die almost immediately. Here a few rave for food, there another frightens away the birds of prey from some putrid carcass that he may regale himself on what a hyena would disdain."

Widows and orphans in the wilderness . . . that was the situation. Axel Eriksson visited wagon after wagon, finding only women and children creeping round without food or medicine, without help, but awaiting the inevitable end with courage. Some died through eating poisonous fruits. A lad named Willem Prins was murdered by Bushmen. Natives buried the dead; the trekkers were all too ill to dig the graves. They were lonely graves, beyond the trade routes; they are lonely today, hundreds of miles from the nearest village.

Traders brought oxen to the stricken families, and an Ovambo chief supplied food. Meanwhile the trekkers at Rietfontein had decided to move. They had been at the spring for a year, game had become scarce and grazing was no longer plentiful. Not far from Rietfontein stands a relic of the occupation – a huge tree on which many trekkers carved their names. It has a hollow trunk, and messages were often left inside for the benefit of later parties.

Some of the Rietfontein people went back to the Transvaal; but in February, 1878, the main body linked up with the Okavango survivors at Leeupan, in the wild country to the west of Grootfontein. Here a meeting was held and Jakobus Botha elected as leader. They had not yet discovered their Promised Land, but they had not lost faith.

Trek! The wagons rolled on to the Etosha Pan, where even these old-time hunters stared in wonder at the vast herds of game. Fountains gushed up among the reeds. They shot many ostriches for the feathers, and though elephants were rare they secured some ivory. Segal, a trader, sold them rice, coffee and other foods they had not tasted for months. This was a pleasant interlude indeed, the happiest period since the start of the trek. But the hardships already encountered told on some of the old people; and Gert Alberts and Marthinus van der Merwe buried their wives at Etosha.

The main body camped at Etosha, and scouts were sent into the Kaokoveld. Led by Gert Alberts, these men examined the springs at Zessfontein, Otjitundua and Kaoko Otavi, and rode down to the sea at Rocky Point. They reported that the land was even finer than Etosha.

Trek! For ten days the wagons crossed the Omaheke, making the first tracks over grassy plains which are little known even today. Some settled at Otjitundua, which they named Rusplaas. Others went on to Kaoko Otavi. It was in June, 1879, that they arrived at these places; and as I have said, the ruins of their stone houses remain to this day – and their graveyards. Seven men, including Marthinus van der Merwe, and nine women and children, died at Rusplaas. The trekkers hunted far and wide from these little villages; they grew wheat and vegetables and planted fruit trees.

The wanderings of the trekkers in South West Africa were not without political repercussions. Some years previously there had been a movement in the Transvaal towards securing a western outlet to the sea. Even before the Thirstland Trek a number of Transvaal burghers had travelled in South West Africa, causing such a scare among the natives that Mahahero had asked the Cape government for British protection. This led to the official mission of Dr William Coates Palgrave, a former hunter and trader, who spent years trying in vain to bring the country under British protection. Palgrave realised that the Thirstland trekkers would make first-class settlers; but both Herero and Hottentot chiefs were extremely nervous about the presence of these people from the Transvaal. In the end Palgrave had to advise the trekkers to settle in the no-man's-land of the Kaokoveld.

While the trekkers were living in the Kaokoveld, two schooners left Table Bay loaded with provisions and other necessities. Axel Eriksson's appeal had been successful. Relief committees had raised five thousand, six hundred and fifty-eight pounds, and the masters of the ships were instructed to land their cargoes on the Kaokoveld coast and hand everything over to the trekkers. They anchored off Rocky Point, found that landing was impracticable, and then returned to Walvis Bay. Messages reached the trekkers, however, and they sent their own wagons to Walvis to collect the goods. In their impoverished state, these cargoes were riches indeed. Without them, they might have stayed in the Kaokoveld. Now they were like giants refreshed, and the *trekgees* flared up again.

At this crucial moment a new and remarkable character appeared on the scene, a trader and hunter named Will Worthington Jordan. Some writers have spelt his name Willem Jordaan, and the error was perpetuated by the Germans when they placed Jordaanhohe on the Kaokoveld maps. Jordan, however, described himself as "an Englishman by birth and education". In fact, he was the son of an English father and a Cape coloured woman.

Jordan soon gained the confidence of the trekkers, and later they regarded him as their saviour. It is a little strange, perhaps, that these Afrikaners from the Transvaal, with their strong colour prejudices, should have placed their faith in a coloured man and followed his advice so gratefully. Jordan, however, was a man of education, fluent in Dutch and other languages, *persona grata* with the Portuguese in Angola, and known to all the chiefs in South West Africa. The trekkers looked upon him as the finest doctor they had ever met (though he had no medical training) and told many tales of his powers of diagnosis and marvellous cures.

Palgrave's offer of a permanent settlement in the Kaokoveld had been rejected by the trekkers on the ground that they did not wish to live under the British flag. They had no means of knowing that a few years later the German flag would be raised over the country.

Jordan then suggested Angola as a suitable home. He knew the weakness of the colony, still at the mercy of rebellious native chiefs after four centuries of nominal Portuguese ownership. Jordan thought the Portuguese would welcome the trekkers, both as settlers and fighting men, and he offered to introduce a deputation to the governor. The trekkers agreed.

Commandant Jakobus Botha led the deputation. Gert Alberts, P.J. van der Merwe and others rode with him through Swartboois Drift; and thanks to the influence of Jordan they received a hearty welcome. The Portuguese promised them two hectares of land for each family, freedom of religion, and freedom from taxation for the first ten years. They would have to submit to the laws of Portugal, but they could use their own language and elect their own representatives to deal with the government.

Trek! Stone houses round the Kaokoveld springs, the irrigated fields and fine hunting grounds were left far behind. Late in 1880 the first parties formed a laager at Swartboois Drift and awaited the rest of the cavalcade.

Some of the girls were swimming in the shallows at the drift when a young crocodile seized Nellie le Grange by the leg. The men heard her screams, but thought the girls were amusing themselves. Cillie van der Walt and several other women then went to the rescue, hauling both Nellie and the crocodile on to a sandbank. They had to throw sand in the crocodile's eyes before it released its grip; and it was a long time before Nellie's wounds healed.

All the wagons crossed the Kunene before the year ended, and on January 4, 1881, the trekkers came at last to the Humpata plateau, about a hundred miles inland from Mossamedes. There were two hundred and seventy men, women and children in the great wagon convoy. A little ceremony was held as the horsemen pulled up outside the first Portuguese fort. Volleys of blank cartridges were fired in salute, and the Afrikaners gave a *wapenskouing* which convinced the Portuguese that they had gained valuable allies against the savage tribesmen.

This was indeed a land flowing with milk and honey. Grazing for the cows was magnificent; and in the forests the trekkers saw thousands of native beehives made of tree trunks. But as these new settlers laid out their village at Humpata thankfully, there were many who looked back down the long trail from the Transvaal and thought of those who had fallen. It was a trail marked out by graves and the skeletons of oxen. Nearly three hundred men, women and children had died between the Transvaal and Humpata, most of them as a result of fever.

It was an untamed world the trekkers had entered, but one with many possibilities. Native carriers had been bringing up supplies on their heads from Mossamedes for the Portuguese, each man taking a sixty-pound head load. The trekkers opened a wagon route. When the government started an immigration scheme from Madeira, the trekkers brought the new colonists to their farms. Thus they were able to save a little money and establish themselves on the land.

At first there were few books for the children in the little school. History books they did not need; their parents and grandparents told them stories of the Great Trek and other sagas more vivid than anything that has been written. Their religious needs were never forgotten by the churches in the Transvaal, and the first minister to visit them, in 1881, was the Reverend J. Lion Cachet.

Eighteen months after the arrival of the trekkers at Humpata a well-known English explorer and hunter arrived there. He was the Earl of Mayo, F.R.G.S., and his impressions of the new settlement in the wilds of Angola have been overlooked by historians of the trek.

The Earl, accompanied by his valet Paul Kelly, left Mossamedes by wagon in July, 1882. He found that comfortable little thatched cottages with stone or mud walls had been built at Humpata. "All the people of the Boer settlement were most kind, obliging and hospitable," he wrote. "A finer set of men I have never seen. Without doubt, during that terrible journey, it was a case of the survival of the fittest." He also noted that the settlers had made clever irrigation canals to bring water to their cottages and gardens.

From Humpata the Earl set off on a hunting trip, accompanied by a trekker named Paul Venter. Natives they encountered were afraid of the horses; for no horses had been seen in that part of Angola before the arrival of the trekkers. The Earl compiled a map of the region, marking several places named by the trekkers – the Honey River, Commandant's Drift and Paul Venter's Pits.

The Earl and Venter travelled south to the Kunene shooting

elephants, and then returned to W.W. Jordan's store at Humpata. "I was suffering from fever, but received some little comforts, as much as the kindly Boers and their wives could offer me," wrote the Earl. He described the Portuguese farmers he had met as *degradados*, men sent into exile for their crimes, some of them murderers.

Senhor Paiva, the Portuguese commandant of the district (went on the Earl), had married Commandant Botha's daughter. The Portuguese at the coast imagined that Paiva was treating the Boers too well, and found an excuse for recalling him; but he was reinstated soon afterwards. Customs duties on goods landed at Mossamedes were excessive, and the trader Jordan found it cheaper to haul his goods all the way from Walvis Bay by wagon. Portuguese farmers were jealous of the new settlers as the Boers grew better wheat.

"At the moment the Boers have no clergyman, but the Commandant holds services and arranges marriages," the Earl wrote. "The elder people have started a school. They know their Bible, and are exceedingly moral and well-conducted."

Soon there were grievances, and the Humpata plateau was not journey's end after all. *Trekgees* had not died out. Only a few years after their arrival some of the settlers had become restless. They told a Transvaal minister named Pelser who visited them that they disliked the Roman Catholic influence in the colony. They were exposed to bands of native robbers, and often they had to fight for their lives.

Jordan had been away in South West Africa on one of his many trading journeys. He knew of this discontent, and had been seeking another territory for the restless ones. He had almost secured land in the splendid Rehoboth country by arrangement with the leaders of the Bastard "republic"; but the Germans had already declared their protectorate over the coastline and the Rehoboth area, and Jordan found them unwilling to recognise a little Boer state within their sphere of influence. So he went to the Ovambo chiefs instead and secured land round Grootfontein, Otavi and the Waterberg. This cost him three hundred pounds in cash, twenty-five guns, one salted horse and a *vaatjie* of brandy. He wrote to London and Cape Town, requesting British protection, and received some encouragement from Upington, prime minister of the Cape Colony. Will

Worthington Jordan was not without skill as a diplomat.

Back in Humpata, Jordan discussed the scheme with the Afrikaners. Forty-six heads of families decided to move south to the new Utopia – only they decided to call it the Upingtonia Republic in honour of Sir Thomas Upington. They elected one G.D.P. Prinsloo as president, reaped their crops and loaded their wagons again.

Trek! All through October and November, 1884, small groups of Angola Boers crossed the Kunene bound for Upingtonia. They planted wheat, mealies and tobacco on their new farms, and built shelters; but Upingtonia proved to be an uneasy resting place. Always in South West Africa there was the threat of war. For some reason the Hereros hated Jordan, and they disputed Jordan's purchase of the land. Jordan turned to the Germans for help, and asked Commissioner Goering for a cannon. This little request went to Bismarck, who turned it down because of the expense. All the Germans did for Jordan was to suggest that the English name of the republic was unsuitable; so it was changed to Lydensrust (Rest after Suffering).

Among the children of this miniature republic was Ben Bouwer (later Brigadier-General B.D. Bouwer, D.T.D., D.S.O.), son of an elephant hunter, Barend Bouwer. The son left a vivid account of his father's exploits. Ben Bouwer was commandant of the little republic's forces. Once, when ambushed and wounded by Bushmen, Ben Bouwer killed eight of his assailants and escaped. When a troop of lions took his favourite horse from beside the wagon, Ben went in pursuit and shot nine lions. In May, 1887, a Grootfontein settler named Rudolph du Toit was on his way back from Walvis Bay when he was murdered by Hottentots. Ben Bouwer mobilised a commando within twenty-four hours of hearing of the murder, found the offenders and fought a battle that lasted three days. All the loot was recovered and the Hottentots who survived were driven off.

After this incident, however, the Grootfontein settlers felt more insecure than ever. Jordan went from chief to chief trying to settle the land dispute. He was on his way to Kambonde in Ovamboland when he met two Boers who had escaped from the Ovambos with their lives. They warned him that his mission was dangerous. Jordan, a most determined man, went on. Details of the final tragedy are not all that clear, but it seems that Maharero had asked

Kambonde to kill Jordan. All that is known is that Jordan was shot dead by Kambonde's brother. The trekkers had lost a friend.

Will Worthington Jordan, a shadowy but fascinating character, had passed out of the story of South West Africa. Soon afterwards President Prinsloo wrote to Goering announcing the end of the republic owing to the hostility of the different tribes.

Trek! Some returned to the Transvaal; a few settled round the Otjimbingwe mission; a fair number went back to Angola. The settlement at Humpata grew as a result of further treks from the Transvaal. There had been two large treks across the Thirstland. In 1893, a third trek, made up of forty wagons, crossed the Southern Kalahari safely. Both the people and the oxen suffered to some extent from thirst; but wild melons were found along the route of the trek and so they came to the Rietfontein outspan and rested. They chose a short route to Angola through Ovamboland, and were involved in a brush with hostile Ovambos. But the incident which caused most comment was the suicide of Frederick van Rensburg, a man of eighty-four, nicknamed Oom Kalwerneus. He seemed to have had a premonition of evil, and on three occasions he had threatened to ride back to the Transvaal on horseback. This plan was naturally opposed. Shortly before reaching Humpata the frustrated old man took a long *riem* and hanged himself.

The last Thirstland Trek to Angola, in 1905, consisted of people who did not wish to remain in the Transvaal after the South African War. It is probable, however, that most of those who took part in the later treks were influenced by letters received from friends and relations who had established themselves in Angola.

All through the years the Angola Boers fought campaign after campaign for the Portuguese. Right up to 1915 the Ovambos gave trouble; but tribesmen who had easily defeated the Portuguese learnt at last that the Boers never lost a battle.

Between campaigns the Boers were in the habit of poaching elephants in the Kaokoveld. At first they found enough ivory in Southern Angola; but when the elephants crossed the Kunene the Boers followed. These raids were carried out on a grand scale; they were well-organised expeditions with a dozen or more white hunters and up to two hundred native scouts and carriers. They left their wives and families in laager on the north bank of the Kunene and plunged into the Kaokoveld to massacre the elephants. Jan Harm Robberts, the hunter who led most of these expeditions, estimated his total bag (from 1894 to 1908) at two thousand elephants. He financed the hunters, equipped them with the finest rifles, and paid them half the proceeds in British gold after the tusks had been sold in Mossamedes.

It was a deplorable slaughter, though no one ever thought of game preservation in those days. They also shot hundreds of rhino and made sjamboks. Africa has seldom seen hunting on this scale, massacres carried out by experts who seldom wasted a cartridge. For months on end they followed the elephant trails, living on elephant meat and mealie meal. Only once did a German patrol corner them; but they had no ivory with them and they bluffed their way out of this predicament and rode hastily across the river. On one occasion the hunters saw eighteen enormous herds of elephants in a valley to the north of Kaoko Otavi. They said there were three thousand elephants in sight that day. You will not encounter such herds in the Kaokoveld today, after those years of ruthless shooting.

I have an idea that the end of the hunting expeditions from Humpata were among the factors which led the Angola Boers to make their last trek. Ivory became scarce after so much killing. (I met the last of the Kaokoveld ivory poachers in Windhoek in 1928; an Angola Boer who had been captured by old Chief Oorlog and handed over to the police.) It is clear, however, that after World War I the "land of milk and honey" was not providing them with the standard of living they had enjoyed in the carefree days of ivory poaching and transport riding. The collapse of the Portuguese currency also hit many of them hard. Some of them remembered Paul Kruger's warning when they left the Transvaal: *"Julle gaan na 'n Roomse land en julle kinders sal Rooms word."* (You are going to a Roman Catholic land and your children will be Roman Catholics.) This had not come to pass, but who could see into the future? Even more real was the prospect of their children losing the faithfully nurtured Afrikaans language. Their early freedom in this respect had been curtailed; and though the community had imported teachers from South Africa, the authorities were insisting upon attendance at government schools where all teaching was in Portuguese.

Thus, after nearly fifty years in Angola, a burning *trekgees* arose again in the community. No one wished to return to the Transvaal. All eyes were fixed on South West Africa, where so many Afrikaners had found homes long after the Thirstland Trek. It is not generally known, perhaps, that at the end of the first twenty years of German occupation there were many more Afrikaners than Germans in South West Africa. At the beginning of this century, Afrikaners formed almost the whole farming population, and the South African War swelled their numbers. When the colony passed to South Africa after World War I there was another strong reason why the Angola Boers should long to rejoin their fellow countrymen.

So in March, 1928, two delegates were sent to interview General Hertzog in Cape Town. Their names were Andries Alberts and Michiel van der Merwe, descendants of the first Thirstland Trek leaders; sons of the men who, in 1880, had gone ahead to Angola as delegates to the Portuguese. General Hertzog was most sympathetic, and a special fund of half a million pounds was created to settle the Angola Boers in South West Africa. The delegates returned with the news that each farmer would receive about eight thousand hectares of land, to be paid off over thirty years. There would be advances for homesteads, stock, windmills, boreholes and dams. Not a single head of cattle, not a horse or donkey or any animal, would be allowed to cross the Kunene River for fear of lung-sickness and other diseases. However, the Union government would compensate them to some extent for the loss of stock.

Trek! Only four families remained at Humpata. Family after family loaded the wagons again. Wagon after wagon rumbled down the well-remembered track to Swartboois Drift. On the south bank they saw the Union flag and assembled to sing hymns of thanksgiving. The little company of two hundred and seventy white people who had gone north to Humpata in 1880 had become an eager cavalcade nearly two thousand strong. With them came a few of the faithful Zulu servants who had accompanied the original trek from the Transvaal. The Portuguese had decreed that no natives were to leave Angola, but the trekkers hid their own retainers under the wagon covers and smuggled them across the drift.

Now almost the whole exiled Afrikaner community were on their way back. Month after month, convoys of motor trucks carried the Angola Boers from Swartboois Drift to their new homes. Each night they camped at water holes they knew, and lit their fires amid the ruins of their old Kaokoveld settlements. I met the first convoy five hundred miles south of the river in September, 1928 – the historic first convoy which brought with it the leader Michiel van der Merwe. But there was one man in that convoy, a patriarch named De Jager, who had seen the whole story. He had survived the Thirstland Trek and returned as a living link with the Voortrekkers. Later I met other old people with great wealth of memory. Listening to them, I found the Thirstland episode coming to life at last with all its bravery and horror. I saw the heirlooms they had brought back from Angola with them; old Bibles, old *riempie* beds and chairs, tables and wagon-chests and guns that had been with them on all their wanderings.

People in South West had been wondering what manner of men these might be who had dwelt in Portuguese territory for so long. All doubts were soon dispelled. The men might wear black, wide-brimmed Portuguese sombreros; but as a whole the trekkers formed a cameo of Transvaal life and custom of last century. They spoke a pure Afrikaans without trace of foreign accent. Everything they had taken with them had been marvellously preserved – their race and religion and language. They were Afrikaners of an earlier day perhaps, but still Afrikaners to the bone.

Most of the trekkers were settled in the Kalahari districts, the dry, grim sandveld that came as a shock to them after the irrigated fields of Humpata. There were very few wealthy folk among the Angola Boers, and so the early years in the sandveld were among the hardest they had known. Families lived on mealie meal, babies went short of milk, and the crushed roots of the *witstamboom* had to serve as coffee. Children went to school after a breakfast of porridge in a saucer. Lambs became fat, then died. Some families were placed a hundred miles from Gobabis, and had not even a donkey cart to visit the village. There were many in South West Africa who predicted that the Angola Boers would never settle down in such surroundings, but that one day they would pack up and vanish like gypsies into Angola again. A decade passed, and the Angola Boers were still there. It became apparent, however, that the struggle on the Kalahari farms was too hard; and in 1938 new farms were surveyed for them in the Outjo district.

Trek! The hard-pressed people moved off hopefully into a land where, according to the farmers, cattle die only of old age. Only now were they nearing journey's end. They settled in the land of bush and granite koppies, camped under the mopani trees, built huts and *hartbeeshuisies* – and finally homesteads. The first solid homes many of the Angola Boers had known arose when their herds of cattle flourished. For the first time in their lives old men bought motor cars.

Yet they still live close to the wild. Not long ago three families on farms were mourning close relatives who had been killed by lions or leopards. On one of those farms the father had destroyed thirty-seven leopards, but in the thirty-eighth encounter the leopard was the victor. In the Outjo hospital there is nearly always someone who has been mauled by a wild beast. Fire victims come for treatment, too, men who have been caught in the huge bush fires that rage in the district. But the saddest tale I heard there was of a little girl who was bitten by a snake on a farm more than a hundred miles from the village. She died long before the doctor arrived.

Lions seize the cattle, too, and one Angola Boer shot fourteen lions in a year. But the rain can be relied upon up there in the north, and the grass grows high. Men who were keeping families on five pounds a month shortly before World War II now have incomes of two thousand pounds a year, and more. In this security the *trekgees* has burnt low. The Angola Boers are no longer a race apart; they are members of an established farming community, the younger ones indistinguishable from other South West Afrikaners.

The *trekgees* has burnt low. But in 1950, seventy-fifth anniversary of the departure of the first Thirstland Trek from the Transvaal, someone suggested that a ceremony should be held at Rusplaas in the Kaokoveld. The authorities gave permission for the people to cross the "red line" for this purpose. And in October the descendants of the Thirstland trekkers drove from all their settlements to stand beside the ruins and hold a service beside the graves.

Not only descendants. Among the six hundred people who gathered at Rusplaas that day was Jan Labuschagne, aged ninety, who was married at that resting place on the way to Angola. And there were two women who had played among the stone houses at Rusplaas as children, and had made the long journey to revive happy memories. At the age of eighty or ninety even a motor car journey into the Kaokoveld is no small undertaking. But all those at Rusplaas had heard a call which was not to be denied when it reached the ears of Thirstland folk. Clearly it sounded down the years, and their response was certain. Trek!

LORDS OF THE LAST FRONTIER

Characters

Here are some fascinating tales of the brave, eccentric and exciting characters who made their way to Africa.

You will find pioneering women such as the indomitable Frau Bulleck and the famous Dr James Barry. Then there are the colonial builders such as Logan of Matjesfontein (now spelled Matjiesfontein) which thanks to the efforts of a modern hotelier, is preserved much as it was when Logan completed it in the 1890s.

The strange tale of the German baron and the castle he built in the desert remains a story surrounded in mystery. And the gallant Hauptmann Schottland is the very stuff of which Buchan used to write.

Here again the results of Lawrence Green's enthusiastic pursuit of an exciting yarn have not been dimmed by time.

Women of the Frontier

1940

Many bold women have faced and defeated the African loneliness. Wives and missionary women, travellers, nurses, flying girls – all these have experienced the terror of vast spaces and taken the risks. But the bravest story I know concerns the struggle of Frau Bulleck, a widow with a young family living on a remote farm in the frontier district of Gobabis, South West Africa.

I first heard mention of Frau Bulleck while passing through the Gobabis outposts with a Kalahari expedition in 1936. The police had warned us that Bushman raiders, wild bow-and-arrow men of the desert, had been stealing cattle on both sides of the South West Africa-Bechuanaland border. Patrol after patrol had hunted the Bushmen unsuccessfully. Farmers were angry – and nervous. It was a state of affairs that had arisen at intervals ever since white settlers had penetrated that far corner. Raids still occur today.

One farm in the district, I was told, had become almost immune from Bushman attacks – the farm Alexeck, about a hundred and forty miles northwards from Gobabis, the home of Frau Bulleck. The Bushmen feared the lonely widow who had chosen to live in a wilderness cut off, for months at a stretch, from police protection and civilisation.

Frau Bulleck's farm lies in Kalahari ranching country, and I travelled close to her boundaries during the journey eastwards into the desert. It was only recently, however, that I learnt the full story of her voluntary exile in that wilderness. Mr N. van B. de Jong, a cattle buyer in South West Africa for many years, told me of his visit to Frau Bulleck and her extraordinary family.

Herr Alex Bulleck was one of the German soldiers who were

granted free farms after the native wars in the territory. He was a famous hunter in his time; but there came a day when he was out unarmed in search of straying cattle, and met a lion. So there was a widow with five daughters and a tiny boy, and only the farm to support them. That was soon after the Great War ended, and the country had passed from Germany to South Africa.

The farm was one of the largest in South West Africa, possibly fifty thousand square miles in area, but unfenced and with limits undefined. Whenever Herr Bulleck had tried to set up fences, the Bushmen had stolen the wire to tip their arrows. There were wooded plains where eland and blue wildebeest roamed; limestone pans overgrown with thorn trees, often containing water holes; and the queer depressions known to the Hereros as *marambas,* apparently dry but with water near the surface.

It was on this farm, in 1922, that Captain van Ryneveld, magistrate of Gobabis, was ambushed and killed by a Bushman's poisoned arrow. Yet Frau Bulleck stayed on with her children.

She had decided, almost on the day of her husband's death, that it would be impossible to support her family elsewhere. On the farm were most of the necessities of life. The herd of cattle was small but sufficient. There could never be a shortage of meat while the game lasted; and the teeming game had seldom been disturbed by hunters. Frau Bulleck clung to the farm desperately, as a last hope.

At first the authorities tried to persuade her to accept a smaller farm close to Gobabis. Two reasons lay behind the offer – the menace of the Bushmen, and the need to educate the children.

Frau Bulleck had already dealt with the Bushman danger with a rifle. She soon became known among the roving Bushmen bands as a formidable enemy. One Bushman chief complained to the police. An official letter, asking for an explanation, reached the widow. And the widow wrote back to headquarters in Windhoek enclosing the hoof of a cow killed by Bushmen as evidence supporting her action. She discouraged official visits, and was finally left in peace. In a more settled land, no doubt, Frau Bulleck would not have achieved this weird isolation. But South West Africa was then, and is still, in the pioneer stage; and strong characters still find scope for their whims. Frau Bulleck held out, against wild men and the demands of civilisation, on her distant farm.

Meanwhile there were the five daughters and the little boy. Frau Bulleck tackled the problem of their education in her own way. She had served as maid in a noble household on the shores of the Baltic. A woman of some education herself, she managed her home intelligently, and with refinement. But few people knew the efforts she was making at that period. Frau Bulleck, as I have said, feared contact with the outside world. Even the German missionaries at Epukiro, about sixty miles away, seldom saw the lonely widow.

During the rainy season of 1929 Mr de Jong planned a cattle buying trip from Gobabis, and decided (more from curiosity than expectation of business) to call on Frau Bulleck. In Gobabis village there was a storekeeper who came from the same German province as Frau Bulleck; a man who bought her farm produce, supplied her with groceries, and had gained her confidence. This man gave Mr de Jong a letter which ensured hospitality. And thus started a series of adventures which Mr de Jong described to me:

"I drove away from Gobabis in a large motor car with two passengers – Father Dohn, a missionary bound for Epukiro, and a tall Herero native servant," recalled Mr de Jong. "The heat was terrific. Owing to the rains I could not take the usual route along the dry bed of the Black Nossob River. I was forced to follow a wagon track through the Kalahari to Epukiro. The sand was so heavy that I travelled in low gear all day, using tin after tin of water for the radiator. When I reached Epukiro in the evening I was exhausted, yet anxious to push on towards Frau Bulleck's farm at night to avoid the heat of another day.

"Now a new difficulty arose. I was told that no one had travelled over the unmade track to the farm for seven months, and the faint trail was overgrown with grass and bush. Not a single native at the mission would volunteer to accompany me as guide. They declared they were afraid of Frau Bulleck, and to a lesser extent of Bushmen.

"Finally I decided to navigate across the unknown stretch of about forty miles by map and compass, a method often used in the little-known Kalahari areas.

"During the night drive something struck my windscreen. I jumped out with my rifle, found a broken arrow, and fired a shot to frighten the lurking Bushman sniper away. My Herero boy now feared the worst, and as we approached the farm he trembled.

"By 3.30 a.m. I had located the dry river banks on which the farm was situated, and at 4 a.m. the howling of dogs announced that I had arrived.

"Two women came out to welcome me. One was Frau Bulleck, the other her eldest daughter, then a girl of twenty-two. I told them I was exhausted and wanted to go to bed; but they had not seen a visitor for seven months and they kept me talking until I dropped asleep in my chair.

"I remember fragments of that conversation. They questioned me excitedly, but the things that interested them most were the trivial happenings in the territory. For example, when I told them that the railway timetable from Gobabis to Windhoek had been altered they chattered eagerly, though they only saw a train once a year when they made their trek to the village.

"I studied the Bulleck household in detail when I awoke about noon. Frau Bulleck and her daughters all wore skin trousers such as the Bechuanas make – wonderful garments of springbok leather, sewn like a patchwork quilt. But even more remarkable were their *kap doeks,* padded handkerchiefs worn round the head in the style that later became fashionable in more civilised places. Their faces had been tanned brown by the sun. When they took off their *doeks,* however, their necks were white, with sharp lines of demarcation between sun-bronze and protected skin.

"The *doeks* evidently shut out sound. As a result Frau Bulleck and her daughters had formed the habit of shouting; and they continued to shout indoors after removing their headgear. They often had difficulty in following me when I spoke in an ordinary voice – I was forced to shout back.

"All of them wore home-made *veldskoens* on their feet, and although the farmhouse was comfortably furnished and neat it was clear that they had to improvise many things. Tallow lights, made from butter fat, were used instead of paraffin lamps. The beds were covered with *karosses* of wild animal's skins. They were without money, newspapers, radio; yet, in spite of living this Robinson Crusoe life, their manners were perfect, nothing was done roughly or carelessly.

"During supper that night I heard an ominous noise from the cattle kraal, rather like a saw cutting through wood. Frau Bulleck looked up from her plate and spoke casually: 'Annie, go out and see what is wrong. I think a leopard has jumped in among the cattle again.' She dealt with the matter as calmly as though a cat was in the rubbish bin.

"Annie took a shotgun with her, but no shot was fired. She soon returned, took her place at table without a tremor, and remarked: 'I found the leopard in a trap. But it's all right, Mother, I did not waste a cartridge – I clubbed it to death.' Anyone who has seen the rage of a trapped leopard will realise the courage of the girl.

"The Bulleck girls were all fearless hunters. Though they had guns, they seldom used them; cartridges were too expensive. They preferred to bring down eland and other large and small antelope with Bushman bows and arrows. Frau Bulleck herself was a marvellous tracker. She assisted the police, during the Van Ryneveld tragedy, by examining Bushman footprints and naming the very men concerned.

"Apart from the farm life, however, the daughters had vague ideas about the world. I asked Frau Bulleck how she expected them to find husbands. It appeared she had made plans for the three grown-up girls, and intended arranging for three young men from her own German town to come out to the farm. This scheme, I believe, was actually carried out; but the men were appalled by the isolation, and the girls remained unmarried.

"At the time of my visit, there was not a servant on the farm. Frau Bulleck and her daughters could deal with every task – branding cattle, chopping wood, repairing wagons, making gates and carts. The only product they could sell was butter fat, which they sealed in tins.

"They had a vegetable garden, with a well eight-five feet deep, dug by the girls. I saw one of them go down a ladder made of *riems* (strips of cattle hide) when the bucket jammed. The homestead was surrounded by walls, but Frau Bulleck's reputation was the best defence against attack by Bushmen.

"I was disappointed in the cattle. The small herd had lacked fresh blood for too long. Nevertheless I bought twenty-eight head, branded them and considered the problem of driving them to the railhead. I could not give my rifle to my Herero boy, as it would have been against the law to supply a native with a firearm; and the Herero was reluctant to go because of the Bushmen. After much persuasion, however, he set off for Epukiro. I took a different route by car. After four days at Epukiro the boy and the cattle had not arrived, so I returned to Frau Bulleck's farm. There I learnt that the cattle had wandered back home, and the boy had waited helplessly for me.

"Frau Bulleck solved the problem by sending two of her daughters off to Epukiro in charge of the cattle. They delivered them safely and my visit came to an end."

Since Mr de Jong's visit, I understand, Frau Bulleck has bought a motor lorry. She is able to reach Gobabis in five or six hours, instead of travelling for days by ox wagon. But her farm is still among the remote places of South West Africa. How many men, I wonder, would have clung to such a lonely home and struggled to success as Frau Bulleck has done.

OLD AFRICA UNTAMED

Doctor James Barry

1951

Doctor James Barry, first woman doctor and greatest male imper-
sonator of last century, has suffered much from the imaginations of
novelists and dramatists. The true story, I find, is more fantastic
than the books based on interludes in her long career. It is all of a
pattern, whether she is duelling in Cape Town, treating yellow fever
in the West Indies, or riding through Montreal in her sleigh.

I discovered Doctor Barry, enough of her to explain some of the
mysteries, in the archives and libraries of Cape Town; in memories
of people who had known her, recorded in old newspapers; and
above all, in the anecdotes handed down in old Cape families and
still told to this day. So I intend to follow her vivid progress through
life without once stretching your credulity beyond the point where
serious historians become restless.

Her origin will probably never be proved beyond doubt. Lord
Albemarle, who described her in "Fifty Years of My Life", says she
was the legitimate granddaughter of a Scottish earl. Britain's sober
"Dictionary of National Biography" confirms the statement. Edin-
burgh University records show clearly enough that the Earl of
Buchan was responsible for James Barry, medical student.

Other writers have declared that her name at birth in 1795 was
Joan Fitzroy, and that the Prince Regent was her father. Olga Racster and Jessica Grove, joint authors of a play and novel based on
her life, believe that her father was the Duke of York, second son of
George III, while her mother was the daughter of a Miss Barry,
daughter of General Barry.

All that can be said with certainty is that throughout her career,
and in spite of her most outrageous behaviour, she remained under

high protection. Everywhere she went there is strong evidence of powerful influence at work on her behalf.

She first takes shape as a character during her student days. Other students wore shooting jackets; she disguised her slim, feminine figure with a long frock coat. Doctor Jobson, who was there at the same time, recalled that Barry was afraid of the rough quarters of the town. He tried to teach Barry boxing, but she was always guarding her chest. Finally she took up fencing and became so skilful with the rapier that the jeers were less frequent.

In 1812, at the age of seventeen, she qualified in medicine. Records of the British war office revealed her career from July 5, 1813, when she joined the army as a hospital assistant. She served in Spain and Belgium, and it is possible that she was present at Waterloo. Then she was posted to India; and early in 1817 she reported for duty as staff surgeon to the Cape Town garrison. She lodged at the Widow Sandenberg's boarding house, No. 12, Heerengracht.

From this moment Doctor James Barry becomes as visible as a film heroine. Not only Lord Albemarle, but many other distinguished visitors to the Cape made a point of describing the queer little doctor.

About five feet in height, she had soles three inches thick fitted to her boots. Lord Albemarle sat next to her at a mess dinner; for Governor Lord Charles Somerset had praised the skill of young Doctor Barry, and Albemarle was anxious to meet her. "In this learned pundit I beheld a beardless lad, apparently of my own age, with an unmistakable Scots type of countenance, reddish hair and high cheek bones," wrote Albemarle. "There was a certain effeminacy in his manner which he seemed to be always striving to overcome. His style of conversation was greatly superior to that usually heard at a mess table in those days. A mystery attached to Doctor Barry's whole professional career. Quarrelsome and frequently guilty of flagrant breaches of discipline, he was sent home several times under arrest. His offences were always condoned at headquarters."

Besides increasing her height, Doctor Barry made her frail body appear more impressive with the aid of towels. The coloured people of Cape Town called her, in Afrikaans, the *Kapok dokter*. *Kapok* means cotton-wool, and they thought she stuffed the shoulders of her uniform jacket with it.

Even then, I suppose, there were people with enough knowledge of psychology to realise that Doctor Barry was over-compensating herself for her physical handicaps. She carried a huge dragoon's sword and wore long spurs. Her temper was hung on a hair-trigger, and her insults, delivered in a high, squeaky voice, involved her in constant trouble.

"I should much like to cut off your ears," she screamed at one high official. This was her favourite threat. One day a clergyman sent Barry a polite note asking her to pull an aching tooth. She flew into a towering rage. "Does this stupid person suppose I am a vulgar tooth-drawer?" she demanded. "If he had personally made this application, his cloth would not have saved his ears."

She then went to a coloured farrier, Thomas, and informed him that the clergyman's donkey needed attention. Thomas arrived at the house with hand vices and pincers. When the clergyman asked what it meant, Thomas replied: "Doctor Barry has instructed me to come without delay to draw the tooth of a donkey."

The clergyman complained to Lord Charles Somerset, who replied: "No one pays attention to what Doctor Barry does or says. You had better join in the laugh against yourself."

Every day the doctor fed her black poodle Psyche at Saunders's confectionery shop. She rode round Cape Town in full dress uniform and cocked hat, on a pony, with an umbrella over her head, accompanied by her black manservant. The padded saddle was of her own design, and once in it she remained firmly wedged.

Lord Charles Somerset spoke of Barry to Albemarle as "one of the most skilful of physicians and the most wayward of men". Somerset spoilt and shielded her to the limit, but she was no respecter of persons, and many a fierce argument she had with him.

Many a patient remembered Doctor Barry with gratitude, however, and passed on tales of her tender ways. One woman at Wynberg must have sensed the doctor's sex, for she told her: "No man could show such sympathy with one in pain."

Among her early patients at the Cape was the dying Lady Brenton, wife of Vice-Admiral Sir Jahleel Brenton. In his reminiscences Brenton wrote: "This extraordinary young man had undergone a most rigid examination before the College of Physicians and had, by the correctness of his answers and the extent of his abilities extorted from them his diploma, with which he had practised with the most extraordinary success. Had not the firm conviction taken place in my mind that the nature of my beloved Isabella's disorder was beyond the reach of human skill, I should have derived the most sanguine hopes from his advice."

This was the period of Napoleon's exile on St. Helena. On the staff at Longwood was Count de las Cases, afterwards Napoleon's biographer. The Count was detected attempting to send a letter secretly to Europe; and in 1817 he arrived at the Cape with his young son Emmanuel. They were housed at the Castle, more or less under arrest.

Las Cases overworked his son as a penman, the lad broke down, and Doctor Barry was called in. Her appearance startled Las Cases, for he wrote that she had "the form, the manners and the voice of a woman". Nevertheless, he was impressed by her advice, for she had been recommended to him as an "absolute phenomenon who had saved the life of one of the Governor's daughters after she had been given up, which rendered him a sort of favourite in the family." Barry cheered Las Cases and often visited him and his son as a friend. Las Cases declared that he found her "very agreeable".

The most persistent story of Barry's skill concerns a difficult maternity case, and had an odd sequel. Barry was called in by Thomans Munnik, a wealthy snuff manufacturer of Riebeek Square, whose wife appeared to be dying in childbirth. According to the legend, Barry delivered the baby by means of a Caesarean operation; mother and baby survived and Barry was fêted at the christening dinner.

Barry was a physician, and in all the array of medical documents bearing on her career I cannot find a scrap of evidence suggesting that she ever practised major surgery. If she had, in those days before antiseptics and anaesthetics, it is doubtful whether Mrs Munnik would have recovered.

But the sequel is beyond dispute. The boy delivered by Barry was named James Barry Munnik. He became godfather to the late General Hertzog, prime minister of the Union of South Africa for many years between the wars. Hertzog's full name was James Barry Munnik Hertzog. One day a Cape Town editor, lunching with Hertzog, began discussing the legend. Strange to say, Hertzog had never heard of it, and seemed to dislike the idea of a link with such an eccentric character.

*

In an era of hearty eating and reckless drinking, Doctor Barry formed her own theories. She bought meat for her dog, but never touched it herself. Her diet was largely vegetarian. She liked fruit, and she took a goat everywhere with her for the milk. Champagne and brandy she drank only when ill; at all other times she was abstemious. Often she advised her patients to bathe in Cape wine, which would have had an antiseptic effect.

I admired Barry most when I read her own medical reports in the Cape archives. There you see her as the outspoken champion of the poor, of the prisoners in the vile gaol, of lunatics and lepers. She exposed scandal after scandal, bringing relief and comfort to wretched souls existing under cruel conditions.

Those yellow pages in the archives weigh the scales heavily in her favour. Her faults arose almost entirely from the life of deception she had adopted. Yet it cannot be disputed that in her work among the lowest of human beings James Barry, first woman doctor, set an inspiring example.

You find her warning the authorities that "ignorant and mercenary shopkeepers" were selling such dangerous drugs as opium and arsenic to the public. She discusses mad dog bite with great common sense, and rejects the use of "eau de Luce" as a cure. A slave boy had been bitten by a puffadder, and in that case "eau de Luce" had proved ineffective. The prompt application of a red-hot iron to the wound was more likely to succeed. And when a malignant epidemic fever known as *rot koorts* broke out in the Zwartland she diagnosed it as the typhus of Europe and laid down the treatment.

Quacks who appeared before Barry for examination as apothecaries, chemists and druggists went away cursing, and without certificates. She fixed the fees which district surgeons could demand. When the town's water supply was under suspicion she inspected the spring in Mr Breda's garden, found it pure and wholesome, and traced the cause of the trouble. The water was cut off at the reservoir every night, so that the empty iron pipes rusted. On her advice the pumps throughout the town were locked at night, the pipes remained full, and the rust disappeared.

Probably the greatest public service she rendered came about when she heard that the lepers at Hemel en Aarde (Heaven and Earth), in the Caledon district, were being starved and were running away. She set out immediately on horseback with the Reverend Doctor Thom and descended upon the settlement officials like an avenging angel. Here are her own words:

"Nothing could exceed the misery of the lepers. Their clothing was dirty and bad, the food scanty and ill-managed. These miserable people were confined to a small space of the really beautiful and ample land allotted to them. The hospital was squalid and wretched beyond description. One of the sufferers remarked that it was surely better to die of disease than of cruelty and hunger."

Thanks to her influence with Lord Charles Somerset and her own efficient methods, the leper settlement was reformed. She ordered a diet of milk, rice, coffee and vegetables, mutton and bread, in quantity equal to a soldier's ration, and remarked: "Keen appetite seems almost part of the disease." And she made sure that ample food was provided. During a later inspection she noted that a place for divine service was needed.

Medieval conditions also prevailed in the Cape Town *tronk*. Doctor Barry went in there with her observant eyes and cleansing spirit; and she must almost have wept at the scene of individual suffering and mass degradation.

"In a dungeon in that place I found Jacob Elliott with his thigh fractured, without crutches, without a bed or pillows, blankets dirty in the extreme, without a single comfort, and in short in such a state of misery that if he had not been under the special protection of Providence he could not have survived. He has not been provided with any sort of medical attention which is so much required in his helpless, painful state. Only once in twenty-four hours has the jailer taken him a bucket of water and the common prison allowance."

Jacob Elliott was typical of the jail. She sent him to hospital and denounced the medical officers responsible for this neglect. But she did not overlook the state of the jail as a whole.

"With the exception of persons in solitary confinement and one or two favoured individuals," she reported, "the whole mass of prisoners are indiscriminately jumbled together, young and old, without regard to morality, if such a thing may be supposed to exist in a place never visited by a clergyman except, perhaps, on the eve of an execution."

Officials guilty of this neglect decided that attack was the best defence. Barry was summoned to appear before a fiscal commission and answer for the slur cast on the characters of these officials. She tore up the summons and refused to answer questions on the ground that she had made her report to the governor and was responsible only to him. The court sentenced her to one month's imprisonment, but Lord Charles Somerset set the sentence aside.

Barry's comment on the proceedings was in the familiar vein. "If I had had my sword on when Mr Fiscal proposed sending me to the *tronk* I should certainly have cut off both his ears to make him look smart."

Some of you may suspect that Doctor Barry was a shrew, ready to quarrel with everyone and everything she encountered. Nevertheless, I think her words ring true. She was a merciful, conscientious medical officer, far in advance of her time.

Turn again to the old records in the archives. On this occasion, March 8, 1824, she is inspecting the lunatics in the Somerset Hospital – thirteen men and two women. "The whole establishment appears devoid of cleanliness, order or professional care," she wrote. "One man Scott, working at a trade as cabinet-maker, seemed perfectly sane. Also a Dane, Martin Jensen. There is a women Francina who is as sane as most people and by no means a subject for a lunatic hospital. Another old female Mina, reported to be over a hundred, is requiring not the miseries but even in the most moderate way the necessities of life. This poor creature had neither bread nor blanket. The others are lunatics, but they require also a little attention."

Barry was concerned about the health of the military and colonial chaplains, who were always catching colds in the Cape winter while performing funeral services in the churchyard. She noted that they were exposed to "sudden and great variations in temperature", and suggested that a sentry box on wheels should be provided, similar to those used in England.

At the Cape, private practice came to Barry without her seeking it. Her queer ways increased her prestige. When she entered a sick room her first act was to clear away everything ordered by other medical advisers. She opened windows, to the horror of people who still believed that fresh air was harmful. If her patient died she declared it was due to the blunders of previous doctors.

It is noted in the records of the early Cape Medical Society that Barry never called in a consultant. The doctors of Cape Town resented it; but several of them were fair-minded enough to praise Barry's skill and not one dared to criticise her methods as a doctor.

It was rumoured in Cape Town that Barry was a "King's favourite" and that Somerset was kind to her in expectation of favours to come. There is little doubt that Somerset was the one person who knew her secret before she arrived. He appointed her physician to his own household and promoted her to the rank of colonial medical inspector when she had been only a few weeks in the colony.

This favouritism had serious repercussions. There was a place in the Heerengracht called Dreyer's Corner, where official notices, poems and squibs were posted on the high wall of Mr Dreyer's stoep. All stopped to read and discuss them. One day an "infamous placard" was left there suggesting an immoral relationship between the Governor and Barry. The author was never discovered.

Another serious incident during her years at the Cape was her duel with an officer named Cloete, later Sir Josias Cloete. Many reasons for the quarrel have been given. According to one account they were riding together on the Cape Flats when Cloete remarked: "You ride more like a woman than a man." Barry slashed him across the face with her riding whip.

Another version has it that Barry and Cloete were at Government House one night and noticed that Lord Charles Somerset was paying attention to one of the guests.

"That's a nice Dutch filly the governor has got hold of," remarked Barry in her most offensive manner.

"Retract your vile expression, you infernal little cad," blazed Cloete in the pompous language of the day.

That a duel was fought there is no doubt; some say with pistols, others with swords. Judge Cole vouched for it in his reminiscences. According to all accounts, no one was hurt. But it is also on record that Cloete was posted to the lonely South Atlantic island of Tristan da Cunha, in charge of the British garrison stationed there to prevent the French from using it as a base while Napoleon was on St Helena.

Barry often accompanied Lord Charles Somerset on tours of the colony, and on one occasion they stayed at the hospitable mansion of George Rex at Knysna. Rex was a character as mysterious as Barry; for he was a son of King George III of England and Hannah Lightfoot, the "fair Quakeress". There in the Knysna forests were two people who kept their secrets all their lives. They may have been related, but there is no record of their conversation.

*

What made James Barry choose a medical career at a time when women were nurses but never doctors? What influenced her decision to join the army and serve at the Cape? The "Dictionary of National Biography" has this explanation: "The motive of her singular conduct is stated to have been love for an army surgeon."

This is one of the points on which all previous investigators are agreed, though they offer neither reasons nor proof. With great temerity I suggest that the man was Andrew Smith, later Sir Andrew Smith, K.C.B.

Smith and Barry were both Scots of about the same age, and their medical courses at Edinburgh overlapped. Smith qualified in medicine at the age of eighteen – nothing remarkable in those days of meagre knowledge and swift training – and he, too, was posted to the Cape a few years after Barry's arrival. Both saw service on the eastern frontier, where the interminable frontier campaigns had started. Both returned to England on leave in 1828, though not in the same ship. It is a curious parallel, but if there was a secret Smith and Barry kept it faithfully. Smith married in England at the age of forty-four.

Whether she was in love or not, Barry tried to cultivate the reputation of being a "lady's man". She was, no doubt, averting suspicion from her sex; but in one case at least she seems to have pursued a girl out of mischievous desire to arouse the jealousy of an officer she disliked. Lord Charles Somerset's daughter Georgina is mentioned among her conquests.

When out of uniform she yielded to the feminine love of finery. One outfit she wore at the Cape has been recorded for posterity – "a coat of the latest pea-green Hayne, a satin waistcoat, a vast cravat fastened with many scarf-pins and a pair of tightfitting 'inexpressibles'" (breeches).

Barry was a snob, and there is an authentic story of a Sunday morning in Cape Town when she entered the Dutch Reformed Church in the Heerengracht in the belief that Lord Charles Somerset was attending the service. When she saw that the governor's pew was empty she departed hurriedly. But the incident had been noted and the town chuckled over a verse found nailed to a tree:

With courteous devotion inspired,
Barry came to the temple of prayer,
But quickly turned round and retired
When he found that HIS lord was not there.

Yet she turned against Somerset, her benefactor, on many occasions, according to the dictates of her conscience or the anger of the moment. Somerset was an autocrat, one of the most unpopular governors the Cape ever had. He suppressed the newspaper conducted by the poet Pringle and the patriot John Fairbairn; and during this "reign of terror" one of Somerset's opponents was banished while another committed suicide. Doctor James Barry came out strongly in favour of the freedom of the Press, and used all her influence with Somerset, but without avail.

On September 1, 1828, this advertisement appeared in a Cape Town newspaper: "Those friends of Dr Barry who propose dining together at the George Hotel, previous to his departure from the colony on Monday next, are requested to put down their names." Thus ended a strange and stormy chapter in her life.

There is nothing to account for the posting to Canada, and the ageing, lonely woman must have felt the cold intensely after a lifetime in the tropics. Little is known of this period in Barry's life, though in fairly recent years there were still people in Montreal and Quebec who had personal memories of her. They said she was vain and quarrelsome; but the only vivid picture of her was of her sleigh rides. She had a magnificent sleigh, she wore musk ox robes, and her two footmen – irritated by her nagging – drove her about Montreal much too fast for her peace of mind. To the last she retained her taste for Government House society.

Her overseas service ended in 1864, and she returned to England with Black John, the negro, and the last of the line of dogs named Psyche. These were sad months, for Barry was often ailing. Ladies of the Somerset family remained faithful to her, however, called at her rooms at 14 Margaret Street, London, and took her for drives in the park.

Barry returned from one of these carriage drives in July, 1865, shivering and feverish. Next morning Black John brought the six clean towels she always wrapped herself in, but she remained in bed and spoke to her servant of her life.

"It was not always like this," Barry told him. "Once I had many friends. I have some still, and those are very good to me, but they are not the friends of early times. They will think of me, though, and if you want help they will remember you for my sake."

She died on July 26, alone. Black John asked the charwoman to lay out the body, and soon she came running downstairs and revealed the truth. A report was sent to the army authorities and a post-mortem was held. A nobleman's valet called for the dog Psyche. Black John's fare back to the West Indies was paid. No will was found. No one claimed relationship with the strange, pathetic little doctor. She was buried at Kensal Rise cemetery with this inscription on the gravestone:

Dr James Barry
Inspector-General,
H.M. Army Hospitals,
Died 26th July, 1865,
Aged 71 years.

Inspector-general was the highest rank to which an army medical officer could rise in those days. Barry had held that rank for more than six years and "Hart's Army List" for 1865 placed her at the head of the list in her branch.

*

Death had revealed the secret and many newspapers informed the public. There was no cable to South Africa in those days, and it was not until September 9 that the *Cape Argus* announced the news of

Barry's death in quaint Victorian style:

"An incident is just now being discussed in military circles so extraordinary that, were its truth not capable of being vouched for by offical authority the narration would certainly be deemed absolutely incredible. British officers quartered at the Cape many years ago may remember a certain Dr Barry attached to the medical staff and enjoying a reputation for considerable skill in his profession, especially for firmness, decision and rapidity in difficult operations. It stands an indubitable fact that a woman was for forty years an officer in the British service, and fought one duel and had sought many more."

Other Cape Town newspapers copied the paragraphs. A reader then wrote to the Cape Town *Advertiser and Mail* as follows: "Your paragraph in last evening's issue relative to the late Dr Barry was no secret to many of the inhabitants of this city, as at the time of his, or rather her, residence here it was currently talked of."

Reminiscences of the doctor were printed in Cape Town, Port Elizabeth and Bloemfontein, and these I have already drawn upon – especially the anecdotes.

Someone remembered that the Munnik family had a miniature painting of Dr Barry. In October 1865 a pioneer Cape Town photographer named G.F. Ashley copied it and supplied a large number of prints to an eager public. The *Cape Argus* commented: "A photograph of this eccentric female has now been published. If the portrait from which the photograph is taken was a likeness of the original, we only wonder the sex of the deceased was not discovered until after her death."

Two years after Barry's death Charles Dickens, then editor of *All the Year Round* magazine, received a manuscript from an officer who had known Barry on St Helena. This contained many fresh details and Dickens, with his strong sense of the dramatic, published it under the heading of "A Mystery Still".

The candid writer described Barry as "clever and impudent, and possibly with no certificate of baptism, but socially a gentleman every inch of him." He said that Barry had a fair allowance from some source, but never spoke of relatives or friends. Barry's tastes were too expensive for army pay; they included a horse and private servant, and a diet of asparagus, peaches and grapes.

"Some called him a toady," went on the writer. "His testiness was harmless, however, and he made friends and kept them. Frail in body and eccentric in manner, he ensured respect by his capacity. He defied the rules of the service with impunity. Once he returned to England without leave and told the angry director-general of the medical department in London: 'Well, I have come home to have my hair cut.'"

This writer asserted that on retirement Barry had expected to be knighted, and had ordered the uniform. Finally he declared that the post-mortem not only revealed that she was a woman, but also that she had been a mother. Many others repeated this story until it became a legend.

Lord Albemarle's book, from which I have quoted, came out ten years later, while the novel by Major E. Rogers was published in 1881. It was not until 1895, however, that some of the essential facts emerged, shorn of hearsay and fiction. Sheer chance, I imagine, was responsible.

In 1895 a surgeon named Bright in the United States navy wrote from the naval hospital at Washington, D.C., to the British medical periodical, the *Lancet,* referring to the tradition of a British medical officer who reached high rank and was found to be a female. "Will you please inform me," asked Bright, "whether this story rests upon any credible foundation or is the mere figment of an idle imagination?"

That opened doors to a remarkable series of letters. Among other it brought to light Rogers, who declared that he had consulted Barry's record at the British war office. There he had found all the details of her overseas service, and the result of the post-mortem. Rogers vouched for the fact that Barry was a woman, but it is significant that he did not mention that she had been a mother. He would certainly have done so if this detail had appeared in the post-mortem report.

Rogers wrote: "She was sympathetic and skilful in her profession – yet what a life of repressed emotions must hers have been."

He added that he had visited her grave and found it neglected, and appealed to the army department to rescue it from oblivion. One final point he made was that Sir William Mackinnon, director-general of the army medical department, had assured him that

Barry was the Earl of Buchan's daughter.

Other correspondents testified that it was a "matter of common repute" that Barry was a woman.

General W. Chamberlayne, who had known Barry in Jamaica, said in his letter that her manner and speech were assumed to repel inquisitive associates. He went on: "When I think of the anxiety, care and trouble she must have experienced for years to keep up the assumed character – possibly first undertaken for the love of some man and then retained for the sake of his character as well as her own – it seems surprising that she could have possessed so many good points. It must have been a life of great misery, continually acting a part so repellent to her better feelings."

At the same period as the *Lancet* correspondence, Dr J. H. (later Sir) Meiring Beck gave a lecture on Barry before the Cape Town branch of the British Medical Association. He had gathered his material from people who had known Barry, and I have drawn on this valuable lecture in checking and presenting the facts.

Surgeon-Major Hamilton, who was present at the lecture, confirmed the story unfolded by Dr Beck. "I am the only person in this room who ever saw Barry," remarked Hamilton. "I met her in Jamaica in 1861. She was then a curiously withered-up creature with no hair on her face at all. At that time there was no suspicion as to Dr Barry's sex."

Mark Twain, visiting Cape Town in 1896, heard the Barry story and seized on it avidly. In "More Tramps Abroad" he unwittingly gave a distorted version. He said that Barry had disgraced herself with her people, so she changed her name and sex to make a new start in the world.

The play by Olga Racster and Jessica Grove was staged in London thirty years ago, with Sybil Thorndike as Barry. Not long afterwards an amateur cast produced the play in Cape Town, and held their rehearsals at the old wine farm of Alphen, scene of the duel between Barry and Cloete.

An investigator called at the British war office in 1919 to consult Barry's personal file. Officials remembering seeing it there shortly before that time; but a long search revealed that it had been stolen. How fortunate that Rogers, novelist though he was, had access to the file before this crime against history had been committed.

Rogers at least was able to set out the important facts in the *Lancet* correspondence.

Barry's memory lingers in the folklore of Cape Town, and her ghost is supposed to roam the mountain slopes above Camp's Bay, where Lord Charles Somerset had his shooting box. Coloured nursemaids still tell the children: "Old Doctor Barry's ghost will catch you if you stay out late."

I prefer to remember Doctor James Barry as the champion of the lepers and the ill-treated prisoners – the brave woman, kind at heart, who found Jacob Elliott with his thigh fractured but "without a single comfort", and eased his pain.

GROW LOVELY, GROWING OLD

Castle in the Wilderness

1953

You may have seen the Windhoek castles on the hills above the town, the white fort at Namutoni or the Zessfontein ruins. South West Africa has a castle grander than any of these, a *schloss* with as strange a story as anything that has come out of Africa. It is Schloss Duwisib to the east of Maltahohe on the edge of the Namib desert.

Schloss Duwisib takes your breath away. You come upon it suddenly, by steep, rough tracks, and there it stands in a ring of hot and barren mountains. You gasp again when you enter the cool baronial hall.

Baron Hansheinrich von Wolf, the man who built it, was a German artillery officer, a drunken and eccentric member of the aristocracy. I am not presenting him as a hero; but there were incidents in his lurid career which count in his favour. He would certainly not have lasted long with the Nazis. Baron von Wolf did as he pleased, and men still speak well of him in this remote district.

Jayta, his small blonde wife, was a granddaughter of the New York homoeopathic medicine manufacturer. Dr Frederick Humphreys. She was born at Summit, New Jersey, in 1881. Her father died, and her mother married an Irish-American lawyer named Gaffney, a friend of Kaiser Wilhelm II. Gaffney became American consul-general in Dresden, and Jayta was staying with him in 1907 when she met and married Hansheinrich von Wolf.

Von Wolf was in disgrace. He had been in the war against the Hottentots holding a remote outpost in the Maltahohe district, and he had lost his field guns in an encounter with a much superior Hottentot force. A more skilful officer than Von Wolf might have driven off the enemy. But the Von Wolf family had a reputation for

160

military blundering. In the Franco-Prussian War of 1870 the baron's father had lost a whole battery. Now the baron had left the Hottentots in possession of his guns and his rations. The baron and the survivors of the garrison rode for their lives and reached Maltahohe village.

I want you to remember this little incident from a forgotten war, for it is the key to the castle – the explanation of something which would otherwise remain a mystery. Baron von Wolf was allowed to resign his commission and any other man would have sunk into obscurity.

Within a few years, however, Baron von Wolf returned to South West Africa and the scene of his defeat. His wife was with him. They landed at Luderitz and started immediately the enterprise which astounded all who heard of it. The baron bought the farm now known as Duwisib, fifty miles from Maltahohe, from the government – fifty-six thousand hectares at the equivalent of threepence a hectare. In other words, he secured about a hundred and thirty thousand acres for seven hundred pounds. Today it is probably worth fifty thousand pounds, including the castle, which cost twenty-five thousand pounds to build in the days when native labour was cheap.

Every ship from Germany brought antique furniture, building material, steel girders for the castle; and an Afrikaner named Adrian Esterhuizen was busy with twenty ox wagons, toiling through the Namib with all this freight. He covered four hundred miles on every round trip, and it took him two years before the last wagon load was delivered on the lonely farm. Meanwhile artisans had arrived, Italian stonemasons and a Swedish carpenter. An army of labourers was at work on the farm, quarrying stone.

While the castle was being built the baron and his wife lived in a hut close by. You must travel to Duwisib in summer, as I did, to understand their hardships. I drove there in the late October heat through country suffering from the most severe drought of the century. Even the springbok were showing their ribs. Kudu, emboldened by hunger, were invading the gardens of the farmers at night. Baboons with the surly appearance of furred louts hung round the farmhouses and moved sluggishly as the car approached. Dead sheep were stacked for burning.

This is a land where trees give little shade; a land where even the scorpion and the puffadder must seek protection from the sun. Duwisib is a Hottentot name meaning "the white chalk place without water". A chalky outcrop in these parts is usually a sign of water near the surface; but the baron had to go down two hundred feet, using a hand drill, before he found the strong vein which still supplies the farm. The original windmill, bearing the name of a Dresden firm, is still working faultlessly.

During the building period the baron and his wife visited the United States to raise more money for their stupendous project. I had it from the old bookkeeper at the castle, the late Herr Herbert Hassenstein, that the baron's military pension was fifteen pounds a month, while his wife's income was fifteen thousand pounds a year.

Towards the end of 1909 the castle was finished. Now come with me to Schloss Duwisib and reconstruct the life of the baron and the blonde little American baroness. They had lived for a full year in their two-roomed hut, and at last they were enjoying to the full the luxuries of the castle. They had no children; yet according to all accounts, and despite the baron's reckless habits, they were a happy couple.

All the outer walls are two feet thick, with loopholes in the sides and iron-barred windows in front. There is a massive tower in the centre, over the arched entrance, and turrets at each corner. Just inside the studded front door the baron's love of horses is shown by rare old coloured prints. Here, too, is a hand-carved chest dated 1700 and valued at five hundred pounds. Within the huge, stone-flagged hall you see old duelling pistols, swords and sabres, and an almost complete set of the famous Spanish Riding School engravings. Narrow stairs lead to a gallery; and from there you look down on glass chandeliers and fireplaces, chairs bearing the Von Wolf crest and old tables. From there you can see the fountain and the flowers in the courtyard, and the palm tree planted by the baron.

From there, in 1909, you would have seen the baron and baroness handing champagne to their guests. Some are German officers who have come to buy horses for the army. Others are bearded Afrikaner transport drivers, the men who helped to bring the castle into being. The administrator of the Maltahohe district is there

Baron von Wolf is a democratic nobleman, and if anyone dislikes his friends they may leave.

Below the hall is the wine cellar, filled to the ceiling with Piesporter and Riesling, Berncastler, Liebfraumilch, Niersteiner and Zeltingen; with casks of beer and cases of Scotch whisky.

There are seven bedrooms for the guests, all with fireplaces and brass bedsteads. Across the courtyard live the servants. The large rooms are oak-panelled, and the baron and baroness occupy a superb suite in one corner. The baronial hall, thirty feet in height, is flagged, while the other rooms have parquet floors.

Modern plumbing was installed when the castle was built. The plans have been lost, however, and the present manager tells me that he will have to dig up much ground if anything should ever go wrong with the septic tank.

One room draws me again and again. The painted ceiling must have a meaning, but it has been lost. It is the small room in the tower over the main entrance, a quaint room with an old mirror. I am told that it is a ladies' room. The painting shows a Zeppelin cruising over the North Pole. Outside the brown earth shimmers in the heat.

*

The baron is a fine pianist and a gay singer. He is in good form on this night of the housewarming. The guests wander through the long rooms in wonder. They see the Napoleon room with the engravings of incidents in the Napoleonic career. (No wonder the unsuccessful artillery officer was an admirer of Napoleon!) They finger the 1735 oak wardrobe with inlaid panels and try, as I did, to discover the secret keyhole. They stand respectfully before the portrait of the Crown Prince in oils, a personal gift to the baron. They admire the gold-chased sword with the hilt designed as a wolf's head, with rubies as the eyes of the wolf. This is the first of many entertainments at the remote castle. It is the beginning of a legend.

Among the guests from Germany who stayed at the castle was Hansheinrich's sister Ellen. She had been tutor to Princess Hermine, who became the second wife of Kaiser Wilhelm II. When she gave up her position as lady-in-waiting her parents thought she had been spoilt, and sent her to Africa to teach her a lesson. Ellen spent a year at Duwisib and taught the Hottentot women knitting – certainly a contrast with her previous life. After the Second World War she was reported to be leading the life of a peasant in East Prussia.

*

You can turn the clock back easily enough at Schloss Duwisib. I like most of all the ancient sideboard in the dining room with its hand-carved grapes and old wineglasses. In this room are the portraits of the baron's father and mother. Here were once set out the silver cups awarded to the baron when his East Prussian Trakehner horses were successful in shows and races. He owned several trophies to his valuable Irish stallion Crackerjack which died of old age on the farm; and more than one to an Australian horse born at sea between Melbourne and Cape Town, and named Neptune by the baron. There are many descendants of these horses on Duwisib, but they are running wild in the remote corners of the farm. His racehorse Hasso cost two thousand pounds.

The best stock was always good enough for the baron. He imported camels from Egypt and Arabia, Hereford cattle, merino sheep from Australia, and in 1910 he had one of the first karakul herds in a country which has since grown rich on the black karakul wool. In the Maltahohe district they say that the baron would have made a fortune if war had not come in 1914. Certainly he spent a fortune.

He spent it on gambling and drinking parties that lasted for days. Every month he set out for Maltahohe village in a carriage drawn by six horses, followed by a wagon loaded with bottles. I saw the chest in which he kept his drinks cool; metal lined, with places for bottles of all sizes, and compartments for ice, exquisitely designed. Maltahohe in those days was nothing more than an administrator's residence, police station, post office stores and an hotel. It was a gruelling trek from the castle to Maltahohe, and the baron once remarked: "If I end up in Hell it will be no worse than this drive."

On arrival in Maltahohe the baron's procedure was always the same. He entered the hotel bar, pulled out his revolver and shot five bottles off the shelves. The last shot was reserved for the lamp. Then the hotel proprietor, who had been jotting down the value of each hit, presented the bill and if the details were correct the baron paid

164

cheerfully. He would pay any amount – provided he had not been overcharged by one pfennig. That was one of his peculiarities. A good-humoured man, he lost his temper only when he was swindled, or when someone drank his beer.

As a gambler the baron appears to have been unlucky. The old bookkeeper assured me that he once saw a cheque for sixty thousand marks (three thousand pounds) signed by the baron after one night's play. There is a hotel manager in Windhoek today who has reason to remember the baron's weakness for cards. One night in 1914 the baron and his friends were gambling in the hotel when the police raided the place. The manager lost his licence. "I had to become a waiter again," he told me. "But I know the baron would have compensated me if the war had not broken out. He was a fine man, that baron."

The baron was elected by the settlers to represent the Maltahohe district in the legislative assembly (which was only faintly democratic) at Windhoek. Von Wolf was popular, I gather, because he never "played the baron". He was far too outspoken for the German officials, and Governor Seitz disapproved of him. The baron went his own eccentric way.

Among the baron's more remarkable exploits was a journey during the boom of 1908 in search of diamonds. Duwisib is more than a hundred miles from the diamond coast; but Baron von Wolf and his friends covered the first sixty miles on camels. Then they came to loose, shifting dunes with never an opening for the camels so they sent the camels back to the farm and tramped on to Meob on the coast. Brack water was found at Meob and they refilled their water bottles. Marching south, they had pegged claims at Sylvia Hill and found a few small diamonds. After that they plodded on to Luderitz, nearly a hundred and fifty miles of heavy going in the sand. You can imagine the baron's thirst on arrival. He drank a bottle of champagne and then sat down to a game of cards that lasted all night.

That was the occasion when the baron decided to give a yachting party. He chartered a sealing cutter, the *Rana,* which had sails but no engine. Baron von Wolf wished to visit Ichaboe Island, the bird island thirty miles north of Luderitz. He was accompanied by the chief of police and other officials; and they brought cases of champagne, beer and rum with them. Every man on the island was invited to drink with them. A strong south-wester blew up while the *Rana* was at the island, and the baron's party was delayed for five days. This worried the German officials, as a mail steamer was expected at Luderitz and they had to carry out their duties. Nothing worried Baron von Wolf, however, until the champagne gave out. Then he asked the headman to pull them across to the mainland, and the Germans walked back to Luderitz with their pockets filled with beer bottles.

There is a painting of Baron von Wolf in the castle, revealing a tall, clean-shaven man, dark with a determined jaw. No portrait of his wife remains, but I was assured she was good-looking. Jayta von Wolf is a shadowy figure, for though many in the Maltahohe district remember the exploits of the baron they have little to say about his wife. She spoke German badly, I gather, but she was a capable woman. On one occasion when the baron and his workmen were drinking beer instead of baking bricks she went to the kiln and carried on the work herself.

Once the castle had been built she was attended by a chamber-maid and a needlewoman. The white staff included a chef, carpenter, farrier horse-trainer, groom, butler and the bookkeeper I have already mentioned. There were many native farm labourers, and one of them, a Hottentot shepherd, died during the typhus outbreak only a few weeks before my visit.

All the buildings near the castle are in medieval style. You can dive into a huge, round swimming bath twelve feet deep, built of the grey Duwisib stone. Under the roof of the manager's house is a blacksmith's shop with old-fashioned bellows. There is an oven for smoking meat. I also noticed, for the first time in my life, stone dog kennels and turreted pigsties. The ring where the horses were trained had its massive walls set at an angle. Vineyards and mulberry trees make a refreshing contrast with the sunbaked surroundings.

It is a self-contained world, this Schloss Duwisib, and it has need to be. Once every eleven years in South West Africa, on an average, the dry rivers run madly, and then there is no way out. Duwisib is cut off by floods for weeks at a time.

Now it is August, 1914, and Baron von Wolf and his wife are leaving Luderitz in the German liner *Gertrud Woermann*. The shrewd baron has observed the storm clouds gathering in Europe, and he does not wish to find himself suffering a second defeat in South West Africa. He is making for Germany to rejoin the army there.

The *Gertrud Woermann* found sanctuary in Rio de Janeiro; but this did not suit the baron's plans. His wife booked a passage from Rio to Rotterdam in a Dutch steamer. She went on board with a huge wardrobe trunk, which was placed in her cabin. A "woman friend" was in attendance – the baron in disguise! Jayta von Wolf told the purser that her friend had left the ship. Meanwhile the baron had hidden himself in the wardrobe trunk.

During the voyage the baron never left his wife's cabin in daylight. The stewards, gossiping in the pantry, were amazed at the amount of food consumed by the petite baroness. She was always asking for sandwiches and fruit to be sent to her cabin. And not only that – she sent for a bottle of whisky a day. Yet no one suspected the presence of the baron.

At Falmouth the ship was searched by British naval officers. They knocked at the door of the baron's cabin, and caught a glimpse of Jayta von Wolf in *déshabille*. This was before the days of ruthless warfare. The American lady was indignant, and the British officers retired apologising. The ship was allowed to proceed to Rotterdam and Baron von Wolf stepped triumphantly on shore. On his return to Germany the little affair with the Hottentots was overlooked, and Major Baron von Wolf was reinstated in the artillery.

In September, 1916, Major von Wolf was killed in action in France. A French officer searched the body, found letters from the devoted Jayta, and forwarded them to her, with other personal possessions of the baron, through the Red Cross. Drunkard, spendthrift and reckless gambler though he was, I think the last dramatic episode in the life of Hansheinrich von Wolf was admirable.

When the baron left Duwisib in 1914 he placed his friend Count Max von Luttichau in charge. Soon after the war ended the estate was declared bankrupt, and it was sold with all its treasures for seven thousand and fifty pounds.

The new owners were a wealthy Swedish couple, the Murmanns. When their son grew up he learnt to fly, and the Murmanns had their own aircraft parked on a large pan near the castle. It is sad to have to record that Mr Murmann died suddenly at Duwisib, and his son, a South African Air Force pilot, was killed in action in World War II. The castle and the farm were sold again, this time to a company for twenty-five thousand pounds. By the sale of a few of the pictures during his lifetime, Mr Murmann had recovered most of the purchase price of the castle.

*

Jayta von Wolf married again between the wars. Her second husband was Erich Schlemmer, consul-general for Siam in Munich. She returned to her home town of Summit, New Jersey, however, before World War II.

Schloss Duwisib lost some of its treasure during the 1914-15 campaign, including a ten thousand pound Persian carpet. The baroness put in a claim for the old silver after the war, but not a spoon could be found. Fortunately the funiture was too heavy to move, and those who looted the carpets and silver did not appreciate the value of the pictures. It stands to the credit of the company which now owns Duwisib that the castle is being maintained very much as it was in the days of the baron.

From the window of the dining room at Schloss Duwisib you can see a distant mountain peak called Wolfsberg. The baron has left his name on the map.

So now I am going to sleep in the stone castle where Von Wolf revelled with his friends. There are no secret passages here, and no ghosts, but there is this mystery.

Why did Von Wolf return with his wife to the scene of his disgrace? He might have lived far more luxuriously in the pleasant city of Dresden; and there is no doubt that he was a man who knew how to enjoy all the amenities of civilisation. Instead, as I have shown, he settled for years at the end of the world, in a wilderness of dust storms and burning summer heat. This was no life for a woman, yet the woman found all the money for this fantastic enterprise and shared the years of exile with her husband. Why did they build this castle?

If you ask the Maltahohe farmers who knew him they will reply:

"Oh, his wife had plenty of money." That is no answer at all, and the riddle would gnaw at my brain tonight if an old friend of Baron von Wolf had not told me the answer.

Jayta Humphreys, before her marriage, had been an early follower of the psychologist Sigmund Freud. When Von Wolf returned to Germany from the Hottentot war she realised that he was a broken man. He had lost his army career, his state of mind was desperate. She studied him with sympathy and rare understanding, and at last the idea came.

"We must go back to the scene of your defeat," she told him. "Only there will you realise what a small thing this is in a whole lifetime. We'll face the people there together . . . build a castle and live in grand style so they will be proud to accept our hospitality. A castle in the desert, Hansheinrich von Wolf . . ."

And so the grey Schloss Duwisib still stands in a far corner of the Maltahohe district, strange monument to a devoted woman's inspiration.

LORDS OF THE LAST FRONTIER

Logan of Matjesfontein
1955

Matjesfontein is only a wayside station to most of you, a gateway to the Great Karoo linked with the name of Logan. Generations of main line travellers have glimpsed the row of red-brick houses which make Matjesfontein unlike any other dorp in South Africa. Within those houses are memories.

Not only Olive Schreiner, but other famous names belong to Matjesfontein's strange past. The whole place is stamped with the personality of James Douglas Logan, the Laird of Matjesfontein, a patriarch in a tradition of his own. He has been dead for thirty-five years, and it is time his story was told.

This vigorous Scot was born in Berwickshire in 1857, and set off to Australia in a sailing ship at the age of twenty. The ship put into Simon's Bay in distress and was wrecked. Jimmy Logan reached the shore with the clothes he was wearing and an abundant supply of self-confidence. He had worked as a clerk on the North British Railways, but the only railway post he could find in Cape Town was a porter's job at the new railway station, then under construction. By the time the building was finished, Jimmy Logan had become stationmaster. The next step, as district superintendent of the Touws River-Prince Albert Road section, took Logan into the Great Karoo for the first time.

Before leaving Cape Town he had married Miss Emma Haylett. He became interested in catering, resigned from the Cape Government Railways, bought an hotel in Touws River and a wholesale wine and spirit store in Cape Town. In the early Eighties Logan decided to invest everything he had got in the Matjesfontein area. When he started there was just a corrugated iron shed beside the railway line. Land was cheap enough, for no one imagined that anything could be done with this desolate country on the karoo edge.

Logan paid four hundred pounds for the farm of three thousand five hundred morgen which he called Tweedside. You must have seen it, fifteen miles south of Matjesfontein, with its three unusual iron gates and long fence running for miles beside the railway line. Altogether he bought sixty thousand morgen, and most of these farms are still in the family. Tweedside was his favourite. He opened up the first artesian well in South Africa on that farm, sank drill hole after drill hole, and planted thousands of fruit trees in an area where no one had ever dared to attempt fruit growing on a large scale. Cherries, pears and many other varieties had come to the karoo. Gums and pines grew up by the thousand on Tweedside. Logan had his own private railway siding on the farm. His farm labourers received free cottages on condition that they kept them clean. If Jimmy Logan found a sign of litter, however, the labourer paid ten shillings a month rent.

Meanwhile he was also developing Matjesfontein village. His own residence, Tweedside Lodge, was connected with the farm by the longest private telephone line in the colony.

The secret of Logan's fondness for Matjesfontein had its origin in his own weak chest, cured by the dry karoo air. He envisaged Matjesfontein as a great health resort. For some years doctors in England had been sending patients to Beaufort West, which was too dusty, and the Nuweveld Mountains, where some found they were inhaling too much grass. Logan believed in the Matjesfontein climate and set about providing amenities.

"Mr Logan insists on his village being as clean as the deck of a ship," wrote an early visitor. "It has the appearance of a smart London suburb, and close by are the golf links, cricket ground, tennis and croquet courts and swimming bath fed by a sulphur spring."

Matjesfontein was designed and built by Jimmy Logan. He imported London lamp posts for street lighting, and they are still there. The village was the first in South Africa to have waterborne sewerage, and the first to be lit by electricity. Logan spent a thousand pounds tracing a watercourse on one of his farms. He discovered a supply that yielded eleven thousand gallons a day, a great find in the karoo, piped the water to Matjesfontein and sold water rights to the railways at a handsome profit. The shipwrecked youth was firmly on his feet.

Cape Town newspapers devoted columns in November 1889 to the opening of the Matjesfontein waterworks. Logan had invited scores of guests, and when he entertained it was done in the grand manner. The train bringing Lady Sprigg, Colonel Schermbrucker, M.L.A. and many other leading politicians and personages, reached Matjesfontein in the morning. Jimmy Logan had organised a cricket match, rifle shooting, pigeon shooting, billiards, and tennis. The Worcester band was there. Shortly before lunch Lady Sprigg turned the wheel and a fountain played on the bare veld. "The luncheon served in the decorated railway shed would have done credit to a first-rate London hotel," declared a newspaper report.

Colonel Schermbrucker declared that Logan had made a paradise in the desert. He hoped that Matjesfontein would become a large town. Another speaker suggested that the name of the place should be changed to Logansville. Mr Logan replied modestly that it was not that he had done so much, but that in the karoo others had done so little.

During the Nineties a stream of celebrated figures flowed up to Matjesfontein. I have never fully understood how this pilgrimage of English aristocrats to the tiny karoo dorp came about, but it was certainly another result of Logan's drive and enterprise. It just became fashionable to make the sea voyage to the Cape and a trip to Matjesfontein. So I was shown Victorian albums filled with signed portraits of the great. Lord Randolph Churchill (father of Winston) was there in June 1891, a fine year for veld flowers. He picked bluebells on the koppies, borrowed a dog from Logan at the suggestion of Rhodes, and went on a shooting expedition to Rhodesia.

The Duke of Hamilton and many other titled people stepped off the mail train at this little village. I cannot imagine what brought the young sultan of Zanzibar to Matjesfontein, but he was there, too, and Admiral Nicholson; and Admiral Rawson, who gave his name to Rawsonville; and Sir David Gill, the astronomer; James Stewart of Lovedale; all sorts of celebrities stayed at Jimmy Logan's hotel.

Olive Schreiner loved the place. She rented the villa which became known as Schreiner Cottage, next to the post office, and took her meals at Logan's railway refreshment room – of which more will be heard. Here she posted her long letters to Havelock Ellis, and looked forward to his replies as she walked alone at dawn on the veld, feeling a "wild exhilaration" as the sun rose. Here, in 1890, Rhodes broke a journey to Kimberley so that he could dine with her.

It was at Matjesfontein that Olive Schreiner wrote "Thoughts on South Africa". She called her cottage "home", and wrote to Logan during one of her absences: "I shall be very glad to come back to dear old Matjesfontein." She gave Logan's son a book for boys inscribed: "From his very loving friend Olive Schreiner." And after hearing Jimmy Logan's stories of adventure on land and sea she advised him to write his autobiography and offered to edit it for him. South African literature has lost rich pages owing to the unwillingness of such characters as Jimmy Logan to put their experiences on paper.

Logan became a great patron of cricket at this period. He arranged the two visits of Lord Hawke's teams to South Africa – they played at Matjesfontein, of course – and he accepted the entire financial responsibility when the early South African cricket teams toured England. When George Lohmann, the greatest English cricketer of his day, broke down in health, Logan offered him a home and an engagement at Matjesfontein. The change to the crisp karoo prolonged Lohmann's life for years.

Those were the days before railway dining cars at the Cape, and passengers took their meals hurriedly at refreshment rooms. In 1892 Sir James Sivewright, minister of railways, gave the catering contract to his friend Logan without calling for tenders or informing any of his ministerial colleagues. This caused a political crisis of the first magnitude. Sivewright defended his action on the ground that tenders had not always been invited in the past. Moreover he argued that Logan was an admirable caterer.

Nevertheless, Sivewright had to resign and the contract was cancelled. Logan then sued the government and was awarded five thousand pounds damages with costs. Merriman and Sauer resigned. The cabinet disrupted by the Logan contract had been known as "the ministry of all the talents". Rhodes had to dissolve and reform his ministry without three of the talented members.

During the official inquiry into the catering contract, Logan stated that he had invested twenty thousand pounds in refreshment rooms all the way up the line from Wellington to Bulawayo. He had intended to spend a further thirty thousand pounds to make these rooms "second to none in the world". Matjesfontein had the best refreshment room of the lot. Nothing was too good for Matjesfontein. Logan served two breakfasts there – one at three shillings and sixpence, where travellers went for "quiet and high-toned society", and a half-crown breakfast for other customers. He had planned a school of railway cookery, to be established at Matjesfontein with a skilled chef in charge.

Another typical Logan enterprise, carried out successfully for years, was the Matjesfontein mineral water factory. There he made all the soda water, lemonade and ginger ale for thirsty karoo railway travellers. The old plant is one of Matjesfontein's many relics.

After his indirect but sensational appearance in Cape politics, Mr J.D. Logan entered the old Cape house in person as Progressive M.L.A. for Worcester and later as M.L.C. for the North West Cape. Again he figured as a stormy petrel, holding the balance of power in an evenly-divided upper house and bringing about the downfall of the Jameson ministry.

Matjesfontein's most crowded months were during the South African War, when it was the headquarters of the Cape Command with twelve thousand troops camped round the village. The Coldstream Guards, Seventeenth Lancers, Middlesex Regiment, all came to know Matjesfontein only too well. Down a side street in the former laundry a Major Douglas Haig presided over a small mess, and Mr J.D. Logan was invited to a champagne party. Private Edgar Wallace of the R.A.M.C. unloaded medical stores on Matjesfontein railway platform. French, Ironside, Roberts all marched down that main street.

Logan built the present double-storeyed Hotel Milner in the early stages of the South African War. The turret was used as a lookout post, while the hotel became a military hospital. Always an individualist, Logan raised his own mounted corps for service in the field and equipped it at his own expense. He was twice wounded and mentioned in dispatches.

One landmark at Matjesfontein that every motorist knows is the granite monument to Major-General A.C. Wauchope in the private cemetery south of the village. Wauchope was killed at Magersfontein, but the body was reburied at Matjesfontein which was, as I have said, the military headquarters of the period. It was the Black Watch regiment that put up the memorial, and Lady Wauchope visited the grave after the South African War. Wauchope's body was never taken back to Scotland, as some writers have stated.

Jimmy Logan had left Scotland, like thousands of other Scots, with only a few pounds in his pocket. After the South African War he returned on holiday, took over a castellated mansion with a baronial hall near his native village in Berwickshire, and became the benefactor of the poor and aged in the district. He still spent much of his time at his beloved Matjesfontein, however, and there he died in 1920. His son, Mr James Douglas Logan, and his daughter, wife of Colonel H.J. Buist, stayed on at Matjesfontein. For many details of the career of the Laird of Matjesfontein I am indebted to them.

Some years ago, when the river at Laingsburg was in flood, I spent a night at the Hotel Milner at Matjesfontein with many other motorists. I saw there one of the most complete collections of South African male and female big game heads I had ever seen, and imagined that these, too, were one of the original Jimmy Logan's enterprises. Many travellers must have gazed in wonder at the array in the hotel dining room. During a recent visit to Matjesfontein, however, I learnt that the present Mr Logan was the collector. He started about thirty years ago. A firm of taxidermists in Pretoria supplied most of them, and farmers filled in the gaps.

There you see magnificent specimens of the wildebeest and waterbuck, kudu, springbok, gemsbok, blesbok, tsessebe and hartebeest. Among the rare heads are those of the bontebok and nyala, and there are horns of the situtunga. Many East African animals are included. "I only shot one of them myself – the red deer from Scotland," Mr. Logan told me. "I was out shooting woodcock in Perthshire, and my gun was loaded with birdshot. Suddenly a stag broke cover. I let drive with one barrel, but it was like shooting against a brick wall. The next shot struck the back of the neck and the stag dropped dead. It caused a stir in the district, as no red deer had been seen in that part of Perthshire for years. But that is the way the fine antlers of a 'monarch of the glen' came to Matjesfontein."

Mr Logan remembers the springbok migration of 1886 across a farm six miles to the west of Matjesfontein. The springbok still visit this area occasionally, and there is a small herd on Tweedside farm. Tweedside is leased as a sheep and wheat farm nowadays, but Colonel and Mrs Buist retain the homestead and grow thousands of tulips.

Most people think of Matjesfontein as part of the karoo, though it is really on the fringe. The true karoo veld begins at Whitehill, a few miles to the north, where the Logan family gave the land for a succulent garden some years ago. This garden has been removed to Worcester, an unwise step in the view of some botanists.

Mr Logan is no mean botanist himself. He has many varieties of succulents in his own garden next door to the hotel at Matjesfontein. Two succulents which he discovered bear his name; and in company with another botanist he found the only yellow stapelia known to science. In a good year, he told me, the veld between Matjesfontein and Sutherland has a more gorgeous display of wild flowers than Namaqualand.

Matjesfontein takes its name from the rush called Matjiesgoed from which mats are made. Early last century a farmer named Coetzee and several of his relatives were murdered there by slaves, aided by Bushmen; and Coetzee's wife was carried off to the Bushman stronghold. She would have been murdered too, but the slaves spoke up on her behalf and she was held prisoner. Then the Bushmen heard that a commando was approaching. They were leading her to the place of execution when the commando under Veldkornet Nel arrived and saved her life. Nel recovered twenty-five thousand rix-dollars in paper money from the Bushmen.

Lichtenstein visited Matjesfontein with Commissioner De Mist a few years later, and found John Strauss, son of a German soldier, farming there. He told them that his father had been among those who were murdered during the rising of the slaves.

Thus the settlement of Matjesfontein is at least one hundred and fifty years old. The railway reached it in 1878, and from Matjesfontein the old Gibson and Red Star Line coaches set out on the run of five or six days to Kimberley. Matjesfontein has never become the town which Colonel Schermbrucker mentioned in his optimistic speech long ago. It is a village of two hundred people with two schools, and its glorious days have departed. Yet I drove away feeling, as I have often felt before, that small places like Matjesfontein have much beneath the surface if you care to uncover it. I understood the fascination it had for old Jimmy Logan, who liked Matjesfontein better than his castle in Scotland; and for Olive Schreiner, who was drawn back there again and again at intervals of years.

Colonel Buist told me that when he saw the Great Karoo more than half a century ago he remarked to another officer that it seemed like a desert. The officer pointed to the bushes and declared that they made the finest grazing for sheep in the world. "Little did I think that I would settle here in 1921 after thirty years as an army surgeon," remarked Colonel Buist. "Yet it grows on you and you get to like it. I don't know why the time passes so fast, or what I have been doing, but I never have an idle day."

That must have been the way old Jimmy Logan felt about it, too. John X. Merriman once said: "I wish there were ten thousand Logans in South Africa." However, there was just that one determined individual, and so there is only one Matjesfontein.

KAROO

Hauptman Schottland

1966

Years before the Kaiser's War, when Fred Cornell and Solomon Rabinowitz were blasting rocks and pounding their samples along the Orange River, they sometimes encountered a fair, blue-eyed, close-cropped, spectacled man known as Alexander Schottland. He was short and powerful. Often he wore German army uniform. He was in fact a Briton, one of the most courageous and successful spies ever employed by the South African and British governments.

I was privileged to spend a morning in London a few years ago with this tremendous yet reserved character. So much sand has blown over the deserts of South West Africa since World War I, so much brown water has flowed down the Orange, that the great military secrets of more than half a century ago may be revealed without bringing army intelligence officers to my door. So here is the true but untold tale of espionage in that thirsty campaign which thousands of South Africans even now have reason to remember.

Alexander Patterson Scotland (for that was his real name), nephew of George Bernard Shaw, was born of Scottish parents in Britain in 1882. He was blind, but at fourteen he suddenly gained his sight. During the years of darkness the boy had developed an ear for music, a nose and a palate. His first job was in a Mincing Lane tea merchant's office, and there he learnt to recognise Darjeeling and Orange Pekoe, Assam or Ceylon with his eyes closed. In later years he formed a Churchillian taste for good alcohol and discovered his ability to drink any quantity of Scotch whisky without ill effects, mental or physical. He also discovered a gift for languages, in which he achieved perfection wit' out effort. This sensitive and restless young man then looked round for adventure, emigrated to

Australia at seventeen, returned to London and worked in a provision business. At twenty he felt his first military longings, and sailed for Cape Town with the idea of joining the army there and taking part in the South African War. But that war ended soon after he arrived, and he found a post in an insurance office. Then an uncle, a director of the firm called South African Territories Ltd., offered him a job as manager of the branch store at Raman's Drift on the German side of the Orange River. Scotland left Cape Town thankfully for an open-air life in the weird frontier country of mountains, sand and bush.

Raman's Drift, a lonely spot to the west of the Augrabies Falls, was on the main route between Namaqualand and the German colony early this century. Men of the Cape Mounted Police patrolled the south bank, and there was a pont at Raman's Drift which carried the traveller with his wagon or horses to the German military post and store across the water. Raman's Drift was a place of refreshment between two deserts. Scotland's firm had another store at Warmbad, some way from the river, and there the Germans had a fort and a large garrison. Horses, mules, donkeys, oxen and wagons were in great demand, and the Germans drew on the Cape Colony for most of their needs. Young Scotland rode about this borderland on horseback taking orders and learning three languages, German, Cape Dutch and Nama. Within two years he had become so fluent in German, his accent so perfect that many people thought he was a German and referred to him as Schottland. And all the time he was selling canned foods and biscuits and soft drinks, and coming to understand his customers. He met that remarkable character old Hendrik Witbooi, an educated man and clever guerrilla fighter. Among the young Bondelswart captains he knew and respected Abraham Morris, son of a white father and coloured mother. The Germans had flogged Morris when he was a boy, but they paid heavily for that later. Morris, a large and powerful man with a strong personality, was also something of a mystic. He had not yet become a hero, but among the Bondelswarts he commanded instant obedience.

Scotland liked this hard country with its stony wastes and deep gorges, sand dunes and unmapped mountains. Here are the oldest rocks in Southern Africa; and his firm held mineral rights over the southern parts of the colony. Here are natural wonders such as the narrow Fish River canyon, two thousand feet deep in places, an enormous, spectacular, twisting gash in the harsh brown sandstone wilderness. Here, in those days, were herds of gemsbok and springbok, kudu and mountain zebra. On the mountain slopes grew aloes and euphorbias; but only in the river beds were green reeds to be seen, and acacia. Over the face of this land of drought wandered the Hottentot nomads with their fat-tailed sheep and goats; a fierce people, but with Bibles. They had guns and wagons, like the white farmers of the frontier. Sometimes they were kind and hospitable; but when harshly treated they became cruel and merciless. They were the finest hunters in the colony and they alone knew all the hidden water holes in the weird and inaccessible world of the Orange River mountains. All the Hottentot clans loved the freedom which they had known in this country for centuries. It was inevitable that they would clash with the Germans, and in October 1903 the rebellion started. No one realised at the time that it was the opening of a long guerrilla war. White farmers were murdered, their farms were plundered. Parched detachments of German troops were ambushed and massacred. Abraham Morris had his revenge in Gungunib gorge, when he wiped out a fairly large German force. Again and again the crafty Hottentots led the Germans into chasms where they lay hidden until the evening; then the deadly snipers opened fire, some with antiquated muzzle-loaders, others with modern Mausers snatched from the bodies of their enemies. Usually the Hottentots escaped in the darkness. I have seen the lonely graves with German crosses under the knife-edge ridges in those gorges. It must have been one of the most nerveracking campaigns (for the Germans) that Africa had ever seen.

The war kept Scotland busy, for his firm was supplying the Germans with vast quantities of goods. One day there was a gathering of staff officers at Raman's Drift, and Scotland was introduced to a Major Wade, the British attaché with the German army. At a suitable moment Wade took Scotland aside and spoke to him quietly. "We've heard about you – you're doing a good job. Learn all you can about the German army and one day you will be a valuable man." Thus in a far corner the career of a brilliant secret agent started.

Flushed with many little victories, the bold Hottentots now dominated the wild country in the south. It was unsafe to travel anywhere without arms, and Scotland was often in danger. A senior German officer solved the problem by pointing out that only those in uniform were permitted to carry firearms, and that Scotland had better get into uniform. Before long Scotland had become Hauptman Schottland, a member of the German staff concerned with the distribution of supplies. No better way of learning about the German army could have been devised. Hauptman Schottland was present at several battles, the indispensable staff officer who kept thousands of soldiers from starvation. Now and again he had to visit the head office of his firm in Cape Town, and there he met Dr Leander Starr Jameson, prime minister of the Cape Colony. "Dr Jim" gave Scotland certain instructions. General Smuts also spoke to the young man who knew the country over the Orange River so well, and in later years they reached a perfect understanding. On this occasion Scotland returned to Raman's Drift with a new official appointment which gave him even greater influence with the Germans. Scotland alone could issue permits for goods from the Cape to cross the river into the German colony. When the war slowly ended in the Warmbad area Scotland was asked to find the Hottentot leaders and arrange peace negotiations. Abraham Morris had gone into exile in Namaqualand, but Scotland tracked down Jacobus Christiaan and brought about an armistice. Scotland had earned the first of the decorations he was to wear, the Order of the Red Eagle, granted by the Kaiser.

Up to 1909 no German suspected that Scotland was anything but a friend. In that year Scotland sensed a change in the German feeling towards him. One night in Keetmanshoop he was invited to the *casino,* the German officers' mess, where he was entertained lavishly and interrogated with no great subtlety. They started with beer and wine, sang and toasted one another. At two in the morning Scotland heard one of his hosts saying to another officer: "We're getting nowhere – bring the whisky." At four, Scotland had evaded all questions and drank the Germans, all but one, under the table.

"Let's go for a ride," suggested Scotland cheerfully.

"Schottland, you are terrible," muttered the last German and fell to the floor.

South African Territories held wide prospecting rights in the south, as I have said. The next awkward incident arose as a result of a reported diamond discovery at Ai-Ais, the hot medicinal springs in the Fish River Canyon. The company had already spent many thousands of pounds in discovering galena, iron ore, copper and zinc, lead and silver. Rumours of gold had been investigated. Ai-Ais had yielded lead, silver and copper; then Scotland had to ride into the blazing, foul-smelling canyon to see whether the diamond rush was justified. In fact, the canyon had been salted by two South African I.D.B. men who had stolen the diamonds from the Pomona fields. Scotland found no indications of diamonds at Ai-Ais. He thought, however, that there might be uranium or some other valuable radioactive substance present in the healing waters. Scotland arrested the I.D.B. men, and both received long sentences. While they were in prison Scotland was accused of acting as an accomplice in the affair. He was brought before a German judge and was able to clear himself of the charges. Nevertheless it seemed that an attempt had been made to deport him, with other British subjects, from the territory. Most well-informed people, German and British, knew that war was coming; but it came earlier, possibly two years earlier, than the Germans had expected.

Scotland was not taken by surprise. At the end of July 1914 he was in Keetmanshoop. He owned one of the very few motor cars in the colony, a Ford model T, and he employed a reliable Cape coloured driver. Just before the outbreak of war Scotland sent his driver to Upington with a bulky parcel hidden in the Ford. The parcel contained all the latest military maps of the colony. Scotland also compiled lists of the German army units, their officers and the places at which they were stationed. He gave full details of the German staff under Colonel Franke; the nine regular companies, one hundred and forty officers and two thousand men; the regular and reserve batteries and machine-gun troops; the six reserve companies; the camel corps and frontier guard on the Kalahari border; the signal and telegraph section and six wireless stations, fixed and mobile; the transport columns, native labour corps, artillery, supply and ordnance depots; the field ambulance units and hospitals. Scotland had also gathered exact descriptions of the German military aircraft and the personnel of the small flying corps. He was able to describe the defensive positions, and to give it as his considered opinion that the ports of Luderitzbucht and Swakopmund would not be defended. His appreciation of the coming campaign, with the movement of Franke's efficient army of ten thousand men, was probably the most valuable and comprehensive document of its kind ever supplied by an intelligence agent in enemy territory. Scotland also included in the secret pack an urgent note to General Smuts; he said that he would be arrested at any moment, and that he was relying on Smuts to do his best for him if the Germans sentenced him to death as a spy. The coloured driver reached Upington safely and delivered the pack to the magistrate. At almost the same moment Scotland was arrested.

Of course Alexander Scotland had not been working alone in the German desert colony. A young officer named Captain Edmund Ironside was there, bearded and disguised as an Afrikaner transport rider. Ironside fell under suspicion, however, and had to slip over the frontier to Rietfontein, thirsty and exhausted. Later in his career he rose to the rank of field-marshal. Another outstanding intelligence officer was Major J.C.W. Leipoldt,* assisted by Captain Richter and Captain Eric Nobbs. (Nobbs, a great agricultural scientist, was able to prevent General Botha's hungry soldiers from devouring the pure-bred flocks of karakul sheep.) I may also mention here a humble but invaluable guide who joined the South African invaders at the opening of the campaign – Abraham Morris.†

Every spy must have a "post office" or other means of communication. Those neat little wireless transmitters of World War II were not available in the days of primitive spark coils. For years Scotland sent his information to a Mr E. Müller in Luderitzbucht. Dusty Müller, as Scotland called him, held the position of British consul there. That was long before the Union had a diplomatic service. Müller was an Afrikaner and the Germans knew him as the man who looked after the interests of the thousands of Cape coloured labourers working for the Germans on the diamond fields. Scotland's reports went out in the sealed diplomatic bag, a method which has

---

* Major Leipoldt's adventures as a treasure hunter are related in "Something Rich and Strange" (Timmins, 1962).
† Abraham Morris went into revolt against the Union Government during the Bondelswart Rebellion of 1922, and was shot dead by a police officer.

been pursued faithfully by spies for centuries. You may not be surprised to learn that when World War I broke out, Mr. Müller was away in South Africa on leave; but he was soon to return to Luderitzbucht as Lieutenant-Colonel Müller, on the staff of Brigadier-General Sir Duncan Mackenzie.

Another colleague in the secret service game was a quiet daredevil with remarkable blue-white eyes, C.K. de Meillon. He had fought with great distinction under General Botha during the South African War; he was captured, but escaped; and when caught a second time he was sent to Ceylon. After the war he refused to take the oath of allegiance and went into exile in Madagascar with Denys Reitz and other "irreconcilables". There he joined the French Army and took part in native campaigns. De Meillon's next move was to German South West Africa, where he secured a mineral concession. He was treated unfairly, however, and decided to return home. I understand that the officer who administered the oath of allegiance in Cape Town heard De Meillon's story and suggested that he should return to German territory as a secret agent. De Meillon agreed, and he was "deported" from the Cape on the ground that he had refused to take the oath. The Germans were now sympathetic, and before long De Meillon found a post as manager of one of the Kaiser's farms. Then he was granted a commission in the German army and fought in the Herero and Hottentot campaigns. Three months before the outbreak of World War I he left the colony unostentatiously and reported to General Smuts. When war came Major de Meillon sailed for Luderitzbucht as chief intelligence officer on the staff of Mad Dunc, the nickname of sixty-year-old high-spirited General Mackenzie. However, the Boer veteran De Meillon soon proved himself to be every bit as reckless as his army commander. When the little invasion fleet reached the coast near Luderitzbucht, De Meillon and a small party of picked men were put on shore at night by the celebrated Captain Wearin of the coasting steamer *Magnet*. (The rowing boat capsized after the scouts had been landed, but Wearin, a champion swimmer, made his way back in spite of the icy water and the sharks.) De Meillon and his men crossed fifteen miles of desert in a roaring sandstorm and were just in time to watch the evacuation of Luderitzbucht by the German troops. De Meillon found a house which had been abandoned so hurriedly that hot coffee and a meal had been left on the table. After refreshing himself he went to bed worn out. Next morning the troopships steamed in unopposed and De Meillon was there to welcome them. Lieutenant-Colonel Müller marched up to the town hall, found a white flag flying, and took the surrender from the *burgomeister.*

So there were two thousand armed men with horses, mules and three-quarters of a million gallons of Cape Town water. The advance into the waterless hinterland started, always with De Meillon riding well ahead of the army and bringing in information and prisoners. Soon the Germans became aware of his presence, and put a price on his head, dead or alive. They had not forgotten his German commission. De Meillon was regarded by some of Mackenzie's staff as too bold, too optimistic and in too much of a hurry. Once he asked for a squadron to intercept and wreck a German armoured train operating in the Aus area. The plan was turned down, but De Meillon carried out many other ambitious forays successfully. Early in the advance he was wounded, but he soon returned to duty. Many of the Hottentots were in his pay, and De Meillon usually had his fingers on the German pulse. One day he made a fatal mistake. De Meillon had formed a strong impression that the Germans would evacuate Aus without fighting. This was contrary to Scotland's appreciation of the German tactics; but De Meillon was so confident that he rode too far into Aus poort. With him were Sergeant-Major Dreyer and three Hottentot guides. He rode into an ambush, and a German officer recognised him. "De Meillon, put your hands up – we've got you," shouted the German.

"I'm going to fight," called back De Meillon, dismounting and lying down behind his horse. This brave man was shot through the head. Dreyer was captured and sent to Windhoek. The Germans sent a wireless message to General Mackenzie stating that the three Hottentots were German subjects and would be hanged. When the South African troops entered Aus they found three Hottentots suspended from a tree. De Meillon's grave was marked by a wooden cross bearing his name, and his spurs were placed on the mound. A huge military funeral service was held on April 25, 1915, and Major de Meillon's widow came from the Cape to attend. One hundred men formed the firing party. Private P.W. Rayner, who had served under De Meillon, wrote: "He was buried where he fell. Cold, ruthless, utterly daring, very lovable, he was a great guerrilla fighter."

Sergeant-Major Dreyer found a truculent man in the next cell at Windhoek Gaol – Hauptman Schottland. Scotland told Dreyer that when he had complained of conditions there the warder had laughed and replied: "Don't worry – you won't be here for long. There is going to be an 'accident' one of these days." However, the message to General Smuts had not been disregarded. Day after day the Union forces sent a wireless message to Dr Seitz, the German governor, to this effect: "What have you done with Scotland? We are holding one of the most important Germans at the Cape as a hostage. Whatever happens to Scotland will happen to him." That saved Scotland's life. He was sent to the prisoner-of-war camp at Tsumeb and then to Namutoni. When the Germans surrendered, Scotland had been imprisoned for nearly a year. He went down to Cape Town by train, sailed for England, and entered the second and even more sensational phase of his life as an intelligence agent.

*

Scotland did not find it easy at first to convince the British intelligence department in London that he would make a useful officer. He could not very well appear in uniform as a *hauptman,* wearing the Order of the Red Eagle; but he mentioned the name of General Smuts and was received by a general. "Do you know anything about the German army?" the general asked. Scotland had to laugh. "I served in it for four years," he replied. Soon afterwards Second Lieutenant Scotland landed in France.

I think Scotland's most courageous exploit during World War I was his discovery of a secret route into German-occupied Belgium and the use he made of it. Scotland reached Brussels in disguise, posing as a German colonial; and there he made contact with a German he had known in South West Africa, a simple fellow who remembered Schottland only as a German. This man found Scotland a post in a welfare organisation. Once again Scotland put on German uniform, working as a counter assistant and barman. Three times he crossed the lines, carrying on each occasion a mass of information. The O.B.E. he received was indeed richly deserved.

Scotland returned to South West Africa when peace came, and there are many old South Westers who remember him as manager of a great meat-packing firm. They also speak fondly of his beautiful wife Roma. He went on to the Argentine in the 1930s. Nazi agents were very active, and he found that they were fully aware of Schottland and his record. Shortly before World War II, during a visit to Germany, an influential German friend asked Scotland a number of questions about South West Africa and the Argentine; then he invited Scotland to his home for an important meeting. Just as coffee was about to be served everyone stood up and in walked Adolf Hitler. There followed a long and close interrogation in which Hitler asked Scotland about his army career, officials he had known in South West Africa, and other penetrating questions which showed that the Hauptman Schottland episode had been studied carefully. "You are an ingenious man, Schottland," remarked Hitler as he was leaving the room. "Now I can understand the reports we have on our files about you." But the reason behind this strange meeting was something Scotland never discovered.

At sixty Scotland was in his old uniform again – as a British major, I had better add. He worked in France for a time at the interminable yet fascinating game of interrogation; but his most important duties were carried out at the London Cage. I have stood outside this quiet mansion near Hyde Park and thought of the Nazis who were taken there to be interrogated by Lieutenant-Colonel Scotland and other giants of the military intelligence world. In those rooms Scotland gathered the evidence which sent Fritz Kneochlein to the gallows for the atrocities near Calais when nearly one hundred British prisoners were murdered. Scotland was the man who tracked down the Germans who ordered the executions of fifty Royal Air Force men after the escape from Stalag Luft III in Silesia. Scotland unravelled the mystery of Rudolf Hess, the deputy *fuehrer,* after that dramatic flight to England which kept all of us guessing and wondering for years. "The information that Rudolf Hess brought, and what transpired during the questioning, remains a closely-kept secret," declared Scotland years after the war. That was Scotland's most important interrogation episode.

Alexander Scotland remained a shadowy figure until the trial in 1947 of Field-Marshal Albert Kesselring in Venice. I need not recall the facts; only an amusing passage while Scotland was giving evidence. The prosecutor said: "Now, Colonel Scotland, I am going to ask you some questions about the German army." The defence objected on the ground that the witness had never served in the German army and could not speak about its organisation.

The prosecutor: "Colonel Scotland, were you ever in the German army?"

"Yes."

Scotland gave no details, but the London and other newspapers filled the gap with rather too much imagination. "Amazing Career of Bernard Shaw's Nephew" runs one headline before me. A relative told the reporters that Scotland had served on the German general staff in both world wars. Perhaps he could not be blamed for this belief. Mrs Scotland was interviewed, and she could only say: "He is rather a mystery man. I knew he did secret service work during the war, but I am surprised to hear of some of his activities."

One newspaper stated that Scotland had a deeper knowledge of the German army than anyone outside the German high command, and this was probably true. Many fantastic stories appeared. It was even said that he had returned to England wearing his German uniform as a *hauptman,* and took a taxi to the war office unchallenged. However, the British authorities (following an old intelligence rule) decided not to deny any of the stories for fear of revealing information. Many people still believe that Alexander Scotland was the hero of a famous spy novel in which the hero, Bretherton, changed sides again and again without detection.

As a result of the publicity someone persuaded Scotland to write a book. This would have been the greatest spy book of the century if only it had been published. Word of the enterprise reached the war office, however, and the very people who had worked with Scotland during the war now appeared in his London flat and ransacked every room. Years passed before his personal papers, files and scrapbooks were returned. After severe censorship his manuscript was but a shadow of the complete masterpiece. The secret of Rudolf Hess and many more remained untold. Scotland acted as technical adviser in the production of a spy film, but this work did not bring him into conflict with his former colleagues of M.I.5.

When I met Alexander Scotland in his London flat he looked

wistfully at some photographs of South West Africa I had brought with me: the mud fort at Warmbad, the ragged Bondelswart Hottentots, the old German buildings in Keetmanshoop, the veld with low, scattered bushes. He sighed and then he spoke: "That is where I learnt the art of intelligence work. It is an art. When I was arrested at the outbreak of World War I, a German officer interrogated me, and that man really taught me the technique of dealing with an enemy. It was in the German colony that I learnt German and the German mentality. In later years I could speak to German prisoners in a way they could understand. They almost forgot I was a British officer interrogating them. Sometimes I would meet a prisoner who had been in South West Africa; then I became Schottland again and we talked as old friends. That was the way I got vital military information. It seemed to them that I was a German talking to Germans."

Scotland pondered for a moment. "I'll tell you another thing. Violence will rarely make a man give you the facts you need. Some men will talk under that sort of pressure, but you can never rely on what they say. I am resolutely opposed to brutality. Germans I interrogated gave evidence in court afterwards and their evidence tallied exactly with what they told me. They never retracted anything. As I said before, interrogation is an art that has to be learnt."

I had always wondered how even the bravest man felt when living behind the enemy's lines as a spy, and I put the question to Scotland. "Did you ever lie awake at night thinking that at any moment you might be taken out and shot?"

"Never!" replied Scotland emphatically. "They could not take me by surprise. I was a German, talking like a German, thinking like a German. No, it never worried me."

Scotland turned again to my photographs. "I really loved that country," he reflected. "It was what I call a personal country. If they saw you could do a job they accepted you and let you do it in your own way. I found the Argentine hostile. South West Africa was a friendly country, the land itself. And so healthy . . . Lord, how well I was during my years there."

THUNDER ON THE BLAAUWBERG

Islands

Green's passion for the sea is evident in these stories of the islands of the South Atlantic. He loved these wild, storm-wracked chunks of rock set down in the ocean.

He was fortunate to travel at a time when pollution on a large scale was virtually unknown. Not only have times changed but so have tastes: modern reaction to the idea of turtle soup and unlimited supplies of penguin eggs – available fifty years ago in London for a shilling each – is not the same as it was.

Green tells of the good and bad old days of Victorian imperialism, sometimes with unconscious humour. When, in 1861, the behaviour of the guana collectors on the tiny island of Ichaboe became too unruly and violent, one of Her Britannic Majesty's frigates, aptly named *Furious,* was sent to restore order.

There is no doubt about the spell which these islands cast over Lawrence Green. He returns to them again and again in his writings. And as he wrote of his efforts to find out why islands hold such power over their inhabitants, perhaps he was subconsciously trying to discover the roots of his own fascination.

Island Treasure

1933

Steam south along the desert coast of South West Africa, south from Walvis Bay for a hundred miles, and you will raise the volcanic rock marked on the chart as Hollam's Bird Islet.

This is the first of that string of queerly-named guano islands owned by the South African government. Here, on a pile of stone, basalt and lava, is the home of the seals. Pelts valued at hundreds of thousands of pounds have been won on this lonely spot – by licensed seal hunters and by daring poachers. Yet the fur seals still haul up out of the cold ocean year after year; first the great male seals, then the females. Desperately the males fight on the rocks of the islet, while the females watch and go to the victors.

Sealing is a risky trade. Few islands are more inaccessible than Hollam's Bird; the surf breaks all round, there is no beach. The seal hunters row in with a whaleboat towards one spot at the base of a forty-foot wall of rock where landing is sometimes possible. A man with a rope lashed round his waist jumps for the ledge. If he misses his foothold he is hauled back to the boat. But once on shore, he makes the line fast to an iron ring-bolt in the rock, and then the sealers swarm up with their clubs.

Years ago the docile, silky seals waited innocently to be butchered. Now they have grown cunning. They post sentinels to warn them of the coming of the raiders. Their eyesight is poor, but they have a marvellous sense of smell. A female seal, cornered with its young, will turn and fight. And if a man shows cowardice, the female will follow him with dangerous jaws snapping viciously.

There is no count of the seals that have been clubbed to death on

Hollam's Bird; but there is a long list of men drowned and men killed by the seals they hunted.

The raiders make a determined rush as the seals lie sunning themselves on the flat rocks. Rifles cannot be used – the bullets would damage the valuable skins. So the hunters club right and left mercilessly, with never a pause until their victims are dead and the survivors have found safety in the sea.

Great care is taken in removing the pelts, for a slip of the knife means a ruined skin. The whaleboat is loaded with pelts, and as the boat, dripping blood, rows back to the ship, sharks follow eagerly in the hope of snatching the skins. Once on board, the skins are salted and stowed away in barrels.

A man may earn four hundred pounds at sealing in the short season of four months. In the early days the schooner *Antarctic* took one thousand, four hundred seals in one day. But the hunter has always lived dangerously. He may remain on Hollam's Bird in one of the nameless graves near the landing place.

The poachers, of course, pay no royalty to the government and thus make richer hauls – if a gunboat does not come nosing out of the fog to seize ship, cargo and crew. The fogs which so often cover this desolate isle – dense fogs that other sailors dread – give protection to the poachers. Before the war, when Germany owned South West Africa, Hollam's Bird was a British possession; and the Germans raided the island so often, and with such success, that the stolen pelts brought down the price of sealskins on the London market. Thousands of skins were taken on foggy days.

Less than a century ago Hollam's Bird Islet was the resort of pirates. Today only the seals, the penguins and the gannets are at home there. Who knows what treasure may lie buried under the white layer of guano on Hollam's Bird?

*

Never did a sea-swept rock receive a more fitting name than Mercury Island. This black, oblong bird sanctuary off the coast of South West Africa has an enormous cavern in its face, and the island contains a maze of tunnels. When the seas rush in, the whole island shakes like quicksilver.

The lonely men who work there for months on end collecting the phosphates have a neat way of demonstrating this curiosity. They place a full glass of water on the table in their hut; and as the great combers go smashing into the cavern beneath, the water spills over the brim. Windows shiver and doors rattle. An eerie place!

"It is impossible to conceive anything more wild and dreary than this isolated spot," wrote a shipmaster in the old South Atlantic sailing directions. "Nothing but the hope of great profits could induce men to imprison themselves in so wretched a dungeon; a sentence of transportation could certainly not be more severe than the banishment the guano gatherers impose upon themselves."

One day, Mercury Island, eaten away by the sea, must collapse like a sandcastle. This great jelly cannot go on shaking forever. The guano men hope that the end will come when they are not there – familiarity with the peculiar movements of the island has driven anxiety out of their heads. Visitors are rare; but when they do make the difficult landing on Mercury Island they seldom feel safe for a moment.

On the summit of Mercury, a hundred and thirty feet above the sea, there is a funnel which they call the Glory Hole. You can hear the noisy waters far below if you listen at the edge of the funnel. Undoubtedly it opens into the great east to west cavern.

There are many stories of the Glory Hole, but no records of exploration. Diamonds are there, they say, and the treasures of those Madagascar pirates who lay in the shelter of the island waiting for the East Indiamen to pass . . .

Three sailors, bolder than any man within living memory, went down in to the Glory Hole eighty years ago. They were never seen again. In some dark corridor, lost or trapped by the sea, they must have died of hunger and thirst.

So the only treasure ever taken from Mercury is the phosphate wealth of the penguins and gannets. There is no fresh water on the island – the tanks are filled by ships bringing supplies from Cape Town. Fish are easily caught, however, and there are always unlimited supplies of penguin eggs – delicacies which cost a shilling each in London.

Mercury Island, trembling like a little earthquake, is not the place for a man afraid of solitude. Yet every season, when labourers are recruited in Cape Town, hordes of applicants line up to sign on. There are compensations. The island is wonderfully healthy; it is said that the strong reek of ammonia from the guano prevents colds. The men live there without a doctor, with only a ship's medicine chest – friar's balsam, castor oil and the like – to cure their ailments.

Work goes on from sunrise to sunset. In the evenings old packs of cards are brought out, and the stakes are cigarettes. The music of guitars and banjos mingles with the crying of the birds and the ceaseless beating of the sea.

And all the time Mercury Island rumbles and shakes – a long but perfectly clear warning that one day it will return to the bed of the ocean.

*

Possession Island, south of Mercury again, is the kingdom of the penguins and scene of a century-old mystery which baffles naturalists to this day.

A wicked-looking island from the sea; glaring white where the guano lies; black rock and white breakers. The wrecked coasting steamer *Nautilus* looms over the southern end of Possession. Beneath the surf lies the sailing ship *Auckland,* lost with all hands years ago.

Possession, the largest of the guano islands, is only three miles long; and like all the rest it has no fresh water. There was a time when water was brought by schooners, and delay meant danger for the large gang of men on the island. Once, indeed, the water ran low in the tanks and the thirsty island crowd scanned the horizon in vain for a sail. So one man, to save his comrades, paddled across the strait for two miles to the mainland and trudged towards Luderitzbucht for help.

They found him dead on a dune outside the town, recognised him as a guardian of the birds on Possession and guessed his mission. The cutter they sent loaded with water barrels reached the island just in time.

After that tragedy the government erected sun condensers on the island, capable of supplying seventy gallons a week – you can still see them rusting on the shore. Today steamers bring fresh water, and it is stored in tanks holding twelve hundred gallons.

The unsolved mystery of Possession is the covering of seal skins which Captain Morrell found there in 1828, many traces of which are even now to be found beneath the guano. Imagine it – an island clad in fur! "The whole island was literally covered with the carcasses of fur seal, with their skins still on them," wrote Morrell. "It was evident that they had all met their fate about the same period. I should judge, from the multitude of bones and carcasses, that not less than half a million had perished here at once."

Morrell suggested that the seals had been overwhelmed and suffocated by one of the terrible, hot whirlwinds that sweep out to sea from this desert coast. But the destruction of the seals would have been repeated many times since then if his theory had been correct. Moreover, the seals need only have slipped back to the sea to escape such a menace. No, some other explanation must be sought. It is possible that the seals fell victims to a plague of which modern science knows nothing. At any rate, seal hair, skeletons and teeth are still dug out of the soil of Possession, almost perfectly preserved by the same chemical which mummifies the bodies of dead seamen on Ichaboe and other islands of the group.

From this graveyard of the seals once came diamonds worth a thousand pounds. Is there another tiny island in the world which has produced diamonds? I doubt it. The discovery of diamonds on Possession came about as a result of the rich hauls which were being made on the mainland – at that time German territory. One of the theories of the origin of these beautiful stones was that they reached the shore from a "parent rock" on the ocean bed. It seemed possible that there might be diamonds on the British islands, too, and government officials and prospectors combed the bird sanctuaries for this new source of wealth.

And on Possession, among dozens of worthless crystals, diamonds were found. A thorough search followed. Washing machines, sieves, picks, dynamite and spades were sent to the island. Ovambo native labourers with experience on the German South West African fields were recruited for the work. A trench three hundred yards long, in a bank of gravel and clay – and the all-pervading seal hair – was dug. Within a few weeks the diamonds worth a thousand pounds, already mentioned, were handed over to the government. Then the enterprise was abandoned. Results had not justified the expense. It was argued that the risk of disturbing the penguins, thus losing the valuable guano deposits, was not worthwhile.

When the Possession Island discoveries became known, however, a syndicate of eager prospectors in Cape Town planned a daring scheme. With diamonds on the mainland and the island, they argued, there must also be diamonds on the floor of the sea. They would dredge for them, and bring up a richer load than any fishermen had ever hauled! The coasting steamer *Nautilus* was chartered, with all the secrecy appropriate to such an adventure, and the prospectors steamed north. I heard the tale from a man who had tried his luck on every African diamond field – a tough, sun-browned Scot, who sailed in the *Nautilus*.

"We lowered our grab buckets to test the bottom near Possession – inside the three-mile limit," he recalled wistfully. "Misty weather, it was, just what we had prayed for. A diamond came up in one of the first buckets. We did not need to test it – we old prospectors knew. And just as we were all crowding round in fine spirits, cheering and slapping each other on the back – just then the sharp bows of a gunboat poked out of the fog. She was the *Panther,* the coastal patrol ship. The Kaiser had issued a special decree that all diamonds found in the sea within the three-mile limit belonged to Germany. We knew the law – and they must have known what we were seeking.

"Then began a game of blindman's-buff. The *Panther* had three times our speed; but the fog was in our favour. A solid white wall shut down between the *Panther* and the *Nautilus*. We should have steamed clean away – but our skipper had forgotten all about Possession Island. The shock as we struck the reef threw us all off our feet. All hands reached the island in the boats, and the Germans could not touch us there. Diamond diggers' luck I suppose – I have known worse."

And there the *Nautilus* remains, wedged out of reach of the gale-driven combers – a silent memorial of old adventure.

The legends of hidden caches of diamonds on Possession are innumerable. I know of two illicit expeditions in search of hoards which were certainly not based on mere rumour. In the graveyard one parcel of diamonds was supposed to have been hidden; among the bleached white crosses of decaying wood, where the bodies of the captain of the *Auckland* and his wife were buried when they were washed ashore.

I can think of many places where I would rather seek treasure at night than in the graveyard of Possession. They say that the *Auckland's* captain and his wife may still be seen resting miserably on the beach near the wreck. Sharks guard the island. The ghost of the woman, they say, has no legs . . .

Such is Possession, island of mystery and diamonds.

*

Ichaboe, near Possession, is the strangest island of its size in the world. This guano-whitened rock is less than a mile in circumference; but every reeking, living inch of it would make a page of adventure.

The discoverer is unknown. Captain Morrell visited Ichaboe a century ago, when charts of the South West African coast were still rough drawings. "This is a fine place for making captive the great leviathan of the ocean, the right whale," he wrote. "The island is literally covered with jackass penguins and gannets." Then, as an afterthought, he added a few words worth hundreds of thousands of pounds. "The surface of this island is covered with birds' manure to a depth of twenty-five feet."

Captain Morrell took fur seals, suggested in his notes that trade might be done with the Hottentots in leopard skins, ivory and ostrich feathers, and sailed away. The idea of taking a cargo of the rich guano never occurred to him. But when his celebrated "Narrative of Four Voyages" reached Liverpool, an enterprising shipowner sent three vessels to search for the island. The brig, *Ann of Bristol,* under Captain Parr, found it; and there began a prosperous trade which continues, as a State monopoly, to this day. The *Ann of Bristol's* cargo was sold in Liverpool for nine pounds a ton, for farmers were just beginning to realise the value of phosphates as fertiliser. Word of the great discovery flew round. Soon a fleet manned by the toughest sailormen of Liverpool was steering south on the long passage to Ichaboe. The place was a no man's land; it was not surprising that the rival crews fought bitterly with knives, belaying pins and fists for the wealth that lay heaped on the tiny islet.

Signs and relics of the bloodstained early history of Ichaboe still remain. Go to the island, as I did, in the coasting steamer carrying water and provisions. The headman will show you the old graves, and tell stories that would seem fantastic if they were not backed by official records, by the wrecks that litter the island shore, and the ring of truth in the voice of a lonely exile. A queer character is Emilio Barbieri, headman of Ichaboe – "Mister Milo" to everyone along the desert coast of South West Africa. Italian by birth, he came to the guano islands in 1895 as a young sailor in a full-rigged ship; and there, save for rare spells of leave, he has worked ever since. A man with the frame and muscles of a wrestler, with a face tanned to mahogany by the suns and the winds and the spray of the South Atlantic. I marvelled at his seamanship as he brought the lean, double-ended whaler out from the surf-beaten shore of Ichaboe. And I was glad to know that he was handling the steering oar when I leapt into the boat and raced towards the stony beach in a welter of green sea.

Mister Milo told me of the foreign legion of broken men who drifted to Ichaboe as sealers and guano collectors – men who left the past over the horizon when they signed on for work on the island. "There was a doctor, struck off the rolls – but he still had his knowledge and he was useful here," recalled Milo. "Aye, and clergymen, too, and men of every nation and colour. There is no drink here; life on the island was good for them."

He led me out to the graveyard and I found that Milo had a store of information gathered from old shipmasters concerning the wild early days of Ichaboe. "There is something queer in the soil of all these guano islands – it preserves bodies just like mummies," he declared. "Under these wooden crosses are men stabbed to death, clubbed and shot. You could see their faces today, after sixty, seventy years – though, *Madre di Dios,* I would not disturb them.

"But once, many years ago, there was a sailor working here; and after a storm this mad fellow found some of the graves with the earth torn away by the wind. Every morning he would go to the coffins, and lift up a lid, and say: 'Good morning, Jack – still here? You've got a darn sight better shirt than mine. I think I'll take it.' He never took a shirt; but one day, after drinking rum from a ship, he went to one of these mummies with a jack knife and cut off the head and ran into the hut swinging it by the red hair. I tell you, his messmates cleared out pretty quick."

Yes, there were odd characters on Ichaboe in the earlies, as Trader Horn would say. On one day in February, 1845, four hundred and fifty-one ships were anchored in the mile-wide channel between Ichaboe and the mainland. Hundreds of labourers were clearing the deposits – seventy feet high the guano was at first, and not twenty-five as Morrell had guessed. They made a hell of the island with their mad carousals and bloodthirsty feuds. But it was not until 1861 that the British naval frigate, *Furious,* was sent to Ichaboe to restore order. I saw the result of that visit in a board nailed up in one of the huts:

> "This island of Ichaboe is this day taken possession of for and in the name of her Britannic Majesty, Queen Victoria, as a Dependency of the Cape of Good Hope. Signed Oliver J. Jones, Captain, H.B.M.S. *Furious,* 21st June, 1861. All claims to rights of Soil or Territory to be made to the Governor of the Cape of Good Hope. God Save the Queen."

Many of the ships that came to load guano in those days were driven ashore in the south-west gales; many relics of these disasters remain. Milo himself lives in a charthouse torn from the poop of a sailing ship, strengthened against the weather by timbers from other lost ships. There is a cannon outside, half-buried, a muzzle-loader of a very old type. And on the reefs of the island lie the skeletons of ships; so many of them that even Milo cannot remember their names.

But Milo does recall the period when the ships that came to load guano were all fast schooners from Table Bay, five hundred miles to the south'ard. One of them, the *Themis,* had been a crack yacht in her time – she won a race across the Atlantic. Most famous of all was the *Sea Bird* and her master, Captain Garcia; "as tough a sailorman as ever laid canvas on a heeler," they said of him. A little packet with fine lines, she was, and seventy men of the guano and sealing gangs would crowd into her salon, hold and fo'c'sle. Bearded fellows with rings in their ears, owning nothing but their mattresses stuffed with sea birds' feathers – sailors to a man. For six months they would work. Then, back in Cape Town, came a great pay day; the seamen's boarding houses would ring with their shanties and all the money would go in the fierce brandy they call Cape smoke. On the island they had lived like Robinson Crusoes; but for a day there were kings in sailortown.

Today, the labourers on Ichaboe are coloured men, and Milo sighs for his old comrades. A few years ago he returned to Italy for a holiday. "My friends were all dead – or gone to America," he said sadly. "People called me the man from Africa. They were all strangers. Everything was different. Perhaps I have wasted my life on Ichaboe – but now I shall never go back to Italy."

One thing has never changed on Ichaboe – the bird population. You watch them as you steam up to the island, like an enormous swarm of flies hovering over a cake. It is really impossible to count them; but the official estimate is forty million. Nearly all are gannets – bodies as white as chalk against a blackboard, wings tipped with black, heads and necks like yellow silk, blue beaks and pale blue eyes. In the southern winter all but the sick and aged birds desert the island. They return in an enormous cavalcade, beating the air into a whirring tumult, as though a squadron of aeroplanes was passing overhead. On this day the gannet millions blot out the sun until they have settled down on Ichaboe. A great sight, seen by few men besides Milo. No one knows where they go to make their homes when they leave on the long northward flight. But Milo knows, almost to the day, when instinct will guide them back to the island. Like snow they cover it in the breeding-season. Every inch is packed with their nests – even a snake could not crawl between them. A gannet eats its own weight in fish every day. Marvellous fishermen they are – you see them dropping from the sky like plummets, wings tightly folded, to emerge a second later with their victims in their beaks.

Years ago an argument arose in South Africa. Which are worth more – the guano-producing birds or the fish? Naturalists calculated that the birds destroy twenty thousand tons of fish a day. The annual yield of guano from all the islands of the coast is about ten thousand tons (and it is interesting to note that Ichaboe, the smallest island, exports the greatest quantity of guano). Those interested in the fishing industry would drive the birds away from their sanctuaries and turn the fish into fishmeal – a food for cattle and poultry. The controversy fills the correspondence columns of the South African newspapers from time to time; but no solution of the problem has been found. The government, however, believes literally that a bird in the hand is worth two in the bush, and there is little likelihood of a change.

So Milo watches over the gannets of Ichaboe year after year – the hermit of the South Atlantic. I can hear them now, in the radio of memory, crying their harsh "para! para!" as they dive incessantly in search of fish for themselves and their young. And on the screen of memory I see those rough, sea-booted men of the Forties who drank rum there, and battled like pirates for the treasure of the island – the men who lie where the gannets roost on the wooden crosses of Ichaboe.

THE COAST OF TREASURE

Leper Isle

1946

Alcatraz of the convicts, Molokai of the lepers, Heliogoland fortress – there is an island in Table Bay which is reminiscent of all three. When you gaze across from Blaauwberg beach and see the full size of Robben Island, with its trees and streets of houses, you may well ask what is to be done with the place.

Robben Island has again become a question mark on the blue South Atlantic. Equipment worth hundreds of thousands of pounds was dumped on the old wooden jetty during the war and hurriedly assembled. Guns, radar and asdic, steamrollers to make an aerodrome, all the material for a degaussing range to beat the magnetic mine . . . in those days there was no doubt about Robben Island's role. You could reach the island from the docks by crash boat within seven minutes. A fine new settlement was built, and a safe harbour provided for the first time. But now? No one seems to want Robben Island, the old place of exile and suffering, shipwreck and strange drama.

On more Sundays than I can remember between the wars I sailed over to Robben Island anchorage in Murray Bay and wandered through the leper settlements; and after the lepers were removed in 1931, through the deserted village. From the people of the island and from old records I gathered an outline of this queer island story. Robben Island, "island of seals" when the first explorers landed, lies only six miles from Table Bay breakwater. A low island, often covered with fog, two miles long and only a mile broad. An hour's sail from Cape Town, yet the island might belong to a different world.

The settlement as I first knew it, twenty years before the evacuation, was a happy place in spite of its purpose as a leper, lunatic and convict station. Prison warders and hospital attendants fishing from the jetty. Healthy-looking nurses in the streets. Hospitality everywhere in those days; in the mansion of the commissioner; at dances in the club; in all the homes of the island. Picnics in fields of lilies, and on the beach on the far side where even now bright beads are washed ashore occasionally from a lost ship.

For a long period there were always at least two thousand people on the island – five hundred officials and their families, a hundred convicts, five hundred lunatics and about a thousand lepers. Even the lepers seemed contented in the days when I sailed over to the island regularly; for the island gave them more freedom than any hospital on the mainland. They had their own gardens and fowls; the government brought their produce and gave it back to them to eat! Robben Island was fortunate in its doctors, too, and their devotion to the patients was magnificent.

The officials drew their supplies from a large government store stocking everything except liquor. A bakery, a dairy, a butcher's shop and vegetables grown on the island made housekeeping easy. Although the road running round the island is only seven miles in length, there were a dozen motor cars in use. The weekly steamer brought a programme for the cinema. If life was not exciting for the inhabitants, it was free from many of the problems of the cities.

Lunatics of the quiet type worked as servants in the village. One elderly patient was always to be seen building boats from fragments of wreckage – odd craft indeed, invariably broken up by the attendants before they were ready for launching. This ruthless, though necessary action did not disturb the old fellow in the least. He simply set to work on a new vessel. Occasionally he varied his occupation by making "coins" with bits of brass, carving an unflattering portrait of Queen Victoria on each one.

Among the dangerous patients was a woman who had set fire to a number of churches, and twice succeeded in producing a blaze in the Robben Island asylum. Well-behaved lunatics were admitted to the staff dances, however, and the daughter of a former commissioner relates that her favourite partner was a murderer who had poisoned several people. He danced well and was most polite.

There have been macabre scenes in the settlement. One night, many years ago, a huge cask of rum drifted on to the beach. The lepers broke out, taking their pannikins, and on the shore there was a mad carousal. In the Eighties of last century the lepers were wretchedly housed and fed. Many complaints brought no redress. So one night they set fire to their hovels and forced the government to build new homes for them.

It is clear that the lepers were not always so well-treated as those I knew. A visiting physician in 1881 reported: "Here I saw human beings kennelled worse than dogs. In a long, low, thatched shed some forty poor creatures were stowed away, most of them unable to leave their beds. They would be burnt alive if the thatch caught fire. Here were black, half-caste and white all mixed together, but no females."

A last scene, worthy of Grand Guignol, in the leper section of Robben Island. The story is true, for I found it in the offical records. A commission arrived to hear the grievances of the lepers, the pitiful appeals of men who thought themselves cured and wished to return to their families; of poor souls driven desperate by long exile. Though leprosy is not infectious and only slightly contagious, the lepers were not allowed to approach the members of the commission, seated at their table. Guards stood between the muttering lepers and the visitors. A member asked why these strict precautions were being taken. "We discovered a plot among the lepers to infect you gentlemen with the disease," answered the head guard. Such are the lengths to which loneliness will move a body of wretched men.

Soon afterwards, Dr W. Ross was appointed superintendent, and conditions improved. In 1886 the island had its own newspaper, the *Robben Island Times*.

Lepers are peculiarly liable to chest complaints, and for a long time it was felt that Robben Island, swept by sea winds and swamped by fogs, was an unsuitable spot for a leper hospital. As the years passed, leprosy decreased in South Africa; among white people, in fact, the disease is showing a tendency to disappear entirely. The cost of upkeep of an island establishment became too high for the number of patients maintained. Finally the lepers were removed to a central hospital at Pretoria and the only people left on the island were the lighthouse-keepers and their families. There has been a light on Robben Island since 1657, when Van Riebeeck erected an iron platform on which a fire was kept burning whenever ships of the Company were sighted off the port.

The staff, who had found life on Robben Island pleasant enough, were reluctant to abandon their solid homes. Every year after 1931 some of them chartered a small steamer and spent a day of pathetic reunion in their ruined gardens. Once a south-east gale arose and marooned them all for several days.

I sailed there often after the settlement had been abandoned. Birds were nesting in the broken windmills. Rabbits scuttled out of the power station which had once lit up the whole island. Sea birds had found shelter in the pretty summer houses and bathing boxes along the shore. The gaol gates had been unlocked for the last time. Grass was growing thickly over the trolley lines that run all over the island; and the trolleys we pushed and rode furiously down the slopes were rusting under the sun. The gardens, once bright with dahlias and carnations, were desolate. The white houses with their red roofs, and the solid grey stone buildings hewn by convict labour will not decay for many years; but the sports ground, the golf course and the cultivated land had dropped back to the wild appearance of the surrounding rabbit warrens. The club had been gutted, the billiard tables and large library sold. Spread out on the floor I found a tattered island flag, bearing the lighthouse emblem. And outside on the uncut lawn there remained a captured German field gun.

Many of the houses stood open, doors and windows swinging to every wind, broken chairs and old official papers littering the floors. The church, more than a century old, was locked. Convicts built the church, too; the hardworking convicts who made life easy and cheap for officials and their families. Life on this leper island, in the twentieth century at any rate, was not the misery you might imagine. I moved among contented groups of lepers entertaining friends from the mainland. Many of them suffered no pain for years at a stretch, and little disfigurement. But in the long buildings, behind the barbed wire fences, were others sorely afflicted, the poor creatures who were leper-lunatics. There I dared not enter.

Murray Bay, where I left my small yacht at anchor, was once the site of a whaling station owned by a Mr Murray. The enterprise had to be abandoned for a queer reason. Makanna the Left-Handed, a

Xhosa chief who had attacked the Grahamstown settlers in 1819, was exiled on Robben Island. He organised a band of prisoners, seized one of Murray's whaleboats and pulled away from the island. The boat capsized in the surf on Blaauwberg beach and Makanna was drowned. The sequel to this episode was that Murray was given notice to quit, and he had to set up his whaling station on the mainland.

Eight condemned criminals, handed over to the English East India Company to be marooned at the Cape (then, in 1618, inhabited only by savages) were the first Robben Island settlers. The directors of the company saw a chance of trading with the Hottentots and establishing gardens for the supply of fresh vegetables to their ships. No volunteers for service in the perilous outpost having come forward, the directors petitioned James I to pardon a number of men condemned to death. Thus the unwilling criminals found themselves marooned on the shores of Table Bay with guns, ammunition, food and a small open boat.

They were left in charge of Captain Cross, who had been a member of the King's Bodyguard – a quarrelsome bully. Cross soon antagonised the Hottentots. He was attacked, and, according to the narrative of a survivor, "shot full of arrows and spears". The criminals escaped in their boat and made for Robben Island as the most obvious refuge. Their boat was so severely damaged while landing that it could not be repaired.

They lived as castaways on dry biscuits they had saved, eked out with penguin eggs and fish. Six months later a ship called the *New Year's Gift* was sighted, and the desperate men set to work to build a raft. Four of the men, afraid to wait for daybreak, paddled off with this driftwood contraption and were not seen again. Their companions, however, were rescued from the island next day and given a passage to England.

There was a grim sequel to this stroke of good fortune. The men stole a purse soon after landing. They were tried, declared habitual criminals, and the old sentence of death was enforced.

Van Riebeeck made Robben Island a penal settlement later in the seventeenth century. His men found hundreds of sheep grazing there; sheep left by British shipmasters some years previously. Van Riebeeck was also the first man to fortify the island with "a six pounder from the Maris". The prisoners, the legions who followed, were kept busy quarrying the blue island stone for buildings on the mainland.

Robben Island has had many superintendents, but the first of them all was Ryk Overhagen of the Dutch East India Company. In 1658, Van Riebeeck's council decided to reward him for his faithful service at the fortress and on land journeys, and gave him this appointment at fourteen florins a month. No doubt a florin went a long way.

Overhagen looked after the sheep and cattle placed on the island for safety from native thieves. He was expected to keep up a flourishing garden and send carrots and sweet potatoes to the mainland. He fired the first signal gun from the island, and carried out experiments with fire beacons to assist ships entering Table Bay. It is recorded that a steenbok was shot on Robben Island during Overhagen's period there, but this must surely have been a captured buck which had been transported to the island. Partridges and pheasants were introduced by Governor Adriaan van der Stel early in the eighteenth century.

The first escape from Robben Island was reported in 1731, when seven men put to sea in a little boat which was no more than a framework covered with skins. Governor de la Fontaine ordered a commando out to search the coast from Blaauwberg to Groenekloof, and four of the fugitives were found. Their frail craft had, of course, overturned in the surf and the other three had been drowned. Many another prisoner risked his life, and lost it more often than not, by paddling away from Robben Island with a raft or barrel.

Captain Cook visited the island in 1776, and not long afterwards came Le Vaillant, the French traveller and naturalist. Le Vaillant wrote: "The island takes its name from the number of marine dogs that are found there. Its unhappy exiles are each day to deliver a certain quantity of limestone, which they dig. In spare time they fish, or cultivate their small gardens, which procures them tobacco and some other little indulgences." On the north side of the island are still to be seen the remains of these old garden boundaries and circular stone walls.

No doubt other unofficial visitors trod the sandy shores of Robben Island long before Van Riebeeck's day. They left little but the inevitable legends of buried treasure. Possibly these pirates were responsible for the introduction of the English wild rabbit, a brown species entirely different from the dassies, hares and rabbits of South Africa, and found nowhere on the mainland. Today the island is an enormous rabbit warren. This is more remarkable than it may seem, for there is not much of the grass rabbits love. Moreover, hundreds of cats that ran wild after a taste of rabbit flesh during the years when the island was occupied, live in the warrens and prey on the rabbits. Robben Island became a sportsmen's paradise in the early nineteenth century. Young officers of the British garrison, sent there as a punishment and to keep them out of debt, shot quail, pheasants and rabbits and enjoyed the good fishing.

Among the few successful escapes from Robben Island was that of two brothers named Carel and Jacob Kruger, sentenced for coining late in the eighteenth century. They made a boat of skins, reached the coast near Blaauwberg and tramped northwards to Saldanha. Then they left civilisation behind for the unknown interior, where no white man had ever been before. Carel Kruger was trampled to death by an elephant – there is still a farm called Carel's Graf in the Prieska district. Jacob lived on as an outlaw for twenty years, with the shadow of Robben Island always over him. Finally he received a free pardon, only to be killed by a lion soon afterwards.

When the British occupied the Cape for the second time in 1806, they retained Robben Island as a penal settlement. A British merchant ship, the *Elizabeth,* at anchor off the island, was boarded by twelve convicts. They seized muskets, locked the captain and crew in their quarters and took the ship to sea. Once away from the island the convicts set the officers and crew adrift in the longboat. These men reached Cape Town safely, and a warship hurried after the *Elizabeth.* The twelve desperate convicts were recaptured and sent back to Robben Island with long sentences.

The stretch of icy water between the island and the docks forms South Africa's "channel swim". Many have attempted it and only a few have succeeded. The first man to swim from Robben Island to the mainland is also the only one – Mr H.C. Cooper, who covered the distance in just under seven hours on September 4, 1909. He used the breast stroke.

It is a far more difficult swim than the English Channel crossing, as the Table Bay water is seldom above fifty degrees Fahrenheit, whereas the Channel is usually above sixty-five. Women seem to feel the cold less than men, and four women have completed the Robben Island swim. Two of them, Mercedes Gleitze (1932) and Asta Winckler (1934) were already famous when they tackled the freezing currents of Table Bay. But the most popular success was one which I watched from start to finish – the great swim by the fifteen-year-old schoolgirl Peggy Duncan in November, 1926. There were sharks about that day, and I was in charge of a small craft chartered by the newspaper which had organised the swim. The contest was nearly called off; but we decided that Peggy Duncan was well protected, and nine hours thirty-five minutes after leaving Robben Island the strong, sunburnt girl reached the old Adderley Street pier. The second woman to accomplish the feat, during the following year, was Miss Florrie Berndt, a Robben Island nurse. In 1930 Peggy Duncan swam the English Channel.

Off the rock-fringed shore of Robben Island lies the "boneyard", the unfrequented stretch of ocean where old ships, stripped of their fittings, are taken out and sunk. You can see the rusty iron, the boilers and stumps of masts of the wrecks of recent years along the northern shore. But of two famous vessels lost there, which stand out in my mind from a long and tragic procession of doomed ships, nothing remains above the surface. One was the mail steamer *Tantallon Castle,* piled up in the early morning of May 7, 1901 in a dense fog with a hundred and twenty passengers on board. The other was the *Dageraad* – and that is a tale of sunken treasure which I shall presently tell.

The *Tantallon Castle* wreck was noteworthy because she was the only regular mail steamer on the Cape run ever lost in Table Bay. She had been passing through fog for some hours before the disaster; but Captain de la Cour Travers had taken soundings and was satisfied that he was on a safe course. Double lookouts had been posted. The captain was on the bridge. Suddenly the lookout shouted a warning – he had seen a patch of seaweed, indicating land close by. Captain Travers had his hand on the bridge telephone; he rang down "full astern". Too late. There was, in the words of a passenger, "a thump, a thud, and a slow, grinding impact" as the *Tantallon Castle* settled down on a reef.

Signal guns were fired, the people of Robben Island hurried to the shore, saw the stranded liner and telephoned to the mainland for help. The master of the little coasting steamer *Magnet,* first to arrive, pitched his own deck cargo overboard and sent a whaleboat across to the wreck. All the women and children were transferred, and then the rest of the passengers. Soon harbour tugs were on the spot, with the *Braemar Castle,* the *Avondale Castle,* the *Raglan Castle* of the same company, and H.M.S. *Tartar* – all ready with tow-ropes and anxious to save the *Tantallon Castle* from total loss. The mails were taken off safely, and most of the baggage, but the ship resisted every effort to drag her away from the teeth of the rocks. Photographs taken that day show her lying broadside on to the swell – a fine ship at the time, with three masts, one funnel, and the first-class quarters aft, according to old-fashioned custom. Captain Travers and the crew left her sadly. Not one life had been lost; but the water was rising in the holds and soon afterwards she broke up. The court of inquiry left the captain's certificate untouched, but considered that he should have taken more soundings. A recommendation that a fog signal should be placed on Robben Island was followed by the government – half the lighthouses and fog signals of the world have been provided only as a result of shipwrecks. So the Robben Island gun, known to thousands of sailormen in after years, boomed over the bones of the *Tantallon Castle.*

Of the *Dageraad* enough is known to establish, beyond doubt, that she was a treasure ship. She was one of a fleet that sailed north from Table Bay in 1694 to salve the cargo of a distressed Dutch East India Company ship named the *Goude Buys* – the Golden Jacket. News had reached the Cape that the *Goude Buys,* after a long passage from Holland, had anchored about a hundred miles up the coast with every soul on board ill. Scurvy, of course – the dread sickness which took such toll of the mariners of Holland then, and for years afterwards. Some of the wretched crew of the *Goude Buys* had landed and tramped overland to the Cape, several perishing of hunger on the march.

When the *Dageraad,* a small, fast yacht, reached the spot, the *Goude Buys* had dragged her anchors and drifted ashore. The coast where she lay, however, is sandy and free from danger; it was easy to salve her specie and cargo. With much precious freight under hatches the *Dageraad* ran back to Table Bay. Fog caused her end, too – she struck the west end of Robben Island and broke up at once. Sixteen of her men were drowned. It was recorded at the time that "the broken chests washed ashore, but the money is still under the sea."

Since then children have found a few golden ducats and silver pieces of eight in rocky pools. But most of it lies, to this day, in the sand of the green depths beneath the long coils of seaweed, caressed by every tide in the strongroom of the cold South Atlantic. Golden coins, no doubt, with guilders and rix-dollars – a romatic hoard awaiting recovery by some diver bold enough to go down there in the sweep and surge of the open ocean. I should like to stand on the beach of Robben Island on the day when the treasure of the *Dageraad* comes on shore.

The most recent treasure unearthed on Robben Island was found, in August, 1944, by soldiers of the wartime garrison who were digging near the lighthouse. They first found a skeleton, then a number of silver and copper coins. I examined the coins – they were French, bearing various dates from 1688 to 1726. The large silver coins, about the size of a five-shilling piece, were handsome and well preserved.

It seemed to the soldiers that the skeleton had not received proper burial. They thought the man might have been a shipwrecked sailor who had died there alone and been covered by the drifting sand. It was just one more tragedy, perhaps, of the island that nobody wants.

SO FEW ARE FREE

"Every Man has his Price"

1956

St Helena is a dot in the South Atlantic, but it has many claims to fame. Probably it is the only island in the world with a population running into thousands which can claim to have lived through more than a century with only one murder.

Old islanders told me all about that murder, from every angle, and described the governor's dilemma when the two murderers had to be executed. I heard queer tales of other crimes within living memory and the crimes of long ago. They traced for my benefit, in old St Helena Almanacs, the career of a character named James Francis Homagee, a Parsee, who was given the choice of death for some unspecified crime in India or the hangman's job on the island. (In the middle of last century it was considered the right thing to go abroad for a hangman.) Homagee never had to carry out an execution. At first he walked round Jamestown with a tin on his head selling fish. Then he became messenger at the castle. He secured a post as clerk and towards the end of last century he rose to be chief magistrate of the island. Homagee certainly made the right choice.

In a dark little room in the castle I spent hours examining the St Helena archives, including criminal records covering hundreds of years. This island has had its full share of cruelty and torture, mutinies and hangings. In a seventeenth century conspiracy thirteen men "in open day" shot Governor Johnson at the castle and escaped in the ship *Francis and Mary*. Rebellious slaves were hung, drawn and quartered, while some were "hanged in chains alive and starved to death".

Records of the quarter sessions and other criminal trials which I studied, some trivial and others serious, bring to life many events which shook island society. Idle, gossiping women, scolds and tale-bearers, mischief makers and scandalmongers were ducked in the sea or whipped. Erring slaves were branded, or burning sealing wax was dropped on their shuddering limbs. One slave who had poisoned several people was burnt to death, and all the blacks on the island had to bring fuel and watch the execution. Soldiers were flogged and drummed out of the garrison with halters round their necks. Thieving slaves had their right hands cut off.

One of the company's officers, who had an illicit love affair with a widow, was called to task by the governor. He insulted the governor, whereupon he was degraded before the garrison, his sword was broken over his head, and he was forced to stand in the pillory with his paramour. Two centuries ago four white men who beat a woman slave to death were fined six pounds ten shillings between them. Often a black would be condemned to death while a white accomplice would receive a light sentence. Until late in the eighteenth century the evidence of a black was not admissible against white people. Elizabeth Renton, who murdered one of her female slaves with a carving knife, escaped for this reason.

Among the earliest entries I found in the council records (1678) was a mention of an inquest on one Thomas Green. "Body taken up," ran the record. "Trial by touching the dead body. Three persons committed on verdict of manslaughter." At this period, too, W. Melling was ordered to ride the wooden horse with a bag of shot at each heel; his crime was "swearing and incivility".

Soon afterwards Elizabeth Starling assaulted and abused the captain of the ship *Charles the Second,* while her husband threatened to beat the captain "and to make the sun shine through him". Apparently the husband was acquitted, but Elizabeth received fifteen lashes on her naked body and was ducked three times.

Two runaway apprentices, Rowland and Eastings, broke into a house, took a fowling piece and killed a sow. Each lad had the tip of his right ear cut off, his forehead branded with the letter R, and a pair of pothooks riveted round his neck. They were also flogged round the town.

Then there was the impudent Corporal Bowyer who married a widow, Mrs Simms, before the circumstances could be considered by the governor in council. Bowyer was reduced to private and imprisoned, while ten acres and eight head of cattle belonging to Mrs Simms were seized.

The court dealt with the apprentice Eastings again not long after the episode of the sow. He was only fourteen, but he had committed so many thefts that some members though he should be hanged. Here is the final decision: "Looking on him as a youth who may become a good man, it was ordered that he be whipped under the gallows and then sent away off the island in the ship *Resolution*." It seems that the *Resolution* was selected because she was a dangerous, leaky vessel which was expected to founder during the voyage to England. However, the sentence was regarded by the directors of the English East India Company as far too lenient. "We are ashamed that our aged governor should be guilty of so great a folly," came the reprimand from London.

John Knipe complained to the island council that Bridget Coales had failed to marry him as promised. She sat on the lap of the butcher of the ship *Modena* and let him kiss her. Knipe asked her whether he was not as good as the butcher, whereupon she called him "down look dog" and compared him with an old dog owned by her father. Bridget had to pay fifteen pounds damages.

According to the records, chaplains and doctors were among the most troublesome of the company's officials stationed on St Helena during the eighteenth century. "Dr Wignall always drunk and nearly killed the governor by giving unsuitable medicines, his excuse being he had nothing else to give," runs an entry in 1725. "The doctor, for drunken and disorderly conduct, placed in the stocks for one hour, and he sung and swore the whole time."

Seven years later it was recorded that Mr White the chaplain and his wife had for a long time "led very scandalous and immoral lives, the woman having been drunk almost every day she has been on the island, and Mr White himself often in the same condition and always rude and troublesome." For sixteen months Mr White had neither dined nor supped with his wife. This conduct was "highly resented by all the good Dames of this place, and we believe, and the woman says, that this cold, unkind usage is the cause of her giving herself up to liquor and ill company." It is not clear from the records how the company dealt with White.

Totty, a slave, was tried for running away repeatedly and living a freebooter's life. Members of the jury had suffered from Totty's raids, and they petitioned the governor to have Totty executed. This was granted. He was drawn on a cart by other runaway slaves to the place of execution and hanged.

Those were hard times for slaves. Moll, a slave woman owned by Mrs Gurling, was sentenced to three hundred lashes (to be given in three instalments) and to be branded on her cheek for breaking into a country house and stealing one rupee. Yet when George Alexander stripped his slave Abigail and beat her cruelly with a rawhide whip, he was fined forty shillings. Even in 1810 a free black named Nancy May was given two hundred lashes for stealing fowls. She was tied to a cart, wearing a paper bearing the words Fowl Stealer, and beaten in different parts of the town.

Ladder Hill above Jamestown was known in the earliest days of the English settlement as Fort Hill. For a century the gallows stood there. People on board ships in the harbour and everyone in Jamestown could see the bodies hanging in chains, according to the brutal custom, as a warning to others.

Sorcerers and witches were burnt to death. Lawyers were deported "lest the people should occupy their minds with litigation". (To this day there is not a lawyer in private practice on the island.) There was also a strong prejudice against such decent folk as the Quakers. An entry in 1680 reads: "William Saddler is discovered to be a Quaker, for which and other bad behaviour he is ordered to leave the island."

Ensign Slaughter, who was accused of slandering the governor, was flogged. If you go through the records carefully to the date when the sentence was carried out, you will discover that the wretched officer was flogged with wire whips and fish hooks tied to a cane.

Men and women, white or black, were usually stripped when flogged. An unusual entry appears in 1733, when a planter named John Long was sentenced for receiving stolen yams from The Briars. The warrant reads: "You are to whip the said John Long publicly with ten lashes, but in regard he hath been a planter here, you may for this first time let him receive the shame of this punishment with his clothes on. You are to make your prisoner fast to the tail of the wooden horse, and read this to him before you whip him."

Soldiers of the St Helena garrison loved their taverns and punch-houses. When these places were put out of bounds towards the end of the eighteenth century, the troops mutinied. Led by a sergeant, they marched out of their barracks with bayonets fixed and drums beating, aiming at seizing the artillery and ammunition depot on top of Ladder Hill. Governor Corneille pacified them for a time; but the mutiny soon broke out again with the officers and a body of loyal men fighting it out with the rest of the company's soldiers. They started with muskets and ended with both sides using field guns. At last the mutineers surrendered. Many of them escaped in the darkness, mixed with the loyal troops and pretended they had played no part in the mutiny. All the known mutineers were tried by court-martial, and ninety-nine were condemned to death. Even in those days the authorities were reluctant to carry out a mass slaughter, so the men drew lots and one in ten was shot.

For stealing a piece of cloth from a sailor in the street, one William Whaley was hanged. Not many years later (in 1800) a slave was hanged for snatching a bottle of liquor from a drunken soldier. These crimes were regarded as highway robbery.

St Helena's most prominent landmark is the great ridge on the north-east coast known as the Barn. It dominates the Longwood plain, and Napoleon must have hated the sight of it; though nowadays some people see an outline of Napoleon on his death bed along the edge of the Barn. Wild goats, descended from the goats left by the Portuguese, have lived in the inaccessible caves of the Barn for centuries. You have to be a fine climber to follow those goats along the narrow ledges, and if you fall the sea is hundreds of feet below. Nevertheless, these perilous heights once provided a sanctuary for a raider who is still remembered on the island.

A party of islanders were stalking the wild goats with shot guns and rifles one day in 1897, when there were more goats than you will find now. Two brothers named Legg were there with George Duncan; and they related this queer tale to Mr Edward Constantine, the history lover, who passed it on to me with meticulous accuracy.

The islanders followed a goat along a dangerous "vein" on the west side, clinging to a precipice which hangs over the sea. Suddenly they came to a cave with an entrance just large enough for a man to squeeze inside. It looked as though the stone "doorway" had been built by human hands. "One man could keep an army out of that cave," Constantine told me. "A push, and an intruder would fall three hundred feet into the sea."

Abandoning the goat hunt, the three islanders climbed into the cave and explored it. They found a bed made of slate and other stones, a pair of blue cloth trousers which fell to pieces when touched, a stone club and a chopper made from the heel of a scythe. A bag contained ten pounds of salt; there was a good razor wrapped in flannel; a whetstone, tinderbox flint and steel; some jerked beef still fit to eat; a bottle of water and a large amount of island tobacco done up in rolls. The cave dweller had made shelves of flat stone slabs. A smaller cave had been used as a kitchen.

This was the lair of an eccentric hermit named Louden's Ben, a deserter from a Portuguese ship. Ben worked on the Longwood farms for some years. Then he went queer in the head, and from time to time he would tell the farmers: "The white goat on the Barn is calling me." He would disappear for weeks at a time. In 1874 he took to raiding the poultry runs and vegetable patches, and fired on the police when they tried to arrest him. After that he was never seen again, though signs of his raids on the farms were obvious enough. Some of the boldest climbers on the island searched the Barn, for everyone knew he was there; but no one imagined that a human being could reach the unknown cave on the seaward side of the Barn where Ben lived. The "vein" followed by the goat hunters must have been enlarged by the passage of the goats when the Leggs and Duncan reached the cave. Few people indeed have visited the place from that day to this, for it is still a most formidable climb. The fate of Louden's Ben has never been settled, for no skeleton was found; but he must have fallen into the sea far below his cave. A rock at the foot of the precipice is known to the fishermen as Louden Ben's Rock.

I have said that St Helena has known only one murder in more than a century. There was a public execution in 1850 (before Homagee's arrival) when a half-caste named Lowry, a slave descendant, murdered a servant girl at Fox's Folly, near Napoleon's tomb.

St Helena islanders are among the mildest and most lawabiding of people. Thus the island was deeply shocked in 1881 when the news arrived that a St Helenan named Lefroy had been found guilty of a revolting murder in a railway compartment on the Brighton train. He had shot and knifed an elderly man and robbed him of money and a gold watch and chain. Lefroy hid in a Stepney boarding house, but his landlady identified him by a portrait in a newspaper. That was the first occasion on which a murderer was caught and hanged as a result of that particular form of publicity.

St Helena itself remained undisturbed by murder throughout the second half of last century, but there was a sinister incident in 1888 which might easily have ended in murder. This was the arrival of Deeming, a fugitive who was "wanted" for the murder of eight women and several children.

Deeming spent some weeks on St Helena in the hope of dodging the police. There was no cable to the island at that time, and no one suspected that he was a murderer. He applied to the farm of Solomon for a position as clerk, but – happily for the island – he was turned down and left soon afterwards. No doubt his murderous instincts would have come to the surface again. Deeming accosted and frightened a number of island girls during his stay, but went no further.

A fugitive of a different sort, but also equipped with an alias, was living quietly on St Helena at this time and for long afterwards. He was a Fenian conspirator from Ireland named Robert Farrell, who had turned Queen's evidence in a murder trial and had been sent abroad by the British authorities. Another informer, James Carey, had been followed out of the country and shot dead on board ship in South African waters by a Fenian who had sworn revenge. With this episode in mind, the British government decided that St Helena would be a safe place for Farrell. And so it was. He spent many years there, and was killed by an accidental fall of rock at Rupert's Bay.

So little crime occurred during Governor Sterndale's period of office (1897-1902) that he was presented with white gloves at all but two of the fourteen criminal sessions over which he presided. Not long afterwards the long, bloodless period was broken. It was late in October 1904 that a young signalman named Robert Gunnell bought a gold chain and pendant in Mrs George's shop in Jamestown. He told Mrs George that this jewellery was a present for his girl, and that he hoped she would marry him. Gunnell went back happily to Prosperous Bay signal station, for he had been accepted.

On the first of November a police constable at Longwood heard the report of a gun in the distance, and thought someone was shooting rabbits. Next day, however, there was no response to a telephone call to the Prosperous Bay signal station. When the police arrived, poor Gunnell was lying dead with a shotgun wound in the back of his head.

Suspicion fell immediately on two brothers, Richard and Lewis Crowie, idle fellows who had already been convicted of several robberies. The Crowies were arrested and taken to the home of Constable Constantine at Longwood. While they were there, Constantine's little daughter saw Lewis Crowie throw a gold watch into the hedge. It was Gunnell's watch.

Soon afterwards the Crowies signed a confession. They had stolen a shotgun and cartridges from Mr Bassett Legg in Jamestown, and then walked to the signal station and told Gunnell that they had been fishing. Gunnell lived alone. He invited the Crowies to tea, and they were about to sit down when one of the Crowies shouted: "There's a ship out there." Gunnell went to fetch his telescope, and while his back was turned one of the brothers shot him from behind.

Lieutenant-Colonel Sir Henry Galway, governor and chief justice, presided at the trial. The jury returned with a unanimous verdict of guilty, and sentence of death was passed. Galway then set about finding a hangman. He thought it would be a difficult task, for there was no official executioner on the island. Among the troops on St Helena was a company of Lancashire Fusiliers. They were paraded at the governor's request, and their captain asked for two volunteers to act as hangmen, each man to receive five pounds. "Volunteers – one pace forward . . . march!" yelled the sergeant-major. Ninety men stepped forward. Two were selected.

Next day, however, Corporal Shoesmith of the police and John Williams, government carpenter, called on Sir Henry Galway and pointed out how unfair it would be to allow so much money to go to outsiders. They were both old soldiers, and they claimed that they should have been given first refusal of the job.

Galway gave them the job. The carpenter built the gallows in the old wood store next to the gaol at the foot of Jacob's Ladder. The Crowie brothers were executed on February 2, 1905. "It taught me that every man has his price," commented Sir Henry Galway. "I must say that those two amateurs performed their duty like old hands."

That was St Helena's last murder, and I think the rest of this century will pass without another call for volunteers. During my month on the island, in December 1954, the skeleton of a European woman aged about thirty was found embedded in sand at Sandy Bay. The teeth were perfect, without fillings. There was no possible means of identification, but rumours that the woman had been murdered ran round the island. Some said it was the skeleton of the actress, Eileen (Gay) Gibson, murdered at sea by the steward Camb and pushed through the porthole. Superintendent Ogborn of the St Helena Police decided against the murder theory. This was probably a victim of an enemy submarine in World War II, washed up and buried in sand, and uncovered more than a decade later by the restless sea.

If you settle on St Helena you can rule out all crimes of violence and sleep with your doors and windows unlocked. Burglaries are rare, and when they do occur it is usually found that the hungry burglar has left the valuables untouched and spent all his time in the pantry.

THERE'S A SECRET HID AWAY

Some Found Happiness
1956

Drive out of Jamestown by the steep Side Path road, and after a mile you may look down on one of those fine country estates for which St Helena is famous. This is The Briars. At a glance you can understand why Napoleon felt so strongly drawn to the place as he rode past during his first day of exile on the island.

The Briars was a yam plantation and government farm in the seventeenth century. When the Emperor noticed it, the place was privately owned and shaded by a variety of beautiful trees. Among the great laurels and palms stood a quaint little pavilion. Napoleon rode up the drive and asked whether he could move into the pavilion immediately.

William Balcombe, owner of The Briars was a fat, wealthy man who lived well. According to island legend, he was an illegitimate son of the Prince Regent of England. He was a banker, ship's chandler, and East India Company's financial agent. Balcombe and his wife entertained generously, and gave dances in the pavilion, of oriental design, which had caught Napoleon's eye. They offered Napoleon their own house, but he did not wish to disturb them. So that day Napoleon occupied the dancing pavilion, a single room with two doors and six windows, while his servants pitched tents and his chef prepared dinner in an arbour.

In recent years the pavilion has become a complete house, the home of the cable station manager. It is still a charming place. I found the view and the climate pleasing; for The Briars stands above the heat of the valley yet below the mists which some find depressing. Much of the original design and ornate decoration remain unaltered. I copied the plaque beside the front door: "The Duke of

Wellington stayed in this house when he returned from India in July 1805. The Emperor Napoleon also lived here from the 18th October until the 10th December 1815, before taking up his residence at Longwood House."

Those were Napoleon's happiest weeks on St. Helena, I imagine. He formed his friendship with mischievous, precocious, fourteen-year-old Betsy Balcombe, with her blue eyes and blonde curls. She stole his papers, accused him of eating frogs, swung a sabre dangerously round his head, denounced him for cheating at cards and slapped the face of the courtier Las Cases. The bungalow where the Balcombes lived is in ruins, but I peered into the cellar where Betsy was locked up all night as a punishment. She spent the dark hours terror-stricken, throwing her father's wine bottles at the rats.

What a place to live, amid such memories! I wandered in the old garden where the wild dog roses called briars grow to this day; and I pictured Napoleon talking to the slave gardener Toby, the man whose freedom he tried to buy. In Balcombe's time this estate produced many of the fruits of Europe and Africa; and after Balcombe had fed his own large household, the surplus fetched six hundred pounds a year. Balcombe had a brewery there, too. Yet in spite of these profitable enterprises, Balcombe ran into debt and finally sold the lovely place to Isaac Moss, partner and close relative of the first Saul Solomon.

The Briars became a silkworm farm in 1828, a man named Walker having paid nine thousand pounds for it. Mulberry groves were planted. A Chinese labourer was sent all the way to China, returning with the silk worms. However, the venture failed. Saul Solomon bought The Briars for four hundred pounds; later the Moss family regained possession of The Briars and lived there for decades last century. Miss Phoebe Moss was responsible for importing and releasing the mynah birds which are now too plentiful, and too fond of fruit. She also introduced South African frogs, but these appear to be harmless.

Early this century the Eastern Telegraph Company bought The Briars and moved up from the house at Rupert's Bay where the cable was landed. Cable companies used to send prefabricated buildings of uniform design to their outposts; and these bungalows now stand among the banyans and bananas. For many years, cables were sent by hand and besides the executives there were forty operators, all bachelors, living at The Briars. The old estate became the social centre of the island. Many servants were employed. The forty bachelors had forty ponies, a bowling green, a library with thousands of books, and a mess where guests were entertained magnificently. Some of the servants built cottages round the estate, so that people talked of The Briars village. It is hardly a village, though it is the only group of houses outside Jamestown on the island which might possibly rank as a hamlet.

Not far from The Briars is Chubb's Spring, where Napoleon sometimes walked. Captain Bennet of the infantry had a house at the spring in those days; and when Napoleon died, Bennet gave his handsome dining room table so that the carpenter could make a coffin.

On the road just above The Briars is Button-up Corner. The change of climate is so sudden that the riders of old buttoned their greatcoats. Near here a path runs to a cottage where the island's lepers are segregated; just two or three afflicted people living amid great beauty. Still climbing, you come to Alarm House, where two guns were placed towards the end of the seventeenth century to fire a signal when ships were sighted. Here, too, is Alarm Cottage, which can be hired by visitors complete with a skilled St Helena cook, and at such a reasonable rate that you seem to have stepped back into the past. On the farm outside you can study the island produce growing abundantly. No house on St Helena nowadays fetches as much as it cost to build. Alarm Cottage, with several acres of good agricultural land, changed hands at five hundred pounds when last it was sold.

Now the road skirts the great hollow called the Devil's Punchbowl and the empty, nameless tomb where Napoleon's body lay from 1821 to 1840. I believe that he only visited the site of his grave once in his life, and drank from a spring. You find a cottage and a caretaker at this spot; once the tomb was guarded by a French army sergeant, but now a St Helenan tends this little patch of France within the iron railings. The caretaker comes out with glasses on a tray so that visitors may drink from Napoleon's spring.

Perhaps you remember the incident when Napoleon's funeral ended and his French followers broke off a few branches from the willow over the grave before returning to Longwood. That willow died soon after World War II, but cuttings were known to have been taken to Australia. Slips from the Australian offshoots were nurtured, on instructions from General Smuts, by the forestry department near Stellenbosch; and they were planted at the tomb on the one hundred and twenty-eighth anniversary of Napoleon's death.

The road to Longwood leads past Halley's Mount, where the seventeenth century comet discoverer set up his telescope to observe a transit of Mercury, but failed owing to mist. It goes on past Hutt's Gate, though there was never a man named Hutt; the huts of the slaves stood there.

Longwood and the neighbouring Deadwood once formed one property known as the Great Wood. Old plans show this large, deep forest. Melliss, writing in 1875, declared there were people still living in St Helena who remembered losing their way in the Longwood gum forests. The area had become a grassy plain with hardly a tree. "I searched in vain for forest trees and shrubs that flourished in tens of thousands not a century ago," wrote Melliss. "Probably one hundred St Helena plants have thus disappeared since the first introduction of goats on the island. Every one of these was a link in the chain of created beings, which contained within itself evidence of the affinities of other species, both living and extinct, but which evidence is now irrecoverably lost." Today it is hard to believe that people vanished in the forests described by Melliss, and were never seen again.

Goats cannot destroy full-grown forests. What happened was that the old trees died and the goats destroyed the saplings. Governor Beatson imported many exotics early last century; English broom and brambles, Scotch pines and gorse, bushes from the Cape. These new growths overran the island and extinguished much of the indigenous flora. Beatson also destroyed most of the goats, but he was too late.

Deadwood Plain, of course, was covered with the tents of Boer prisoners of war, mainly Transvalers, in the first years of this century. Old people in St Helena still speak well of the prisoners. They had the sympathy of the islanders, and it was considered a huge joke when they succeeded in eluding their guards and reaching the taverns of Jamestown unobserved. One man, an Englishman by birth who had fought for the Boers, married an island girl and opened a bakery. Boer Smith, as he is called, was still living in retirement on the island while I was there. Indeed, he had only left the island once, to see his mother.

Such a wealth of history, so much literature has grown up round Longwood that I had intended to skirt Longwood Old House with no more than a passing mention. The Napoleonic legend has overshadowed an island which has seen many dramatic episodes apart from the Captivity period. However, I spent a morning at Longwood and became hypnotised, as so many other writers have done before me.

I saw Longwood almost as Napoleon left it. You may remember that the old farmhouse reverted to its original purpose after Napoleon's death. For some years the farm was owned and worked by a member of the Moss family. The rooms, sacred to all who respect the relics of history, became storerooms and stables; even the salon where Napoleon died. Souvenir hunters looted the place and scribbled their names on the walls. Even the wallpaper was torn off by visitors. Rats took up their abode in ceilings and floors.

France gained possession of Longwood a century ago, and some restoration was carried out. Longwood has known many vicissitudes, but in recent years no money has been spared in preserving the historic farmhouse. Furniture and other articles used by Napoleon have been sent back to Longwood, some from France, others from different parts of St Helena. I saw the globes of the earth and sky, bearing the marks of Napoleon's fingernails. There were the sideboards used by the priest Vignali when he celebrated Mass. The original copper bath, where Napoleon lay dictating his memoirs, was back in its place. And I rolled a ball by hand over the billiard table, following Napoleon's custom.

I walked in the garden, too, along those deep paths which Napoleon followed because the hated sentries could not see him. Bending under the wind was a tree of the cypress species, and an evergreen oak, which were there in Napoleon's day. I thought of the years of wind and rain which the French exiles endured at Longwood. (The island golf club is at Longwood, but few people who know the island would care to live in such an exposed spot.) Napoleon needed the garden walls and the pergola with the passion vine.

Longwood must have been an unfortunate place in Napoleon's day. I went up the stairs and walked under the slate roof, and I was surprised to hear that the servants lived in those crowded garrets over the rooms of Napoleon's staff. At one period there were more than fifty people, masters and servants, herded in this farmhouse.

In the yard I noticed a small outbuilding attached to a wall and inquired innocently: "Was that Napoleon's lavatory?" My guide replied with dignity: "The Emperor used only a commode."

Labourers digging in the garden while I was at Longwood brought to the surface scraps and fragments which called the Captivity to my eyes more vividly than any of the museum pieces. They found buttons of the St Helena Regiment, coins bearing the names of Solomon, Dickson and Taylor, and the very broken glass of the wine bottles which caused so much trouble with the Governor, Sir Hudson Lowe. Perhaps you did not realise that even Napoleon was supposed to return his empty bottles. They disposed of a thousand bottles of wine a month at Longwood. I will not say they drank so much, for there is evidence that Napoleon's servants sold wine to the soldiers of the guard. Sir Hudson Lowe was appalled by the cost, and asked for the return of the empties. To show their contempt, Napoleon's servants broke many bottles deliberately. Lowe was extremely angry when he found the shattered glass in the garden, and threatened to cut off the Emperor's wine. So the gardeners still unearth these relics. The pieces they showed me were fragments of champagne bottles, with thick green glass.

Across the valley from Longwood stands a country house now called Teutonic Hall, but once the residence of the Miss Polly Mason who was said to have signalled to Napoleon. She was an eccentric old maid who rode about the island on an ox. Napoleon liked visiting her; but there was never a love affair with her or anyone else to lighten Napoleon's exile. Napoleon's servants, however, left children on the island. His valet, Marchand, had two children by an island girl named Esther Vesey, and was rebuked for it. All the servants were more or less free to roam Jamestown, thus adding a very small French strain to the island mixture.

Thousands who call at St Helena, spending part of a day before their ship moves on, carry away nothing more than a few impressions of Jamestown and the drive of five miles to Longwood. This is better than nothing, but there is time for more. St Helena is an island of quaint and beautiful names and memorable places. Anyone who fails to gaze upon the Sandy Bay scene misses one of the seven wonders of the seas. This district is part of a great volcanic crater; a basin composed of naked black mountains, fantastic peaks, volcanic vents, ridges and ravines, varied by the rich green botanical wonders of the island summit.

I looked out over this staggering panorama from Rose Cottage, home of the Lunns, who were previously in Uganda. They bought Rose Cottage and an acre of garden for seven hundred pounds a few years ago. Pheasants are a nuisance in the garden, but they have fowls and ducks, rabbits and sheep. A very old Seville orange tree probably came from Spain or Portugal. Plum trees yield enormous crops.

Mr Lunn pointed out the Sandy Bay landmarks. Most prominent of all is the spiral rock called Lot, rising nearly three hundred feet above the hill on which it stands. It has been climbed, but only at great risk. Mutinous slaves once took refuge in a cave at the foot of Lot. They held out for days, rolling stones down on their attackers. According to the records, "a brisk young man named Worrall" climbed Lot behind and above the slaves. "Then they hove down rocks in their turn and beat down the chief of the slaves so much bruised that he died, at which all the people in Sandy Bay had great satisfaction, for they had suffered much from them."

Beyond the Lot rock are Lot's Wife and the Asses' Ears. Here, too, in the volcanic upheaval are the Devil's Garden and the Gates of Chaos. I saw the black face of Cole's Rock, where the slave-owner Cole was just about to flog one of his men when all the other slaves turned on him and threw him over the cliff.

Jenkins, the man whose ear caused so much trouble when it was cut off by the Spaniards – the War of Jenkins' Ear, you remember – once lived in this crater. He was governor of the island in 1741, and his old house Lemon Grove has a plaque in the wall. Some of the East India Company's gardens were in this huge bowl, irrigated by the best stream in the island. Date palms are old and enormous, and there are many pomegranates. Virgin Hall, a very old estate, still produces fine vegetables and bananas of the best flavour. Rats feed on wild olives. The Sandy Bay beach, where a party of Boer War prisoners seized a boat and tried to escape, has been washed away. Fishing boats no longer use it, and there are times when even a turtle would find landing dangerous. Barracks and cannon of the old fort on the shore have fallen into the sea.

Grandest of the residences above Sandy Bay is Mount Pleasant, visited more than once by Napoleon. The owner at that time was Mr (later Sir) William Doveton, born and brought up on the island, and possessed of a simple island outlook. Napoleon brought his own food from Longwood, and Doveton thought it was indeed a sumptuous breakfast – champagne, cold pie, potted meat, cold turkey, curried fowl, ham, dates, almonds, oranges, salad and coffee. Cason's is another high estate, named after an officer who commanded the troops under seven governors. Bamboo Hedge is a flax mill nowadays. Blarney House, Blarney bridge, and the old dairy farm called Fairyland are also in this neighbourhood.

You will have gathered that St Helena is an island of quaint and beautiful names. Dolly's Chop House has vanished, but Distant Cottage is still there; far in the south of the island beyond Lot's Wife Wood. West Lodge has a ghost legend. A slave was flogged to death there, and a slave orchestra played to drown his cries. They say you can still hear that music. Someone played a practical joke there on a soldier of the St Helena garrison during World War II. The victim had to have mental treatment.

Mount Eternity, Rosemary Hall, Myrtle Grove, Wild Ram Spring, Spyglass, Blue Point, Willow Cottage, Chinaman's, Rock Rose, Lazy Point, Silver Hill . . . my large-scale St Helena map is worth the five shillings I paid for it at the Castle. The names remind me of many a ramble, and many an eyrie where I stood and dreamt of all the pages of this dramatic island's story. Such a place was the High Knoll fortress. I found the massive doors wide open and the whole place deserted, from dungeons to powder magazines; deserted except by the wild goats that seemed to accentuate the weird atmosphere. I thought of the old mutineers who were blindfolded and shot against the grey walls last century. I remembered that Boer prisoners who tried to escape were locked in this fortress. And I felt glad that I could walk out without a sentry to stop me, and find my car and drive away.

Knollcombes is a happier memory. Sir George Bingham once

lived there; the man who saw a fourteen-year-old slave girl with her back bleeding after a whipping, and thereupon started the movement which led to the abolition of slavery on the island. But the house Bingham occupied was in ruins, thanks to the white ant which has eaten so many St Helena homes. I discovered fragments of a spinet, the piano of the eighteenth century, lying among the remnants of furniture. Knollcombes is now the property of a retired army officer. He was planning a new house on the old place. I walked round the garden with him, and saw that he would have peaches and guavas on his table, and pine logs to burn, and pheasant in season. St Helena is a long way out of the world, but those who do not fear solitude will find peace there.

Just above Knollcombes is the Baptist chapel, and the graveyard where Boer prisoners who died on the island were buried. Two of them were boys of sixteen, two were men over seventy. All the names are inscribed on the two memorial pillars. The graveyard is always neat. In a neighbouring cemetery there is an impressive obelisk in memory of Governor Hudson Ralph Janisch, who was also an historian and an astronomer. Only one previous official born in St Helena had become governor. Janisch was the eldest son of G.W. Janisch, confidential clerk to Sir Hudson Lowe during the Captivity. He never left the island, but became a magistrate and then served various governors so well that he was recommended for the highest position himself. When he was appointed, however, the governor's salary was reduced from two thousand pounds a year to nine hundred pounds. Hudson Janisch had the confidence of the islanders, and governed them well from 1873 to 1884, a hard period in the island's history, when more than fifteen hundred St Helenans emigrated to the Cape. Janisch was the first official to recognise the value of the archives in the Castle at Jamestown. He indexed the records and found many episodes for his "Extracts from the St Helena Records". His descendants left the island and settled in Cape Town, but some of them still visit the island where the first two Janischs helped to make history.

Four generations of Janischs have ridden on the tortoise which is pointed out to every visitor in the grounds of Plantation House, the governor's residence. Visitors are informed that this tortoise (probably from Mauritius) is a living link with Napoleon. In fact, it was landed as recently as 1858, when there were already two giant tortoises of the same species chewing the governor's lawn. One died in 1877, and the shell was sent to the London Natural History Museum. There was an aged female which the millionaire Rothschild tried to buy, but his offer was refused. This tortoise was accidentally killed by falling over a cliff. The survivor is a male, but its exact age is unknown.

Plantation House, with its farm of more than a hundred acres, is one of the island's oldest and most pleasant estates. The house was built in 1792, but Sir Hudson Lowe added the present library, billiard room and other amenities. St Helena is the starting point in a colonial governor's career. There must have been many past governors who rose to much greater positions, but who looked back wistfully on their years in charming little Plantation House.

Doubtless the heyday of Plantation House was the Captivity period, for Sir Hudson Lowe's salary was twelve thousand pounds a a year. Lowe had two large farms producing free of charge the food which enabled him to entertain generously. The company's slaves worked as labourers, and there were many skilled Chinese on the estate. But I do not think Lowe ever enjoyed himself. He was too worried, too full of fear that Napoleon would escape, too conscious of his responsibilities.

Rooms at Plantation House have old brass plates with the positions of those who occupied them many years ago: Governor's Room, Admiral's Room, General's Room, Baron's Room. One room is labelled Chaos, and here a poltergeist is said to disturb the fine old furniture occasionally. I must say that the friendly and homely atmosphere of Plantation House did not suggest a haunted mansion to me.

One memorable Sunday, thanks to Inspector Ogborn of the police, I circumnavigated St Helena in the motor launch *Yellowfin*. Several islanders among the inspector's guests confessed that it was the first time they had cruised all the way round their lonely island. We towed a gig as a lifeboat; for it might mean shipwreck if the engine failed on the uninhabited, wave-lashed stretches of the island's weather side.

At first the coastline was familiar, for I had been out fishing with Charlie Wade as far as Egg Island. There were the goat tracks across the seaward face of Ladder Hill, often used by daring islanders following stray goats, or gathering wild pepper and wild tobacco on the cliffs, or hunting wild rabbits in the caves. I still shudder when I think of the precipices surrounding that island. Many islanders have gone out, never to return; though all knew that they had either fallen to their deaths or been swept off the rocks. Charlie Wade told me about three brothers who had all vanished at different times. "Must have bin a drowning family," remarked Charlie calmly.

Every valley has its ruins. Steering west about from Jamestown, you come first to Breakneck Valley, barred by a Dutch wall. Young's Valley was defended in the same way, but the name is fairly recent. It seems that Young had a garden with yams and bananas in the narrow valley, and lived there happily until his wife fell ill. The doctor advised him to move, for the valley is isolated. Then his wife died.

"Same man Young what was dwelling here drowned hisself two years afterwards," Charlie Wade ended. "He was a bit daft, see . . . jumped over."

My favourite St Helena valley, the place I would select for a retreat from civilisation, is Lemon Valley. More than two centuries ago a Dutch squadron from Table Bay landed soldiers there, but the English threw large stones over the cliff and beat them off. Nevertheless, the Dutch captured the island and built a dizzy fort on the cliff overlooking the Lemon Valley landing place; and they threw the usual defensive wall across the mouth of the valley.

Lemon Valley was once the watering place of the East India ships. Then a landslide occurred, and the taste and colour of the water were affected. However, there is a stream which never dries up, and though the lemons have vanished there are still a few guava and banana trees. A solid stone house, used as quarantine station and barracks for the garrison in World War II, now lacks doors, windows and floors. As I roamed the deserted valley I felt that a hermit who was also a handyman could soon put things in order, grow enough fruit and vegetables and catch enough fish to support himself.

This time the *Yellowfin* slipped past my imaginary paradise. I saw the bird rocks again, where the black crabs come out into the sunshine. There was Creepy Cove, so called because it is impossible to climb along the cliffs unless you creep on all fours. Then came Horse Pasture Point, with the sea booming in the caves at water level; noddies nesting in a guano cave.

Egg Island is a huge white waterless rock where the Dutch set up cannon and left a few unhappy soldiers to repel invaders. At rare intervals the tide will allow you to walk from the island to the mainland. Police sergeant Dillon told me that he explored Egg Island with Dr Gosse, the historian, some years ago and found some cannon balls, coins and military buttons. Dillon was in the guano trade before he joined the police. He knows the rotten rock of his native island, and he spent months working desolate Bosun Bird Islet at Ascension. ("We had to dig our own 'graves' in the guano to sleep on Bosun Bird – and the lice nearly ate us up," Dillon recalled.) Dillon said there was guano on the cliffs at Frying Pan Cove, inside Egg Island, but it was a dangerous place for a boat. The usual system was for a man to be lowered over the cliff in a bo'sun's chair with a bag between his legs. This man chopped the solid guano off the cliff with a hammer, filled the bag, and then sent the bag down to a boat. If there was an overhang, the man in the chair drove pegs into the cliff, then made the chair fast to dead-eyes on the pegs and hauled himself below the bulge. It was a pretty desperate game, he declared, and only a few men on St Helena had the nerve to do it. With guano at fifteen pounds a ton it was more or less worth the risk. Frying Pan Cove was a nightmare, however, because you had to work without the aid of a boat. Moreover, the men who lowered the chair could not see what the man in the chair was doing. The sacks of guano had to be hauled up the cliff when they were full. Special whistle signals were given for each stage in the operation.

Members of the Phillips family are about the only real guano experts left on St Helena, apart from Dillon. There is old man Phillips working with a son-in-law. Another son worked with the team, but one day they hauled up the chair and there was no one in it. "Maybe a stone struck him," suggested Dillon. "He must have fallen out of the chair and got drowned."

From the *Yellowfin* I saw the five rocks and islets where the sea birds nest: Egg, Peaked, Speery, George and Shore Island. All are close inshore. Speery is the most dramatic; a pinnacle rock where you would imagine that even the birds would find it hard to move.

Yet men climb that rock, work the guano and sleep on the summit.

Most common among the sea birds is the white-capped noddy, known to the islanders as the noddy bird. Another species of noddy (called blackbird locally) is vicious, and men collecting guano have to guard their heads. But the most spectacular bird of these waters is the red-billed tropic bird (the trophy-bird of the islanders), which nests in the cliffs. They have a way of dropping off the ledges to launch themselves in the air, and it is said that they cannot rise on the wing from level ground.

Many birds of St Helena were captured alive or shot for sale to visitors up to about sixty years ago. Tropic birds were killed for their plumes, which then adorned women's hats. The interesting St Helena sandplover, or wire bird, was trapped and sold in cages. This land bird is believed to be the only indigenous bird of the island; it was noticed by very early travellers. Fortunately the trade in birds was stopped towards the end of last century, or several species would have been exterminated by now. Major E.L. Haydock, the ornithologist, located only about one hundred pairs of wire birds on the island a few years ago.

Dillon told me there must have been rare birds on St Helena "in the before days". He found a pair of avian feet on Shore Island once, large feet different from the feet of any bird frequenting the island today. These mysterious skeleton feet were buried deep in the guano, and Dillon is still wondering what the whole bird looked like.

"Sea's a bit rugged today," declared the islanders as the *Yellowfin* plunged into the seas off Sandy Bay, and the spray came over. But as we left the last of the bird islands astern the launch was running before the trade wind, moving easily until she came into the calmer waters of Prosperous Bay. There the party landed, and I looked up to the heights and saw the old, disused signal station where poor Gunnell was so stupidly murdered. Dillon told me a happier story of Prosperous Bay. He once found a four hundred pound turtle some way inland, where it had gone to lay its eggs; and he sold it at five-pence a pound. Here, too, are more ruins – the battery and a fort built to keep any possible friends of Napoleon away from the anchorage.

It was at Prosperous Bay that the English landed in 1673 to recapture the island from the Dutch. Captain Kedgwin took four hundred men on shore, using a clever negro slave named Black Oliver as a guide. It was long odds against the assault succeeding, for the whole force had to scale a cliff with a last perilous section which demands a rope. A fine climber named Tom climbed the last section without any sort of aid, and then lowered a rope by which the four hundred men reached Longwood Plain. As each man came up, hand over hand, he called out: "Hold fast, Tom!" (This point on the cliff has been marked as Holdfast Tom on the maps ever since then.) Meanwhile Captain Munden was bombarding Jamestown from the sea. The Dutch surrendered. Prosperous Bay gained its name as a result of the British victory. Someone had to climb down the Holdfast Tom cliff when Napoleon died, for there is a gypsum deposit there and this was used for the controversial death mask. Another account, however, states that the gypsum was fetched hurriedly from George Island by whaleboat.

Sail on round the sinister cliffs of Turk's Cap and the Barn, round Buttermilk Point, past Half Moon Battery and you come to Rupert's Bay. This opens up another secluded, almost forgotten yet lovely valley which seems to be waiting for an escapist.

Rupert was a prince, son of the King of Bohemia, who anchored in the bay to refresh his ship's company a couple of hundred years ago. Ever since then the islanders have called it Rupert's Valley. William Burchell the botanist of South African fame occupied a house in Rupert's Valley early last century. He landed on St Helena by accident, became deeply interested in the plants, and stayed on as schoolmaster. For five years he investigated the botany and geology of the island, and he sent many specimens to England. It was due to Burchell's experiments that the island was proved to be a suitable place for coffee and cotton. He sailed for the Cape in 1810, to embark on the expeditions which led to greater achievements.

Freed slaves were housed in Rupert's Valley a century ago. Many thousands of slaves rested there, recovering from the ordeal of the holds, before they were sent on to work as free labourers in the West Indies. Melliss the naturalist boarded a captured slaver just as she anchored in Rupert's Bay in 1861, and gave this impression: "I picked my way from end to end in order to avoid treading upon the slaves. The deck was thickly strewn with the dead, dying and starved bodies. A visit to a fully-freighted slave ship is not easily to be forgotten; a scene so intensified in all that is horrible almost defies description." Bishop Gray was another shocked visitor to Rupert's Bay at that period. "If anything were needed to fill the soul with burning indignation against that masterwork of Satan, the Slave Trade, it would be a visit to this institution," he wrote. "There were not less than six hundred poor souls in it. Of these more than three hundred were in hospital; some affected with dreadful ophthalmia; others with severe rheumatism, others with dysentery, the number of deaths in a week being twenty-one."

It was a slave ship, of course, which brought the white ant to St Helena. Within thirty years Jamestown had been devastated, and the ant had created havoc all over the island before the end of the century.

"In the shipping days," as the islanders say, when fifteen hundred ships a year called and it was not so hard for a man to earn a living, Jamestown was overcrowded. One governor of a century ago suggested that a suburb should be built in Rupert's Valley. This was done, but a scheme for linking the two valleys by a tunnel was never carried out. At that time, too, a governor sent to England for a wooden prefabricated building called a "model gaol". It was set up in Rupert's Valley. Not long afterwards a prisoner who disliked all gaols, model or otherwise, put a match to it. Within an hour it had been destroyed. Other buildings of the period are still there, but mainly in ruins. One good double-storeyed house, with a plaque in honour of Burchell and palms and bananas, is used by the cable company; for you can see the deep-sea cable emerging from the ocean and crossing the beach. The whole waterfront is barricaded in the familiar St Helena fashion by an old fort wall. A chimney and boilers were pointed out to me as relics of the South African War, for they formed a distilling plant to supply the prisoner-of-war camps.

Shortly before World War II a solitary leper was living at Rupert's Bay, passing the time with a gramophone and a number of old records. He is no longer there, and I imagine that it would not cost much to rent a house in the valley.

I walked along the cliff paths one Sunday afternoon from Jamestown to Rupert's Bay, and it was a walk to remember. Often I dared not look over the low stone wall. There is an inlet along the route called Rowland's Cove, scene of several fatal accidents owing to rockfalls and people slipping over the edge. St Helena is an island of incredible residences, and I saw one that afternoon. The house was built into a ledge in the cliff, there was a palm tree apparently growing out of the rock, and you could have dropped a fishing line into the sea from any of the front windows. A painter could have made a remarkable canvas of that quaint eyrie, but I was always conscious of the heights.

Well, you have circled St Helena and the launch *Yellowfin* is back on her moorings off Jamestown in the bay which has known so much sea adventure. I fancy that I can see the earliest sailors of all landing on the beach, taking what they wished in goats and swine and fruit, carving records of their visits on rocks and trees, and sailing away with their memories of the uninhabited mid-ocean paradise. "Providence has bestowed upon it all that is best of air, earth and water," declared François Pyrard. "Nowhere in the world, I believe, will you find an island of its size to compare with it."

Some people in St Helena still hold that opinion, and they are not all islanders. There are others among the white community who regard themselves as exiles; they wish their lives away, looking forward always to the next holiday in England, or the next transfer to some less isolated colony. What is the truth?

There is no truth for all. I was told of a woman, suffering acutely from a nervous complaint, who went to stay with well-meaning friends on St Helena; for they thought the utter peace of the island would cure her. Instead, it brought on the most serious emotional attack she had ever known. The ship left, and she felt trapped. It was claustrophobia in a dangerous form. Heaven alone knows what would have happened to her if a ship had not put in by sheer chance a few days later and carried her thankfully away.

Another woman who was merely bored after a year or two on the island remarked to me: "I prefer bridge to conversation here. You go round and round meeting the same people and hearing the same subjects discussed time after time. It's like going on for years in the same ship with the same passengers. A man has his work, but a woman is to be pitied."

Then there was the wife of a well-educated, well-travelled man who had nevertheless spent most of his life on the island. She had been born elsewhere. "I am afraid that I am here for life, and I feel it," she summed up. "I dare not make close friends, for in a few years they pass on to a tour of duty elsewhere and are lost to me. In any case it is hard to make friends – the circle is too narrow."

Yet I remember, too, a man who seemed happy – a settler who had tried other paradise islands and left them in disgust, and found peace on St Helena. The war had been unkind to him, I know, and he deserved to find what he had been seeking. "I don't see why I should be called an escapist simply because I have chosen to live in a place where the people do not hate one another," he declared.

I cannot quarrel with that test, but there is another which I would have to apply successfully to find the island of my dreams. It is pleasant to see well-nourished people round one. You can enjoy your own meals far more if the general standard of living is not so very far below your own. Now as I have said, the St Helena people are not starving. Certainly they are not well-fed. I gave a small boy a shilling for carrying my fish up from the wharf, and asked him what he would do with the money. He looked up at me in surprise. "Give it to my mother to buy bread," he replied. "Lots o' people here werry poor, mister."

Just before I sailed from St Helena I was taken to see a woman of ninety-seven. Her father and mother had been slaves. She had married at twenty-one, and her marriage had lasted for seventy-one years. Her tiny cottage looked out over a wide expanse of ocean, but she was almost blind. I expressed my sympathy, wondering what the secret of her peaceful mind might be.

"Oh, it's not so bad," smiled the old woman. "I've had a contented life, my daughter looks after me – and I can still see the sunset."

THERE'S A SECRET HID AWAY

241

Ascension Island

1958

Ascension is a grim, unlovely island with an atmosphere as weird as anything you will find on the face of the oceans. It has seen much suffering, many tragedies. Yet those who live there now will tell you in all sincerity that it is one of the happiest isles in the world, a place they are in no hurry to leave. Their strange affection puzzled me for a long time.

Passengers in liner after liner have gasped at the sight of this lonely and desolate volcanic cinder in mid-South Atlantic, and they have steamed away thanking God that they were not being left behind. Here, you would imagine, a castaway would have died of thirst in the days before the island became inhabited. And you would be right.

I, too, failed to perceive the spell of Ascension; but when a place baffles me I become all the more determined to wring the secret out of it. This was not easy. Thanks to the governor of St Helena and the Union-Castle Line, however, I was able to land twice on the island. Thanks to the cable men and their wives, who voyaged with me and talked of their island years, I believe I know the secret now.

You must have two special permits to visit Ascension, one from the master of your ship and the other from the governor of St Helena or the Ascension magistrate. The captain has to keep an eye on the weather, for the notorious rollers may come up while you are on shore and then you may be marooned on the island until the next ship calls. Thus the privilege of landing is seldom granted.

Only the occasional eccentric like myself wishes to go on shore there. "I saw a land not lying before me smiling in beauty, but staring in all its naked hideousness," wrote Charles Darwin when he gazed upon the Ascension landscape. He could not discover a tree anywhere. A later American visitor summed up the scene as "Hell with the fire put out".

Ascension consists of the summits of forty small, extinct volcanoes. The shape gives a very rough impression of a bell, twenty miles round the rim and rising to nearly three thousand feet where Green Mountain peak thrusts into the clouds. It is a fantastic mass of cinders, streams of black lava and sand, weird hills and volcanic craters. Geologists say the island is fifty thousand years old, a very recent arrival above the surface. (St Helena, regarded as a "sister" island, is possibly the oldest ocean island in the world.) Ascension is still almost naked, and many more thousands of years must pass before it is properly clothed. Devil's Ashpit, Devil's Punchbowl, Devil's Riding School and Dead Man's Cove; these are sinister names. Dust and lava, scorpions and mosquitoes; a desert island indeed, a hideous, sunbaked wilderness.

Ascension, this weird Ascension, reminds me that the cable service has never brought forth an author to reveal to the world a life that remains hidden as though behind a curtain of secrecy. These men, and their wives, spend years in strange and sometimes romantic isolation. Their exile may be pleasant, it may be an ordeal; often and often the elements of drama must be present. Yet not a word comes out. For years last century, all this century, the submarine cables have been spreading out along the trade routes, linking remote atolls and ocean islands and the cities of the world. Cable men have been stationed all along those routes, and they lived through all sorts of vicissitudes. They have known joy and sorrow and appalling loneliness, and survived dangers. In their messes they have discussed the most fantastic experiences. But not one of them has put it down for posterity. What do you find in the *Zodiac,* the magazine of the cable service? Search the whole set, and you will find little more than descriptions of dinners and cricket matches and a few travel pieces admirably illustrated with photographs. I once met Edgar Middleton, a former cable operator who wrote a play called "Potiphar's Wife" and made eighty thousand pounds. But he never drew on his memories of life on a cable station for that or any other work. Never have I encountered such neglect of such a magnificent theme.

So here is Ascension, one of those lonely cable stations which no one has dramatised, an island with a great question mark hovering over its barren shores. It was on Ascension Day in 1501 that Juan de Nova sighted the clouds massing round the peak. He sailed up into the shallows and anchored. Certainly he and his men were the first human beings to set foot there; and possibly they left the goats, mentioned by many visitors, to serve as food for castaways.

Before long Ascension (like Table Bay) became known as a pillar box of the ocean. Friar Navarette, a late seventeenth century caller, remarked: "Sailors of all nations are in the habit of leaving letters here, sealed up in a bottle and placed in a certain hole in the rock. Letters are taken away by the first ship that passes in the opposite direction." A beacon on the south-easterly point of Ascension marks the spot, and it is still known as Letter-Box.

All the very early callers were Portuguese, and they made a track up the mountain. This path can still be traced, from North-East Bay to the summit. They may also have placed the wooden cross on the present Cross Hill, overlooking Georgetown. One manuscript (which I found among the logbooks and diaries of old Ascension in the British Museum Library in London) suggested that a sailor had been buried there with the large cross above his grave.

Britain did not take possession of Ascension until 1816, but British ships called at the island for a century and more before that date. Struys, a Dutch writer, said that in 1673 the English were using Ascension as a rendezvous. "The whole island," Struys reported, "is white with the dung of mews, cormorant and a sort of wild geese that come thither to breed and also to prey upon the dead fish which lie in heaps upon the shore."

Just two centuries after the discovery the first castaways lived on Ascension. They were Dampier and his men; William Dampier the former buccaneer returning from a voyage of discovery round the coasts of Australia on behalf of the British admiralty. His ship, the two-decker *Roebuck,* had sprung a leak and the pumps could not cope with it. Dampier had to beach his ship on the south-east coast of the island, between Pumice Cove and Pillar Bay. (Timbers and spars, black with age, were discovered there in recent years, probably relics of the *Roebuck.*) Then he sent his men ashore on a raft with their chests and bedding.

Dampier had time to order the sails to be unbent for use as tents. He also saved a puncheon and a thirty-six gallon cask of fresh water, and a bag of rice. Unfortunately there were thieves among the crew of fifty, and some of the precious stores vanished. They suffered from thirst, but on the sixth day Dampier saw the goats in the valley and followed one to the "drip" which is known to this day as Dampier's Springs. Here the rain is held by a layer of clay and led over a moss-covered rock where maidenhair fern grows. It is no more than a trickle, but it saved Dampier and his men.

Half-way up Green Mountain is Dampier's Cave, where the castaways lived on land crabs, sea birds, turtles and goats. According to island tradition, Dampier buried a treasure near the cave. Many a hopeful naval expedition, many cable exiles have searched for that treasure, but always in vain. If you go back (as I did) to Dampier's own account of the loss of the *Roebuck* you will find no mention of treasure. Dampier complained that he lost his own books and papers after beaching the ship. That was his only serious grievance. He described a tree which he found with a carving: an anchor and cable and the year 1642. After forty days on Ascension they were all taken off by three British men-o'-war and an East Indiaman. Dampier, of course, was in command of the expedition a few years later which marooned Alexander Selkirk (Robinson Crusoe) on Juan Fernandez, and was again in command when the castaway was picked up after five years.

Ascension's next castaway died but told his tale in a diary found beside his skeleton. It was a quarter of a century after the Dampier episode that Captain Mawson of the British ship *Compton* landed and found the bones and the grim message. (This was another Ascension relic which I studied in the British Museum library.) The diarist, evidently a seaman, had been marooned on Ascension as punishment for some grievous offence which he failed to describe. They left him a Bible, a tent, a cask of water, a little wine, a hatchet, two buckets, an old frying pan, a fowling piece without ammunition, a tea kettle, onions, peas, rice, and salt.

Very soon the ordeal began. Finding himself in a desert, the castaway was reluctant to consume his own small larder. "I feel great dread and uneasiness, having no hopes remaining but that the Almighty God would be my Protector," he wrote. He climbed a hill in the hope of sighting a ship or seeing food in any shape, but he was rewarded only with a "raging hunger". On the hill summit he left his useless gun with his shirt made fast to it as a tiny signal of distress.

After a time he succeeded in killing a few sea birds, which he skinned, salted and dried in the sun. Turtle helped him to vary his diet, but never did any man find less enjoyment in the noble flesh. The need for a supply of fresh water was always on his mind, and before long he went inland to the south carrying a few onions. All he found was a growth like purslane, which he ate, and some other roots and green herbs which he was afraid to eat.

On his return to the beach he planted the remaining onions, hoping for a crop. The diary reveals that his mind was wandering. Often he saw apparitions, and it is impossible to follow his routes over the island. One passage, however, reads clearly enough: "I found a turtle with whole eggs and flesh and made an excellent dinner, boiling the eggs with some rice. The remainder I buried for fear the stench should offend me, the turtles being of so large a size that it is impossible for one man to eat a whole one while sweet."

He fished without success. On one expedition he found a hollow place with a stream of fresh water (probably Dampier's Springs), but it seems that he lost it again. His shoes were worn out, crossing the clinker, and his feet were cut severely. This may have accounted for his failure to return to the water. At all events the last pages of the diary refer to his "great thirst" which could not be quenched with sea birds' eggs or turtle blood. Here is the end of the miserable castaway's story. "I am become a moving skeleton, my strength is entirely decayed, I cannot write much longer. I sincerely repent of the sins I committed and pray henceforth no man may suffer the misery I have undergone. For the sake of others I leave this narrative behind me to deter mankind from following such diabolical inventions. I now resign my soul to Him that gave it, hoping for mercy in . . ."

Captain Cook brought the *Resolution* to Ascension during his great voyage in search of the unknown Southland late in the eighteenth century. He, too, was repelled by the bleak landscape. "The dreariness of this island surpassed all the horrors of Easter Island and Tierra del Fuego, even without the alliance of snow," Cook remarked. "It was a ruinous heap of rocks."

Cook's men found a wreck on the east coast of the island, a ship which had been on fire and had been beached. "The distressful situation to which such a set of men must have been reduced in this barren island, before a ship could take them up, drew an expression of pity even from the sailors," Cook wrote. Cook was short of fuel, however, and he took on timber from the wreck to keep his galley stoves alight. He also captured twenty-four turtle, which lasted his ship's company for three weeks.

Ascension became a British colony and a permanent settlement at the same period as Tristan da Cunha, and for the same reason. Napoleon was a prisoner on St Helena, and islands which might have been used by Napoleon's friends as bases for an escape plot were seized and garrisoned. Thus, in 1815, law and order came to the isle of turtles in the shape of two British men-o'-war, *Peruvian* and *Zenobia.* They landed a twelve-pounder carronade, and left young Lieutenant Cuppage there with a sloop's crew. One year later the island was formally commissioned as H.M.S. *Ascension.* But the settlement became known as Garrison because the garrison lived there, and the name has stuck in spite of the later, more dignified title of Georgetown.

Garrison looked like an African village in the early years, with a stone tenement for officers, tents for seamen and marines, hovels for the Kroomen from West Africa. Rain was collected in casks and iron tanks. Apparently the hardships were known at the admiralty, for the captain was granted a special allowance of four shillings a day.

After the death of Napoleon the admiralty decided to abandon Tristan, but to retain Ascension as a sanatorium for the crews of men-o'-war who were operating against the slavers along the fever-stricken shores of West Africa. The island served the purpose well except on those tragic occasions when ships brought the deadly yellow fever with them. "Sores heal rapidly, fractures unite quickly, inflammatory complaints are not obstinate, and everyone enjoys uninterrupted good health," reported a naval officer of that period.

Captain H.E. Brandreth of the Royal Engineers, who surveyed the island in 1829, was responsible for the amenities which made life worth living. He not only planned the defence, but also designed the water scheme. Water has been precious on Ascension ever since

Dampier nearly died of thirst. Seldom has there been too much of it, for heavy rain falls in the settlement only at intervals of years. Rivers may run like the *wadis* of Egypt for a day, but then the greedy clinker absorbs every drop.

At first the garrison used water brought from St Helena and other places in barrels, as the rainfall and Dampier's Spring never supplied enough. Brandreth built a catchment area like the Gibraltar scheme on a small scale, and the pipeline from Green Mountain to Garrison was laid. It was never possible to supply much water to ships. Sun condensers were used at one time, and a plant came later for distilling a couple of thousand gallons of fresh water a day from the sea. Anyone who wanted his laundry done had to supply the water out of his day's ration.

Brandreth also bored in a ravine, penetrated a bed of lava, and made a well that yielded a thousand gallons a day for some time. The well dried up and was forgotten, and a later attempt to revive this source failed. Some believe there is an underground river at Ascension. Sounds as of running water are heard, but this water, if it exists, has never been brought to the surface.

I came across Brandreth's own description of Ascension in an old report. Some of the marines employed on the farm had their wives with them, and Brandreth found a little red-cheeked Devonshire woman living in a cave at Dampier's Springs. Her husband had scooped out a parlour and bedroom, each eight feet square, plastered and whitewashed and with canvas on the floors.

"People rarely complain of life on the island," Brandreth declared. "The secret is found in constant occupation, the brilliance and elasticity of the atmosphere, the remarkable salubrity, and the good sense, tact, judgment and temper of the commandant."

But the shadow of yellow fever always lay across the early settlement. Malaria claimed some, but others recovered. Yellow fever could not be treated in those days. So today Ascension is an island of cemeteries. Many a grave recalls those tragic years when the old gunboats anchored there with fever-racked crews under awnings, and buried their dead by the dozen. One such ship, H.M.S. *Bann,* arrived in 1823 with yellow fever on board. The disease was passed on to the shore garrison, and one-third of the people died. Only sixteen of the *Bann*'s crew survived.

This lesson was not forgotten. When the stricken H.M.S. *Bonetta* arrived in the middle of last century, no member of her company was allowed in the settlement. *Bonetta* anchored opposite a landing known as Comfort Cove, and all hands landed. There they died, one by one, some digging graves for their shipmates and then scooping out their own graves before they became too weak. Every day the men of the garrison left food and water close at hand, but they could not save the *Bonetta*'s men. Last to die was the *Bonetta*'s surgeon. He cared for his patients to the end, and he was found dead in the shallow grave he had made for himself. They changed the name of the place after that. Modern charts show it as Comfortless Cove.

Captains of H.M.S. *Ascension* had almost unlimited power during the long decades when the island was as isolated as any ship at sea. (Today the cable manager also acts as magistrate; but the cable linking the island with St Helena and the outside world limits his authority to some extent.) A captain of last century was not only in command of the "stone frigate". Visitors found that he was also governor, sole legislator, chief executioner, dockyard superintendent, coroner, public prosecutor, jailer, and president ex-officio of all local societies, the canteen, library and sports club. As a rule the commander was a naval officer, but officers of the Royal Marines also held the post.

One such potentate was handed an official document by the surgeon reporting the arrival of a baby. This stern disciplinarian added the word "approved", and his initials. For a long time babies born "on board" H.M.S. *Ascension* were deemed to have been born at sea, and their births were registered in the parish of Wapping.

Wives of naval officers did not always live in harmony. Not all of them were willing to take precedence according to the ranks of their husbands; even the front pews in church were contested until a wise captain decreed: "Let age take the higher place," I have an extract from the *Admiralty Gazette* describing the wretched state of affairs in Georgetown at the end of last century, when ten officers' wives formed cliques and would not speak to their rivals for months on end. When some matter had to be settled, they wrote letters. The wives of petty officers and marine non-commissioned officers were far more human, and the cottages where they lived are still called Harmony Row.

One captain was advised to try the experiment of punishing the husbands for the sins of their wives. He made inquiries and then rejected the idea. Some of the wives would have loved to have seen their husbands suffer. This captain finally resigned his appointment in despair, pointing out that he could handle any ship afloat, but not the womenfolk of H.M.S. *Ascension.*

Naturally, the queer life of Ascension was not easily imagined by those who had never seen the place. Long ago the wife of a naval captain stepped on to the jetty and inquired: "Where is Government House – and the governor's carriage?"

"Yonder is the captain's cottage, ma'am, and here is the island cart," replied a seaman politely.

Mrs Gill, wife of an astronomer royal, spent six months on Ascension with her husband eighty years ago in an effort to fix the true distance of the earth from the sun. She found housekeeping difficult. When she went to the bakery they gave her a stale loaf. A bell rang at seven in the morning and everyone ran out for a tiny ration of fresh milk from the mountain. "Vegetables?" she asked. "Only sweet potatoes, and none of those till next Friday," was the answer.

"Where shall I find the butcher?" Mrs Gill inquired.

"There ain't any butcher," replied the cook with a grin. "The sheep and bullocks are starving for food and water, and hardly any are killed that have not fainted first."

"But surely there are plenty of fish?" persisted Mrs Gill.

"Generally, ma'am, but not when the rollers are in."

Ascension has watched many dramas of the sea. Men in open boats have sighted the peak with dry throats and thankful hearts. Many a slaver was brought there as a prize, and many a negro stepped on shore at Ascension as a free man. So many West Africans were living there at one time that a "suburb" of Garrison was known as Krootown.

Two men-o'-war which lay for years in the anchorage at Ascension were H.M.S. *Tortoise* and H.M.S. *Flora.* It was in 1844 that the *Tortoise* arrived as permanent guardship, and she swung at her moorings there (latterly as a coal hulk) until early this century. *Flora* became guardship in 1865, and was transferred to Simonstown as depot ship seven years later.

Flora nearly came to grief at Ascension. She was lying there one night, an unrigged frigate with many sick naval ratings from West Africa on board, when her mooring cable snapped. Slowly she drifted before the south-east trade wind. For a time no one noticed the movement; but at last someone remarked that the lights of the settlement were growing faint. They dropped anchor just before the ship reached deep water. She remained at anchor on the island shelf, and was brought to safety later. *Flora* had very little food and water on board. If she had been blown away from the island, the officer in command on shore would have had no seaworthy vessel to send after her. In those days before wireless *Flora*'s crew and the invalids would probably have perished.

Tortoise was evidently capable of putting to sea during one critical period when Ascension almost dried up. All hands were in danger of dying of thirst; but *Tortoise* made sail, headed south for St Helena, and returned in great haste with her holds filled with barrels of water. She cannot have been a fast ship with a name like *Tortoise,* but she got back in time.

Britain almost abandoned Ascension in 1881, and the useless garrison of five hundred Royal Marines was withdrawn. The place was costing forty thousand pounds a year, and it was no more than an occasional coaling station. Germany tried to secure the island a decade later, offering South West Africa in exchange. However, the British admiralty objected. The island was left with a very small garrison during World War I, although an attack by a German raider seemed probable. Soon afterwards the admiralty decided to "axe" H.M.S. *Ascension* in the same way that other units of the Royal Navy had been dealt with. Finally, in 1922, the white ensign was hauled down and the Eastern Telegraph Company's manager became magistrate and ruler of the island.

Memories of the Royal Navy cling to every corner of Garrison, just as they do in Simonstown. The long occupation is ineradicable. All buildings in Garrison and on the mountain are still owned by the Admiralty, and let to the cable people on indefinite lease. Names such as Bunghole Square, in the middle of the settlement, recall the days when rum casks were handled there. I found Admiralty Cottage in ruins, eaten by white ants. Years ago it was the lovely home of the naval captain on Cross Hill. Once I met a doctor who had taken over the hospital from the naval surgeon when the navy departed; and in that hospital he found an operating table that went right back to Nelson's day, a fearsome, bloodstained board with rings so that the terrified patients could be lashed in position, while arms or legs were sawn off without an anaesthetic.

A brass port light from some forgotten man-o'-war supplies the red light outside the police station. (The navy also put up a jail which remains empty nowadays for years at a time.) In little St Mary's Church, which the navy built in 1843, there are tablets on the walls in memory of seamen who were killed at sea; seamen who fell on Green Mountain; seamen who died while serving on the island. And I remember the little baptismal font of grey Ascension limestone, where so many of the island's babies have been christened.

Many of the bungalows in Garrison were built a hundred years ago, and rebuilt by cable officials with bricks made from lava. I found them charming. Always the main room is the open verandah, shaded by jalousies, but open to the endless sweep, sweep, sweep of the south-east trade wind. Without the breeze, life on Ascension would be intolerable. Now and again the wind swings round and blows from West Africa. They call that a coaster, for it is a hot and damnable wind; and everyone feels irritable until the comforting south-east trade comes again.

In the bungalows are pieces of furniture now becoming antiques of a sort, the standard mahogany furniture which the old Eastern Telegraph Company supplied to its exiles in far places . . . wardrobes, chests-of-drawers, great sideboards bearing the company's crest. Kitchens have paraffin refrigerators, blue flame and pressure stoves.

Cable people live outside most of the time. Meals are served on the verandah, and many sleep on the verandah. It is a place for the happiest possible sundowner parties, with little polished, dusted tables everywhere and pink gins and snacks and curios such as only cable men can gather during their years of service in the queer outposts of the globe. Yes, a place where tales are told as the sun goes down, tales of life in the solitudes that only the cable men know.

Each house in Garrison now has a forty-gallon water tank, and in these days of a small population each person is allowed seven gallons a day. When I landed for the second time in April, 1957, the island had been suffering from a drought. One tank on the mountain had run dry. The whole supply would have lasted for another twenty days; and then rain fell on Green Mountain.

In the later naval days a windmill pumped salt water to a tower and every household enjoyed salt water baths. This vanished pleasure is still spoken of with regret.

Green Mountain is the paradise of this weird island world. As you drive out from Georgetown, away from the brave little bath-watered gardens of bougainvillaea and Cape daisies, petunias and zinnias; as you enter the ferocious lava wastes it seems unlikely that the island can relent and offer a normal picture of beauty. Six miles to the summit, and the first half of the journey shows you only the craters, the sharp clinker that cuts your shoes to pieces, the sullen hills, the red, black and grey dust; and the once-molten lava, set just as it was when it stopped flowing, in wave after wave. Men have been lost in the lava desert, and found delirious and half dead from thirst.

I walked away from the jeep at One Boat, listening to the sound of my feet on the brittle clinker, the clinker that rings like broken china. Has the whole island been explored? I doubt it. There must be far corners cut off by fissures and inaccessible owing to the jagged, universal clinker. At night the clinker shrinks and "whispers" in a menacing way. The ash takes on strange shapes of man and beast. It is better to cling to the road.

Landmarks on the Green Mountain road are God-be-thanked, a tank with a tap on the pipe line, One Boat and Two Boats. The boats are ships' gigs sawn in half and placed upright beside the track as milestones; relics of naval humour. At nine hundred feet the road rises suddenly, and you begin to realise how the marines and West African negroes must have toiled when they built this route to the summit. They followed a design with many zigzag turns called ramps; safe enough if you ride or drive carefully in daylight, but seldom used at night.

Coarse grass appears on the uplands, with aloes and prickly pears beside the road. At seventeen hundred feet you see Cape grass, mat grass and cow grass; much better fodder for the thousand and more sheep on the mountain.

Green Mountain is a mountain in the making. Nothing larger than flowering shrubs and ferns grew there early last century. When the navy took over, men-o'-war brought not only trees from all over the world, but tons of good earth for the mountain farm. Now it seems that the trees and vegetation have influenced the climate. Records kept during a decade since World War II suggest that the cooler air above the pastures and cultivated belt has precipitated a higher rainfall.

Ascension's finest trees are to be found in the ravines, where soil and moisture favour growth. Gums, cedar trees and Cape yews are established there. Many other trees came from the West Indies. On the slopes, eucalyptus, araucaria, juniper, acacia and castor oil trees were planted. Port Jackson willows and Scotch fir have survived the droughts. Slowly, very slowly, the trees are creeping down the mountain. Centuries hence, Ascension may be covered to the same extent as St Helena.

Above two thousand feet, round about the oasis near the summit, comes the great transformation. Here are lanes as green and scented as any in Devon; here is the farm with its coconut palms and banana clumps, roses and geraniums, wild raspberries and wild ginger and vegetable gardens, gorse and guavas and blackberries. The buildings stand as monuments to the men who built the road and the farm in the mid-ocean clouds – possibly the strangest farm on the face of the earth. The old sanatorium for fever-stricken seamen, the Red Lion barracks with its clock tower (where the rum was issued), the solid houses, cow byres and pigsties like slate-roofed cattle palaces; these were built to last for centuries. They had to drive a tunnel through the mountain for an aqueduct; a dark tunnel with a guide wire along one side. Newcomers are advised to cling tightly to the wire and jump over an imaginary hole in the floor. This ancient Ascension joke still succeeds.

Pass through the tunnel and you look out over Breakneck Valley, one of the steep places where necks have been broken. It blows hard on the mountain. Watch your step on the paths above the precipices. Up here, too, is the cottage where a shepherd hanged himself; yet another reminder of the grim pages in Ascension's past. Sherry and Bitters Corner strikes a more cheerful note. It was named because the bracing winds at that spot gave the navy men keen appetites.

Finally there is the dew pond, a cemented pond on the very summit in the old crater. This man-made beauty spot far up in the mist belt is surrounded with bamboos. Blue lilies, goldfish and frogs make the pond interesting. And beside the pond is a long, rusty anchor chain, used last century to haul heavy loads up the mountain. According to an Ascension custom with a forgotten origin you must hold the chain and wish . . .

General Godfrey Mundy, who visited the island nine years after the occupation, found seven horses there. He rode over the hills and valleys of volcanic ashes, up Green Mountain, to the hamlet of half a dozen houses built like an eagle's eyrie three hundred feet below the summit. They gave him a breakfast of "beefsteak" and "veal cutlets", both made of turtle meat. The general found that English potatoes and sweet potatoes were being grown, with pumpkins and plantains. West Africa supplied such items as calaloo (a tropical spinach), peppers and cassava, bananas and melons for the early garden. Cape gooseberries were among the first fruits. Every ship brought new plants. It became the custom for officers stationed there to contribute some useful botanical item; now it is a tradition, and no cable manager departs before he has planted a tree or flower which Ascension has not seen before.

Stand near the summit of Green Mountain when the sun is going down, and in clear weather you will observe a spectacle which is, I believe, peculiar to this island. Face the east, and a gigantic shadow of the mountain is projected slowly across the ocean. When the shadow reaches the horizon it rises and presents a distinct shadow of Ascension's peak against the eastern sky.

This island lacking fresh water and timber attracted many early visitors because of the turtles. Captain Leslie, a British shipmaster who called late in the eighteenth century, declared that the Ascension turtles were the finest in creation, "fat and large and in the highest perfection for eating of all I ever tasted".

Another tribute came from Captain George Young of H.M.S. *Weazle,* who put in at Ascension for turtle because most of his men were suffering from scurvy. He reported that the turtle "saved many a good man's life".

Ascension's turtle is the green turtle, *Chelonia mydas,* the only true sea turtle which an epicure will touch. (The fat is greenish in colour, hence the name.) Giants among the green turtle weigh nearly half a ton. No male turtle has ever been identified on Ascension. Only the females land there, always between Christmas and June, always on dark nights, lumbering up the beaches far beyond high water mark. Then each female digs a sand pit with its flippers and deposits fifty to sixty eggs. They have always been allowed to lay their eggs before capture. Turtle experts, by the way, do not talk of males and females, but of bulls and hens.

When you find the same delicacy on your doorstep every day it soon becomes unattractive. Thus the luxurious turtle soup does not often appear on Ascension menus; not only because a licence is necessary to "turn" a turtle, but also because turtle soup takes three days to prepare, and only on great occasions is it worth the effort.

They made a noble effort in 1957, when the Duke of Edinburgh landed. Mrs G. Elliot-Pyle, who simmered the royal soup, informed me that she used the "calipash", the greenish flesh from the belly. Marrow bones, herbs and spices, fresh basil from the mountain, fresh thyme and parsley and tomatoes went into the pot. Turtle fat, celery and more turtle meat were added on the second day; and on the third day the nourishing soup was strained and clarified. Mrs Elliot-Pyle made enough soup for eighteen people on that occasion. Crawfish with lettuce salad, tiny pork chops with swedes and mashed potato, and a *mousse* of coffee, rum and raisins completed the Duke of Edinburgh's lunch.

Compare this menu with the experiences of a sarcastic army officer who visited Ascension in the Eighties of last century. Among his notes I found these remarks: "Ascension produces nothing but turtles, rats and wideawakes. A starved bullock is slaughtered on Saturdays, and salt junk and groceries are served out by the purser's steward. The fortunate possessor of a bunch of carrots or a half-crown cabbage is in a position to give a sumptuous dinner. Water is so scarce that it is served out like a ration of rum. What a charming place; nothing to do to pass the time, nothing to eat and nothing to drink."

Turtle kraals, built early last century in a creek where the tide ebbs and flows, are now used as playgrounds and swimming pools by the children. The seamen and marines of old would often capture a hundred, two hundred turtles in a night and keep them in those kraals. A thousand turtles were shipped to England in one year for the King, the lords of the admiralty and other distinguished people. Each turtle was marked on the belly shell with the name of the owner. Casualties occurred during the long voyage under sail, and the seamen in charge of the turtle would report to the captain: "I don't like the looks of Lord Melville this morning, sir." Another day the news would spread: "Duke of Wellington died last night." A tradition arose, however, which was observed in all British men-o'-war: "The King's turtle never dies."

Men of the old Ascension garrisons were issued with fresh turtle meat almost every day. It was cooked like beef or mutton, but nothing could disguise the richness and most of the men detested it. I was amused to see, in an old naval diet sheet drawn up for prisoners in the cells: "Turtle soup will be served twice a week." However, some of the soldiers must have enjoyed it, for I found a diary which read: "We have turtle in various ways – soups, broth, excellent cutlets like veal, and in pies which are very good." Nevertheless, a glass of fresh milk has always been more deeply appreciated on Ascension than a plate of turtle soup.

Another entry in the records showed that an early captain of the island had gone on board a visiting ship which had a cargo of horses, and had exchanged four turtles for two horses.

Turtle hunters slip a noose over the back and fore fin, twist the rope round a stick, and use the stick for turning the turtle over on its back. Turtle crawl out on to Long Beach and Dead Man's Beach, close to the settlement; they have never learnt to avoid man. But man handles these monsters from a bygone age with care, for a blow from a flipper may break a wrist.

Ten weeks after the eggs have been laid, the sun has done its hatching and tiny young turtles emerge from the sand to start their perilous journey towards the sea. Many are devoured by sea birds. Others reach the water only to be swallowed by the fierce and expectant conger eel. I have a pair of hollow baby turtles, killed and preserved by St Helena islanders working on Ascension; these are among the Ascension curios, prized by all old cable men who have been stationed there. The turtles appear to have been "blown" like birds' eggs, but the islanders keep this process secret.

Cockroaches are not prominent residents, as a rule. Years ago heavy rain fell, high grass appeared where only clinker had been known before, and with the grass came a cockroach invasion. Every house was raided. Officers of an American man-o'-war were being entertained at this period, but a dance at the club had to be abandoned. The dance floor was a moving carpet of cockroaches, and the servants could not sweep them away fast enough.

Nothing like that has occurred again though clothing is still eaten by cockroaches. One still hears tales of raids on houses and gardens by land crabs, however, and these are more ferocious than cockroaches. Some are nine inches long, with huge mouths; vicious monsters coloured brown or yellow or reddish purple. They live among the cactus of the craters, and always they are eager to find carrion. "One of the most revolting sights I ever saw was a swarm of land crabs devouring a dead sheep," a cable man told me. "There is an island legend of a shepherd who fell asleep and had his eyes picked out by the crabs, and I can believe it. I know the story of the shepherd who had his watch stolen by land crabs is true, for the watch was found in a crab hole."

Captain Brandreth found the land crabs so troublesome that he trained a pack of dogs to hunt them. The crabs fought back, rearing up defiantly with raised claws, and nipping their enemies from their burrows so that the dogs howled with pain. Rats and crabs are always at war. On the run, the rat usually succeeds in getting in a deadly bite. But a rat that enters a crab hole is lucky to emerge alive. Crabs also tackle the very young rabbits with confidence, but leave the older rabbits alone.

Roasted crabs form one of the island's snacks. Take a small bore rifle to Cricket Valley if you fancy crab hunting and you will return with a good haul.

Ascension provides glaring examples of man's folly in setting one animal against another. Rats swam ashore over a century ago and bred in such numbers that the first British commander decided to wipe them out. He sent for cats, which fled to the remote corners of the island and preyed not on rats but on poultry and the useful wild guinea fowl. So another commander imported dogs to hunt the cats. Dogs have never flourished on Ascension because the clinker lacerates their feet. The dogs faded out, and today two sheepdogs on the mountain farm are the only members of their tribe.

Rats of Ascension are of two species, a black, glossy-furred rat of the mountain and a brown rat in the settlement. Darwin considered that the variations were due to their different environments on the island. Tiny "clinker" mice are also found, but these do little or no harm.

Naturalists studying the reversion of domestic animals to the wild state will find good material in the Ascension cats. I am a cat lover, but I would think twice about taking one of the tigerish Ascension breed into my home. After centuries of freedom they have developed ferocious canine teeth. "Tame" specimens guard their owners' houses like dogs, rushing at visitors. They will also follow their owners at heel from house to house. "Beware of the cat" is a warning you will do well to heed on Ascension. A cat will bite unexpectedly and run. Babies have to be guarded. It is a firm rule on the cable station that no one may keep more than one cat. I think cats would be banned entirely if they were not so useful in keeping the rats and land crabs out of the houses.

Every cat, tame or wild, knows when the wideawakes are breeding. Every home loses its dubious pet, and the whole cat breed goes to the haunts of the birds to prey on the chicks. Some of the wild cats are so bold that they have been detected killing very young lambs on the mountain slopes.

Turnips were ruined by wireworm on the farm some years ago. Pairs of rooks were sent from England to destroy the pest. The rooks nested, the young birds learnt to fly; and then one day the whole rook colony left Ascension, never to return. Mynah birds were brought from Mauritius after that episode. But the only birds which have really proved an asset to Ascension are the guinea fowl and red-legged partridge. They add a touch of luxury to the island menu. General Mundy, who visited the island early last century, said the guinea fowl got up in enormous coveys and flew as strong as pheasants. In one year, two thousand guinea fowl were shot for the table. Wild cattle roamed the mountain in those days, but they became dangerous and were exterminated by the garrison.

Ascension's rabbits are the descendants of Cape (probably Robben Island) rabbits set free by some shipmaster many years before the island was occupied. So many have been shot that the rabbit may share the fate of Juan de Nova's goats. The scanty vegetation cannot support a large rabbit colony. It was during World War II that

American service men shot the last of the wild goats, that tough breed of goat which had roamed mountain and plain for nearly four and a half centuries.

In the queer world of nature on Ascension Island the lumbering turtles are rivalled in sheer fascination by the graceful sooty terns. Millions of these mysterious sea birds invade the plains of the island; not at the same time every year, as you might expect, but at intervals of about nine months. No one knows where they go when they depart. Many questions about the sooty tern remain unsolved.

Wideawakes, they call them on the island. I heard the parent birds calling to their young at dawn one morning on Wideawake Fair, and became aware immediately of the origin of the name. They scream in such lively chorus as they greet the day that there can be no doubt about their wakefulness. Wideawake Fair is their age-old home on the island, a number of flat spaces between hillocks close to the south-west coast. No doubt the noise of many thousands of birds reminded someone of a busy country fair ground.

Wideawakes have an enormous range, and they breed (sometimes in immense colonies) from the West Indies to the Pacific isles. I believe that Ascension is their greatest nesting stronghold. Sometimes the curtain of birds is dense enough to black out the sun. No one who has seen these sea swallows with their long, slender wings and forked tails on Wideawake Fair ever forgets the spectacle. Walk among them, and many remain unafraid and refuse to take to the air. Dr James P. Chapin, assistant curator of birds at the American Museum of Natural History, estimated that he saw one hundred thousand terns at once on the main Wideawake Fair, and there were many other "fairs" in the neighbourhood. Thus it would be no exaggeration to say there are a million, possibly two million wideawakes on Ascension.

Dr Chapin was called to Ascension Island during World War II, after American engineers had built a mile-long runway down Wideawake Fair. They had completed the formidable task in three months so that not only bombers but fighters might cross the ocean in greater safety. And then the birds imperilled the whole vast enterprise. Pilots naturally hated the birds that rose in screeching clouds when they opened up their engines. One wideawake smashed through the cockpit windshield of a Flying Fortress and wrecked the radio. Always there was the danger that the birds might be caught in air scoops or openings in the engines.

So the army tried poison and bullets, smoke candles and flares and regular explosions. The birds went on laying their eggs under the aircraft. Dr Chapin studied them with the trained eyes of an ornithologist, and noticed that the birds moved away if their eggs were broken. He recommended the organised destruction of the eggs, and soldiers broke the eggs at the rate of forty thousand a day. The plan succeeded.

When I drove down the great runway called Wideawake Field the Americans had returned to Ascension, and they were building a guided missile station with the same energy they had displayed in wartime. But there were no birds to bother the occasional postwar transport aircraft landing on the old mid-ocean runway. The wideawakes have not been wiped out, as many people feared. But they have moved on.

I stood there at dawn beside the hill at the end of the runway, watching the birds swarming up to greet the day, racing out to sea to prey on small fish. And when full daylight came I saw something else which reminded me all too vividly of another desert I knew in wartime. It was a bomber in ten thousand fragments, scattered over the hillside which it struck years ago. I have seen many wrecked aircraft on the field of battle, but nothing so small as that tragic American bomber which failed to lift in time.

Wideawakes are unpredictable birds. One season long ago their breeding grounds were flooded, so they remained on Ascension for nearly a year, laying their eggs again. It seems that they cling to the island until they have a young bird ready to take to the wing with them. When the armies of wideawakes migrate from Ascension they do not fly away in long columns like cormorants, heading for some destination. Wideawakes scatter, with no line of flight to betray their intention.

I said there were possibly two million wideawakes, and by this time the people on Ascension must have eaten millions of their eggs. Though the bird is small, the green egg speckled with dark spots is the size of a hen's egg. A flavour is hard to describe, and possibly for that reason the wideawake's egg has been compared with that of the plover. I found the wideawake's egg more fishy, but not unpleasantly fishy. The white is glutinous and clearer than a hen's egg, while the yolk is a pumpkin colour. Some housewives on Ascension use the eggs in puddings, pancakes and omelettes, and fry, boil or poach them. Others will not look at them.

If you want to be absolutely sure of your wideawake's eggs, draw a circle in the clinker, take all the eggs out, and then wait until the birds have laid fresh ones. You can have them every day for two or three months. The birds and their eggs receive a certain measure of protection at the present time. Old naval garrisons, however, must have revelled in these eggs. Island records show that in one week the men gathered one hundred and twenty thousand eggs. And a remark passed by a rating on Queen Victoria's day has been preserved: "I fear summat must be wrong wi' me. Last season I could eat as many as four dozen of them wideawake eggs at a sitting. Now I can only manage two dozen."

Those bygone, turtle-fed sailors had a nickname for Ascension. They called it Soup Island. It should have been Soup and Egg Island. St Helena people regard wideawake eggs as a great delicacy. Every islander working on Ascension is permitted to collect two dozen eggs for export, and every southbound liner carries a shipment to the "sister island".

Fresh patches of bird guano whiten the lava in many places. Holes in the clinker are filled with ancient guano deposits, and scientists have stated that an extinct species of penguin or albatross may have nested there. This guano has been worked at intervals with more or less success. English Bay, along the coast to the north of Garrison, was the headquarters of a guano company and some of the buildings are still there. (Their lights misled a liner, which ran aground but floated off safely.) Steam down the west coast of Ascension and you come to Bo'sun-bird Islet, a guano rock with a bird population which is of great interest to scientists. I met a St Helena islander who lived and worked on this appalling rock thirty years ago; one of the most frightening places I have set eyes upon during a long search for strange islands.

Bo'sun-bird Islet rises sheer from the sea in a manner which I dislike intensely. It is close to the coast, yet a large ship could pass in safety in the deep water between islet and shore. Only a skilled mountaineer could survive there. The islet is a massive column

262

three hundred feet high, with about an acre of flat land on top. Coloured pale yellow with guano, it is like a monstrous old tooth jutting up from the clear blue water. A rope ladder hangs from a projecting rock, and thus explorers and guano workers gain access to the islet and the narrow, perilous track leading to the summit. How the first visitor secured a foothold without the rope ladder is a mystery.

My informant, Sergeant Dillon of the St Helena Police, told me that he was fifteen years old when he joined the guano workers. They spent five days at a stretch on Bo'sun-bird, taking their boat to Garrison every weekend. "We had to dig 'graves' for ourselves in the guano if we wanted to sleep in safety at night," Dillon recalled. "Otherwise we might have rolled off the islet into the sea. There is a recess, you can't call it a cave, about halfway up, and we made that our home – but always in bitter discomfort. The top of the islet was impossible. Birds and lice eat you up on top."

One party of American naturalists visited Bo'sun-bird Islet shortly before Dillon worked there. They were members of an expedition sent to the South Atlantic islands in the schooner *Blossom* by the Cleveland Museum. These five men endured the hardships of the islet for a fortnight, their hands and feet pecked and cut by the birds, choking in the all-pervading guano dust. But they studied the bird life thoroughly and brought back many specimens.

Bo'sun-bird is the breeding place of the Ascension frigate bird, classified two centuries ago by Linnaeus and now known to be at home only on this islet. With a body the size of a hen, it has a wingspan running up to ten feet. Males and females have black plumage. Frigate birds attack other birds fiercely and unexpectedly like the fast-sailing frigates of old; hence the name. A frigate bird will overtake the slower booby or tern, and if the victim does not disgorge its fish immediately, the frigate bird will deliver a crippling blow with its sharp hooked bill. Frigate birds are also known as man-o'-war hawks. (The species found in the Pacific islands are sometimes domesticated and used to carry messages, like pigeons.) Eggs of the frigate bird, white and oval and larger than a duck's egg, are a favourite delicacy among the St Helena people on Ascension.

The Bo'sun bird which gave its name to the islet is the red-billed tropic bird, a white-plumed bird with long tail feathers like white streamers. Wideawakes also jostle for space on the summit. The blue-faced booby breeds on Bo'sun-bird Islet, and rivals the terns and tropic birds as a diver.

You have seen that Ascension is not entirely a desert, but the appeal which this island possesses for many people may still elude you. I will tell you how the secret of Ascension was revealed to me.

It is five in the morning and very dark offshore as the motorboat carries me towards the rock in Clarence Bay which they call Tartar Stairs because of the steps cut in its face. They fish for man-eating sharks from this jetty. A long swell breaks noisily on Dead Man's Beach as we moor the motorboat and step across into the dinghy to go alongside the steps – Bruce of the cable station and I, the eccentric visitor, and two St Helena boatmen.

As the boat rises and falls, as the surf crashes a few yards away, Bruce warns me that landing will not be easy. I assure him that I am at home in small boats and will be in no danger. Bruce then leads the way, reaching for the rope that hangs above the steps. He misses the rope and falls headlong into the dark, noisy sea. I remember the sharks. One boatman and I drag Bruce over the side, while the other boatman shows great skill in keeping the boat out of the surf. During a lull we make the steps at last. Thus I arrive in Ascension for the second time, and walk reflectively round Garrison while Bruce is changing his clothes.

Here is the centre of Ascension's little capital, the double-storied Exiles' Club with the clock presented by Queen Victoria in the naval days. It has wide open doors, and wicker chairs on the long balcony; and I can see that for decade after decade the men and women of Garrison have found pleasure in their drinks on that balcony in the cool trade wind. (No doubt the pleasure is heightened by the fact that whisky is still under six shillings a bottle and gin three shillings.) Here they talk of the life they have known on cable stations as far apart as Cocos and Rio; the lonely places of the earth and the great cities and the crowds. They talk with the voice of experience, and I am still wondering why Ascension ranks so high in their affections. I gaze round the club in search of inspiration.

Three huge turtle shells hang from the walls. The oldest bears the names of every Royal Navy and Royal Marine commander; the next lists the cable managers; and the third gives you the American officers in command of the air base. That first turtle reminds you of

Ascension's tragic past, for it records three commanders in the middle of last century who died on duty and one who was removed.

What is the secret? Before I landed today one cable man told me he had spent two years on the island, the regular period, and had just volunteered to stay on for another six months. (This man had been stationed previously for fifteen years in Alexandria, which is no mean city.) I thought of the farmer who was engaged by the navy as a young man and spent almost his whole life happily on Green Mountain; a brokenhearted old man who had to leave when the navy departed. I recalled a doctor who worked on Ascension for many years, refusing every offer of transfer. Once he went to England on leave and hated it. He said that his return to Ascension was the happiest day of his life.

Yet this was the same island which men once dreaded. "A scraggy, barren rock," wrote a seaman two centuries ago. "Were it not for the famous large turtle it would be known only as a mark in the middle of the ocean to be shunned by navigators." And there was a British general who declared: "St Helena is a rock, Ascension is a cinder."

So what is the secret? A new day is flooding over the neat bungalows and sheltered gardens of Garrison, and I hope it will bring the answer. I can see old Fort Thornton now to the eastward and another battery of Georgian and Victorian cannon to the west. This place is a nautical and military museum starting with the rusting junk of Napoleon's day and ending with aids to atomic warfare piled up on Long Beach by the United States air force. If they land any more drums of fuel there will be no room for the turtles to lay their eggs. But it is not the grey breath of old wars or threat of new ones that holds people on this island. Or the many reminders of past tragedies. I can distinguish the old naval cemetery close to Dead Man's Beach, a name which it gained one day when the rollers swept over the graves and tore them open and littered the beach with skeletons and coffins. Such events only deepen the mystery.

Perhaps they love the beaches and the sea, you say? You must pay a fine of five pounds if they catch you walking on the island beaches; that is, if you come back alive. The treacherous sea that desecrated the cemetery has a way of taking people by surprise on the golden sands. Rollers flood Long Beach and the football field, break over the jetty and damage the crane. Once a nursemaid and two young children were swept away suddenly, never to be seen again, leaving the captain of marines and his wife to grieve for them.

So now the only bathing place is Comfortless Cove, where the cables are brought on shore. Comfortless is a sheltered place among the rocks, with a red-roofed cable house and a banana-leaf hut for bathers. Even here it is dangerous to go far out. Fishing is forbidden while bathers are in the water, because the bait attracts fierce barracuda and sharks. And all the time someone has to watch the narrow entrance to the cove to see that the man-eaters do not enter.

Fishing? I can imagine a keen angler revelling in the fishing. "One afternoon ten of us fished from the pontoon near the jetty," a cable man told me. "We caught over one hundred fish, mainly the local rock-cod." Tunny and wahoo are caught easily enough from motor boats offshore. Every year the "fly" arrive in millions, fish of the *marsbanker* (horse mackerel) family, and are chased right up on to the beach by the tunny. You can pick up stranded *marsbankers* and cavally on Long Beach by the dozen if you get there before the shrieking sea birds.

Cavally are often speared from the pontoon, smoked and sent to St Helena. Crawfish are easily caught in nets, and you can find oysters and crabs to vary the shellfish menu. Most plentiful of all the Ascension fish is the black turbot or trigger fish (just "blackfish" on the island), a scavenger which loves seaweed and will clean the hull of any ship in the anchorage. Finest table fish is the conger. Each householder pays seven shillings and sixpence a month, which covers the cost of sending a fishing boat out on every calm day. Each afternoon a selection of fresh fish are dropped into all the kitchen sinks on the island. For that reason the cable people eat meat for lunch, as a rule, and plan fish suppers.

What else has Ascension to offer? Good mutton from the mountain, and occasional beef steak flown in from America, bananas from the island farm, wild guavas for making jelly, and paw-paw, grape fruit, grenadillas and tomatoes. A little mineral water factory in Garrison produces sodas, ginger beer and tonics at twopence halfpenny a bottle. And for the vases on verandah tables there are the mountain flowers called "poppers" that come down wrapped in ferns and wild ginger leaves. Or carnations from your own garden if you have been careful.

I think the cable wives like the island because housekeeping is easy, because everyone is healthy and young children flourish. A year or more may pass without a death on the cable station. (There were about fifty white people when I was last there, and one hundred and fifty St Helenans.) With a library and an open-air cinema, tennis courts and the worst golf course in the world (thanks to the clinker) no one need be bored.

You can still live more cheaply in Ascension than in the cities. All a man needs in the way of clothes are shirts, shorts and tropical mess kit. A motor car is not a necessity, though cars have been used there since 1931, and there are now several modern cars as well as the original pioneer baby car and a number of motorcycles. The navy had a system of rails and trolleys throughout Garrison, but tarmac and dust roads have been made since then. But even now it is impossible to avoid the cruel clinker. A set of tyres lasts for no more than three thousand miles. No one becomes attached to Ascension because of the motoring, for it is no pleasure; merely a means of reaching the mountain and the American zone.

Green Mountain, which I have called a paradise, explains some of the charm of Ascension, and there is no doubt that without that mountain the island would be regarded as a melancholy rock of exile. It is the contrast that makes a stay on the mountain so memorable. The cable men take one week's local leave every six months. On the mountain they can walk and climb and breathe a different air. Above all they enjoy the fire in the grate at night, something unknown down below.

As I stand here on the club balcony gazing out over Garrison the St Helenan servants are going to work. There is no mystery about their love for Ascension. They sign contracts for two years, and most of them try to remain longer before returning to their own poverty-stricken island. Ascension gives them security and good meals for two years at a stretch. A trained male cook receives seven pounds a month, and regards it as wealth. Some of the St Helenan cable employees earn extra money by cooking and doing other housework in their spare time.

Everyone finds work to do on Ascension, for that is one of the obvious ways of living happily in isolation. From top to bottom you meet people doing more than one job. The cable manager has two desks in his office; one for the problems of submarine telegraphy and wireless; the other for use when he has to sit in judgment as magistrate or deal with the administration of the island. Another cable official acts as club secretary and lay reader in church. The doctor is also the island registrar and marriage officer. With only one ship a month to handle, as a rule, the harbourmaster is easily able to manage the canteen and act as clerk of the court; and his wife is the postmistress. When your shoes need mending you take them to the baker. The butcher is a first-class cook and waiter. Joshua, the power house attendant, will cut your hair.

In the dawn, before the sun blazes harshly on the abominable clinker, Garrison makes a mellow and comfortable picture of a self-contained, seaside world. Now I can understand something that baffled me for a long time. A bachelor like myself might easily suffer from "Ascensionitis" in this place, a well-known form of nerves or state of dissatisfaction which cannot be cured with gin at three shillings a bottle – though some have tried. But a man with a family might find this easygoing life very much to his taste. (As for his wife, one of them remarked to me: "I like Ascension because there are no social problems – everyone knows his place.") It is a friendly place. If you have travelled the world you must know that people in small, remote places tend to share their pleasures and usually manage to create a more hospitable, mellow atmosphere than the lonely people of the cities.

All day and all night the busy cable lines from Britain and South America, West Africa and South Africa, chatter away through the Ascension listening post. You would say that these people could never forget the urgent outside world . . . but they can. Ascension, the contented little suburbia in mid-ocean, has become their world. They are concerned with their own affairs, and satisfied with the safe and cheerful daily round in Garrison, with the mountain as an outlet when the clinker becomes monotonous.

They leave Ascension with their memories of the cries of the wideawakes, the chirping of millions of crickets after the rare rain, the tremendous crashing on the beaches when the rollers come up, the loudest sound of all. They remember the starlit nights and quiet dawns, and the sun coming up serenely over the wide, unbroken ocean. And if you told them that Ascension was a grim, weird island they would look at you in wonder. Ascension gave them peace of mind.

SOUTH AFRICAN BEACHCOMBER

Isle of Dead Ships
1960

In days of sail the Tristan da Cunha islanders became famous for their bravery in rescuing shipwrecked crews. Many sailing ships passed the peak of Tristan to check their chronometers, and some called at this "larder of the South Atlantic" after months at sea for fresh meat and vegetables. Thirteen sailing ships were lost on the Tristan group last century.

The hospitality shown by the islanders to survivors brought them honours and awards: a signed portrait of Queen Victoria, gold watches, cash and stores. After the wreck of the *Allanshaw* the British government sent a gift of a hundred pounds to Tristan. This was the strangest disaster of all.

Not that the other shipwrecks lacked drama. A great Tristan lifesaver for half a century was Peter Green. He was shipwrecked there himself in the schooner *Emily* and remained to become the patriarch and ruler of the island. Under his guidance the islanders risked their lives and shared their last crusts with castaways. One crew had to be fed for nearly a year before they were taken away.

In the Hagan home on Tristan I saw the nameboard of the American ship *Mabel Clark* forming part of the panelling over the fireplace. One of her crew married a daughter of Peter Green; and indeed shipwrecks supplied almost the only fresh blood in this little community. No wonder so many Tristan children were named after ships that had come to grief there! The bells that call the Tristan islanders to church are the bells of the *Mabel Clark*.

Rats came to Tristan when the *Henry B. Paul* was wrecked in the Eighties of last century. Those rats have impoverished the island. They also brought the ferocious fleas which sent me, and the naval chaplain, to the cruiser's sick bay for ointment after the ordeal of nights on shore. It was suspected that the *Henry B. Paul* and another ship, the *Edward Vittery,* were run aground at Tristan for the insurance money. However, the ordinary hazards of the sea were such that four large sailing ships were lost on the Tristan group between 1870 and 1872.

The loss of the *Allenshaw* was different from all the others. One of her crew, an able seaman named Paddy Saunders, settled in Cape Town. He had been in three shipwrecks within two years, and he would go to sea no more. I owe the story of the *Allenshaw* to Saunders; while the sequel formed another of the experiences of my old islander friend John Hagan.

The *Allenshaw* was a full-rigged iron ship of sixteen hundred tons, one of James Nourse's "coolie ships". She sailed out of Liverpool in February 1893, bound for India with a cargo of salt; and as a rule she picked up indentured Indian labourers at Calcutta and carried them to Natal, Mauritius and other places. But this was the last voyage of a fine ship. She was classed 100 A1 at Lloyd's; she had a full crew of real seamen; and she was doomed.

She was doomed because her thirty-year-old Irish master, Captain A.C. Thomson, was a madman. No one knew that when the *Allenshaw* sailed. It was not long, however, before everyone realised that Thomson was a hermit. He talked to Stewart Waters, the mate, and the other two officers only to ask questions or give orders, and rarely did he speak to any of the men before the mast. When the *Allenshaw* reached the open sea he came on deck once a day at noon with his sextant to fix the position.

Paddy Saunders found that three men in the fo'c'sle held masters' certificates, while two others had served as officers. Several of them owned sextants, and they annoyed the master and mates by working out the ship's position from time to time.

Saunders also remembered that five seamen squinted. Old sailor-men regarded even one cross-eyed shipmate as unlucky; five were deadly. In addition, an apprentice named Roberts chanced to remark that every ship he had sailed in had been wrecked. So the *Allenshaw* had more than enough Jonahs to sink her.

"I could see that the captain was worried about something, but I only found out what it was later," Saunders told me. "He never talked to me. I studied him during my trick at the wheel, however, and his abnormal state of mind was obvious."

Thirty days out, and the captain's madness became a little more plain. He ordered the men to remove all equipment from the lifeboats – masts and sails, oars and rudders, water and food. Everything was stowed away below and the boats were swung inboard and lashed securely.

On the morning of March 23 the peak of Tristan was sighted dead ahead, and the fine ship *Allenshaw* raced towards the island at twelve knots with all sail set. At two that afternoon the *Allenshaw* was still heading for the island. All hands, with the possible exception of the master, knew that she was too close for safety.

One of the seamen who held a master's certificate went to the wheel at two that afternoon. He tried to edge away from the island, altering course to the south'ard from time to time when the captain went below. But the captain had a telltale compass in his cabin, and soon he ran up the ladder shouting: "Damn you, keep her on her course."

Some of the men went to Waters, the mate, and begged him to take charge of the ship before it was too late. Waters was a careful Scot, a married man with a family. He was afraid to make the move which might have lost him not only his job but his certificate. How often in the history of the sea has a mate taken it upon himself to lock up his captain and take command of the ship?

So all hands stood waiting for the end of the *Allenshaw,* and most of them must have felt their hearts beating faster. Until the last moment they hoped that the captain would give the order to alter course, but never a word did he utter. At two forty-five that afternoon the captain went below and Waters called to the helmsman: "Mind your helm, we're getting close to the land."

"Helm coming up, sir," called the man at the wheel.

Even then the ship might have been saved; but at that moment the captain returned on deck, sent Waters for'ard, and put the ship back on her course for destruction. Next moment the ship grated, jarred and struck heavily. "Let go all sheets and halfyards," yelled the mad captain.

She remained fast, listing, with the seas breaking over her.

"Get the boats away," the captain ordered.

This was no easy matter in view of the state of the boats. They cut the lashings away, however, and one lifeboat and the gig were launched at last.

Captain Thomson sat by himself in a damaged boat with his arms folded. "Come on, sir – jump for it," Waters shouted to him. "We'll pick you up."

"Never mind me – save yourselves," called back the captain. Soon afterwards a sea struck the boat and the captain was washed overboard and drowned.

Twenty-six men were now afloat in the two boats in a rough sea. They had no oars, thanks to the captain, but they tore up the bottom boards and paddled away from the ship. Roberts, the "Jonah" apprentice, an able seaman named McDonald, another seaman and the sailmaker, were clinging to the mizzen rigging. Evidently they thought they were safer there than in the lifeboats, and hoped the boats would return for them when the sea was calm.

That afternoon several islanders, including seventeen-year-old John Hagan, were gathering penguin eggs from the Cave Point rookeries. They saw the *Allenshaw* strike, and watched two boats making for the line of surf. Hurrying down to the shore, the islanders were in time to point out the safest landing place. One boat upset in the surf, and the exhausted men would have been drowned if the islanders had not rushed into the sea and dragged them out of the breakers. John Hagan found that he had saved the life of young George Collis, third mate.

Soon afterwards the *Allenshaw* broke her back, snapped in two amidships and sank. Part of the mizzen mast still jutted above the surface with the four men who had remained on board.

They were in great danger. Two of them, a seaman Bompach and the sailmaker, swam for the shore and were hauled out of the surf more dead than alive. At daybreak the sea was a little calmer and the islanders ventured out to the wreck in one of their canvas boats. They picked up a few cases of stores, but saw nothing of the seaman McDonald and the "Jonah" apprentice Roberts. The mizzen had gone during the night, taking the two men who had been clinging to it.

So the survivors pulled round to the Tristan settlement with the islanders and were taken into the homes of the fifty people living

273

there at that time. Peter Green, the ruler, celebrated his eighty-fifth birthday while they were there. George Collis was given shelter by John Hagan's mother. Collis and Hagan became inseparable.

Fortunately the Cape station flagships, H.M.S. *Raleigh,* had called a few days before and left a good supply of tea, cocoa, coffee, flour and other groceries which the islanders could not produce. Food was more plentiful in those days, for although the rats had arrived, there were fewer mouths to feed. Paddy Saunders, who stayed with Betty Cotton, spoke to me fondly of the shredded crawfish fried in butter, and the potatoes mashed in milk and butter, served in that household.

"Money, liquor, tobacco and swear words were all unknown among the deeply religious Tristan islanders while we were there," Saunders recalled. "Some of the girls were so shy that I was never able to talk to them the whole time I was on the island."

Early in April the barque *Clan Ferguson* appeared off the island. Waters, as the senior officer, intercepted her and asked for a passage. His request was refused, and the master would do nothing more than accept letters. Two weeks later the Italian barque *Beppo* was intercepted. Again the captain sailed on without the *Allenshaw's* survivors.

"I suppose they took us for a gang of pirates," commented Paddy Saunders. "The Italians threw two of our fellows into the sea and cut the boat painter. We were a wild looking crowd by that time – bearded and in rags."

However, a humanitarian captain was on the way. He was master of the German barque *Theodore,* and he agreed at once to take the whole crew. The men had been on Tristan for three months.

Two of the *Allenshaw's* mates decided to remain on Tristan. One of them, G.H. Cartwright, married one of the Hagan girls and stayed on Tristan for a year before bringing his wife to Cape Town. The other officer who had come to love the lonely island was George Collis; and he, too, lived on Tristan until Cartwright and his wife left.

But that was not the end of the story. An inquiry into the loss of the *Allenshaw* was held in Cape Town, with Mr P. Nightingale presiding and Captain M.H. Penfold as nautical assessor. Waters told the court that he had read the sailing directions and knew that it was not safe to approach within two miles of the southern shore of Tristan. He had warned Captain Thomson that he was going in too close, but his words were disregarded. "I did not speak again because the captain was a difficult man who disliked interference," Waters declared. The court found that there was nothing to show that Captain Thomson of the *Allenshaw* was not sober. "Unhappily the disaster resulted in the loss of his own life and two of the crew, besides the total destruction of a fine ship and cargo," the magistrate went on. "The loss was due to a very great error of judgment on the part of the master. The first mate, seeing that the ship was close to the shore, should have remonstrated with the master. However, the court considers that this admonition is sufficient."

Apparently no one felt like informing the court that Captain Thomson was suffering from some mental disease when he sailed the *Allenshaw* deliberately on to the rocks of Tristan. One secret which never reached the court was revealed to me by Paddy Saunders. He went round to the scene of the wreck several weeks afterwards with some islanders who were anxious to see whether anything useful had drifted ashore.

"I found a waterproof wallet containing a portrait of a girl and some letters she had written to Captain Thomson – among them a letter breaking off her engagement to him," Saunders told me. "It seemed that no good purpose would be served by keeping the letters and I burnt them on the spot."

So that was the secret of Captain Thomson's madness. One more sequel to the wreck of the *Allenshaw* rounds off this weird story.

John Hagan landed in Cape Town towards the end of last century, knowing nothing of the world outside the lonely island. "I had five pounds in my pocket and a lot of hope in my heart," Hagan informed me. "I had no friends in Cape Town, but I knew that I had a staunch friend in George Collis, wherever he might be."

Collis went back to sea and sailed as master in a number of ships. Strange to say, he called only once at the Cape, and then his friend John Hagan was away up-country. Nevertheless, they kept in touch for more than half a century. Collis sent presents which were treasured by Hagan – a set of whale's teeth, a walking stick and other things. "I shall never forget the kindness you and your mother showed me," Collis wrote.

Collis settled at Westgate-on-Sea in England when he retired. He often talked to his friends of Tristan, and planned to revisit the island in a small yacht. This scheme had to be abandoned, however, owing to ill-health. Shortly before his death in 1947, Collis wrote to his old friend John Hagan: "I want to leave you something to remember me by."

Hagan was in bed with heart trouble, an old man living with difficulty on a small pension. He had the doctor's bills to meet, and he was worried about the money he still owed on his house at Woodstock.

Then came news of the death of Collis, the friend of his youth. Later there arrived a letter from a lawyer. Poor old John Hagan had inherited fifteen hundred pounds.

That was the end of the story of the *Allenshaw,* fifty-five years after Hagan had risked his life in the Tristan surf and made a lifelong friend.

EIGHT BELLS AT SALAMANDER

Tales of the Sea

These stories of ships and the harbours which shelter them are typical of the offbeat and interesting tales which Lawrence Green revived and presented to his readers.

"Russian Armada off the Cape" is a strange account of the Russian fleet's ill-fated expedition in 1904 to fight the Japanese – then an isolated and secret race. It illustrates the differences between the primitive life of the ordinary Russian sailor and the luxurious existence of his officers. It was contrasts such as these which were, even then, building resentments which would lead to the Russian Revolution in 1917.

When Green wrote "Three Men Survived" in 1960, he remarked that there were probably still some people living who lost friends or relations in the *Drummond Castle* which sank in 1896.

Today, a quarter of a century later, there can be nobody left who remembers this shipwreck. Time has taken away much of the tragedy and left the drama and excitement. Death was minutes away for all but three of the two hundred and forty-five passengers and crew who celebrated their final night aboard the liner on her voyage from Cape Town to London.

The boisterous history of Port Elizabeth is made even more vivid by the accounts of two old-timers who clearly remembered the city in the 1850s, when it was little more than a village.

These and other dramatic records of lone sailors, stranded castaways, and the mysterious legend of The Flying Dutchman are all to be found in this selection of nautical Green.

The Story of Simonstown

1947

One harbour on the shores of South Africa is still stamped as plainly as Portsmouth with the marks of the Royal Navy. This corner of England is called Simonstown.* These white-faced houses, rising in steep terraces from the waters of False Bay, have watched much drama of the sea. In the traces that remain, figureheads and tombstones, old masonry and cannon, you may see the shadows recalling centuries of adventure.

Simonstown has not been transformed like the ships that find anchorage in the bay. Where are the pirate brigs now, the frigates, corvettes, sloops, even the early iron-clads with their sharp prows? It is not so long ago since wicked black slavers were towed in here to be broken on the beach. Not long, indeed, since *Erebus* and *Terror* sailed in, fresh from their conquest of the Antarctic.

Winter gales in Table Bay drove the Dutch East India Company to seek a more secure anchorage. They found it in the bay then known as Yselstein; and before long a hospital, powder magazine, forges, slaughter house and staff quarters appeared beside Simon's Bay. Forts were built, garrisoned and armed so that cannon balls could be sent red-hot from the furnaces to stop an invader. A martello tower still stands, the only one of its kind in South Africa; a somewhat mysterious building which is supposed to have been used by the company as a lookout station.

Some of the old, shuttered houses in steep alleys and cobbled lanes were built in the days of Dutch occupation. Others, with their

---

* Since Green wrote this tale the official name of the town has reverted to the historic "Simon's Town". – *Ed.*

dense gardens of cactus and aloes, were there when H.M.S. *Pluto* steamed into Simon's Bay in 1828, the first steam-driven fighting ship to visit the southern outpost of the Navy. Admiralty House, purchased for about ten thousand pounds, has been in the possession of the navy for well over a century, a stately residence indeed with its bougainvillaea and famous lawn.

Among interesting relics in the grounds is a headstone in memory of Mr Percival George Duddy, midshipman, who died off the Cape of Good Hope on April 26, 1828, after a lingering illness borne with extreme fortitude and resignation, occasioned by a fall from the mizzen top. *Aet.* 16 years . . . a small token to departed juvenile worth. Two guns below the croquet courts bear the royal arms of Portugal; they were taken from a Portuguese slaver.

Simonstown's oldest house is probably The Residency, next to Admiralty House. The Residency, used as police court and magistrate's office, is believed to have been the residence of the governor in Dutch East India Company's days. It was a naval hospital early last century. Lord Nelson walked on the flag-stoned stoep as a young lieutenant. In one of the cells opening on to the courtyard are the original stocks into which prisoners were locked long ago. Some of the doors at The Residency were once cabin doors on board an East Indiaman.

It is recorded that one bygone admiral, whose flagship had an evil reputation for rolling in the long Cape combers, always travelled by bullock wagon when his ship sailed round from Simon's Bay to Table Bay. For a long time the weekly wagon was the only official link between the two towns. In summer the Table Bay anchorage was preferred, for then the south-east hurricanes swooped down on Simon's Bay with such violence that once a flagship was cut off from communication with the shore for a fortnight.

From this base strange coasts were surveyed; ships left for tropic seas and the southern ice; foreign craft were brought in as prizes; naval expeditions were sent inland to take part in the little wars of South Africa. The convict ship *Neptune* lay off Simonstown for weeks, guarded from the angry colonists. Sail-driven, paddle-driven, screw-driven – a long procession of ships. There was the *Badger,* commanded by the young Lieutenant Horatio Nelson, afterwards a hulk in this harbour. Some ships were kept in commission for more than fifty years, H.M.S. *Seringpatam,* for example, which became the flagship of the Cape station after service as a coal hulk! Such changes are not seen today.

Ships from this port prowled round St Helena when Napoleon was there, and sailed without authority in an attempt to blockade the Plate and seize the Argentine. Tales of all the peril and tragedy of the sea were heard in these streets. Mutinies, floggings, hangings; there was even a "Court of Piracy" held on board one old flagship. As the years passed, the roll of lost ships grew longer; ships that met disaster on unchartered rocks, like the *Birkenhead,* or struck icebergs in the Southern Ocean. There was a convict ship once, the *Guardian,* which was brought waterlogged to the Cape after a struggle that lasted nine weeks.

After the Napoleonic wars the ships from Simon's Bay concentrated on a new enemy, the slavers. Here was a chance for midshipmen, some of them officers who became famous in the service. They chased the slavers into every creek from Sierra Leone to the Congo and further south, and escorted many a captured vessel into Simon's Bay. There was a slave depot for the freed cargoes in Simonstown then – Black Town, the people called it. The naval cemetery on the hillside remains as evidence of many desperate fights with privateers and slavers; it reflects, too, the toll of the seas and the African climate.

There were times when the long main street of Simonstown was paved with gold for the storekeepers who traded with the navy. Before the Suez Canal, the inns were crowded with officials and fine women bound for India – a gay throng, known humorously as "Hindoos", eating their curries and drinking their punch and wine. Squadrons of French, Russian and American ships called, too, and on such occasions life in Simonstown was more brilliant than the far larger Cape Town, twenty-two miles away. Huge wooden buildings were erected specially for the naval balls, and fireworks entertained those outside.

No doubt there are people in Simonstown who remember the New Bedford whalers, the dingy "spouters" that called at Simon's Bay in scores to fill their water casks. These smoky black square-riggers must have presented a sharp contrast with the smart and gleaming men-o'-war in the anchorage. A large iron cauldron, excavated near Simonstown recently, and thought to be a hundred years old, recalled the stirring days of whale chasing in False Bay. Whales were dragged on shore, cut up and "tried out" in the pots on the present Seaforth bathing beach. I heard the story in Simonstown of an American whaleship captain who arrived there after a voyage that had lasted two years. "What luck?" he was asked. "Wal, I haven't got any whales yet," he replied, "but I've had a darned good sail." The shore whaling industry at Simonstown flourished for years, and I believe it would not be impossible today to find a harpooner and boat's crew. Years ago I knew an aged Tristan da Cunha Islander, William Cotton, who had settled at Simonstown with his son George, and had taken part in many whale hunts. Sperm whales and humpbacks visited False Bay in great numbers, even in the early years of this century. One day the watchers on the mountainside sighted the fountains of thin vapour betraying a school of whales. There was an American whaleship at anchor, and her boats were soon away, racing the local boats. A wounded whale smashed one of the Simonstown boats and tossed it in the air. One of the American harpooners then saw his chance, leapt on to the whale's back and killed it with a skilful thrust of the lance.

For nearly thirty years an aerial railway ran from the dockyard to the naval sanatorium on the mountain top. Steel towers supported the wire rope and the neat passenger car. Apart from sick men, thousands of others, including the Prince of Wales, made the trip. Naval ratings bound for the rifle ranges, and parties hurrying to beat out mountain fires, were carried by this railway. It closed in 1932, when a motor road was built to the summit.

The dockyard at Simonstown was once policed by a special little force recruited from the London Metropolitan Police and naval pensioners. They wore a distinctive uniform, very much like London bobbies, except in the heat of summer. Then they appeared in cool white duck.

Simonstown has known the strain of several wars since the day in 1795 when the red-coated English soldiers took the town. Undoubtedly the most feverish period was from 1939 to 1945, when the blackout was complete and the dockyard worked to a higher tempo than ever before. The peacetime payroll of five hundred men grew to more than five thousand men and women. Early in the war the

Carnarvon Castle was transformed from a mail ship to an armed merchant cruiser. During those grim years, ships damaged in collision and shattered in battle were dry-docked, repaired and sent into battle again. Altogether three hundred and thirty ships were repaired at Simonstown. *Queen Elizabeth, Queen Mary, Mauretania, Aquitania* and *Empress of Britain* were among the two thousand ships that called during the war years.

Yet Simonstown does not change much, as I have said. Old ships have departed; *Rattlesnake, Monarch, Boadicea, Raleigh* and tiny vessels like *Tickler, Gadfly* and *Griper* are seen no more at the moorings. The inn kept by Mynheer Vanderskippe has vanished. But seamen still march past the old-fashioned houses. London seems much nearer to the Simonstown tradition than does Pretoria. Simonstown, indeed, is in touch with the ports and the oceans of the world, through the ghosts of men and ships.

TAVERN OF THE SEAS

Man Overboard

1960

One day in 1926 the Union Castle freighter *Ripley Castle* steamed in from the United States. As a waterfront reporter I went on board hopefully to find out whether anything had happened during the long, hot run. "There's a trimmer named Tony Madison who might tell you a story," remarked the chief officer, Mr John Crombie Brown.

Tony Madison, I found, was a thirty-five-year-old American of some education who had never worked at sea before signing on aboard the *Ripley Castle* in Philadelphia. In the tropics, he told me, the work in the stokehold became unbearable for a new hand. The "black gang" staggered about half-naked, almost blinded by the flames licking out of the glowing furnace doors. Sweat ran hot on their necks and arms and trickled into their boots. Even the old hands cursed between the clanging of shovels and grinding of barrow-loads of coal from the bunkers.

It was like that one Sunday night just after the *Ripley Castle* had crossed the equator. The ship was steaming at ten knots with a gentle following breeze, which meant no air at all down below. Eight bells sounded midnight, and Tony Madison tumbled out of his bunk in the fo'c'sle, grabbed a piece of ship's biscuit, swigged a cup of water, and stumbled away over the dark well-deck, up the ladder, along the deck to the "fiddley" and down to the stokehold.

Ventilators and wind bags were useless that night. The firemen were roasted alive, but steam pressure had to be maintained, the relentless fires had to be fed. Cleaning the furnaces was agony, for when the red-hot coals came tumbling out they had to be sluiced with water, and that filled the stokehold with steam.

At last the strain became too great for Tony Madison. The leading fireman saw that he was fainting and ordered him up on deck for a breath of air so that he might recover his strength and carry on down below during the rest of the watch. Half-dazed, with head swimming and eyes aching, Madison crawled up the steel ladder.

"I caught a glimpse of the stars – and then the sea closed over my head," Madison told me. "It seems that in my half-conscious state I must have staggered to the side and slipped between the rails into the South Atlantic. As I came to the surface I heard a tremendous noise of foaming water, and saw the creamy wash of the propeller only a few feet away. I cannot imagine why I was not sucked in and cut to pieces."

The shock roused Madison and he shouted wildly. But the lights of the ship were moving steadily away, and he realised that there would be very few hands on deck in the small hours of the morning; just the lookout on the fo'c'sle and one or two men with the officer of the watch on the bridge.

Madison made up his mind that he would keep afloat until he was worn out. The water was warm enough. He struggled out of his boots and trousers and swam slowly in the wake of the ship. It was calm, with only a long swell moving the surface. Each time he came to the top of the swell he could see the lights of the *Ripley Castle* moving steadily southwards. No one had heard him.

"I was almost certain that I was doomed, but I plodded along after the ship with a slow breaststroke," Madison went on. "One faint hope kept me going – that I would be missed in the stokehold and that someone would search for me and raise the alarm. I did not see any visions of my past rising before me; that comes later, I believe, when you are half-drowned. As a matter of fact I did not do much thinking. I just concentrated on keeping in the wake of the ship so that if she did put back to look for me I would be there."

Madison's thoughts were beginning to wander when he was brought back to reality by a sharp pain in the hip, followed by a stab in the calf of the left leg. He grabbed at his calf, and his hand closed over a large fish. The thought of sharks had occurred to him, and he felt relieved. Then he realised that a shoal of voracious fish might be dangerous, and he felt sorry that he had kicked off his trousers.

Sea birds fluttered down close to his head, and Madison thought they might try to pick his eyes out. He had not seen the lights of the ship for some time, but at that moment the swell lifted him and he saw them clearly. "That's the last I shall ever see of the *Ripley Castle*," he told himself. But he kept on swimming.

Meanwhile the end of the watch came on board the *Ripley Castle,* and one of the firemen pointed out that Madison had never returned to duty. By that time Madison had been in the water for forty-five minutes. When the report reached the captain, he swung the ship round dead in her track and steamed back at full speed.

Madison never knew how they found him. He was growing exhausted and sleepy when suddenly he noticed something red – a steamer's port light – right alongside him. He called, with the last of his strength, and saw a lifeboat being lowered. They dragged him over the side of the boat, and he went to sleep at once.

That was Madison's tale, confirmed by Captain Sinclair, master of the *Ripley Castle* and Mr John Crombie Brown, chief officer. For years I remembered that story when other vivid tales, heard along the waterfront, had passed out of my mind. I never really understood how Tony Madison had been found, at night, in the wide South Atlantic, one and a half hours after falling overboard.

More than twenty years afterwards I went on board the mailship *Pretoria Castle* to talk to Captain John Crombie Brown, commodore of the Union-Castle fleet and soon to retire from the sea. Captain Brown was known to his crews as Eternity Brown, for he held Bible classes in his cabin for all who cared to attend. I knew that Captain Brown had been round the world in sail and had served through two world wars. He must have had many escapes and adventures; but I was not prepared for the answer he gave me when I asked him to recall the most desperate episode of his sea career.

"It was that affair of Tony Madison," declared Captain Brown. "I felt conscience-stricken about Madison. This is not the story you heard at the time – it is a much stranger story. You see, Madison had been to me the day before he fell overboard and asked me how he could make his peace with God. I was thinking about my own problems at the time, and I told Madison to call later. When I heard he was missing I felt guilty. He would probably be drowned, and I had not told him.

"So I prayed that I might be given the chance of speaking to Madison again. I asked God to save Tony Madison from the sharks. Then I posted men all along the rails with orders to listen carefully for a shout.

"The ship came back to the position where Madison had gone overboard. I strained my ears and heard the faintest cry, so faint that I wondered whether I was imagining it. Fortunately another man had heard it, too. So I took charge of the lifeboat. As the men pulled away from the ship's side I had to make up my mind which way to steer. Where was the man? I believed that God would answer my prayer, and I steered at random into the darkness. There was dead silence as I shouted: 'Madison ahoy!' Then I shone my torch and saw Madison's head close to the boat. We had him – after he had been in the water for ninety minutes. My prayer had been answered."

*

You might not imagine that an episode such as the escape of Tony Madison could happen twice. It happened again in 1955 with a sixteen-year-old German cabin boy named Wolfgang Horst Emrich as the survivor. His chance was estimated at a million to one. His own ship steamed on for two hours without his absence being noticed, and *he was picked up by another ship*.

Wolfgang fell overboard in exactly the same way as Madison. He was making early morning coffee in the galley of the German tramp steamer *Stechelhoern* when he felt dizzy with heat. He went on deck to cool off, and next moment the ocean smacked him hard in the face. No one heard his shouts.

The *Stechelhoern* had left Las Palmas a few hours previously. She was forty-five miles south when Wolfgang fell overboard. Wolfgang kept his head, noted the course of the ship, then turned in the opposite direction and started the long swim back to Las Palmas.

"I felt lonely," he said. "The wind blew spray into my eyes. I choked when the sea filled my nose and mouth. But I managed to get rid of my boots, then my clothes, so that I was swimming with nothing but my belt with my seaman's knife."

He needed that knife. First a jellyfish wrapped itself round his right arm and stung him painfully. With the aid of the knife he scraped it off. Then a shark circled round him. He could not see whether it was a man-eater or a harmless species, but when it brushed against him he plunged the knife into the shark's side. The shark made off, taking the knife. "I felt lonely again without my knife," said Wolfgang.

Salt water he had swallowed made him vomit. His arm, his eyes and his stomach muscles were sore. But he kept on swimming, using the breaststroke to save his strength, and taking his direction from the sun.

At eight-thirty that morning the captain of the *Stechelhoern* was informed that Wolfgang was missing. He turned back immediately and sent out a wireless request for a search to all ships in the neighbourhood. Captain Arthur of the *City of Lucknow* was not far from the position where, according to the German captain's estimate, Wolfgang had fallen overboard. Captain Arthur altered course and called for all available hands. Eight passengers helped.

Zigzagging again and again over a square of ocean, the *City of Lucknow* carried out the search, faithfully and efficiently, hour after hour. Wolfgang had been in the water for more than five hours when Captain Arthur decided to search an area two miles beyond the point given by the German captain. "I cannot explain what made me do it," declared Captain Arthur.

Cadet Cornes, staring with sun-puckered eyes across the great waters from the stern of the *City of Lucknow*, heard a seagull scream, and followed it down to sea level where a flock of seagulls flew round an object in the water. Was it food? A fragment of driftwood? Suddenly Cadet Cornes leapt to the bridge telephone. He had sighted Wolfgang.

A well-drilled crew took the lifeboat away in record time, with the second officer urging the men to row faster and faster. They were not going to lose him now. They did not lose him.

Wolfgang was found by the surgeon of the liner to be suffering from pneumonia, exposure and jellyfish stings. It was impossible to send him back to the *Stechelhoern*, and he remained in the liner's sick bay for days before he recovered. He owed his life to the fact that he was a strong swimmer (winner of many contests); to the hovering seagulls; to the watchfulness of a young cadet; and to something more, a mysterious impulse felt by John Crombie Brown in the search for Tony Madison and Captain Arthur when he turned in a certain direction without knowing why he was doing it.

So Wolfgang Emrich landed in Cape Town and found himself, as an anticlimax, in the immigration detention barracks. It seems that if you are picked up miraculously at sea you still rank as a stowaway. That did not last long, and Wolfgang returned to Germany as a passenger. "It all sounds a story tall enough to arouse the envy of Munchausen," commented a Cape Town newspaper. "Yet it happened. We wonder whether any of our readers with a memory for amazing rescues and freak escapes can recall any more surprising than the survival of Wolfgang Emrich."

Nearly thirty years had passed and they had all forgotten Tony Madison, the man who was picked up in total darkness as the answer to John Crombie Brown's prayer.

It happened a third time on the Cape run in April 1957, when an Italian seaman, Giovanni Sigona, jumped from the steamer *Northern Gulf* because his shipmates had made his life a misery. He was not trying to commit suicide. "I felt sure some other ship would find me," declared Giovanni Sigona.

He was in the cold water one hundred miles west of Cape Town for thirty hours before a ship came along. Thoughtfully the Italian had provided himself with two cork life jackets and a copper bar to fight off sharks. He floated, numb with cold, until the tanker *British Premier* came along and rescued him. Giovanni Sigona recovered in a Cape Town nursing home.

These were all miracles indeed. Let me add a few points which may not be generally realised. In calm weather a ship can often follow her track in reverse by keeping to the "lane" of rubbish which marks her passage. Litter may remain afloat long enough to lead the way back to the person who has fallen overboard. Such a person may be sighted by a keen lookout with binoculars at a distance of four miles.

If you search the modern records of the sea you will find comparatively few people who have fallen overboard accidentally as did Tony Madison and Wolfgang Emrich. It was different in the days of sail. But now any shipmaster will tell you that the "man overboard" is usually attempting suicide. On rare occasions people are pushed overboard. Not long ago a senior Union-Castle captain stated that in forty years at sea he had never known one person to fall over-board by accident.

EIGHT BELLS AT SALAMANDER

Russian Armada Off The Cape

1960

Signalman Harvey called his wife and gave her the telescope. It was the most dramatic scene he had ever known during his years in charge of the lookout station on Signal Hill. "Russians all right – sixteen of 'em," he announced. "No good calling them up though. They must be thirty miles offshore."

For days everyone from Cape Town to Cape Point had been awaiting news of the Russian fleet. An incident early in the voyage had almost led to war between Britain and Russia; and it seemed possible that the incident might be repeated when the blundering Russians entered South African waters. Night after night the Simonstown batteries had been manned at full strength. Even in far-away Natal, fifty mounted police troopers had been sent to the coast to stand by the obsolete guns on the Bluff and Durban beach.

It was 1904, and Tsarist Russia was at war with little, unknown Japan. The Japanese, who had only recently emerged from mediaeval ways, had been winning battle after battle on land and sea in the Far East. So the Russians had assembled a great fleet in the Baltic to steam across the world and vanquish their enemies.

It was a mighty fleet on paper. Manned by better seamen, it might have been a powerful fleet. But the Russians were doomed from the moment their Tsar gave his approval.

Russian naval officers of that period sought comfortable shore billets rather than sea experience. They preferred vodka and pink champagne, graft and bribery, to gunnery and manoeuvres. Among them were counts and princes; cruel, self-indulgent and inefficient. They knocked their men down and ordered floggings without allowing the victims to speak in their own defence. They wore uniform arrogantly at all times; on shore and afloat, usually with dirty collars. They smoked their little Russian cigarettes at all times, on and off duty. The ratings, many of them recruited far inland and poorly trained, were stupid *muziks*. Sometimes they were mutinous.

Such was the personnel of the fleet which was sent out under the elderly Admiral Rozhestvensky to meet those patriotic fanatics, the Japanese. Rozhestvensky had forty ships and twelve thousand men; but he had to steam eighteen thousand miles and he needed half a million tons of coal for the voyage. Only the Russians could have planned such a fiasco.

Only the nervous Russians could have mistaken trawlers in the North Sea for Japanese torpedo boats. In the confusion that night they sank a British trawler and killed two British fishermen. They also opened fire on each other and killed a Russian priest. Britain sent an ultimatum to Russia.

Although the incident was settled when the Russians paid full compensation, some uneasiness remained. King Edward VII wrote to his foreign secretary: "I really think that we see daylight, and what has been a most grave and serious incident may pass away quietly, and perhaps we may be on a better footing with Russia later. They must, however, see that the world cannot tolerate their fleet opening fire on any ship they meet that comes within reasonable distance."

Rozhestvensky had been warned during the voyage that he would encounter fishing vessels in South African waters, and that any repetition of the North Sea incident would be "highly undesirable". He was inclined to be truculent. Russian agents had informed him that a flotilla of schooners, armed with torpedo tubes and disguised as fishing craft, were awaiting him at Durban. It was said that Rear-Admiral Sionogu of the Japanese Navy was in charge of this secret mission. So Rozhestvensky replied that any fishing vessel which approached or tried to break through his squadrom would be ruthlessly destroyed. Hence the suspense in Cape Town as the Russians moved southwards.

It was a slow progress. The queerly-assorted Russian fleet was led by the eighteen-knot flagship *Kniaz Suvaroff*, a heavily-armoured battleship of fifteen thousand tons with three sisters, *Borodino*, *Alexander III* and *Oryol*. They were painted black, like most Russian warships, with yellow funnels. They had twelve-inch guns and rams. But other ships were less impressive. The old battleship *Oslyabya* seemed to be top-heavy. Another ship, *Dimitri Donskoy*, had been a square-rigged frigate; now, with engines that gave her only ten knots, she was on her way to a naval battle.

One vessel named *Kamchatka* was purely a repair shop, and it was not long before the naval ratings and civilian engineers on board came to blows. Another ship was filled by a plant which provided drinking water from the sea. A white hospital ship, the *Oryol* (not to be confused with the battleship) was regarded by the Russian seamen as a floating palace and haven of rest. Thousands of men longed to be taken ill and transferred to her. Morale was low in the doomed fleet of Admiral Rozhestvensky.

Rozhestvensky had many nightmares, but coal loomed even larger in his mind at first than the Japanese enemy. His ships needed ten thousand tons of coal a day. He could not expect help in any British or Portuguese colonial port, but the Germans were friendly and the French were observing a sort of benevolent neutrality. Sixty colliers and storeships of a German line had been chartered. Early in November 1904, Rozhestvensky met them at Tangier, his first African port. There he decided to split up his fleet.

His reasons were obscure, but it is possible that he feared some of his ancient iron-clads might capsize off the Cape if they ran into heavy weather. All the ships were overloaded. Many of them carried too great a weight of armour above the waterline. In some the stability had been affected by unnecessary top-hamper in the shape of amenities for officers. It was a Russian naval tradition that officers should live in luxury. Rozhestvensky had ordered the officers to stow coal in every corner, including their own cabins; but the top-hamper remained.

Food was another problem. Strange to say, this grim and inefficient navy fed its men fairly well. Peter the Great had hanged three pursers for serving bad food. Now the men expected liberal rations of tea, meat and vegetable stew, and a quarter of a pint of vodka a day. Every ship was stacked with barrels of salt meat, biscuit and cases of vodka. With all this cargo, the Russian fleet steamed with lower decks almost awash.

So only the most seaworthy ships came by the Cape route. They were the up-to-date flagship and her sister battleships, the older *Oslyabya*, the odd but seaworthy old *Dimitri Donskoy*, the cruisers *Admiral Nakhimoff* and *Aurora*, transports, store ships and colliers and the hospital ship. All the rest went through Suez to meet their new admiral at a Madagascar port.

It was slow, as I have said, and the Russians soon felt the heat of the tropics. While they coaled at Dakar an officer dropped dead. Mutiny after mutiny was reported by harassed captains. Rozhestvensky signalled threats all round the suffering fleet, and some he carried out.

He had two nieces among the high-born nursing staff in the hospital ship. One night an unexpected searchlight revealed a boat from the *Dimitri Donskoy* with a lieutenant, two midshipmen and a nurse in it, returning to the hospital ship after a party in the old frigate. According to a French newspaper, the admiral placed the three officers in an open boat with food and water and ordered them to row back to Russia for court-martial. In a circular the admiral referred to the "example of profound depravity" set by these officers, and declared that everyone might reap the consequences.

They coaled again at the French port of Libreville in equatorial Africa. Owing to faulty navigation they crossed the equator more than once trying to find the place. When the admiral landed at this wild spot, French officials told him that cannibals had eaten two white men shortly before his arrival. However, the seamen bought monkeys and parrots, and all hands enjoyed the pineapples, bananas and mangoes. Some of the captains wished the divers to examine the hulls of their ships for defects, but there were too many sharks about.

Great Fish Bay was the next coaling port. This is a huge sandspit harbour in Angola, the last Portuguese desert outpost before South West Africa is reached. Of course the Russians had no right to be there, but they knew the bay was inhabited only by fishermen. However, the Portuguese gunboat *Limpopo* (with one small gun) greeted them and asked them to leave. Rozhestvensky sent an insulting reply. The *Limpopo* steamed away to carry the news to the governor-general, and Rozhestvensky delivered his final message: "Goodbye, little one. Pleasant passage. By the time you have crawled to the Royal Navy for help, not one of us will be here."

Then came Luderitz, a cheerless, open roadstead but a port where the small German population welcomed the Russians. A gale blew up soon after the fleet arrived. After a delay the coaling started; but warships and colliers were damaged as they rolled heavily side by side. "Men are going out of their minds in the fleet," wrote Chief Engineer Eugene Politovsky to his wife. "It is impossible to sleep as the rats have greatly increased. Some of the ships have lost their anchors. The divers fear sharks, but they have to go down all the same."

At last the coaling was finished. A sub-lieutenant in the battleship *Oryol* had gone mad, racing about the decks shouting: "The Japs are waiting for us. We shall all be sunk." But the hospital ship had gone on to Cape Town (where she was admitted under the Red Cross flag) and the demented officer had to be locked in his cabin.

"Happy voyage and all success in your venture," signalled the German commanding officer at Luderitz as the Russians rolled away to sea again.

Thus the first sight Cape Town had of the Russians was the handsome white hospital ship *Oryol*. There had been incidents, however, before this arrival. Early that year the British freighter *Beckenham* had left London filled with cordite for Japan, and it was thought that the Russians might try to intercept her somewhere in African water. But the *Beckenham* had kept well away from the ordinary steamer tracks, and had reached Japan after sixty-nine days at sea without calling anywhere or sighting another ship. Two Russian ships prowled along the South African coast after that in the hope of seizing ships laden with contraband. They were the *Smolensk* and the *Petersburg*, armed merchant cruisers. In August the *Smolensk* had stopped the British freighter *Comedian* near East London, but had allowed her to proceed to Durban after a search. British men-o'-war then set out in search of the Russians, finding both of them at Zanzibar.

Now the Russians had become visible to everyone and all Cape Town stood on the South Arm and stared at the *Oryol* with her clipper bow, band of red along the bulwarks and red cross emblems on her funnels. She reminded many people of the Union-Castle mailboat *Scot*, and indeed she had been a British passenger liner before her conversion.

A launch flying the white ensign paid a courtesy visit to the *Oryol* while she was lying in Table Bay. Soon the ship came alongside the old Loch Jetty for water and fresh food. Privileged visitors were allowed on board. Mr Knight, a shipping agent who also acted as Russian consul, arranged with Captain Laklimatoff for reporters to inspect the ship. Everyone was courteous, but few spoke English.

However, the reporters were shown the launches which were intended to dash among sinking ships in battle and pick up the wounded. The operating theatre on the boat deck had four tables. The hospital staff of eighty included a French Red Cross surgeon and twenty Russian sisters. They wore brown or grey uniforms with the red cross on their aprons. Patients lay in hammocks on the upper deck; they were mainly seamen injured in coaling accidents.

Mr O. Hansen, a shipping clerk on duty while the *Oryol* took on stores, told me that the Russians were extremely worried about Japanese secret agents. One of the Cape coloured labourers had Mongolian features, and he became a marked man as soon as he stepped on board. "A Russian officer, with signs and gestures, made it clear to me that this man would have to be removed," Mr Hansen said. "I found that the officer spoke German, and explained to him in this language that the labourer was harmless. He accepted my word, but I could see the Russians watching that man's every movement until the ship left the docks."

One day the Russian officers went on shore in a body and sat down to a gay lunch at the Metropole Hotel in Long Street. Then on December 19, the Tsar's Name Day, there was a party in the hospital ship and she was dressed with flags.

Baron Ostensacken, the officer in charge of supplies, told the reporters that the hospital ship carried enough medical stores and food for a year. She took on additional medical comforts during her stay. But the item which caused wide comment – even in the newspapers – was the amount of alcohol ordered from Cape Town firms. Not only did the ship take on many cases of wines and spirits; the officers, and individual nursing sisters, also placed huge orders. No doubt they needed it before the interminable voyage ended.

Meanwhile the naval and military authorities at the Cape prepared for a Russian "invasion". Ships in Cape waters were advised to show clear lights. It was rumoured that the Russian fleet would call at Simonstown for food and water, though under the rules of war they would not be permitted to remain in harbour for more than twenty-four hours.

The *Cape Times* remarked: "Under the iron rules of neutrality we cannot do much to help the squadron on its way. We will nevertheless regard it with the sentiment which common humanity inspires towards a band of men who have embarked upon a voyage of so much hazard. The adventure is one of which no one can see the end; but if the matter is brought to the issue of battle, it is certain that at least some of the proud ships which are now passing along our coasts will never return."

Some uneasiness was caused by the fact that the British naval force in Simon's Bay consisted of just two ships, the flagship H.M.S. *Crescent* and the small gunboat *Thistle*. Three other gunboats were lying at moorings out of commission. It was announced, however, that a large body of police (about one hundred and fifty men) had been drafted to Simonstown to prevent "disgraceful scenes". The behaviour of Russian seamen on shore was notorious.

But if the Russians lost their heads again at sea and opened fire on innocent fishermen there was no great fleet to deal with them. The people of Simonstown found some comfort in the marching of the Royal Garrison Artillery gunners through the streets every night at eight. They manned the Upper North, Lower North, Noah's Ark and Craig's batteries, returning to their barracks every morning. One unhappy incident was reported. A marine sentry on duty at a magazine shot the sergeant of the guard through the leg. It seemed that the sergeant was creeping up to see if the sentry was asleep and failed to answer when challenged.

Probably the most ludicrous touch was provided by the Table Bay Harbour Board, which posted a notice on the customs house at the foot of Ebenezer Road: "Owing to the approach of the Russian fleet, the S.S. *William Porter* is to be kept in perfect readiness day and night, with steam up. By order." The *William Porter* was an antiquated little tug with an oversize funnel. (Some time later she was towed up the west coast but capsized before reaching her destination.) No one ever explained the part which the *William Porter* was supposed to play.

As it happened, there was no need for the British flagship or the tug to intervene. Signalman Harvey and a few others watched the passing of the fleet on December 19 from Signal Hill. The Cape Point lighthouse keepers sighted them and asked the nearest ships to "make their numbers". The request was ignored.

On board the Russian ships the rounding of the Cape was a great event. It coincided with the Tsar's Name Day, which the hospital ship *Oryol* had celebrated in Table Bay Docks before hastening after the fleet. There were banquets in the wardrooms at sea, and vodka flowed on the messdecks.

Engineer Politovsky wrote to his wife that day: "If we double the Cape in safety, then thanks be to God. We are steaming near the shore. It is hilly, dark and treeless. Table Mountain is distinguished by its height and summit. The swell is tremendous. The ships are rolling. It is fearful to look at *Nachimoff* and *Donskoy*. Near Cape Town we met an enormous four-masted ship flying the American flag. She was coming towards us. We are expecting to meet three suspicious schooners."

Another officer recorded sighting Table Mountain at eleven in the morning – "a glorious country which reminds one to an astonishing extent of the other end of the Old World, the North Cape." He added that the cruisers were a pitiful sight off the Cape as they were nearly shaken to pieces, while the battleships dived deeply into the swell.

The fleet was running before a gale. It was just as well that wind and sea were astern, as some of the ships might have capsized if they had felt the weather on the beam.

Not long afterwards a sealed bottle was washed ashore on one of the Cape beaches, and the *Cape Argus* published a translation of the letter it contained, written in Russian by one of Rozhestvensky's seamen: "Oh fisherman who may chance to find and read this letter, pray for those who are being sent to their death and pray that this terrible war may soon be brought to an end."

Commenting on the letter, the *Cape Argus* said: "We hope the fleet will be recalled before it is too late. The ships are ill-found and the officers untrained. The whole world may well hope, for the sake of humanity, that this mournful armada may yet turn back ere it be too late."

But the mournful armada did not turn back. A modern Trafalgar was fought in the Sea of Japan when the Russians steamed out of the fog and the Japanese fleet in formidable line ahead joined battle with them. Between the hours of 2 p.m. on May 27, 1905 and the following midnight, the Russians had lost over thirty ships worth over thirty million pounds, while four thousand of their seamen were killed. The Japanese lost only three torpedo boats. Rozhestvensky, seriously wounded, was taken prisoner. Russia had to sign a peace treaty and Japan became a great power.

Such was the drama Signalman Harvey and his wife glimpsed from Signal Hill that day late in 1904. They watched a turning point, and many of those at sea must have sensed the ultimate disaster.

EIGHT BELLS AT SALAMANDER

Sea Gypsies
1960

Men and women have sailed across the oceans and reached the harbours of South Africa in much smaller craft than the Phoenicians used, smaller vessels than Chinese junks or Arab dhows. I have always made a point of listening to the sea gypsies, especially the lone hands, for they are not as other men.

Some of these adventurers wrote their own stories, and often told them well. I am more concerned here with the unknown or forgotten ocean wanderers, including the men who sailed far and wide long before Slocum and my dear old friend Harry Pidgeon circled the world.

It is hard to say when the first cockleshell navigator set out deliberately to conquer the oceans. I have found mention of a Portuguese seaman, James Bottellier, who sailed from India in 1539 in a cutter eighteen feet long and with a beam of six feet. His motive, according to the English traveller Samual Purchas, was to "recover the favour" of King John III. He coasted along Arabian and East African shores, "doubled the terrible Cape", missed St Helena completely, but survived all the perils of the Atlantic. Purchas noted that Bottellier "came yet safe to Lisbone and was worthily welcomed for daring to encounter Neptune's strongest forces notwithstanding such weak furniture."

Possibly there is a detailed account of Bottellier's voyage in some dusty filing cabinet. Historians are aware that the archives of Portugal still hold much drama in documents which have not yet been properly examined.

I have mentioned two famous American circumnavigators, but Richard Cleveland of Salem, Massachusetts, has been forgotten as a master of small craft even in his own country. Cleveland sailed from France to Cape Town in the little cutter *Caroline* at the end of the eighteenth century. He dreaded Spanish and French privateers more than any heavy weather. His vivid logbook reveals a character (like Harry Pidgeon) who never touched "wine, porter, ale, beer or any beverage stronger than tea or coffee." He never smoked. At sixty-eight he claimed that his life had been free from illness. This was at a period, according to Cleveland, when "drinking grog and chewing tobacco were two essential requisites for making a good seaman."

Cleveland's firm in Salem had sent the first American merchant ships to Cape Town and Mauritius. After serving his time as a cadet, Cleveland bought the *Caroline* at Havre for one thousand dollars and set off on a trading voyage of his own. His cargo of manufactured goods was valued at three thousand dollars.

I could not discover the exact size of the *Caroline*, but young Cleveland noted that many tried to dissuade him from sailing, as it was considered dangerous in such a small craft. Seamen engaged one day would desert the next. Finally he set out with a mate, two landsmen and a boy. "The mate could fish a spar, caulk a seam or make a bucket or barrel," Cleveland recorded. "He was steady and faithful, and saved me much anxiety."

Another man had been a Prussian grenadier, but he was a coward aloft and knew little English. The cook was a tall negro. The boy was French and vivacious. He had served in a French man-o'-war and had learnt English in an English prison; but Cleveland remarked sadly: "His choice of words did not indicate much care in the teacher."

As the little *Caroline* steered south, a privateer with lateen sails fired on her. The balls fell short, but the privateer used her sweeps and came alongside. She was French, and when her captain found that Cleveland was a neutral in the war between Britain and France, he was allowed to go.

Table Mountain was sighted on March 21, 1798, and by this time the *Caroline* was short of food and water. A man-o'-war's boat met Cleveland, and he was taken to Government House to see Admiral Sir Hugh Christian and give him the news of Europe.

"We had many visitors, attracted by the boyish appearance of the master and mate, the queer characters in the crew, and the long voyage," Cleveland wrote. (They had been at sea for five months without a single port of call.) "Some believed we were French spies, and our voyage was the principle topic of conversation in Cape Town for a week after our arrival. My ship was searched for dispatches, and letters I was carrying for gentlemen in Mauritius were all broken open."

However, the papers were returned. Cleveland accepted an offer of five thousand Spanish dollars for the *Caroline*, made by the British admiral. Soon afterwards the *Caroline* left for India with a naval lieutenant in command. She was never heard of again.

Cleveland visited the lookout station on the Lion's Head summit, where a man signalled the approach of vessels with small brass cannon and flags. "The habitation of the signalman is so confined that his residence would be considered a cruel punishment were it not voluntary," Cleveland said. "It is a mere dog kennel, partly formed by the rock, barely sufficient to shelter one person in a sitting position from the weather. A slave brings him his daily provisions and water. This is the only opportunity the recluse has for conversation during the day. My visit was a Godsend, and he begged me to repeat it."

Some time later Cleveland found himself in Calcutta, and there he bought a newly built twenty-five ton cutter for five thousand rupees. He sailed this little ship to Mauritius with a cargo of oil, wax and ghee, and sold her there at a profit. At another period he owned a small English cutter, the *Dragon*, and sailed her far and wide in Eastern waters. Today the feats of Richard Cleveland would place him in the front rank of those who handle small craft successfully in deep waters. The voyages of his little cutters long ago have been overlooked by the historians of the sea.

*

How many people in South Africa remember Captain J. C. Voss, the Canadian who sailed the dugout canoe *Tilikum* over the ocean? Voss was not a circumnavigator (though he could have circled the globe had he wished) and so he never gained such fame as the great Slocum of the same period. But the voyage of Captain Voss from

British Columbia to England was a grand effort of seamanship; memorable, too, because of the interesting episodes which occurred while Voss was in South Africa.

It was in the summer of 1904 that a Cape Point lighthouse keeper looked over the eight hundred foot precipice at dawn and saw the schooner-rigged canoe with three masts sailing past. A visitor who was there suggested that it was a Venetian gondola which had put to sea. In fact, the thirty-foot canoe had been hollowed out of a single red cedar tree trunk by Alaskan Indians. She drew only twenty-four inches of water aft. Instead of a bowsprit she had a weird Red Indian hand-carved figurehead. Yet there was room in this narrow-gutted craft for one hundred gallons of fresh water, provisions for three months, and Voss himself.

Voss had designed a sea anchor. He selected the frail *Tilikum* to show that a small craft could ride out any weather with this equipment. The original owner, a Red Indian, sold the canoe to Voss for a few pounds and a flask of whisky. Voss added a lead keel, sand ballast, decks, and masts carrying two hundred and thirty square feet of canvas. If anyone climbed a mast, *Tilikum* heeled over.

Voss took on a shipmate when he could find one. Unfortunately his first companion fell overboard in the Pacific, taking with him the only compass. Voss completed the run to Sydney with only the sun and stars to guide him.

He reached Durban just after Christmas in 1903 and was met by a tug. "Where are you from?" shouted the tugmaster.

"Victoria, British Columbia."

"By Jove, you have got a nerve."

"Absolutely necessary to get along in this world," Voss called back.

An old friend from Canada, living in Pretoria, suggested to Voss that he should rail the *Tilikum* to the Transvaal. This he did, and the *Tilikum* was exhibited at the Wanderers Ground as "the first deep-sea vessel ever to visit Johannesburg".

Pretoria also saw the *Tilikum*, but the little ship met with an accident there while navigating on dry land. A horse took fright at the figurehead and kicked it off. General Louis Botha shook hands with Voss during this visit and remarked: "I would rather go through another South African War than cross the ocean in the *Tilikum*."

Voss transported the *Tilikum* down to East London by train, and continued his cruise to Algoa Bay. He arrived there just after a great gale, and found a small fleet of full-rigged sailing ships wrecked on the beach.

The little *Tilikum* was driven into Mossel Bay by one gale, and rode out another off Danger Point with her sea anchor. And so she came past Cape Point at last with a light southerly wind helping her into Table Bay.

Voss told the reporters that a whale had risen suddenly, towered over him and almost overwhelmed the *Tilikum*. The canoe had also been pursued and stabbed by swordfish. He had been followed by sharks for thousands of miles. "There was nearly always one on the leeside – I suppose it could see the man at the helm, and was tempted by the sight of meat so close to the water," recalled Voss calmly. But he said that his narrowest escape was when he had cramp in the stomach. No medicine gave him relief, and he thought it was appendicitis. In the end he took mustard and warm water, and that cured him.

His favourite medicine, however, was sea water. He cured himself of seasickness with salt water, and took a small dose every morning.

Voss was a small man with a great appetite. He believed in regular meal hours in all weathers at sea; porridge and ham and eggs for breakfast; a stew of tinned meat, potatoes and onions for lunch; more stew for dinner; and a final meal of tea, hard tack and butter just before turning in.

Thousands paid to see the *Tilikum* in a circus tent in Cape Town. Here, too, Voss found a new shipmate, a man named Harrison who had suffered from tuberculosis and thought the voyage would do him good. So these two mariners sailed away, the *Tilikum* loaded with presents from well-wishers. Most of the parcels contained food: roast chicken, roast turkey, roast goose, wines, brandy and whisky. They anchored off Robben Island for a feast.

Voss had intended to shape a course for Pernambuco without calling anywhere. However, poor Harrison was so seasick that Voss touched at St Helena seventeen days after leaving Table Bay. Harrison had eaten practically nothing, and the salt water treatment had failed to cure him. He remained, thankfully, on the island when Voss sailed.

Tilikum made Pernambuco safely, then crossed the Atlantic again, ran up the Channel and ended her voyage at Margate. She had covered forty thousand miles in three years. Voss, it is sad to relate, died in 1922, at the age of sixty-four, as a poor bus driver. His exploits at sea had brought him neither fame nor fortune.

EIGHT BELLS AT SALAMANDER

Three Men Survived

1960

Probably there are still people living in South Africa who lost friends or relations in the *Drummond Castle* wreck. That was the most serious disaster to a South African liner ever known in peacetime, and rarely even in war records will you find a heavier death-roll. There were just three survivors.

Captain W. W. Pierce of the *Drummond Castle* belonged to a seafaring era in which the names of shipmasters appeared in almost every shipping advertisement. They were not paid much, but they were greater figures than they are today. At the end of a happy run the passengers often presented the captain with an illuminated address. One selected a certain ship because one's favourite captain was in command. And of course the captain who gained a pleasant reputation in this way might also find himself promoted to a larger and better ship.

I have always doubted the wisdom of making a social lion of a sea captain. He has problems to solve on the bridge without having to entertain a charmed circle at the captain's table and elsewhere. However there is not much of that sort of thing as there used to be. Nowadays the purser and his staff do most of that work admirably.

But after a careful study of the evidence I think that the loss of the *Drummond Castle* may have been due to Captain Pierce attempting to do two jobs at the same time. No modern liner captain would dream of acting as Captain Pierce did on the night the *Drummond Castle* was lost.

For years after that wreck, whenever the *Drummond Castle* was mentioned, many knowing people in South Africa would repeat an entirely false rumour. "Of course, all the officers were dancing," they would say. That was obviously untrue, though there was a dance on that night, and another entertainment at which Captain Pierce had been present.

Captain Pierce had spent his whole sea life in the old Castle Line; first as an apprentice in their sailing ships; later in command of the full-rigged ship *Pembroke Castle*; then as an officer in their steamers and as master of the coasting steamer *Courland*; master of the intermediate passenger liner *Dunbar Castle* (built in 1883); and finally in command of the former mail steamer *Drummond Castle*, transferred to the intermediate service two years previously.

Passengers called the *Drummond Castle* the "dear dilatory *Drummond*", for she was no flyer. Nevertheless, they liked her spacious cabins and they knew she would be steady in heavy weather. She was a ship of nearly four thousand tons, fifteen years old, with one funnel. First, second and third-class passengers were carried. In the first class she had marble baths and a drawing room with a grand piano. She had been "modernised" not long before her last voyage, and the novelties included electric light.

Gaily the crowd waved the packed *Drummond Castle* out of Table Bay Docks on May 28, 1896, before going home in hansom cabs and horse trams. The liner steamed out in fine weather, her passengers looking forward to the English summer at the end of the run of three weeks. Las Palmas was the only port of call. Seven passengers joined the ship there, making a total of two hundred and forty-five souls on board – a hundred and forty-one passengers and a hundred and four officers and crew. The ship left Las Palmas on June 12 for London.

On the night of Tuesday, June 16, the *Drummond Castle* had crossed the Bay of Biscay and was closing in with the coast of France near the dreaded Cape Ushant, graveyard of ships. Ushant is, of course, an island, and there is a narrow channel between island and mainland used by coasters. Between Ushant and a small island to the south runs the Fronveur Sound, and at the entrance to the south is the reef called Pierres Vertes. Ushant is known to the Bretons as the "island of terror".

It was a night of drizzle and thick fog, but the passengers hardly noticed the weather. Dancing was followed by a farewell concert in the first saloon. A series of the *tableaux vivants* beloved by Victorian audiences had been organised. These included Babes in the Wood.

Among the first-class passengers was a cleanshaven mine accountant names Charles Marquardt, and Englishman of thirty-five with a fine physique. As he was the only passenger to survive the wreck, his narrative is important. Marquardt recorded the fact that the captain appeared at the end of the concert, remained for five minutes and made a pleasant little speech in reply to a vote of thanks.

Two seamen were saved from the wreck. One, named Godbold, remembered hearing the last songs and the laughter at the concert, and he saw Captain Pierce returning to the bridge. The third survivor was a quartermaster named Wood.

All three survivors agreed that the concert ended at about ten-thirty. Some of the passengers strolled on deck afterwards, but it was so wet that most of them went to their cabins. Ushant light, which should have been in sight, was hidden by the fog.

At eleven Marquardt was in the smoking room, talking to a naval warrant officer, Boatswain Motyer, one of ten naval men travelling as passengers. Marquardt asked Motyer whether he was thinking of turning in.

"No. Whenever there's a fog on I never go to bed," replied Motyer. "I stay on deck all night."

No sooner had he spoken when they heard a loud grating noise and the deck tilted. "That's a collision," guessed Motyer. They rushed out. It was very dark. The bridge telegraph rang loudly as they ran forward, and the engines stopped.

Marquardt noticed that the bow was low in the water. He saw the seamen ripping the canvas covers off the boats, and hurried to his cabin for his life jacket. He also grabbed an overcoat, expecting to spend a cold night in an open boat. However, no boat left the doomed *Drummond Castle*. There was no time. Marquardt had only just regained the deck when the ship slid forward at such an angle that he found it impossible to stand.

"The only person I noticed on deck was a fellow passenger named Hinds," recalled Marquardt. "He asked me for a life belt, and I told him he would find a spare one in my cabin. I made my way to an awning stanchion and hauled myself up on to the rail. A tremendous roaring filled the air as the engineers opened the valves of the boil-

310

ers to allow the steam to escape. All the lights went out. A moment later I found myself in the sea."

Marquardt heard one scream, but most of the people had been trapped down below, and the escaping steam covered the cries of those who were drowning. Another deafening noise was caused by the rush of air through the portholes as the ship went down.

It seems the *Drummond Castle* remained on the surface for no more than four minutes after striking a reef. (It was the Pierres Vertes reef which I have mentioned.) The *Titanic* gave her people nearly three hours to launch the few boats they had; but the six boats along the superstructure of the *Drummond Castle* never left the davits.

Once the ship had gone, Marquardt heard people shouting in terror. A spar drifted past him and as he grasped it he saw that eight or nine others were holding on for their lives. But they had not the stamina of Marquardt. They dropped off, until Marquardt found himself with only Fourth Officer P. S. Ellis.

Ellis and Marquardt made a triangular raft of driftwood. It was so frail that they could not raise themselves clear of the bitter sea; but it was something that floated and they clung to it together for a long time. Ellis slipped off exhausted. Marquardt remained, with bodies drifting past him. The raft broke up at last, but he still had the spar. Now and again he came within reach of a fruit box, and ate some oranges and tomatoes. He was twelve hours in the water and almost unconscious when an Ushant fisherman named Berthelet picked him up.

Godbold the seaman was attending to the awnings when the ship struck. "Clear away the boats!" shouted an officer from the bridge. The second officer and carpenter went forward and reported: "She's making water fast." Godbold went to his boat station. There was no panic, but four passengers tried to climb into his boat before it was ready. "Let's get the boat swung out first," Godbold told them. "Then we can save you."

But as he spoke everyone was swept away. The ship had dropped off the reef into deep water. "Such a cry went up as I hope I may never hear again," Godbold declared. "It was the united voice of the doomed. Some who had not been drawn into the vortex were struggling for life. From the sea came pitiful appeals."

Godbold was hurled across the boat deck by the water. He was close to the bridge, and he remembered seeing Milne, an elderly quartermaster, at the wheel, his face illuminated by the paraffin binnacle light. All the electric lights had gone out. Milne remained at his post as through petrified, gripping the wheel and staring at the compass.

"I went down and down," reported Godbold. "I was between the bridge and the funnel, and I feared that I was inside the funnel. It was the most ghastly moment of my life. Yet somehow I came to the surface when I could hold my breath no longer."

Fortunately the sea was calm. Godbold saw that it was strewn with deck fittings, seats and wreckage. He found a hatch. For about half an hour the cries for help rose from the dark sea. Then there was an awful stillness.

Someone groaned close by, and Godbold recognised a trimmer. "It's cold, isn't it," said the trimmer. Then he let go and was drowned.

It was the coldness of the sea that killed many of the people that night. There was enough driftwood to keep a number of them afloat, but they could not stand the temperature.

Godbold heard another groan. This time it was the quartermaster Wood. "Got room for two?" inquired Wood. Godbold helped him. At dawn the tide carried them near the shore, but a current swept them out again. They went through nine hours of agony before the Breton fishermen hauled them into a boat. They were half-dead with cold. The fishermen stripped them, rubbed them, put their own warm clothes on the two seamen. At eleven that morning Godbold and Wood were carried on shore. They were put to bed, but they could not sleep. Soon they crawled down to the beach to see whether any others had been saved.

*

Marquardt sent the first news of the disaster to London. He drank hot tea and brandy and slept for two hours after his rescuers had landed him; but when he awoke the tragedy dawned on him and he wrote out the telegram which was to bring the merciless shock of sudden death into hundreds of homes.

"*Drummond Castle* total loss off Ushant," telegraphed Marquardt to the Castle Company. "Am probably sole survivor." The two seamen had landed elsewhere, and he had not yet heard of their rescue.

Above the anguish of the disaster there comes down the years a memory of the kindness and humanity of the Breton fisherfolk who cared for the three survivors and buried the dead. The men were at sea fishing when the first bodies drifted ashore. So the sad task of carrying the dead to the lifeboat station (which was turned into a mortuary) fell upon the women.*

A French naval tug, *La Laborieux*, joined the fishing fleet in the search for survivors. There were no more survivors.

Two thousand people, every man, woman and child on Ushant who could walk, formed the great funeral procession on Saturday, June 20, 1896. They were poor as only a fishing community could be, but they wore their Breton costumes and the graves were piled high with flowers. Coffins they could not provide for all, and many of the seventy-three bodies washed up were buried in common graves. Marquardt, Godbold and Wood always remembered the continuous tolling of the bell as the long procession reached the graveyard.

Marquardt had another ordeal to face when he reached London two days later. He found the Castle Line offices filled with frantic wives and mothers. Stricken with grief, they held up photographs and begged for news. Some were worried without cause. "Many a young Englishman has disappeared from view in South Africa, and his relatives at home are terrified lest he should be lying stark and dead off Ushant," wrote Marquardt. "So much there is to anxious hearts in the slightest similarity of names." But for many the news was as bad as it could be. Day after day Marquardt sat in the Fenchurch Street shipping office to be interviewed by inconsolable crowds of mourners.

Cape Town heard the news on the morning of June 18, and the *Cape Argus* brought out a special edition with a full passenger list. Two daughters of the Cape Town city engineer were among the lost:

---

* Queen Victoria issued a special *Drummond Castle* commemorative medal as a token of gratitude, and this was awarded to about two hundred and fifty Ushant islanders for trying to save life or recovering bodies.

Geraldine Olive, aged fifteen, and Beatrice Olive, thirteen. Sub-Inspector Martin of the Cape Dockyard Police, Mrs Andrews, wife of the manager of the celebrated Hatherley distillery, the whole Mercer family of Barberton, were other victims. Mrs Barnett of Johannesburg and her daughter had just escaped death in the frightful Glencoe railway disaster only to perish in the *Drummond Castle*. Towns all over South Africa were in mourning.

South Africa had such a small white population in those days that nearly everyone knew someone on board the *Drummond Castle*. Every flag in the country went to half-mast. Every theatre and concert hall was closed. Sir Gordon Sprigg, prime minister of the Cape Colony, spoke on the disaster in the House of Assembly that afternoon and moved the adjournment as a mark of sympathy.

It was a tremendous blow for Sir Donald Currie, as his Castle Line had not lost a single passenger during the quarter of a century that they had been operating. The court of inquiry absolved the company from all blame, for the ship was well-found and properly manned. Captain Pierce was rightly found responsible for the loss of the ship. The court declared that he was going too fast in view of the fog, and that he should have taken soundings to check his position. This would have informed him that the ship had been set inshore by the strong current.

Godbold joined the British lightship service, and had a second narrow escape when a steamer cut right into the anchored lightship. Once again he found himself struggling in the water, but rescue came much more quickly on that occasion. It was the *Drummond Castle* that shattered Godbold's nerves. Years afterwards he said that the tragedy would live with him to the end of his life.

The *Drummond Castle* went down in thirty fathoms. She had gold on board, and in 1929 the Italian diver Franchesci reached the liner from the salvage ship *Artiglio*. He reported a thirty-foot rent in the hull near the bows, and brought up a fragment of steel plating. (This is now in Lloyd's marine insurance museum in London). But the gold still lies with the drowned people off the rocky island of Ushant.

Would the *Drummond Castle* have been lost if Captain Pierce had not left the bridge that foggy night to make his pleasant little farewell speech in the saloon? Perhaps she would have met the same fate. She was nearing the end of the run and the captain was in a hurry. It would not be so dangerous today, with echo-sounding, radio direction finders and radar. Yet liners slow down in fog even now for fear of colliding with blind vessels which are not equipped with modern devices.

On land and sea and in the air it is usually the human factor that causes the greatest disasters. Captain Pierce sank the *Drummond Castle*, and she went down fast.

EIGHT BELLS AT SALAMANDER

Fire And Ice

1960

Fire at sea brought twenty-seven men, women and children, and the corpse of a small boy, to the Namaqualand coast one hundred and twenty years ago. It was a miracle that any of those people, tormented by thirst in the open boats and in the Namaqualand desert long ago, should have survived the ordeal.

Thanks to a logbook kept by Captain Adam Yule, master of the brig *Australia*, the narrative comes to life as clearly as though the victims were talking. The diary reached the National Library of Scotland in Edinburgh, and I found a copy in the British Museum library in London. Further research in the Cape Town newspapers of the period and the Cape archives enabled me to fill all the gaps in the narrative.

I know the coast where those poor souls landed. It is now the diamond coast, guarded so carefully that no one would escape observation for long. But in the past it was a dead man's coast indeed, as isolated and dangerous as the Skeleton Coast to the north. The old Dutch seamen dreaded the whole waterless stretch to the north of St Helena Bay. There the *Goude Buys* was lost; and of seven men sent on shore to fetch help, five died of hunger and thirst. There too, the hooker *Meteren* ran ashore. Five men were drowned, eighteen reached the shore, but only nine arrived in civilisation. Thirst claimed the other nine.

Captain Yule never imagined any such danger when he sailed from Leith on October 2, 1840 in command of the new and well-equipped brig *Australia*. He had two mates, a carpenter, steward, cook, four seamen and three young apprentices as crew. The five cabin passengers included a Dr Alexander Byers and three young women; while in the steerage there were five men and a young orphan family named Chisholm, two boys and three girls.

It was a dangerous cargo the *Australia* carried: turpentine, vitriol, sulphur, tar and coal, with some wine and spirits. Nevertheless, Captain Yule followed the insane custom of the period and neglected to keep his lifeboats ready for use. The long boat, most important of all, was used as a stall for two live bulls! You will soon realise, however, that in every other way Yule was a fine seaman and a courageous leader.

After a call at Rio the *Australia* steered across the South Atlantic for the Cape. She was running before a strong, fair wind with all sails set on the evening of December 27, and was about six hundred miles from Cape Town. The passengers walked on deck as usual, then retired to their cabins out of the cold. Before nine the captain gave the mate his night orders and went below. In the passage he smelt burning. He thought one of the women had set alight to something in her cabin. However, his investigation showed that the whole cargo was ablaze. "The interior of the vessel was like the womb of a volcano," Yule wrote in his log. "It was impossible to put out the fire. I saw that the ship was doomed."

Captain Yule lost no time in telling his passengers that in spite of the heavy sea that was running they would have to take to the boats. Some were frantic with terror. Others tormented him with questions. The rest remained silent and trembling, smitten dumb in the presence of death.

First the seamen had to drive the bulls out of the long boat and sling them into the sea. One bull went beserk, and valuable time was lost in securing and killing it. By the time the boat had been unlashed and the tackles hooked on for launching, the smoke had become so dense that it was impossible for the men at the davits to breathe. They had to run in and out of the smoke. However, the long boat went over the side at last and was made fast to the stern, where the air was clearer. Even there the passengers were blinded by smoke. The ship was rolling heavily. Flames were pouring out of the fore hatch and the decks were blistering underfoot.

In that ghastly situation Captain Yule remembered everything that should have been done before the ship left Scotland. He ordered the steward to provision the boats while the mate rolled two water casks aft along the deck. The rigging and sails were alight by this time, but the passengers were calm and the children did not cry. Then the mate clambered down into the long boat to help the sailors take on the heavy water casks.

One cask fell into the sea and was lost. The other dropped on to the mate and a seaman, bruising them severely; but this cask was saved.

A skiff was launched, and Captain Yule put the three women into it with two seamen to look after them. It soon became obvious that the skiff was overloaded. This was partly due to the fact that two men passengers had hidden themselves under some canvas below the seats.

Yule and six others were still on board. They launched a small boat from the main deck, and Yule lingered for a moment surveying the frightening destruction of his ship. "I stood, the last living thing among the glare of the burning mass," he wrote. "The mainmast fell as I got into the boat."

Night had fallen. Yule was hoping that the boats might remain fast to the burning ship until dawn, when some vessel which had been attracted by the fire might rescue them. However, the lines between ship and boat caught alight, and at midnight the three open boats were drifting separately.

Yule noted at this time that the fire had probably been caused by spontaneous combustion in the coal. (Later he informed Mr J. van Ryneveld, civil commissioner at Clanwilliam, that the chafing of deals and the cargo through heavy rolling, or the breaking of vitriol bottles, might have been responsible.)

On the first night Yule took charge of the long boat. There were seven in the skiff and four in the small boat. But the small boat nearly capsized during the night, and so her people had to transfer to the other boats while she was set adrift. That made nineteen in the long boat and nine in the skiff. Both were deep in the water. And they were a long way from land.

Daylight brought no friendly sail, so Yule took stock of his resources. He had thirty gallons of water, half a gallon of rum, half a gallon of brandy, a few bottles of wine and some wine glasses. He estimated that it would not be prudent to issue each person with more than one wineglass of water a day; and in this he proved to be remarkably correct. Two small bags of bread had been saved, but some of this had been damaged by salt water. Two hams, two cheeses and a few canisters of preserved meat completed the list. Yule had taken his sextant, chronometer, nautical almanac and chart with him. He had a Bible and psalm book. Flannel shirts and blankets had been stowed in the skiff.

At six in the morning Yule informed everyone that they would be on short rations because it might take ten or twelve days to reach the coast. Then they improvised sails, using oars for masts, and ran before the south-west wind.

Yule had to wash out the long boat, which was filthy after being used as a cattle-stall. The spray came over at first, but the carpenter rigged a bulwark of blankets on the weather side to give more shelter.

"The people pleaded for water, but I refused," Yule recorded. "The cries for water were heartrending, especially the children in the skiff. They did not want food. Water was the only cry. Some began to drink salt water in spite of my warnings. Two people in my boat and two in the other became delirious. They were the ones who had taken salt water. All I could do was to issue the water three times a day, one tablespoon being the ration for each person at a time."

Often they were drenched by the spray. The chronometer was put out of action; but Yule, a skilful navigator, was still able to find his latitude and fix his position by dead-reckoning. Yule and the mate steered the long boat, though most of the work fell on Yule, owing to the mate's injuries. One night the long boat shipped a heavy sea. She would probably have foundered if Yule had not foreseen the danger and ordered the men to keep buckets close to them for bailing.

At dawn on the ninth day the people in the skiff hailed Yule and informed him that the orphan boy John Chisholm had died during the night. Four people in Yule's boat were gravely ill. One of them, George Peat, was dying.

However, when the sun rose that morning it showed the hills behind the Namaqualand coast. The shore was twelve miles away, and they were closing in with it fast. Everyone stared eagerly and thought of the same question. Was there safety ahead, and fresh water – or death in the surf?

Yule ordered the small skiff to go on ahead and search for a safe landing. It seemed a hopeless task on that rockbound coast where tremendous breakers were crashing and no opening appeared. Mercifully the wind and the heavy ground swell from the south-west went down as they approached the shore. The skiff ran for a narrow channel. It struck a rock, and some fell overboard. Lightened in this way, the skiff was carried right up on the beach. All came safely through the surf.

Yule followed with the long boat, unaware of the fact that the skiff's crew were trying to signal him to land elsewhere. He took their warning signs for encouragement, and dashed among the breakers into the channel. He, too, collided with the rock and the long boat remained fast on it. There was deep water between boat and shore. Yule urged everyone to jump overboard before the next wave engulfed them. The seamen saved the women and children. Just after landing the storm burst again and the boats were thrown far up on the beach. They were safe for the moment, with their remaining foot and water intact – but with the body of little John Chisholm, and the dying George Peat.

Captain Yule had discovered by means of his sextant that they were about eleven miles north of the Olifants River mouth, which is about two hundred miles from Cape Town by road. Life now depended on finding water on the spot or marching to the river. It seemed like madness to remain on that beach; yet the leader was forced to stay there for a time. His people were wasting away, their strength had almost gone, and he could not drive them forward. The seamen put up tents of spars and sails. These castaways who had been unable to rest in the boats found it a luxury merely to stretch themselves out on the sand. After the usual water ration had been given out they lay down and slept.

Yule could not sleep. He rose, looked round for traces of water or cultivation, and saw nothing but the dry sand and scrub of the Namaqualand coast. He scanned the veld to the horizon, but there was no house or hut. Not even the tracks of a living creature could be seen in that wilderness.

Wallace the mate was awake, too, and Yule discussed the problem with him. Could they launch their boats again and make the

Cape? Both officers agreed that it would be impossible. There was nothing for it but to march southwards under the burning sun until they came to civilisation. Yule decided to allow his weak flock to rest all the next day, and to set out before dawn on the following day.

That afternoon the body of John Chisholm was covered with the Union Jack. A grave was dug and Yule read the burial service. Next morning George Peat died, and there was another ceremony. "They lie side by side on that desert shore," Yule wrote. Everyone must have wondered whether there would be a third burial – or more.

They all went out in different directions searching for water that day. A succulent plant was found, but the sap proved to be undrinkable. Some collected shellfish, but these were of doubtful value owing to the salty flavour. It was hot in the tents, and Captain Yule noticed that it was much cooler on a rise above the beach. The people had so little energy left that Yule had to bribe them with wine before they would move the tents.

Prospects for a successful march seemed poor. Nevertheless, the women devised canvas bags to hold the provisions. All the water was poured into bottles and jars, and distributed among the men who were regarded as reliable. Yule thought the water would last for six more days, provided he did not increase the ration.

"We are like the last remnant of a famished garrison," Yule's diary reads at this stage. "The scene is appalling, for thirst is maddening. Everyone is suffering from swollen limbs and walking with difficulty."

On the march next day Yule had to rest his company when they had covered only one mile. The loose sand was a torment, and sometimes the thorn bushes delayed them. Always there were the appeals for water to be resisted. It was so hot that the men stripped off their shirts. Somehow they covered another mile, and then everyone rested again.

"I had to persuade them to go on, for there was no shelter from the sun, and our chances were growing darker every moment," Yule recorded.

At noon they were following a coastal cliff when they noticed two huts on the beach below them. I know that spot. There is an island called Elephant Rock separated from the beach by a narrow channel. It is an island where the seals breed, raided by the Hottentots of old and by white people since the beginning of last century. Unfortunately there were no white people in the huts on that day when the survivors of the *Australia* passed by.

Yule and his men shouted, but there was no answer. They considered climbing down the cliff to see whether there was water in the huts, but no one felt strong enough to make the effort. (Later they learnt that there was water on the spot, but the barrels were buried and they would not have found them.) Soon after the huts had been sighted the weary cavalcade reached a path leading into the interior. Some of Yule's party wanted to follow it. Yule decided to stick to the coast. "The coast was cooler, and most likely to lead us to safety," Yule wrote. "If we lost our way in the wilderness at night we would have died."

They covered six miles that day, and camped on a promontory exposed to the sea breeze. No sooner had they halted than Yule made a shocking discovery. A male passenger, an old man who often fell behind, had thrown away his coat in an anxiety to keep up with the others. He must have been delirious, for there were two full bottles of water in the pockets. Volunteers went back to look for this lost treasure, but they never found it.

Yule, that conscientious and thoughtful leader, had a still heavier blow in store for him that evening. He went round collecting the life-giving water bottles from his trusted carriers. Dr Alexander Byers should have handed him two bottles, but he had only one. He had yielded to temptation and drunk a full bottle of water.

"I kept this crime from the other members of the party, as I feared they might kill the doctor," wrote Yule.

So the forlorn company prayed together as usual, and slept. They were within a few miles of help, but with so little water, and in their depressed state, they might have perished within sight of the river. Dew fell during the night, and a little rain, but they had no means of catching it. Some tried sucking the wet blankets, only to find that they were saturated with salt from the boat journey.

"I could not fail to notice the distressing condition of the people in the morning," Yule went on in his diary. "Faces were bloated and disfigured, lips were rent and chapped, arms and legs were swelling. I did not think that some of them would hold out until the next night.

However, I pretended to be cheerful, though I did not feel it. I pointed to some mountains away in the south-east, and told them there was always water in the mountains."

Captain Yule was right about the utter exhaustion of his party. They struggled along for three-quarters of a mile next morning and then collapsed. Yule issued a ration of water. They sang a hymn. Then the purgatory of walking began again. Another mile and another rest. The old man who had lost his coat was almost finished. His face and limbs were covered with sores.

Yet the time passed, and rising ground appeared ahead. The mate thought he could see the river entrance. Yule ran forward. "There were the broad waters of the Olifants River, and the fertile river banks," he wrote joyously. "I could see a whitewashed dwelling house and other buildings on the far bank, and clear blue smoke from the chimney. We prayed, and I served out water. As we were still a mile from the river I kept a small portion of water."

They had carried their flag with them on the march, and now they waved it. The farm people saw them and sent a boat across. Yule gave out the last of the water. As the boat approached the survivors sang the Twenty-third Psalm.

Someone hailed them in English. "Water!" gasped the survivors. "Can you take us to water?" The Englishman (who turned out to be a sailor working for the Elephant Rock sealing company) told them there was an excellent spring on the other side of the river. Yule and the women went first. In three trips they were all across and slaking the thirst that had been torturing them, night and day, for weeks. Those last eleven miles on foot along the coast had brought them closer to death than the voyage of six hundred miles or more in open boats.

The farmers near the river mouth were Willem Louw and the same Hendrik van Zyl and son mentioned by the traveller Sir James Alexander in his account of his journey to the Orange River a few years earlier. Francis Truter was also there, visiting the river with his mother-in-law on a fishing expedition. All these people treated the sick and tattered castaways with the utmost kindness.

"A whole sheep was cooked, and we were also offered part of a wild buck shot that morning," Yule wrote. "But our hearts were too full for keen appetite and the people wept with relief and gratitude."

Louw's farm was on the south bank four miles from the sea. He could not provide food and shelter for twenty-six people. Some needed careful nursing. However, Truter's mother-in-law, Mrs Wolfaardt, offered to look after the three children, giving them clothes and treating them like a mother. The three women were sent by ox wagon to Mr Richard Fryer, storekeeper at Donkin Bay, a journey of about four miles to the south of the river. Fryer sent the wagon back loaded with provisions, luxuries and medicines, and instructed his shepherd to kill as many sheep as the people might need. Fryer, who was a field cornet, also notified the civil commissioner at Clanwilliam (Mr J. van Ryneveld, already mentioned) and asked him to make arrangements for transporting the party to Cape Town. That was a long trek, not without difficulties, over a century ago.

Days passed, however, before the emaciated people of the *Australia* were ready to move. "Symptoms of hardship and exposure appeared, loathsome blotches and swellings of arms and legs," recorded Yule. "Strange to relate, the women and children stood up to the hardship better than the men, setting a fine example of patience and endurance. Mr Thomas Harris of London, a cabin passenger, was in a most pitiable condition. He could not leave his bed. One leg burst. His hand had to be lanced with a razor. We were afraid he would die, and when the time came to depart for Cape Town we had to leave him behind in charge of the doctor."

Most of the company began to recover after five days. Then came an incessant craving for food. "It was impossible to satisfy our appetites, and we were in danger of creating a famine in the generous Dutch households," declared Yule. "Sheep were killed daily. We also enjoyed the wheat pounded in mortars and boiled, or ground in a mill for bread."

They left the Olifants River in ox wagons on January 19, with Truter as conductor on the first stage. "The yoking of fourteen or sixteen oxen was like getting an East Indiaman under way," Yule reported. "The chattering of the Hottentots was very amusing. But the scene on parting from our dear friends was most affecting. The Dutch families were weeping aloud. Mrs Wolfaardt could hardly bear to be separated from her orphan family. Even the Hottentots were crying. Our friends followed the wagons for some way and then stood waving. Thus we left the kind strangers who had entwined themselves round our hearts. While memory holds I trust that we shall never cease to pray for the richest blessings on the heads of our benevolent friends of the Olifants River."

Yule reported that the ox wagons often lost the way during the journey to Cape Town. Water was scarce in that wilderness of bush and sand. Sometimes the wagons were almost capsized. Yule wrote: "We nearly suffered a second shipwreck in the desert, to the great alarm of the ladies."

They passed the Piketberg mountain. Everywhere the farmers were most hospitable. "Our dress, speech and psalms astonished them," Yule mentioned. "Then, on January 28, we reached Cape Town at midnight and experienced the luxury of a good bed for the first time."

Captain Yule interviewed Colonel Bell, deputy governor, and pointed out that his ship's company were penniless. A short account of their plight appeared in the *South African Commercial Advertiser*, however, and money flowed in. Bell was able to distribute a hundred and twenty pounds in cash and clothing among passengers and crew.

Two of the steerage passengers decided to remain at the Cape. The other passengers were shipped on to Australia, while Captain Yule and the seamen returned to Scotland. Mr Van Ryneveld rendered an account to the government (which I found in the archives) for twenty-four pounds to cover the cost of the three ox wagons which he had requisitioned. Thus ended a forgotten drama of Cape seas and the grim coast of Namaqualand.

I put down the logbook of Captain Adam Yule with regret. This heroic Scottish seaman had gripped me not only by reason of his modesty but with many a telling phrase. He was incredibly stupid in keeping live bulls in his lifeboat, but he atoned nobly for his mistake during the long days and nights of ordeal on sea and land. And not many thirsty and worried leaders would have forgiven the doctor for stealing that bottle of water.

EIGHT BELLS AT SALAMANDER

Ghost Ship Of The Cape

1965

A ghostly ship, with a ghostly crew,
In tempests she appears;
And before the gale, or against the gale,
She sails without a rag of sail,
Without a helmsman steers.

LONGFELLOW

Surely there must be something more than pure imagination in the
Flying Dutchman legend? This ghost ship of the Cape is the most
famous of all sea phantoms. It has inspired poets, novelists and
dramatists, and Wagner based an opera on the fearful tale. How did
it arise? Was there ever a blasphemous Vanderdecken or a real
Flying Dutchman?

I have searched far and wide for the answer, finding many other
ghost ships and many different versions of the grim story in various
languages. Let us tremble with the poets before going on to comb
the libraries and study logbooks and Dutch East India Company
journals. Sir Walter Scott alluded to a phantom ship in his poem
"Rokeby," and his notes reveal that it was the *Flying Dutchman* he
had in mind:

Then mid the war of sea and sky,
Top and top-gallant hoisted high,
Full spread and crowded every sail,
The Demon Frigate braves the gale;
And well the doomed spectators know
The harbinger of wreck and woe.

Scott gives the impression that the legend was known to seamen
in the first half of the seventeenth century. His version is an unusual

one, for he speaks of a *Flying Dutchman* loaded with great wealth. Murder and piracy on board the ship were followed by an outbreak of plague among the wicked crew. She sailed from port to port offering the illgotten wealth in return for shelter; but every harbour shut out the *Flying Dutchman* because of the plague.

So the ghost ship still haunts the Cape of Good Hope where the crimes were committed. "She is distinguished from earthly vessels by bearing a press of sail when others are unable, from stress of weather, to shown an inch of canvas," Scott wrote. He remarked that the cause of her wandering was not altogether certain, and declared that the sighting of the *Flying Dutchman* was considered by mariners to be the worst of all possible omens.

Scott's friend, Dr John Leyden, referred to the *Flying Dutchman* in his poems "Scenes of Infancy":

> *Scenting the storm the shadowy sailors guide*
> *The prow in sails opposed to wind and tide;*
> *The Spectre Ship, in livid glimpsing light,*
> *Glares baleful on the shuddering watch at night,*
> *Unblest of God and man! – Till time shall end,*
> *Its view strange horror to the storm shall lend.*

Leyden made his *Flying Dutchman* the ship that started the slave trade.

Far more familiar is the Vanderdecken version, in which the captain of that name is driving his ship mercilessly off the Cape in heavy weather. Sails are lost, decks are flooded, and the seamen beseech him to give up the attempt to round the Cape. Vanderdecken lashes himself to the wheel and carries on, swearing that even God will not force him to change his mind.

His blasphemous oath is heard. Out of the dark clouds falls a brilliant shaft of light, and the Holy Ghost steps on the the high castellated poop. Vanderdecken draws a pistol from his belt and fires. His arm falls withered at his side, and the Holy Ghost delivers sentence: "You have defied the wrath of God, and now you will sail these seas until the end of time. You will know thirst and hunger, but never will you know calm seas again. Henceforward you will bring misfortune to all who sight you."

It is an illogical legend without a moral, for the punishment of Vanderdecken should not have brought Divine vengeance on an innocent crew and other unhappy seamen throughout the centuries. Nevertheless, the undying tale lives on in many forms.

Charles Edwin Markham, seldom quoted but one of the most distinguished American poets of last century and this, could not resist the ghost ship. He conveyed beauty and terror in his poem:

> *Strange ware are handled on the wharves of sleep:*
> *Shadows of shadows pass, and many a light;*
> *Flashes a signal fire across the night;*
> *Barges depart whose voiceless steermen keep*
> *Their way without a star upon the deep;*
> *And from lost ships, homing with ghostly crews,*
> *Come cries of incommunicable news.*

Thomas Moore, national poet of Ireland, gave a more sinister picture:

> *Oh! hurry thee on – oh! hurry thee on,*
> *Thou terrible bark! ere the night be gone,*
> *Nor let morning look on so foul a sight*
> *As would blanch for ever her rosy light!*

A little later came John Greenleaf Whittier, the Quaker poet who usually found his subjects deep in the Massachusetts countryside. Her is his ghost ship:

> *What weary doom of baffled quest,*
> *Thou sad sea-ghost, is thine?*
> *What makes thee in the haunts of home,*
> *A wonder and a sign?*
> *No foot is on thy silent deck,*
> *Upon thy helm no hand;*
> *No ripple hath the soundless wind*
> *That smites thee from the land.*

Edgar Allan Poe, that wayward poetical craftsman, used prose for his description of the phantom:

"Casting my eyes upward I beheld a spectacle which froze the current of my blood. Directly above us hovered a gigantic ship . . . Her huge hull was of a deep black. A single row of brass cannon protruded from her open ports. But what mainly inspired us with horror and astonishment was that she bore up under a press of sail in the very teeth of that supernatural sea, and of that ungovernable hurricane."

W. Clark Russell, the sea novelist, visited Cape Town in the Eighties of last century. He met an old Kapenaar who claimed that his great-great-grandfather had known Vanderdecken and the *Flying Dutchman*. Vanderdecken called at Table Bay for tobacco and fruit. It was on the return from Batavia that Vanderdecken provoked the Divine wrath. According to Russell's informant, the *Flying Dutchman* had a curious low-built bow with a mass of timbers curving at the head to a thick cutwater. Her bowsprit reared up at an angle of forty-five degrees, and a heavy square yard was rigged below it. She was pierced for eight guns. The hull was painted yellow. On a lofty poop of "castle" design the ghostly Vanderdecken stood, trumpet in hand, hailing any vessel that approached him. Vanderdecken always wanted to send letters to Holland; but if any ship hove-to and complied with his request, she was doomed.

Russell founded a novel of his own, "The Death Ship", on the legend, and drew this picture of Vanderdecken: "His eyes were extraordinarily piercing, with cruel brilliance in them such as may be noticed in the insane. The lower part of his face was hidden in hair, but the skin was pale, of a haggard sallowness, expressed best in paintings of the dead, where time had produced the original whiteness of the pigment. I could readily conceive that the defiance of his heart would be hell-like in obstinacy."

I am extremely dubious about the Clark Russell story of a real Vanderdecken. The resounding name should appear in the journal of the Dutch governors, but I have never come across any reference to it. Others have mentioned a Captain Bernard Fokke, the reckless master of the Dutch East Indiaman *Libera Nos*, who was said to have cased his masts in iron so that he could carry more sail. According to this legend, Fokke diced with the devil and made a pact which resulted in some almost miraculous sea passages. Once he was supposed to have sailed from Holland to the East Indies in ninety days. His ship vanished with all hands during a later voyage, only to reappear off the Cape as a ghost ship manned by skeletons. Fokke himself is seen on the poop with an hourglass, watching the passing of the centuries.

Van Straaten is the central figure of another version which appeared in the Netherlands, while German seamen spoke of a phantom named Falkenburg. In essence, these characters all belong to the *Flying Dutchman* legend, Der Flieginde Hollander of Wagner's opera, Victor Hugo's *la sloop fantome*, the Wandering Jew of the oceans. Only in Wagner's opera will you find a love interest.

> *Yet that weary man from his woes might win exemption*
> *God's angel showed him how he at last might find redemption.*
> *Ah, weary seaman, coulds't thou but attain it!*
> *Pray unto heavan to send him a wife faithful unto death,*
> *At anchor every seventh year, to woo a wife he comes ashore,*
> *But though he woos each seventh year, in vain he doth their love*
> *   implore.*
> *"Hui! the anchor loose. Yo-ho-he. Hui! and hoist the sail.*
> *   Yo-ho-he."*

Perhaps he brought the *Flying Dutchman* into Table Bay to search Cape Town for the girl who would remove the curse; but you will scan the port records and search the local folklore in vain for such an episode. Yet the legend lives on, and from Scott to Kipling the poets have felt impelled to visualise the demented Vanderdecken. I think Kipling's glimpse is among the most vivid:

> *Strange consorts rode beside us*
> *   And brought us evil luck;*
> *The witch-fire climbed our channels,*
> *   And flared on vane and truck:*
> *Till, through the red tornado,*
> *   That lashed us nigh to blind,*
> *We saw the Dutchman plunging,*
> *   Full canvas, head to wind!*

Let us not forget the great Coleridge, however, whose "Ancient Mariner" is a ghastly creation indeed:

> *Like one, that on a lonesome road*
> *Doth walk in fear and dread,*
> *And having once turned round walks on,*
> *And turns no more his head;*
> *Because he knows, a frightful fiend*
> *Doth close behind him tread.*

In the British Museum library I found a long, anonymous account of a meeting between an unnamed British passenger ship and the *Flying Dutchman*, written early last century. All on board the

British ship were so nervous that the chaplain brought up his prayer book and read the service for those distressed at sea. Vanderdecken sent a boat across with four men. One weatherbeaten Dutch seaman reached the deck with letters in his hand. The chaplain asked how long they had been at sea.

"We have lost our count, for our almanack was blown overboard," replied the seaman. "Vanderdecken only wishes to write home and comfort his friends."

To which the chaplain replied: "Your letters, I fear, would be of no use in Amsterdam even if they were delivered, for the persons to whom they are addressed are probably under very ancient green turf in the churchyard."

The unwelcome seaman wrung his hands. "We have been long driving about here, but country and relations cannot easily be forgotten," he cried. The he laid the letters on the deck and placed a bar of iron on them. A sudden squall arose, and the man returned to his boat. "Let no one touch the letters," ordered the British captain. "Case them upon the deck by nailing boards over them, so that if he sends back for them, they are still there to give him." The carpenter went for his tools, but while he was gone the ship pitched violently and the letters were whirled overboard by the wind. There was a cry of joy among the sailors. Soon there was a change for the better in the weather. The night watch being set, the rest of the crew went to their bunks.

*

Not only the poets, but hard, unimaginative seamen kept the legend alive. Captain after captain reported sighting the *Flying Dutchman*, some long ago, others in our own time, British men-o'-war among them. In the records of the Royal Navy there is an eighteenth-century account of a mutiny in a British man-'o-war in South Atlantic waters. To scare away inquisitive vessels, the crew rigged their ship to resemble the *Flying Dutchman*. Then they turned pirate. Off the Cape they met the real *Flying Dutchman*, and so terrified were they that they sailed into port and gave themselves up.

Captain Owen, R.N., who charted long stretches of the South African coast, declared that he saw the *Flying Dutchman* through his glasses. The encounter appears in the logbook of H.M.S. *Leven*, dated April 6, 1823. Owen was off Danger Point and bound for Simon's Bay when he thought he saw his consort, H.M.S. *Barracouta*, sailing to leeward. This appearance surprised him as *Barracouta* had been ordered elsewhere. Owen bore down on the other ship and saw a boat being lowered. He sailed away hurriedly, for he knew the *Flying Dutchman* legend and the penalty for taking letters.

Owen and his men reported sighting the *Flying Dutchman* again during that passage, and again a boat was lowered. The *Leven* did not attempt to make close contact. When she reached Simon's Bay she waited for a week and the *Barracouta* arrived. They compared logbooks, and it was found that the two naval ships were three hundred miles apart when Owen had intercepted the mystery ship.

Far more famous was the encounter witnessed by Prince Albert Victor and Prince George of Wales, later King George V. The young princes were both midshipmen, cruising in H.M.S. *Bacchante*, one of the largest men-o'-war of her time. Lord Charles Scott was the captain. The meeting was entered in the logbook as follows:

"July 11, 1881. During the middle-watch the so-called *Flying Dutchman* crossed our bows. She first appeared as a strange red light, as of a ship all aglow, in the midst of which light her masts, spars and sails, seemingly those of a normal brig, some two hundred yards distant from us, stood out in strong relief as she came up. Our lookout man on the forecastle reported her as close to our port bow, where also the officer of the watch from the bridge clearly saw her, as did our quarterdeck midshipman, who was sent forward at once to the forecastle to report back. But on reaching there, no vestige nor any sign of any material ship was to be seen either near or away to the horizon. The early morning, as the night had been, was clear, the sea strangely calm. Thirteen persons altogether saw her, but whether it was the *Flying Dutchman* or one of the other few alleged phantom ships which are reputed to haunt this area must remain unknown. *Tourmaline* and *Cleopatra*, which were sailing on our starboard quarter, flashed signals asking whether we had seen the strange glow, and if we could account for it. During the forenoon watch the seaman who had this morning first reported this phantom vessel fell from our fore-topmast crosstrees and was killed instantly.

Towards the end of our afternoon watch, after quarters, our ship was hove-to with headyards aback while we buried him. He was a smart royal-yard seaman, one of the most promising hands in the ship, and every man on board feels sad and despondent at his loss."

This was not the only death. The admiral in command of the squadron died at the next port of call.

Blue distress signals were seen by officers, crew and passengers of the S.S. *Pretoria* in 1879, and the steamer altered course. An old-fashioned sailing ship was sighted, but she vanished suddenly before the *Pretoria* came within hailing distance. This episode was regarded by those on board the steamer as an encounter with the *Flying Dutchman*.

Once, and once only in the long story of the *Flying Dutchman*, have I discovered a report in which the ghost ship appeared to have played a benevolent role. The main story is completely true, and forms part of the American whaling history.

Captain George Howland of the New Bedford whaler *Canton* was a deeply religious man who would not hunt on Sundays. He was off the Cape of Good Hope in November 1890, and for a week he had been trying to steer eastwards to the Indian Ocean whaling grounds. He was baffled by strong head winds and sudden eerie calms; and at last all on board became convinced that some supernatural force was working against them. In the fo'c'sle the men spoke nervously of the *Flying Dutchman*, and even among the officers there was a feeling that a curse had descended on the ship. Howland decided that neither the *Flying Dutchman* nor a curse was responsible for the weather. He thought it was Divine intervention, and when the wind sprang up he ran before it, course north-north-west. "Let the wind take us where it will," Howland told his mate. "Perhaps there are whales in this direction."

After steering north-north-west for twenty-four hours, the look-out at the masthead sighted two lifeboats, dead ahead. The barque *British Monarch* had been abandoned on fire twenty-four hours previously, and here were her men in the boats. They landed the rescued seamen, and rounded the Cape without a sign of Vander-decken or the freakish winds that had troubled them on the last attempt.

London newspapers in 1911 published a message describing an

American whaler off the Cape that had almost collided with a sailing ship believed to be the *Flying Dutchman*. Cape Town papers early in 1939 described a queer experience in False Bay, when people on the beaches saw a sailing ship beating up towards Muizenberg. They were puzzled, for there was a flat calm over the bay. It seemed that the ship would run into the breakers at Strandfontein, but just before reaching the shallows, she vanished. Many onlookers that day swore they had seen the *Flying Dutchman*.

Finally there is the statement by Admiral Karl Doenitz of the German Navy, the man responsible for sending out the U-boats during World War II. He said the submarine crews saw the *Flying Dutchman* or some other phantom ship off the Cape of Good Hope. "When they returned to their base," Doenitz added, "the men said they preferred facing the combined strength of the Allied warships in the North Atlantic than know the terror a second time of being confronted by a phantom vessel."

Some of these U-boats were sunk later, and the survivors remembered the Vanderdecken legend.

ALMOST FORGOTTEN, NEVER TOLD

On the Wind of a Dream

1965

Look back with me through the long years of sail, gaze upon the vanished fleets that once filled Table Bay, and hear faint echoes of the departed comrade's story.

Often and often I have enriched my hoard of stories of forgotten ships. Sometimes a diary or faded newspaper cutting would give me a little drama. Once I made notes from a ledger that had gathered the dust of a century in a Cape Town attic. It held the reports of all the masters of all the ships that had anchored in Table Bay during five years early last century. Slavers and pirates, famous and infamous vessels sailed again as I turned the pages of exquisite old handwriting.

Cape Town people have always loved to gather on the waterfront and stare at interesting ships and their people. Important ship visitors appear in our history books; but many strange and fascinating tales were lost or overlooked or hidden from the public eye.

Life in the Dutch East India Company ships was dangerous rather than romantic. Mentzel, the mid-eighteenth century traveller, remarked that "most of the sick people are usually cured through the zeal and skill of the surgeon and the excellent medicines of the company". This hardly tallies with his later statement: "The crew look more dead than alive when they come to the Cape of Good Hope, but breathing its pure air and having fresh and wholesome food they recover their bright and healthy appearance."

Possibly it was scurvy that was responsible for the disappearance of a new ship called *De Groet* in Mentzel's time. After leaving the English Channel she was never seen again. Then there was the *Rygersdal,* wrecked near Dassen Island. More than one hundred of her crew had died during the voyage, and the survivors were too ill to handle the ship. Ninety-three were drowned when the ship ran ashore and only twenty managed to save themselves.

The death toll in the Dutch ships of the eighteenth century was about ten per cent of the crew. If foreigners had not signed on, the Dutch would not have been able to keep up their large merchant navy. In spite of all the risks, the Dutch East India Company became at one period the wealthiest corporation in the world. Each summer fleet from India carried to Holland goods valued at millions of pounds. No wonder there were pirates lying in wait for lone vessels separated from the main fleet.

Suspicious craft roamed the Cape coast early last century. The register had an entry about a large cutter, the *Empress,* which put into St Helena Bay for supplies. "She can mount fourteen guns, but has them principally in the hold," ran the report. "Shows but very few people. She was at the anchorage several days, and in constant trade with the farmers." Was she a pirate? Her master said he was bound for Algoa Bay, and after leaving St Helena Bay she disappears from the records – with her formidable armament.

I found that H.M.S. *Tees* had been struck by lightning during her passage to the Cape. Two of her men were killed and five seriously injured. The foremast was shivered and many sails destroyed by fire. I imagined that this must have been a rare accident, but the old register gave details of another ship, the Dutch brig *Prince William,* which was almost put out of action by lightning. Her masts were damaged, sails were set on fire, the rudder was broken and the ship developed so many leaks that the pumps had to be manned constantly. She was foundering when the British ship *Nimrod* came in sight, helped to make repairs, and escorted her into Table Bay. The *Prince William* was beached on arrival, and she never sailed again.

Slavers appear in the shipping records almost throughout the last century. I found the arrival of the slaver *Sylph* in Table Bay in 1819, manned by British bluejackets. They had landed more than three hundred slaves at Sierra Leone and brought their prize to Table Bay. Other nations had not yet abolished the slave trade, and Portuguese schooners often called at the Cape with hundreds of slaves under hatches. The *Matto Grosso,* a Portuguese brig listed in the register, had four hundred slaves on board. She was bound from East Africa to Cuba.

Dhows carried slaves in Indian Ocean waters long after the South Atlantic had been cleared of the filthy trade. Several dhows, seventy-ton vessels, were brought to the Cape by Commander Jago R.N. of H.M.S. *Rapid* in the Sixties of last century. "Galla slaves", as they were called, were settled in the Cape Colony in the late Eighties. I believe a wooden ship that puzzled many people in the dunes beyond Muizenberg early this century was one of the last of the captured slavers.

Stowaways appeared in the old register now and again. The master of the little barque *Harriet,* from Port Jackson to London in the 1820s, called at Table Bay and reported: "After having been at sea for a few days I discovered sixteen men and five women secreted in the ship." I am still wondering how so many people were able to hide on board the *Harriet,* and I suspect the crew of helping them.

On May 23, 1821, the British ship *Nerina* reached Table Bay, and the register stated that she had two cooks on board for Napoleon's household. Before they could be sent on to St Helena, H.M.S. *Beaver* arrived with the news that the emperor had died.

Indiamen, the large and stately vessels of the Honourable East India Company, usually bypassed Table Bay when homeward bound from China and Bengal. They preferred St Helena for provisions. However, the register listed some that put into Table Bay; such famous ships as the *Earl of Balcarras,* the *Marquess of Hastings* and the *Duchess of Atholl.*

These were luxurious ships by the standards of those days, and their passengers included wealthy officials, merchants and their families. One old description mentioned the ships with their bows rich with scrollwork and gilding, the huge, swelling figureheads, quarter-galleries and sterns enriched with mermaids and carved flowers. Down their gangways came women in crinolines and ringlets, and "ayahs gay as tropical birds with little pale English children clinging to them".

*

Cape Town has seen French naval ratings with red pompoms on their caps in recent years. They have been calling here for a long time. I wish that I could have watched the French corvette *Uranie* sailing into Table Bay in 1818; for she had Rose de Freycinet on board, a remarkable woman who sailed round the world disguised as a man.

Captain Louis de Freycinet, her husband, was a distinguished geographer who had been sent off in command of *Uranie* by King Louis XVIII on a scientific "voyage of curiosity". An artist accompanied the expedition to paint strange peoples. Rose cut her hair, wore blue trousers and a long blue coat, and hid in the captain's room until the ship had left the coast of France. Then she surprised the ship's company by appearing in a bonnet and high-waisted dress.

Rose and her husband stayed with a French merchant in Cape Town. In her diary she commented on the south-easter: "When this wind blows one cannot stay in the streets without being blinded by the fine sand," she wrote. "The streets are straight and spotlessly clean, lined with charming houses, well built and delightfully neat." They called on Lord Charles Somerset, and she recorded that he lived like a Viceroy with a retinue. Somerset, a widower still in the forties, talked to Rose for the whole evening. "Perhaps this was due to his adoration of our sex as a whole – people reproach him with loving us a little too much," Rose went on. "Should we regard that as a fault? Yes, for he who loves all loves little."

The voyage of the *Uranie* ended in shipwreck on the cold and uninhabited Falkland Islands. They all lived as castaways for months until a ship arrived by chance.

Cape Town became very much aware of France in the 1860s, when whole armies and ships' companies of sailors filled the streets. They were on their way to fight in China. Thousands stepped happily off the men-o'-war *L'Entreprenant* and *Andromeda,* the *Rhone* and *Garonne.* One day there were five thousand French soldiers in the transports at anchor in the bay. Their bands played in the town. Officers dined at Government House. Local writers gazed in astonishment on the strange uniforms, and one bewildered wit declared: "Their close-cropped heads, long coats, exaggerated style of unmentionables, eternal gesticulations and desperate attempts at fraternisation with all classes have made them the most entertaining set of animals that could have been imported."

Of course the *vivandières* and *cantinières* were there, too, uniformed women with feathers in their hats and bottles of wine on their backs. Cape Town stared at the soldiers and gaped at these camp followers. Some of these women wore campaign medals like the soldiers. There was the almost inevitable street fighting when the Frenchmen, accustomed to mild table wine, were inflamed with "Cape smoke". Newspapers reported that the French had thrown a number of American seamen off the stoep of the Argus Hotel.

The visit ended on a happier note, and one newspaper summed up: "We have entertained our gallant friends as well as we can. We have given them dinners and balls and murdered their language. They have shown themselves delighted with all our attempts, eating the dinners, dancing their legs off at our balls and never laughing at our bad French. Indeed, their politeness is inimitable."

*

Russian ships called at intervals throughout most of last century. The frigate *Pallada* arrived in 1853 with the novelist Goncharov serving on board as admiral's secretary.

Goncharov drove from Simon's Bay to Cape Town, stopping at Rathfelder's Halfway House (now the Eaton Convalescent Home) for a breakfast of omelette, cold tough beef and hot tough ham. He was unlucky at dinner, too, "There was curry, served everywhere from the Cape to China every day," he wrote. "It consists of beef or some other meat, now and then of chicken or venison, even of crayfish and particularly of shrimps, cut into small pieces and boiled with a pungent sauce composed of ten or more Indian peppers. Moreover they serve as well some kind of special almost poisonous sauce from which the dish gets its name."

The young Russian writer was more favourably impressed with the Table Bay waterfront. "An embankment with a railway track stretches far out into the water," he noted. "It is always crowded with sailors of different nationalities, with masters of ships and with common or garden gapers from the town. And there's something to gape about! In front is the immense bay with lots of ships; small boats scurry to and fro; far away is a sandy spit and beyond it the Tiger Mountains. Behind you are the three gigantic mountain masses and the gay lively town . . . At one spot I saw the notice 'omnibus office'. I ask where they go and they mention the nearest places, which are about forty or fifty miles from Cape Town. And they drove there long ago in ox wagons, escorted by crowds of Hottentots, to hunt for lions and tigers. Today it's necessary to go four hundred miles for lions. Towns, roads, hotels, omnibuses and noise have driven them far away. But tigers and jackals are to be found everywhere; they roam the mountains surrounding Cape Town."

Goncharov was reluctant to leave Cape Town, in spite of the curry. "It's painful to quit a familiar house or street, a favourite walk or a good man," he remarked. "So I was sorry to leave Room No. 8, Hottentot Square, the botanic garden, the view of Table Mountain and our hostesses . . . In front of me lies sea and sea and sea."

Apparently there was no trouble during the visit of the *Pallada*. Five years later a Russian squadron arrived, men-'o-war and transports bound for China. Simonstown was full of Russian and British sailors, and the men clashed in the main street. According to the *Cape of Good Hope Gazette,* the Russians were quiet and inoffensive, while the British were like a set of bulldogs eager for a fight. It seems that a crippled English soldier who had lost an arm in the Crimea taunted a Russian. Soon afterwards about one hundred and fifty Russians were facing a hundred British sailors (led by a marine), both sides being equipped with legs of tables, chairs, sticks and stones. After a number of men had been knocked senseless the Russians were driven to their boats at the jetty. Mr Rennick, the chief constable, tried to stop the fight and had his arm broken. Some of the British seamen appeared in court after this incident, and were fined.

Another squadron of Russian ships called in July 1872, and Duke Alexis, the senior officer, presented three hundred pounds to Cape Town charities. But the men of the Russian corvette *Bogatyo* spoilt the good impression left by the Duke. When she departed, a newspaper commented: "Cape Town will be glad to get rid of this dirty and drunken crew."

Here is a barque-rigged British man-o'-war, H.M.S. *Chanticleer,* sailing into Table Bay in 1829 on a scientific mission – to ascertain the true shape of the earth. I found the private journal kept by her surgeon, Dr W.H.B. Webster, in the British Museum library.

Captain Henry Foster was in command, a man who had been with Parry in the Arctic. The *Chanticleer* carried out some Antarctic exploration during her voyage. Her first Cape port was Mossel Bay, and there Dr Webster examined the shells on the beach. He said that the paper nautilus shell was found there occasionally, and that the British Museum had offered one hundred pounds for a specimen. A Cape Town merchant had discovered one of the rare shells and claimed the reward. Dr Webster picked up nothing of value, but he enjoyed the oysters.

Soon after the ship anchored in Table Bay three Malays were hanged. After the executions the bodies were beheaded, and the heads were displayed on poles outside the town as a warning. Dr Webster said the Malays were horrified, as they believed that a maimed body would not be admitted into paradise.

Cape Town had twenty thousand people at that time. Dr Webster described the dazzling white houses with stoeps shaded by fig trees. He thought Government House was "humble-looking but perhaps comfortable". Webster admired the Hottentot drivers, the horses and oxen, the Dutch wheelwrights, and the wine wagons creaking in from the country. He visited a farm beyond the Cape Flats, and noticed the extraordinary stillness after the noises of the ship. His bed was scented with fragrant herbs to offset the odour of the cow-dung floor.

Coffee was brought in at six in the morning. Then came breakfast, with fish, meat, tongue, venison, ham, eggs and tea. Tiffin was at eleven, dinner at two, and coffee was served at three-thirty with sweetmeats eaten with tiny silver forks. Tea at six and a good hot supper at nine rounded off the generous menus of the day.

Webster joined a tortoise-hunting expedition at the vlei, but the party returned with only ducks and land crabs. That night there was a Hottentot dance, with twenty slaves capering to the *gorah,* a calabash with strings, played by a grey-bearded slave musician. Webster called on Sir John Truter, who lived close by. On his return he found that the slaves had been burning sweet-scented herbs in the farmhouse to drive away devils. Next day most of the Malays were drunk.

The scientists of the *Chanticleer* caught a giant sunfish in Table Bay, more than seven feet in length. They also collected shells which Webster called *Caput medusae,* valued at ten guineas apiece. During a visit to Robben Island he saw quail and penguins, rabbits, seals, lizards, chameleons and scorpions. The island, he declared, produced the finest cauliflowers in the country. "Some say that South Africa is a paradise, others a dreary waste," wrote Webster. "The truth is between them."

*

Sailing ship passengers who had reason to feel pleased with their treatment often entertained their captains on arrival in Cape Town. "A splendid dinner was given at the George Hotel in the Heerengracht by the passengers in the barque *Mary* to Captain Hornblow," runs one news item. "This was a compliment to his kindness, attention and hospitality during the passage from Madras, in spite of severe gales."

Many fine little sailing ships were owned by Cape Town merchants last century. Let me recall the little-known voyage in 1814 of the *Good Hope* of one hundred and fifty tons. St Helena was a prosperous island in those days, taking as much grain and wine, salted meat, live sheep and cattle as the Cape could supply. So the *Good Hope* left Table Bay with a cargo of food and drink for the island. Month after month passed, and the *Good Hope* seemed to have vanished from the face of the South Atlantic. Ships that had left the Cape long after her reached St Helena safely. It was feared that the *Good Hope* had been captured by the hostile French or gone to the bottom.

However, the *Good Hope* appeared at St Helena eleven weeks after leaving Table Bay. Her captain and crew had eaten a great deal of the meat and drunk their fill of the Cape wine during the long voyage. When the pilot climbed on board the captain and the man at the wheel were far from sober. The captain had drunk so much that he had been unable to take proper sights. Having missed St Helena completely he had sailed on to the West African coast to get his bearings.

My extracts from the shipping register include this note: "The doctor died at sea and was put in a cask of spirits." (Lord Nelson's body had been treated in the same way some years previously.) This old sea custom had all sorts of repercussions. For example, I have a record of a ship that landed brandy at St Helena from the Cape, and some time later the importers found a body in one of the barrels. An inquest was held, but the mystery of that unidentified body remains unsolved to this day.

Among the well-known Cape shipowners of last century was Captain James Murison, who brought his brig *Rosebud* to the Cape in the 1830s. Murison was a kind-hearted old seaman, shrewd and honest. He carried many of the early settlers to Natal.

Captain Murison left the sea to organise the anti-convict movement. He became a bank and insurance company director, and acted as agent for steamers running to Britain before the Castle Line started. Apart from the *Star of Africa*, his firm had the *Flibberty*, the *Gondola* and the fast *Silver Cloud;* and they traded from the Pacific slope to the China Seas, from Brazil to Mauritius. Yet the enterprising Murison hardly ever left Cape Town during half a century in business. He was a Sea Point pioneer. Every ship in Table Bay had her flag at half-mast when Murison died.

Among the colonial vessels of the mid-nineteenth century was the barque *Enterprise,* not to be confused with the S.S. *Enterprize,* the first steamer to reach Table Bay. The barque *Enterprise* sailed away under Captain Collison and was absent on one voyage for five years. The captain explained that he had been trading in the Arctic and had been trapped in the ice.

These episodes lifted at random out of the dust and the dark are typical of the thousands of forgotten adventures that were told in the taverns of Cape Town when sail ruled the oceans of the world. Few people saw the beauty of sail in those days. But poets like C. Fox Smith have revealed the romance of those vanished fleets:

> *And I watched while her helm went over,*
> *and the sails were sheeted home,*
> *And under her moving forefoot the bubbles*
> *broke into foam,*
> *Till she faded from sight in the greyness –*
> *a thing of wonder and gleam,*
> *For the port of the Past on a bowline –*
> *close-hauled on the wind of a dream.*

ALMOST FORGOTTEN NEVER TOLD

Bay of Lost Cargoes
1969

Old sailormen have told me that Port Elizabeth once had a seafaring quarter as rowdy and dangerous as old Cape Town's waterfront streets. The surfboat crews of Algoa Bay, they declared, were every bit as bold and skilful as the Table Bay watermen. Just as Table Bay skippers feared the winter north-westers, so the ship masters of last century dreaded the black south-easters at Algoa Bay.

Algoa Bay must be paved with lost cargoes, everything from steel rails and other "Glasgow jewellery" to slabs of marble and galvanised sheets. Hundreds of anchors have rested in the mud for centuries. Thousands of fathoms of valuable anchor chains have been abandoned there, enough to hold the fleets of the world. When bales and cases dropped from the slings the Customs men known as "tide waiters" recovered some of the flotsam on North End beach; but Algoa Bay has swallowed greedily fortunes in heavy freight that should have gone to the shore in lighters. Those who know only the modern all-weather harbour can have little idea of past hardships and disasters. Again and again the builders of walls and breakwaters were defeated by the violence of the sea, and Port Elizabeth had to wait more than a century for the secure basin of today.

I can remember the windswept anchorage where passenger ships and tramps plunged and bucketed with strings of lighters bumping heavily against their sides. Gangways were smashed, passengers had to enter tall baskets and trust the magnificent natives of vast experience who handled the rattling steam-winches and lowered them safely to the decks of tugs. The trade of the port was carried on over the years in spite of wild and frightening storms and all too many shipwrecks. In the days of sail a strong south-easter must have been a nightmare for those afloat. Ship masters took compass bearings of Fort Frederick and Bird Rock and anchored in six fathoms, grey sand over clay. October to April were the months they feared. When haze appeared on the horizon; when the air became cold and damp; when the port office hoisted a warning, then careful masters made for open sea. Some trusted their ground tackle, but if their cables parted the surf claimed them and they pounded on the sand. Others hesitated, tried to claw off the lee shore; their topsails carried away, mainsails split and they became victims of the heavy, breaking seas. Often by the next morning a fine ship would have become a mass of tangled rope and shattered timber.

As long as the wind blew from the west, Algoa Bay offered safe anchorage. When it veered to the east of Cape Recife a swell rose and the lighters became hard to manage. Black south-easters filled the sky with dark clouds and masters realised the danger before the gale warning was signalled from the shore. Tarpaulins were dragged over the holds of the lighters and all cargo work came to a halt. Small craft made for the shore. Ship after ship veered out more cable; sixty fathoms became seventy, eighty, a hundred, a hundred and twenty, and men wondered whether the great chains would stand the test. Steamers with their fires burning were safe enough, for they could use their engines to relieve the strain or move out to sea if necessary. Sailing ships had to rely on anchors and chain and springs. Their crews stared across the anchorage to see how others were faring and caught occasional glimpses through blinding spray. Landmarks became invisible. They heard the roaring of the gale, the surf on the beach, the nerveracking creak and groaning of the windlass. All night there would be the lightning and the rain; the wind blowing at seventy, eighty miles an hour; men working frantically by the light of storm lanterns; rockets going up, tar barrels ablaze as signals of distress. Dawn would show the black cloud masses still racing overhead. Dawn on the beach would bring sorrow to all who set eyes on the doomed and the dead. Sometimes the crowds on the beach were able to count the men in the bows of a wrecked ship, but they had to watch them drowning, one by one.

Years ago during an early visit to Port Elizabeth I was advised to call on two old citizens named Josephus Winter and Thomas Morgan. After this lapse of time I can hardly believe my own notes, for these men talked freely of the 1850s. They remembered Port Elizabeth as a place of sandy roads like an up-country village; a Main Street crowded with wool wagons; postcart drivers with bugles; masses of foam blowing across Jetty Street and across Market Square during a south-easter. They had seen a sailing ship break away from her anchor and drive right through a wooden jetty, leaving a wide gap. Then she met her end of the rocks. They talked of the wreck of the *Charlotte,* a troopship bound from Cork to Calcutta under sail. She was no *Birkenhead,* for everyone on board seemed to have been panicstricken. The *Charlotte* carried one hundred and sixty-three officers and men of the Twenty-seventh Regiment, eleven women and twenty-six children and a full crew. She put into Algoa Bay for provisions and water, and while at anchor there a south-east gale blew up. Almost everyone in the town went down to the foot of Jetty Street to watch the drama. "Above the fury of the wind and sea we could hear the cries of the women and children," recalled Mr Winter. "They saw the danger even before the ship parted with her anchor." The captain of the *Charlotte* got a little sail on her and tried to beat out of the bay, but it was hopeless. The troopship crawled along just outside the breakers, parallel with the shore. Off North End beach the mate jumped overboard and was drowned in the surf. Survivors declared that the mate had tried to persuade the captain to beach the ship on the sand. When the captain refused the mate said he was going to give himself a sporting chance of reaching the shore, and went to his death. The *Charlotte* struck the rockiest part of the foreshore and broke in half. The harbourmaster sent a rocket line across, but no one in the *Charlotte* touched it. Then he sent out a lifeboat at great risk. "A panic at this time seized the crew and troops," reported the harbourmaster. "In defiance of repeated hails from the shore they jumped overboard. I launched the boat in a fearful surf and several times pulled alongside. The boat filled and was driven on the rocks after several men had been washed overboard." Mr Winter said the *Charlotte* broke up rapidly, but the stern came so close to the shore that a number of people were saved. At daybreak hardly a fragment of the troopship was to be seen at the place where she had struck. Sixty soldiers, eleven women and all the children were drowned, and the total death roll was one hundred and fifteen. Port Elizabeth regarded the *Charlotte* disaster as a mystery. As a rule people facing death are stirred to action, but nearly all on board the *Charlotte* seemed to have been paralysed by fear. By the way, this wreck which was described to me by eye-witnesses occurred as far back as 1854. Captain Salmond, who tried to organise the rescue, was awarded a gold medal, and this has been preserved in the Port Elizabeth Library.

South-east gales brought work for the local shipyards. They caulked the damaged ships, fitted new rudders, fashioned new mainmasts and topmasts and rigged ships of all sizes. When the *Star of Empire* was dismasted and abandoned, the Port Elizabeth craftsmen fitted her out again and sent her to sea as the *Lady Grey*. Famous little Cape Town traders were calling at Algoa Bay a century ago: the *Lord of the Isles,* which went on to Mauritius for sugar, the guano island vessel *Alert,* Captain James Glendinning's *Admiral,* the *Anna, Albatross* and *Jonquille.* Port Elizabeth builders launched a schooner of their own in the middle of last century, the *Penguin,* for communication with Bird Island. They had their own whaling industry, too, started by Frederick Korsten, the Dutch aristocrat and merchant who was there before the settlers arrived. He was also a farmer and shipowner. Korsten's ship *Helena* sailed to England and he opened up the sealing and guano trade with the Algoa Bay islands.

Whaling flourished all through last century, the fierce old-fashioned whaling which made bull-fighting seem a sport for timid people. Algoa Bay had several great harpooners. Rival whalermen kept a sharp lookout from the Donkin Reserve or St Croix Island, and a smoke fire was the signal that a whale had been sighted. Right whales swam into Algoa Bay to calve from June to September each year. When the lookoutmen saw a "blow", the crews rushed down to North End beach and launched the narrow, double-ended boats. Portuguese harpooners were among the pioneers. One daredevil named Fernandez often jumped from the boat on to a whale's back to drive the lance home. Searle, another skipper, used a small harpoon gun fired from the shoulder; it had a kick that usually knocked him over, but when the dart exploded in the right spot the whale died quickly. Among the last of the North End whalermen was Old Darby, a fearless Malay. He once brought in a huge sperm whale, sixty feet long and valued at eight hundred pounds. They had their blubber pots on North End beach, and all the poor (and the dogs) of Port Elizabeth gathered there to feast on discarded fragments of fat whale meat. Whalebone was cleaned and sold in those days of corsets, and unwanted parts were dumped at sea. But the great skeletons remained for many years as relics of the hunting. Mr Herbert McWilliams, the well-known architect and yacht designer, uses the old cauldrons as flowerpots at his home on the Swartkops River. The vertebrae of whales decorate his garden. Among his nautical museum pieces are the figurehead of H.M.S. *Medusa*, one of Nelson's flagships; ships' lanterns, a signal cannon, bells and bollards and anchors.

Port Elizabeth had its pubs in the very early days, the Red Lion Tavern and the Robinson Hotel. In the 1840s came the Phoenix Hotel, named after the pioneer paddle steamer *Phoenix*, that traded along the coast. Cobb's coaches, drawn by eight horses, started from the Phoenix. By the middle of last century there were rather more bars and canteens than the little town needed. Strand Street, which had a vile reputation, was the resort of smugglers, drunken seamen, escaped convicts and army deserters. Here the thirsty sailorman could refresh himself at the Standard, the Prince of Wales, Kromm's, Ted Sasse's, the Caledonian, the Admiral Rodney and other hotels and canteens. In this unlighted quarter, known as Irish Town, beachcombers slept in surf boats and defended themselves against a horde of rats. Here the stevedores fortified themselves with brandy before pulling off to ships in the bay. Often they needed strong drink for their boats capsized again and again in heavy weather. People loved to watch the surf boats coming in and waiting just outside the line of breakers for a word from the coxs'n. At the right moment the coxs'n would dip his long steering oar and shout; the men would pull together and come roaring in on the crest of a wave. Once the boat touched, all hands would jump into the water. With shoremen helping they would lift the heavy boat with slings and spars and rush her out of reach of the sea. Passengers were carried on shore by natives.

Irish Town was tough, but an Irish priest named Father Murphy restored law and order. He rode a black horse and carried only a cane. When the black horse died he acquired a white horse; and an admirer called his hotel the White Horse in honour of the priest's steed. Thanks to Father Murphy's influence the Roman Catholic prisoners in the little wooden gaol were allowed out on Sundays to attend Mass. For three decades Father Murphy visited the Irish emigrants who settled in Port Elizabeth. He died nearly a century ago, but the man and his famous horses have never been forgotten.

Port Elizabeth had a German colony in the 1850s and they gathered at Hirsch's Hotel, the Commercial in Queen Street. It was not only the fountain with goldfish and lilies that attracted them. Hirsch also provided sausages and pumpernickel, Bavarian cheese and pretzels. His cooks transmuted the plain local cabbage into a legendary *sauerkraut,* shredded and flavoured with caraway seeds, garnished with apples and onions and frankfurters. Hirsch imported the typical German herb liqueurs as well as the Rhine brandies and Steinhaeger gin; and he kept an unfailing stock of regional beers to suit the exacting palates of residents and sailors. There came a time when the German colony in Port Elizabeth formed a Deutsche Liedertafel, gathering under a huge imperial coat-of-arms with black, white and red ribbons. They drank and sang and ate rollmops, and when the glasses were raised the toasts could be heard in the street – *Prost! Zum Wohle! Zur Gesundheit!* Strange to say, a favourite meeting place of the German colony late last century was the Britannia Hotel.

Other early hotels in Queen Street were the George and Dragon, the Oddfellows Arms, the Rose and Shamrock, Fountain and Albion. The Vine in Sea Lane was known for some reason as His Lordship's Larder. Queen Street also had, as a contrast, a garden filled with one of the finest collections of ships' figureheads ever seen in South Africa. Mr Tee, the owner, did not exactly welcome shipwrecks; but he was always on the spot when wrecks were put up for sale, and the auctioneer could always rely on a bid for the figurehead. In this way Mr Tee became the owner of a nautical museum far more romantic than the rusty anchors, chain and other marine equipment that surrounded the George Hotel in Main Street. Where are they now, those crude yet robust wooden statues of classical figures and naval heroes, those famous men and women staring with sightless eyes towards the oceans they had lost? These images of good luck were not always works of art. Some came from the benches of ships' carpenters, though now and again a shipowner commissioned a brilliant woodcarver and adorned a prow with a delicate figurehead that brought the whole ship to life. Mr Tee had a stupid-looking man with a walrus moustache between two lovely female effigies in flowing robes. There was an eagle from a Yankee whaler and a lion from some unknown wreck. Carved from pine and brightly painted, these were relics of the golden age of sail.

Dick Smithers, an American who made a living by breaking up wrecks, was among the Port Elizabeth characters towards the end of last century. He ran a boarding house as a sideline, and his dances with a pianist and three fiddlers were described as the best entertainment value of the period. Smithers charged an entrance fee of one shilling. Of course there were scenes of wild disorder when seamen of the different nations clashed, when fists and belts came into action. But on happier occasions the sentimental mariners gathered round the orchestra and sang with tears in their bloodshot eyes:

> *But a maiden so sweet lives in that little street,*
> *She's the daughter of Widow McNally;*
> *She has bright golden hair, and the boys all declare*
> *She's the sunshine of Paradise Alley.*

Among the picturesque corners of Port Elizabeth early this century was the Chinese market garden. Chinese growers took their vegetables from door to door in pannier baskets. Even in those days some people enjoyed the authentic Chinese dishes; meat and fish cooked with sesame or peanut oil and mild spices; mushrooms and bamboo shoots, shrimps and almonds and soya sauce; cakes flavoured with powdered ginger.

Malay fishermen carried their fish on long bamboo poles. Their mosques were at the lower end of Strand Street. The fishermen moved to South End later and lived in wattle and daub huts. Like the Cape Malays, this colony at Algoa Bay loved picnics on holidays, and they streamed out to the Swartkops River in their carts. The fezzed men favoured brown suits with gold watch chains; women appeared in dazzling clothes. They danced their own *volkspele* and they sang:

> *So lank as die rietjie in die water lê*
> *In die water lê, in die water lê*

So lank as die rietjie in die water lê
Blommetjie gedink om my.

Mr McWilliams, the architect I have mentioned, has pointed out that the city has a number of very narrow buildings. He traced this peculiarity back to the days when wooden spars from wrecks were used as main beams in new buildings. A spar twenty-seven feet long would span a roof or floor; and so many a frontage was determined. Port Elizabeth owes its deep, narrow buildings to the gales in Algoa Bay.

*

Port Elizabeth once watched the daily movements of the most remarkable train in the country. It was not a train to boast about, for it carried the refuse of the town; a train of trucks loaded with eighty tons of household rubbish. People called it the Driftsands Special. It ran for the first time towards the end of last century and completed its unromantic task during the first two decades of this century.

Drifting sand menaced Port Elizabeth in the 1870s. First it was deposited on the beach and blown inland; then it seeped back into the bay at the wrong spot and threatened the harbour. The dune area, with sandhills thirty feet high, was known as the Downs and became a landmark for ships in Algoa Bay. Reclamation started almost a century ago; convicts planted Port Jackson willows but the sand still appeared to be gaining. People spoke nervously of Port Elizabeth being engulfed by sand. So a railway line was built into the heart of the sandy desert and the Driftsands Special whistled off for the first time. Convicts spread the refuse over the dunes. Self-sown tomatoes, pumpkins and acacias grew out of the sand. Stable sweepings yielded unexpected crops of oat hay. But still a yellow cloud of sand arose in a strong breeze and fell on the decks of ships miles away at sea. Only after years of constant work was the desert transformed into the pleasant Humewood resort of today. And only a few railway lovers mourned the passing of the Driftsands Special. Mr E.P. Dimbleby, the Port Elizabeth editor, once told me that the sight he always gazed upon in wonder mixed with horror was the fantastic horde of flies which hovered over the train and accompanied it to its destination. One fly does not make very much noise, but those millions of flies buzzing in unison almost rivalled the engine-driver's whistle.

A more fragrant train is the Apple Express which brings the apple harvest into Port Elizabeth from stations as far away as Avontuur. Early this century it set out as the Walmer Coffee Pot; but those locomotives have gone. It might also be known as the Orange and Pear Train, for the Langkloof orchards fill the trucks with these fruits. And there are times when the aroma of tobacco is wafted through the countryside from the Apple Express. It is a narrow-gauge railway, two feet six inches wide, built at one-third the cost of South African standard gauge. Railway lovers flock to a miniature railway, but during the fruit season they have to make way for more profitable cargoes bound for the harbour.

HARBOURS OF MEMORY

Treasure Trove

There's something about the idea of buried treasure which stirs the heart of the most conservative stay-at-home.

And when you read Green's stories of "sunken wrecks and buried hoards", of Kruger gold and missing diamonds, you might even be tempted to rush off with a shovel and start digging.

For if he is to be believed – and why not? – Southern Africa is littered with troves left behind by soldiers of war and of fortune.

When, in 1962, he wrote of rare coins, the ordinary little tickey (the threepenny bit) was a familiar coin to everyone. Now it sounds as exotic to the ear as the doubloon or the sovereign.

And could there be, somewhere buried deep in the earth, or lying near the surface waiting to be found, the other half of the fabulous Cullinan diamond?

The Seitz Diamonds

1940

Oom Chris Botha, cousin of the famous South African statesman, first put me on the track of the Seitz treasure legend. I have been gathering the threads for a long time. Now I have it all – one of the most remarkable authentic diamond yarns ever whispered about in Africa.

Well past seventy, Oom Chris Botha has few grey hairs in his beard. He resembles the late General Louis Botha strongly; and though his career has been less distinguished, it has not lacked adventure. We were travelling towards a remote goldfield in South West Africa, and sleeping on the veld at night, when Oom Chris asked me whether I had ever heard of the diamonds hidden by the Germans in that territory during the Great War.

Oom Chris, of course, has not missed one of the wars of his time. When the invasion of German South West Africa by Union troops was planned in 1914, he was granted field rank and led the way through the coastal desert. It was a country he had known ever since 1889, when he had gone elephant hunting with the explorer Chapman. But even Oom Chris could not tell me the full story of the diamonds worth five hundred thousand pounds, that came at last, after weird wanderings, into the hands of the Union government. Others have filled in the gaps, however, and the tale can be told.

After the surrender of South West Africa, Major J.G.W. Leipoldt, D.S.O., chief intelligence officer of the Union general staff, was sitting in his office in Windhoek in August 1915 engaged in a fascinating task. He had been instructed to find out whether the German military authorities had handed over all their arms and equipment. Many partially destroyed letters and documents had been collected in the abandoned offices of Windhoek, and Major Leipoldt, with the patience of the true detective, was piecing the fragments together.

One document absorbed all his attention. It had been found in the German military paymaster's wastepaper basket, and it proved to be a travelling and subsistence claim for one sergeant and six men, forming a diamond escort from Luderitzbucht to Windhoek. The date was after the declaration of war.

Major Leipoldt had previously suspected the presence of a large hoard of diamonds. The German governor, Dr Seitz, and treasury officials had declared that working on the Luderitzbucht coast diamondfields had ceased when war broke out; and that the whole output of about fifty-eight thousand carats had been shipped away to South America in the steamer *Gertrude Woermann*. Major Leipoldt, however, had reason to believe that the Germans had carried out a feverish recovery of diamonds after the declaration of war for a special purpose – as emergency cover for an issue of paper marks. He passed on his theory, but his superiors lacked imagination. "There is no possibility of any diamonds being in the country – attend to your duties and do not waste time on diamonds," came the order to Major Leipoldt.

But the Major knew that the paper currency of a defeated colonial government would not be accepted by German banks and other cautious people without security. The Seitz notes, as they were called, aroused his suspicion whenever he saw them. And here at last was a clue.

Major Leipoldt, ignoring the official snub, made further inquiries into diamonds. It soon became clear to him that great secrecy had been observed in collecting the "parcel", and that even the high German military officers knew nothing of the fate of the diamonds. He might, of course, have gone direct to Dr Seitz and accused him of concealing property which should have been handed over under the peace treaty. But his hands were tied by his orders. General Smuts himself had written to him, in reply to a private note, advising him to leave diamonds alone.

Fragments of code telegrams came into Major Leipoldt's possession. They revealed that the governor and his finance minister had both mentioned diamonds in messages sent to the magistrate of

Luderitzbucht on the outbreak of war. The magistrate, however, would know nothing of the hoard after it had passed out of his hands.

Next in the chain of evidence came a queer and grim report from a native informer. The intelligence department employed a number of natives to send word of people hiding or burying things. The report stated that a few nights before the surrender, convicts had dug a grave in the Grootfontein cemetery. When the work was finished, the Germans had shot the convicts. (This appears to have been correct. The German attitude towards the natives in South West Africa never showed respect for human life.)

Grootfontein is a pleasant subtropical farming settlement in the north of the territory. Dr Seitz and other civilian officials went there after Windhoek had been abandoned; and Major Leipoldt remembered this fact when he considered the cemetery story.

About this time Major Leipoldt was mixing with the many German civilians who had been allowed to remain in the comfortable Windhoek hotels, and he was spending his own money entertaining them in the hope of securing further clues. Very soon it will be seen that he had reason to regret this diplomatic hospitality.

Major Leipoldt decided to investigate the story of the grave. He and another officer visited the cemetery at night with the native informer. There was no coffin in the grave; but they found signs suggesting that a small box had been buried and later removed.

Another native informer led them towards the first really important discovery. This man declared that convicts had been digging at night in an apple orchard on the Tigerquelle government experimental farm outside Grootfontein. More murders had been committed. Major Leipoldt confined himself tenaciously to the diamonds. He inspected the orchard, found a withering apple tree where the ground appeared to have been disturbed, and dug. Eight feet from the surface two boxes were exposed. Here at last was a promise of success.

The first box contained silver plate, engraved with the Hohenzollern arms, and intended for the banquets in Windhoek arranged in honour of the visit of the crown prince. In the second box were the personal papers and decorations of Dr Seitz – and something more, an inventory book. This book gave full details of the diamonds from

Luderitzbucht as they were packed in Windhoek. There was also a letter to a German sergeant, a man described as "a hard-boiled Prussian non-commissioned officer with a high sense of duty and a slavish respect for nobility and his officers". As this was the man responsible for burying the diamonds and shooting the convicts, he will remain nameless.

Major Leipoldt made inquiries about the sergeant, and also about a high German official. He was informed that just after the surrender the sergeant had trekked out to the east of Grootfontein, where the Kalahari wilderness begins. He had been accompanied by one native, and he had taken two pack mules. The sergeant had returned after three days, and it came as no surprise to Major Leipoldt to learn that the sergeant had returned alone.

The high German official was found to have made a number of suspicious journeys between Grootfontein and Windhoek. He was searched on the train, and it was proved that he had contravened the martial law regulations by carrying a number of uncensored letters. Among them were letters from the ex-governor, Dr Seitz, who thus became liable to prosecution.

The night after the official's arrest Major Leipoldt was entertaining some German women at one of the hotels in an attempt to gather further information. He had to have his stomach pumped out after the party, and the medical officers diagnosed digitalis poisoning. This unpleasant interlude prevented him from taking part in certain further stages of the search, though he was in time for the finish.

By this time, of course, no one was sneering at the diamond legend. At a meeting of high Union officials it was decided that Dr Seitz should be brought before a court of inquiry. There was one legal difficulty. The diamonds had been the property of the producing companies, and it was not known whether the German government had commandeered them, or whether it had merely taken charge of them in the capacity of a trustee. Under the Treaty of Khorab, when the Germans surrendered, all government property had to be disclosed. It was thought that Governor Seitz might cover himself by stating that the hidden diamonds were the property of the Regie, the diamond control organisation.

It was a delicate situation, for the Union officials were still without knowledge of where the diamonds were hidden, and they could not use the Prussian methods of the period to extract that information.

Major Leipoldt suggested making contact with the wild Bushmen of the area where the sergeant had taken the diamonds to their final hiding place. He pointed out that the unseen Bushmen watched every white traveller in that territory, and that even if they had not witnessed the digging they would be able to follow the sergeant's tracks to the spot.

The high official was approached with guile, and it was pointed out to him that Dr Seitz would not care to face a charge of smuggling letters. All this unpleasantness would be avoided if the diamonds were revealed. The official gave nothing away, but he agreed to discuss the matter with Dr Seitz.

These manoeuvres failed. A party of military officers (including Major Leipoldt) and civilian officials then interviewed Governor Seitz at Grootfontein to bring matters to a head.

His Excellency treated them to a memorable display of temper. (Drawing a tooth is simple in comparison with relieving a German governor of diamonds worth half a million.) Dr Seitz declared, in a sense truthfully, that he did not know where the diamonds had gone. He was informed that proof had been secured that the diamonds had been in his possession in Windhoek. General Berrange, the senior military officer present, ordered a search of the personal belongings of Dr and Madame Seitz. This revealed nothing more striking than bags containing about one thousand eight hundred pounds in gold sovereigns in one of Madame Seitz's trunks. The money was returned, but Dr Seitz was still an angry man when the party went back empty-handed to Windhoek.

It was decided that Dr Seitz should be brought to Windhoek, when General Beves, the military governor, would make a final demand. Dr Seitz duly appeared and, bluffing to the last, refused to hand over the diamonds.

"Well, Your Excellency, you refuse, and in so doing you fail to comply with the Treaty of Khorab," pointed out General Beves. "The peace treaty is therefore now at an end, and we are going to impose a levy on the country to meet the cost of administration."

Dr Seitz asked for time to consult his legal advisers, and the party dispersed for lunch. The Union section enjoyed their lunch, with the exception of Major Leipoldt, still suffering from the effects of digitalis. After lunch Dr Seitz gave in. He named two Germans who were to be escorted to the hiding place of the diamonds.

And now the tale is taken up by Lieutenant Collingwood Selby of the South African Mounted Rifles, stationed at Grootfontein, now living in retirement in Cape Town.

"You are to proceed with escort consisting of two N.C.O.s and ten men to Otjituo," his orders read. "Three Germans will travel with you and will be under your charge. You and your escort will be present while they are digging for certain articles which are supposed to be buried there. You will not take the parcels over, but will allow the Germans to keep them. Your duties are to prevent the three Germans running away and also to prevent them being robbed."

Selby and his men trekked with the Germans for sixty miles into desert country, covering the distance on horseback, accompanied by a cart, between daybreak and five in the afternoon. The spot indicated by the Germans was a few miles from Otjituo, the last police outpost in the territory, on the way to the Okavango River. Selby suggested waiting until the next day before starting digging; but the Germans were anxious to finish their disagreeable task. So after a few hours' rest they all went to an antbear hole pointed out by one of the Germans – the only man in the party who knew the exact spot. In the moonlight Selby watched them dig out a soldier's tin kit box. It was padlocked.

The box, with locks untouched, was taken by cart to Otjituo police camp. There the whole party spent the night, Selby and the Germans sharing one room, with a guard outside the door. During the trek back to Grootfontein next day several diamonds were found on the floor of the cart. A corner of the tin box had rusted through, and more diamonds could be seen through the crack. Selby then gave the Germans a blanket to lash round the box, and the journey ended without further incident.

Narrating his part in the affair twenty-three years afterwards, Selby seemed little moved by the drama. "It was my own camel-hair blanket," he remarked, "and I never received it back."

Box and blanket went by train to Windhoek. A gathering of Union and German officials, half-eager, half-despondent, gathered to witness the formal opening of the box in the Raadsaal of the government buildings on the hill. It was regarded as an historic occasion.

Dr Seitz had brought with him, as diamond expert, a Dr E. Reuning of the Deutsche Koloniale Gesellschaft. (This was one of the geologists who, twelve years later, helped to uncover the diamond wealth of Alexander Bay at the Orange River mouth.) The rusty box was broken open. It was found that ants had entered through the hole in the corner and carried red soil with them.

Before the burial of the box there had been a number of separate bags, each one containing the output of a company. The white ants had eaten the canvas bags and it was impossible to distinguish one parcel from another. One stone, however, stood out among the rough white crystals from the Namib. This was the Ariams diamond, a magnificent lemon-tinted specimen of forty carats, valued by Dr Reuning at five thousand pounds. This had been found in an inland district and had been the property of the German government. Altogether the stones weighed seventy-five thousand carats. They were sent down to Cape Town and sold for five hundred thousand pounds after the war. Dr Seitz maintained to the last that he had committed no breach of the local peace treaty as the diamonds (apart from the Ariams stone) were not German government property.

Some time afterwards it was learnt that Dr Seitz was acting in accordance with a plan made soon after the Agadir incident in 1910. Secret instructions were sent from Berlin to Windhoek detailing the procedure to be followed in the event of war. The diamond companies at Luderitzbucht, instead of handing their outputs over to the Regie, were ordered to entrust them to the magistrate. This was done, as related, but German attention to detail broke down during the hurried evacuation of Windhoek, and the telltale evidence reached Major Leipoldt's desk. A less determined officer, discouraged and left to work in defiance of orders, would certainly have allowed this prize to slip away. When Dr Seitz was repatriated he would probably have carried the little tin box with him to the Fatherland as a small but valuable fragment saved from the wreckage of war.

What actually happened was that the Union government, after

the sale of the diamonds, applied the former German taxation formula, taking about two hundred and fifty thousand pounds and handing the other half of the proceeds back to the diamond companies.

Such a haul naturally aroused thoughts of personal rewards in the minds of several men who had taken part in the long and difficult treasure hunt. Major Leipoldt himself made no move until he was informed that a select committee of the Union house of assembly was to investigate the claim of a former secret agent, a German employed by the Union authorities, to a reward for services leading to the recovery of the Seitz diamonds. This naturally led Major Leipoldt to put forward a claim on his own behalf, and further claims on behalf of one assistant and the widow of another. The secret agent failed dismally in his attempt. The Leipoldt claims were dismissed, mainly on the ground that the officers concerned had secured the information in the ordinary course of duty. The verdict has a familiar official ring about it, but it did nothing to soothe the memory of the digitalis poisoning. And Selby, who made no claim, has lost for ever his camel-hair blanket.

Yet there is still a possibility that the dogged Major Leipoldt will find treasure. He is now government land surveyor in Springbok, Namaqualand. He has in his possession a secret German dossier marked Lobengula – another relic of his work as chief intelligence officer in Windhoek. The authorities would have laughed at that, too, as they laughed at the fantastic diamond yarn. So Major Leipoldt seeks the Lobengula treasure alone – the gold and diamonds and ivory that, as every Rhodesian pioneer knows full well, were carried away by a trusted impi after the burning of Bulawayo.

Every year, when his leave falls due, Major Leipoldt studies his clues to the Lobengula millions. He has made five long journeys to Angola in search of this wealth.

It is hard, perhaps, to place much faith in legends of buried treasure. "These charts – I think the fairies have the making of them, for they bewitch sober men," said Raleigh. But I know enough of Major Leipoldt's quest to make me wonder whether I shall not have the privilege one day of recording another piece of work as brilliant and as successful as the discovery of the Seitz diamonds.

OLD AFRICA UNTAMED

Money, Money, Money
1962

Coins from sunken wrecks and buried hoards were sometimes brought to the newspaper office where I worked, the owners acting on the principle that journalists know everything. As a young reporter I took these coins to a white-haired expert, a sub-editor of the conscientious old school named Arthur Rogers. You will find the A.S. Rogers collection of coins in the Africana Museum, Johannesburg. He loved the Kruger coins.

Rogers, like other collectors all over the world, regarded the old Transvaal Republican issues as the most interesting coins ever minted. He had some of the tokens used as small change last century; the unofficial copper and brass pieces put into circulation by different firms and the silver which the Reverend John Campbell ordered for the Griquas. But all these were mere tokens. South Africa had no real money of its own until the Transvaal Republic began issuing coins. These are the coins which appear in so many treasure tales. Kruger gold still comes to light unexpectedly. Here is the money that has created the legends.

First you should realise that English silver money coined from 1816 was legal tender in South Africa for more than a century. Arthur Rogers showed me coins bearing the portraits of British monarchs from George III onwards; coins which had circulated from the Cape to the Limpopo; the very coins used by the Voortrekkers on those occasions when the barter system broke down.

President Burgers started the coinage of the Transvaal, and with the money there arose certain mysteries that have not all been solved to this day. (Perhaps that explains the fascination the Transvaal coins hold for collectors.) Burgers sent three hundred ounces of gold from the pioneer goldfield at Pilgrim's Rest to a Birmingham firm in 1874, and eight hundred and thirty-seven *ponde* were minted. Each pound cost twenty-six shillings to produce. They caused a storm in the Volksraad, for there were some who thought that it was wrong to reproduce the "graven image" of the president (who was a clergyman) on a golden coin.

No more Burgers pounds were minted. Collectors have noted two varieties, one in which the president was depicted with a coarse beard and another, from different dies, with a finely-pointed beard. The coarse version, in mint condition, has fetched a hundred pounds at sales in recent years, while seventy-five pounds is a fair price for the fine beard.

So here is treasure if you can find it. Pounds of the Burgers and Kruger periods are not likely to be found in lofts and wagon chests nowadays, though some must lie undiscovered where they were hidden long ago. I must warn you, however, that any coin which has been mutilated for use as a watch chain ornament or brooch has lost much of its value. Some such coins have been cleverly restored, but dealers know how to detect a "plugged" hole. Beware of all "pierced" or "clawed" coins.

Specimens have been found of other Burgers coins in various metals, but these are not listed in catalogues and their origin is mysterious. Professor E.H.D. Arndt has suggested that they may have been minted as samples by an enterprising German firm which was anxious to secure a contract.

Kruger coins, including the gold, circulated freely in South Africa up to the 1920s. Sovereigns and half-sovereigns vanished during the gold standard crisis, but the silver coins only began disappearing about halfway through the 1930s. Arthur Rogers always admired the fine condition of the Kruger crowns, half-crowns, florins, shillings, sixpences and tickeys. He said that most of these coins had been hoarded during the first three decades of the century by people who expected them to rise in value. Then they had given up hope and put them back into circulation. If they had held on, they would have seen the rise. Some of the bronze pennies minted in President Kruger's day are now worth about thirteen hundred times their original value.

First of the Kruger coins were those minted in Berlin and ranging from the golden pound to the bronze penny. Once again there was an outcry when the coins arrived, for keen observers noticed the famous wagon error. The designer had engraved a continental type of wagon with two shafts instead of the traditional "ship of the veld" with a single shaft. The wheels, too, were wrongly drawn. So the coins were hurriedly withdrawn. Some went into the melting pot, but most of them were carefully preserved by far-sighted people who knew that errors in coins and postage stamps usually mean higher prices.

Among the rarest of the Kruger coins is the overstamped 1898 pound. The normal 1898 appears below the Arms of the Republic, and on the other side, below the bust of President Kruger, you will discern the figures 99. This was done because the 1899 dies had not arrived from Berlin, and the mint authorities wished to record their activities during the year 1899 on their coins. Only one hundred and thirty of the overstamped pounds were struck, and they are now extremely valuable. Clever forgeries have been noted. A genuine 99 in perfect condition has realised two hundred pounds at auction, but only about a quarter of that amount would be secured for a worn specimen.

Another great Kruger rarity, which is also something of a mystery, is the celebrated Sammy Marks gold tickey of 1898. Collectors look upon these as patterns rather than as coins, for they were never intended to be put into circulation.

As you know, Sammy Marks was the genial Jewish mining magnate and industrialist who became friendly with President Kruger and often advised him on money matters. According to legend, Sammy Marks was given the use of the Pretoria mint for one day as a reward for his services; and it was then that the golden tickeys saw the light. This is most unlikely. On the other hand it is clear that Kruger allowed Marks to satisfy a curious whim, and that the tickeys were minted in 1898 at his request.

No one knows why Sammy Marks selected the humble threepenny die for his purpose, stipulating that the coins should be struck in gold instead of silver. They were otherwise identical with the ordinary tickeys, and two hundred and fifteen of them were produced. Some say that Sammy Marks wanted to give his wife a necklace of these coins. Another version brings up the gorgeous picture of a huge Johannesburg dinner party at which each guest would receive a golden tickey as a souvenir. All I can say with certainty is that forty grains of gold went into each coin, the value in those days being six shillings and sixpence.

It is possible that Sammy Marks had seen and admired the single gold threepenny bit minted in Pretoria in 1894, and had decided to have some of his own. The golden tickey of 1894 is a complete mystery. Only the one solitary example (now in the Pretoria mint museum) is known. Catalogues list it with the peculiar sign reserved for coins which are so rare that their values cannot be estimated. Possibly it was to have been presented to some distinguished visitor who never arrived.

Sammy Marks tickeys, of course, possess a definite value. They have been rising steadily ever since they were struck, and at an auction sale in 1960 a good specimen fetched two hundred and fifty pounds.

June 1900, and Lord Roberts was closing in on Pretoria. The mint shut down, and most of the gold went off with General Smuts on the last train.

Besides the minted coins, the gold included a number of circular blanks, some just plain discs, others with raised rims. They had been carted hurriedly away before the final process which would have given them President Kruger's profile and the republican coat-of-arms. These became known as *kaal ponde* – naked pounds.

Nobody knows how many *kaal ponde* were put into circulation, but they were used to pay the men in the field. They are listed at six pounds ten shillings to seventeen pounds apiece, according to condition. As they had no milled edges and no designs, forgers had a happy time producing good imitations. Nevertheless, the experts have ways of identifying the real thing.

Please do not confuse the *kaal pond* with the *veld pond*. In the *veld pond* you have a fine example of wartime ingenuity. This is a greater rarity than the *kaal pond,* a handsome gold coin with a story.

It was in September 1901 that General Ben Viljoen set up his headquarters at Pilgrim's Rest, a relatively peaceful area. Whole families, refugees from wartorn districts, settled there and lived fairly normal lives until the end of the war. General Viljoen's fighting men included the Lydenburg commando.

Such a community needed money. The authorities had some bar gold from the mint. They scraped the plates on a number of small gold mines in the district, and planned a currency. At first it was thought that small squares of gold would suffice. However, the natives who were supplying food wanted something more like a sovereign. Mr P.J. Kloppers, a school teacher from Holland who had been serving on commando for three years, offered to design and mint a proper coin.

Kloppers was given the title of chief of the *Staatsmunt te Velde*. He made dies and engraving pencils, improvised the machinery, and turned out nearly one thousand coins which came to be known as *veld ponde*.

Each *veld pond* had the Z.A.R. monogram on the obverse with the date 1902, and the value *Een Pond* on the reverse. They had milled edges. Altogether a remarkable effort in view of the fact that the mint was nothing but a hand punching machine worked on the screw and press principle.

Kloppers used twenty-four carat gold, which was soft and easy to work, and made his coins a shade larger than the standard golden pound. They were worth twenty-two shillings apiece from the start, and Dr Alec Kaplan's 1950 catalogue fixed a top price of forty pounds apiece. Of course many of them disappeared, while others were largely ruined when they were pierced.

Forgeries of the *veld pond* are common, but these are easily detected. The first forgeries appeared before the end of the South African War, and they form a mystery which has never been solved. Lord Kitchener issued proclamations on the subject, and Lord Milner specified penalties. If the forger was known, he was certainly never brought to trial.

Kruger coins, I may say, still rank as legal tender in South Africa. Your chances of finding a Sammy Marks tickey or a *veld pond* in your change, however, are hardly as bright as the Transvaal gold from which they were minted.

SOMETHING RICH AND STRANGE

A Last Glance at the Kruger Millions

1962

For sixty years, South Africa has been divided over the Kruger millions. Some believe firmly that a vast sum of money is still lying there in the Transvaal lowveld where it was hidden so that it would not fall into the hands of the British invaders. Others say there were never any millions to hide. I think the truth may be found between the two extreme views.

You may wonder why I am telling once more a story that has found a place in dozens of South African books and innumerable magazine and newspaper articles. First of all, because my interest in this great Transvaal legend was aroused when I discussed it with men who were present during the drama. Secondly, because a South African treasure survey without the Kruger millions would be like a picture of Cape Town without Table Mountain. And finally, because many writers have presented episodes in the classic mystery, but no one has tried to give the whole story.

Let me say at once that if this treasure is ever found and revealed, it will not run into millions. And let me add that I am sure there are still small fortunes in gold buried between Pretoria and the Portuguese frontier. Men were murdered, men were hanged, as a result of quests for the treasure. I do not think the mere rumour of gold is enough to cause murder. Those men must have touched the money before the triggers were pulled.

Mr James Gray, a former editor of the *Pretoria News* and a most conscientious historian, once went to great trouble working out President Kruger's financial resources. He found that at the outbreak of the South African War, the Transvaal treasury held only sixty thousand pounds. However, the government commandeered gold worth four hundred and sixty-two thousand, eight hundred and fifty-three pounds one week before war was declared. This was the output of the Rand mines which was just about to be put on board the mail train at Johannesburg for Cape Town and shipment overseas.

All the mines closed down soon after war broke out, but the government insisted on the work going on. In this way, President Kruger had millions at his disposal; nearly three millions in fact.

Figures compiled by the Transvaal Chamber of Mines show that from November 1899 to May 1900, the mines yielded one million, nine hundred and twenty-nine thousand, eight hundred and seventy-five pounds. There was an official raid on the banks and the mine safes, and this produced three hundred and four thousand, four hundred and forty-four pounds in gold. All those sources give a total of two million, seven hundred and fifty-seven thousand, one hundred and seventy-three pounds.

What a treasure to bury in an antbear hole! However, the Transvaal authorities had to pay for the war. Incredible though it may seem, the cost in the early stages was only eighty thousand pounds a month; then it doubled.

According to Gray, there was still one million, four hundred and twenty-five thousand, five hundred and ninety-three pounds in President Kruger's coffers when Pretoria was abandoned. About six hundred thousand pounds was sent to Europe in the form of bar gold for the purchase of munitions. President Steyn and other Boer leaders received three hundred and fifty thousand pounds in notes and coin for their needs in the field. Sundry creditors were paid one hundred and ninety-four thousand pounds and President Kruger and his party took about one hundred and fifty thousand pounds to Europe with them for propaganda and other purposes.

So now the millions have dwindled. But you will notice that large amounts were distributed, and that many people in all sorts of emergencies may have buried money of their own, or money which had been entrusted to them, or money they had stolen. In fact, we know they did so. Hoards of various sizes have been discovered at intervals ever since the war ended, and these caches of Kruger pounds are still being found.

Is there a hoard greater than all these previous hidden treasures?

One consignment, part of which may have gone astray, was the five hundred thousand pounds in gold bars sent by Dr F.E.T. Krause (then military governor of Johannesburg) to President Kruger at Machadodorp at the end of May 1900. This treasure was entrusted to the *veld politie*.

It reached Machadodorp all right, and several republican officials remembered seeing the gold there, packed in paraffin boxes like bars of soap. Everyone knew what the boxes contained. I have seen a statement by one official reading as follows: "It would have been easy to have helped myself to some of the boxes, and so to have covered myself for life."

There has always been a suspicion that some of this bar gold was hidden. Mr J.A. Stubbs, a detective inspector in the old Transvaal railway police, cross-examined many of those who were at Machadodorp during President Kruger's last day there. He summed up: "I am satisfied that the story of the Kruger millions is a myth. But the fact remains that in tales of buried riches there is invariably a substratum of fact, though frequently distorted."

Colonel Deneys Reitz suggested that certain railway trucks with armed guards were responsible for the origin of the treasure legend. They were unloaded at night and cases were taken away into various parts of the bushveld. "Like everyone else, I was sure that a hoard of gold was being buried secretly," recalled Colonel Reitz. "Long afterwards I asked General Louis Botha what was in the boxes, and he told me. It was ammunition."

However, the fact that small fortunes went astray was confirmed by Colonel Reitz. He knew an Irishman named Jack Hindon who found sixty thousand pounds in the van of a wrecked train. Hindon, an honest burgher, put the money on pack horses and set off with two other men to hand it over to his commandant. They rode through the night, and before dawn the other men disappeared. Hindon followed the spoor in daylight. It led him towards Lydenburg, and before long he found the body of one of the dishonest guards. He never caught the other man, and the money vanished with him.

Colonel Reitz also knew of a treasure of one hundred and twenty ounces of bar gold hidden near Hectorspruit in 1902, and several tins of gold pounds buried in the same neighbourhood. Several expeditions have searched for these treasures. Trees have been found bearing the patterns of nails which seem to have been the favourite marks of men who buried Kruger gold. Whether the gold is still there I cannot say.

*

I have not yet mentioned specifically the Kruger gold that left Pretoria just before the British forces reached the capital in June 1900. There is still an element of mystery about this hasty removal of about seven hundred and fifty thousand pounds. Mr Ernst Meyer told me the story.

It was on a farm in the Gobabis district of South West Africa that I met Mr Meyer, thirty-six years after the episode which he described to me. Ernst Meyer and his brother Alfred, born in Switzerland, were clerks in the mint in Pretoria during the South African War. Their chief was another Swiss named Jules Perrin, who had a jeweller's shop in the town.

Ernst Meyer told me that the work in the mint went on up to the last moment, as though they were living in normal times. He could not understand it then, and he had always been puzzled by the delay in getting the gold out of the threatened capital. Meyer, a staunch republican, knew that the gold would be badly needed for the conduct of the war. Yet the British were almost at the gates and nothing was being done about it.

In the end Ernst Meyer rode off on his bicycle in search of General Smuts, found him at breakfast in his Sunnyside home, and told him that a large amount of gold was in danger. Smuts was taken by surprise. He thought the gold had left Pretoria long before that morning.

Smuts acted immediately, for he knew that the British flying columns were reaching out towards the Pretoria-Delagoa Bay railway line. A special train was ordered, consisting of engine, one closed truck and a passenger coach. This was the last train operated by the Transvaal Republic to leave Pretoria for Machadodorp.

Ernst Meyer and a small party of armed men travelled with the gold. British troops fired on them as they left the town, but they drove on furiously and escaped. They passed through abandoned stations, and sometimes they had to move rolling-stock out of their way before they could proceed. But on arrival at Machadodorp, the tired and hungry Meyer had the satisfaction of informing President Kruger that the gold was safe.

President Kruger made it clear that he had given orders about the gold long before that day. Someone had blundered, and the mystery has never been explained.

Ernst Meyer settled in Angola after the South African War, and was granted a farm in South West Africa in 1928, under the settlement scheme in which so many other exiled Afrikaners took part. The money he saved helped to prolong the resistance of the republican forces in the field. It consisted of gold bars, rolled sheets of gold, bags of smooth *veld ponde,* clippings and shavings of gold. Some of it was minted in Germany and found its way back to the Transvaal via German South West Africa.

Dr W.J. Leyds, the former State Secretary, who went into exile with President Kruger, stated emphatically: "I can positively declare that no government gold was buried either before or after the departure of President Kruger for Europe. The President would have spoken to me about it, and moreover all the circumstances were against it."

Certainly there was no official policy which resulted in the burial of gold. But that individuals hid various sums after the gold had been distributed – that is beyond doubt.

*

My next informant, one of the most accurate and valuable I have ever known, was Colonel H.F. Trew of the South African Police. He served in the war and afterwards as an officer in the South African Constabulary. It was his duty after the war to issue permits to anyone who wished to search for buried treasure.

Treasure expeditions were so common at that time that official application forms were printed. It was laid down that all treasure found must be handed over to the government, and a discoverer would receive one-third of the value. Each party had to be accompanied by a policeman.

Trew, as district commandant of Pretoria, met a great many treasure hunters, including some dubious and dangerous characters. And the most dangerous of all was Phillipus Swartz. Swartz had been a commandant in the Transvaal forces. He was a large man with a black beard, greatly feared by the natives.

The origin of the treasure that Swartz undoubtedly discovered will never be known now. According to an account which I have read, Swartz was out hunting for the pot with one companion when he came across a human skeleton and a number of leather saddlebags filled with gold bars and Kruger coins. They hid the gold, rejoined the commando and kept the secret. Swartz's companion was killed in action.

It was in May 1903 that word reached Trew that Swartz and another white man named Van Niekerk and two natives had gone into the bushveld to the east of Leydsdorp. It was reported that they were searching for the treasure in the neighbourhood of a little place called Phalaborwa, near the Selati River. And they had no permit. Moreover, Swartz had returned alone. He had visited Mrs Van Niekerk on her farm, and told her a story so unconvincing that a suspicion had arisen. Had Swartz found treasure and done away with his companions?

Corporal Bonsfield, Trooper Ferguson and two other white troopers and a Hottentot guide Andries, were sent out in search of Swartz. It seems that Mrs Van Niekerk had been aware of the object of the expedition on which her husband had disappeared. Andries had been with Swartz and Van Niekerk when they had set out to recover the treasure, but he had become frightened and had escaped.

Andries led the police from camp to camp. One day someone fired on them, but they could not find the hidden sniper. That night they heard a pack of jackals scraping up something in a donga, and Bonsfield investigated. He found a human skull, other bones and a ring bearing the initials C. v. N. These relics were brought back by the patrol.

At almost every kraal now they gathered news of Swartz, but for days he kept ahead of them. Then they heard that Swartz was delirious with malaria in a hut not far away. The arrest was easy. A wagon was sent out and the feeble Swartz was placed in Pietersburg gaol.

Some of the highest British officials at that time were convinced that President Kruger himself had ordered the burial of millions in gold to prevent it falling into British hands. Lord Milner was sure of it. Smuts wrote of the legendary millions that continued, after the war was over, "to spook in the minds of great British statesmen" as a vast fortune hidden in the veld, to be used against Britain in future campaigns.

So a number of highly-placed civilians visited Swartz in his cell and tried to extract the secret. They failed. Swartz was put on trial in Johannesburg for the murder of Van Niekerk. After a trial that lasted three days Swartz was found guilty and sentenced to death. He went to the gallows in Pretoria prison without revealing the site of the treasure.

Nevertheless, the doomed man did say a few words about the gold. While he was in Pietersburg gaol, members of the police escort gave him tobacco and an occasional glass of brandy. Swartz told one of them: "The money is ours, and no damned British government shall ever have it."

Colonel Trew placed this sidelight on record: "Before Swartz was hanged he assured the police officer in charge of the case that he had found treasure. He complained bitterly that one of his friends, whom he had sent after his arrest to dig up some of it to pay for the defence, had robbed him of most of it."

Trew added: "Many years afterwards I discussed the case with the lawyer who had first appeared for Swartz. The lawyer had asked Swartz for a substantial amount to pay counsel before the main trial. He was told to go to a certain place in Pretoria at night, and the fee would be handed over. There he was given the money in a black bag. A large number of the coins showed traces of having been buried for a long time."

Trooper Ferguson held the opinion that Swartz had moved the treasure in small amounts by pack mule towards the Portuguese border, hiding various sums in dumps along the way. He was sure that a great deal of the hidden gold remained undiscovered.

The lawyer who received the buried gold was Colonel H. Mentz, later a cabinet minister. Colonel C.F. Stallard, who became a member of the Smuts cabinet in World War II, was the barrister who defended Swartz at the trial. The judge who sentenced Swartz to death was Sir James Rose-Innes; and he declared years afterwards: "This was the most remarkable murder trial in my experience."

*

Trew accompanied one Kruger gold expedition himself. A tall man of forty-five came to his office; a man with a dead white face and jet black beard. "To me he always looked like my idea of the devil," noted Trew.

The name of the devil was Faurie. He said that while he was a prisoner of war in the Ceylon camp, a dying man had given him the position of a large treasure in bar gold and *veld ponde*. He wanted a permit to search for this fortune.

Trew asked for more details. Faurie said that his informant had been a member of the party guarding the gold. The train had been held up in Nelspruit station. That night they had stolen some of the boxes and hidden them in the bush. The spot was marked, and the dying man had drawn a map. They were to search for a small tin bath in which the sovereigns had been buried.

Faurie was unwilling to lead an ordinary policeman to the treasure, but agreed to Trew being present. Trew secured a permit, and he and Faurie left one night on the Delagoa Bay mail train. A wagon was waiting for them at Nelspruit, loaded with food, picks and spades.

The map showed three large trees forming a triangle, and the treasure was shown in an open space in the middle of the triangle. Naturally there were many such places in the bush. Faurie examined a number of them carefully, looking for marks on the trees and an iron spike driven into the earth above the bath.

Several days passed in this way. Trew had no confidence in his companion and slept each night with a loaded revolver in his blankets. Faurie complained about this habit on the ground that there might be an accident. Trew assured him that police officers did not fire their revolvers accidentally.

One morning when Trew woke up, Faurie was absent. Faurie rushed into camp a little later, however, and informed Trew that he had found the right spot, but the treasure had gone.

Trew suspected that Faurie had found the treasure and buried it elsewhere to avoid paying away any share in it. Faurie showed Trew a spot which corresponded with the treasure map. A depression in the centre had been dug up some time before their arrival; and in the grass they found a tin bath. After a great deal of digging Faurie satisfied himself that no scrap of treasure remained, and then they returned to Pretoria.

This was not the last of Faurie, however. Trew met him on two more occasions, both memorable.

Faurie called at Trew's office a few weeks after the treasure hunt and announced that he had discovered the man who had removed the treasure. He mentioned the name of a man who had acted as a British intelligence agent during the war. This man, said Faurie, had a wagon with a false bottom. He had gone into the bushveld, dug up the treasure, and had next appeared at Delagoa Bay with plenty of money to spend. Trew was impressed by the story and instructed one of his detectives to make inquiries. The trail ended at Delagoa Bay, for the man had sailed for Europe from there. The detective confirmed an important point in Faurie's story. The man had plenty of money.

Four years passed, and then came the second meeting. Trew had sent a detective named Hill out on a murder case – murder by poisoning. Faurie was the murderer. Perhaps you remember the case. It arose out of the quest for the lost half of the Cullinan diamond.

Colonel Trew remarked long afterwards: "I have often wondered what my fate would have been in that lonely bushveld camp if we had discovered the Kruger gold. Would I have been offered a glass of brandy to celebrate the event?" So the legend of the Kruger millions never dies. Thousands in gold bars and coins were taken into the Transvaal bushveld, and some of the treasure rests there still.

This legend provides a link between great names in the South Africa that is still within living memory. Great names on the one hand, and also some of the worst criminals the country has ever known. Von Veltheim, the tall German killer, returned to South Africa ten years before his death; a prohibited immigrant using the Kruger millions as an excuse. Not a year has passed since the South African War without discoveries of Kruger gold and reports of new clues to a greater hoard than any that men have yet recovered.

It is the true gleam of gold that keeps South Africa's greatest treasure mystery alive.

SOMETHING RICH AND STRANGE

They Dug Up Fortunes
1962

No, the Kruger gold does not drop into your hand any more, but Kruger gold and other coins do come to light unexpectedly in every corner of South Africa. Here are the treasures, large and small, that have been found; the historical treasures that some prefer to gold; and the queer and romantic legends that still lead us out on the road of dreams.

If you are inclined to sneer at all buried treasure tales, just consider the many official reports of mysterious hoards that have found their way into government coffers. Start with this item of revenue acknowledged in 1904 by the Transvaal auditor-general: "Balance of treasure found on a farm in the Pretoria district, ownership of which cannot be established – four thousand, three hundred and forty-nine pounds, thirteen shillings and sixpence."

In the same year a Mr S. J. Kemp (cousin of the General Kemp who became Union minister of lands) was stated to have dug up a large sum in gold near Louis Trichardt's Drift in the Northern Transvaal. I understand that this was bullion taken by mule wagon from Pretoria shortly before the British forces entered the capital; but I admit freely that I have not been able to find the chapter and verse of this interesting story.

However, I can remind you of the happy experience of two workmen who were putting down the foundations of the Union Buildings in 1911 on Meintjes Kop, Pretoria. On the site of the present west wing they found two wooden boxes containing bar gold. These honest men handed the gold over to the authorities and received half the value as a reward. This worked out at one thousand pounds each, in the days when a thousand pounds was a small fortune. And that find has been recorded officially.

Monuments have an irresistible lure for some treasure hunters. The underlying idea appears to be that a treasure buried near a permanent landmark cannot be lost. The people of Roodepoort in the Transvaal put up a memorial at Vlakfontein in 1913 to the burghers who fell during the Jameson Raid. So many treasure seekers desecrated the site with shafts and tunnels that the Historical Monuments Commission had to lay down a solid bed of cement.

Skanskop Fort, near the Voortrekker Monument at Pretoria, was one of three forts built after the Jameson Raid to defend the capital. This is another legendary treasure site.* Again and again the authorities have refused to grant permits to dig for treasure.

Graveyards attract a certain type of treasure hunter. I am not in favour of ghoulish pursuits, but I must mention the incident which you will find in the records of the Dutch Reformed Church at Kroonstad. Children were playing in the grounds soon after the South African War when they dug a number of Victorian sovereigns out of the sand. A church official then organised a proper search and brought up three thousand pounds in gold and silver. No one claimed the money. In the end it was shared by the church, the official and the children.

Possibly the largest hoard to be uncovered in recent years received wide publicity in 1949, when two natives were charged with theft at Harrismith, Orange Free State. They had called on various people in the district and elsewhere, offering to exchange gold Kruger pounds for one pound paper notes.

Evidence showed that one native had bought a motor car, two trading stores and a flour mill. Both natives were acquitted. The explanation given by one of them, that he had found the gold in a hole near a bridge, was accepted. This native was an educated man, he had written down the number of gold pounds as he had counted them. *He had found sixteen thousand pounds.* Those which had not been spent were produced in court. I believe the native was allowed to retain the gold.

Innumerable smaller hauls have been made, often by natives. A

* Klapperkop Fort, Pretoria, has a similar legend. In October 1961, an underground chamber was discovered by the caretaker. It contained ammunition of the South African War period.

cooking pot filled with Kruger gold and Victorian sovereigns was turned up by the plough on a farm in the Louis Trichardt district in 1951. It had been buried by a witchdoctor a quarter of a century earlier; and the native commissioner awarded the money to the witchdoctor's widow. She had known that the money was hidden somewhere and she gave a feast to celebrate the end of a long quest.

Then there was the Zulu who was working in a garden in the middle of Pietermaritzburg early in World War II when he dug up golden sovereigns and half sovereigns. He should have kept his mouth shut. His yell of delight attracted a crowd, and very soon two hundred people – white, Indian and native – were grovelling in the earth.

No one knows how much money was found that day. The newspapers reported that the police had recovered very little of it. When the owners of the property dug hopefully in other parts of the grounds they found nothing. Apparently the money had been there for a long time, as dates on the few coins seized by the police ranged from 1840 to 1880. This hoard may have been military pay that went astray during the South African War.

Thefts from the mines explain many chance discoveries of gold bars and amalgam (a compound of gold and mercury) in and around Johannesburg. Here again natives have been lucky. One native dug up a lump of amalgam worth one thousand, three hundred pounds in a back garden on the Rose Deep mine shortly before World War II. A schoolboy found a bar of gold under a stone on the old Geldenhuis mine site. It was worth four hundred and sixty pounds and he received one hundred and seventy-two pounds as his reward.

Nqutu, or more properly Ingqutu, means "the stunted one" in Zulu, and under the stunted Nqutu hill on the fringe of Zululand there have been many treasure hunts. Some say that a white trader buried his gold, and then the Zulus murdered him. Others declare that the Nqutu treasure is a South African War hoard, buried by the Boers when they were leaving Natal.

At all events it seems fairly certain that in 1911 an iron box full of Kruger gold was dug up by natives on the bank of the Wilge River. Apparently the magistrate heard about it and the police investigated; but the natives retreated behind a solid wall of ignorance which no white man could penetrate.

War veterans who knew about the treasure said there was more than one box. They are still searching for the other boxes.

Once a treasure has been found, some of the romance departs. If you prefer the legends to the gleam of true gold, there are legends in almost every corner of Southern Africa.

Johannesburg has a famous treasure legend – the gold bars valued in 1900 at more than a quarter of a million pounds, and buried in the grounds of the Fort when the British armies were advancing on the town.

The Fort, of course, really was a fort in those days. It was put up soon after the Jameson Raid to command the Pretoria road and East Rand approaches; and even before the stout walls arose there was a rumour that a rich gold reef had been struck by the builders. Hospital Hill became the scene of a gold rush.

No shot was ever fired from the Fort and after the South African War the place was turned into a prison. Several decades later a Mr H.A. Young gathered evidence bearing on the treasure from people who claimed to have watched the burial of the wooden boxes containing the gold bars. Several people, unknown to one another, pointed out the same site.

It was not until June 1948, however, that a syndicate obtained a permit to search the grassed ramparts and exterior gardens of the Fort for gold. The gaol superintendent was upset because he was sceptical about the treasure and feared the seekers would disturb his rose garden, one of the finest in the city. Members of the syndicate had to deposit thirty pounds with the public works department to cover possible damage.

One member of the syndicate was a woman who declared that her father had seen the treasure buried. Pilot holes were sunk without success. A spiritualist then went into a trance and indicated another site. Convicts dug up the ground, but failed to uncover the gold bars.

Pieter van Jaarsveld, who was finding water and gaining fame at that time as "the boy with the X-ray eyes", then came on the scene. He failed. Electronic devices remained unmoved. The convicts struck some rusty iron pipes and old beer bottles, and that was all.

Knowing old citizens of Johannesburg will tell you that the treasure of the Fort and a large cache of Kruger sovereigns were found and carried away secretly during World War I. A nice haul it would have been, if indeed there was something more than beer bottles under the grass and the roses.

Another treasure on the Rand with a similar story is the Witpoortje Gorge hoard near Krugersdorp. Five gold bars were buried here, according to legend, to avoid seizure by the British forces; and the Republican policeman who hid the gold cut the letters V.D.M. on a rock as a clue to the site. Many searchers have found the letters, but no living person seems to know what they mean or how to proceed.

You will have noticed how the South African War runs through many of South Africa's treasure tales. It is easy to understand people burying wealth at a time when all was in chaos and the banks were closed.

Vice-President Schalk Burger was supposed to have sent two wagonloads of gold out of Johannesburg when the British were advancing. A wheel broke, the wagons were attacked by natives, and the guards buried the gold near the fort on the Pretoria road at Buccleuch. That area has been searched again and again.

Sometimes it is British money that crops up in these tales. Hattingspruit in Natal has a koppie with a house which was once a British military headquarters. People saw bags of money going from the bank at Dundee to this house, so that the troops could be paid. One night just before pay day, the Boer forces attacked Hattingspruit and the British cleared out. Before they left, however, a native saw British officers taking the bags of money up the koppie.

The native was unable to observe the exact hiding place, and so every rock, every stone has been turned over many times since the South African War ended. Dynamite has been used without success.

One keen treasure hunter heard of the Hattingspruit treasure and dreamt that he would find it buried under a peach tree on the koppie. When he visited the koppie for the first time he found it was sprinkled generously with wild peach trees; and though he dug round many of them he had no luck.

So famous is the Hattingspruit legend that the usual clairvoyants and other mystics have been called in to show the way to the treasure. The money is said to be guarded by ghosts, so that night searches are carried out only by the boldest hunters. So far, the only money found has been Kruger silver coins discovered in old mine workings near the koppie.

Another almost identical story is told of a British army camp of five thousand men guarding the railway line between Warrenton and Mafeking. The pay, running into thousands of pounds, was placed in paraffin tins and buried. Heavy fighting occurred, and the men who buried the money were killed. An old Hottentot saw enough of the proceedings to start a legend that still sends expeditions out into the veld.

A war treasure near Potchefstroom has been tracked back to an eccentric character nicknamed "Wilde" Theunis Steyn. This long haired, bearded man and his son lived like hermits in the forest and kept a large herd of cattle in a kraal. The father was a clever cattle dealer, and had saved about five thousand pounds when he heard that Potchefstroom would soon be occupied by the British forces.

Wilde Steyn then filled several large sweet bottles with his gold Kruger pounds, wrapped them in the skin of an ox, and buried them near a thorn tree. He may have moved the hoard from time to time, as he did not even trust his son.

Steyn was captured and interned. When he was released, he returned to the woods; and it seems that he could not find the spot where he had left his money. He spent the rest of his life searching for it, sleeping in a hammock with his shotgun close at hand. Many people in Potchefstroom knew Steyn and his story, but no one can say whether the money is still there. It is possible that it was found and taken away by Steyn's son shortly after World War II, for a native who helped in the search changed a Kruger sovereign in the town not long afterwards.

Some war treasure legends ring true, others are dubious. In the Bathurst district of the Eastern Province they still discuss the Bowker treasure, which I am prepared to accept as gospel; and in the Calvinia district there is a story of a shot spy's fortune which appears to carry the stamp of truth.

Miles Bowker, leader of a group of 1820 Settlers, brought the family silver with him, and this included many valuable heirlooms. He farmed at Tharfield, in the Albany district, in the days when the settlers were constantly menaced by savage hordes.

Rain was beating on the roof of Tharfield one night in 1834 while the Bowkers were at dinner. Silver candelabras lit up the long table. Suddenly a horseman arrived and hammered at the door. "The natives are coming – thousands of natives have crossed the border," he shouted. "Make for the fort!"

Before they left the farm the Bowkers wrapped their silver in the huge tablecloth and buried it in an antbear hole below a milkwood tree. Then they drove their wagons to Bathurst and fought the invaders successfully. But years passed before they were able to return to their farm. The homestead was standing, but it had been looted. Fire had destroyed the milkwood tree.

Every generation of Bowkers has searched for the silver plate bearing the family coat-of-arms. No trace has ever been found. Mr Ivan Mitford Barberton, the sculptor, who is a member of the family, tried an electronic detector which locates metal up to a depth of eight feet. All he found were some old ploughshares.

If the Bowker silver is recovered it will go to the Albany Museum in Grahamstown, where many relics of the 1820 Settlers are preserved. But it looks as though Tharfield has its grip on that fine old silver.

The spy I have mentioned was a De Villiers, working for General Smuts during his invasion of the North West Cape. De Villiers was provided with a large amount of money, between fifteen hundred and two thousand pounds, according to legend. He buried it on a farm between Clanwilliam and Calvinia, recording details of the spot carefully in a notebook. He intended to draw on this hoard from time to time.

De Villiers was captured and shot. At first no one realised the significance of the diagram in the dead spy's notebook. In due course the book and other personal possessions were handed over to a brother of the spy. Long after the South African War had ended the brother heard the story of the money and grasped the meaning of the diagram. He went to the farm, but the owner discouraged him. It appeared that many people in the district had known of the shot spy's fortune, and it was common knowledge that the money had been found.

*

When the South African War was over you might think that farmers and others with money would have placed their faith in banks. Nevertheless, many still preferred to hide their wealth. That was the custom, a widespread custom if not a universal one.

My old friend, the late Mr J. Sauer van Pletsen, encountered many such people when he was doing legal work in the country districts. He knew old-fashioned people who kept thousands of pounds in wagon chests under their beds; and the strange thing about it was that, as far as he could remember, no one ever robbed them. Perhaps they were tougher customers than the robbers.

One day Mr van Pletsen was drawing up a will for an old couple when they opened an iron-bound chest and showed him a collection that would have driven some antique dealers frantic with greed. They had old Cape silver galore, it seemed: teaspoons and tablespoons, soup ladles, and other expensive items in silver from France and Holland. Van Pletsen estimated the value of the contents of that chest at well over one thousand pounds.

According to Van Pletsen, the hoards buried or hidden on farms were seldom lost because the farmer always told his wife where he had placed the money. At one time coffins were in great favour; the unused coffins that all lonely farmers kept in readiness, stored in the loft.

A wealthy farmer, craftier than some, decided that the ordinary coffin was too obvious. He was a large man, and he designed a huge coffin for himself. This hardwood coffin was extremely heavy; and when he had made a double-bottom and filled it with gold it became heavier still.

He told no one of the hiding place. He was killed in a riding accident, and sorrowfully the widow asked the farm labourers to bring the great coffin into the house.

Four men failed to lift it, but six men carried the coffin to the front door – six men, straining and panting. Fortunately the widow had observed the struggle. She measured the coffin, discovered the false bottom, and recovered the gold that might easily have gone to the grave with her husband.

Years ago someone discovered that coffins were ideal for keeping dried fruit in good condition. Farmers who had been using coffins as money boxes then displayed some ingenuity in finding new hiding-places for their money. Graveyards were the choice of those who argued that even a thief would not disturb a graveyard.

Van Pletsen knew an aged farmer who insisted on repairing a well at the back of the homestead. His sons wished to spare him the effort, but he insisted on going down the well in a bucket, and he stayed at the bottom for some time. After his death the widow instructed her eldest son to go down the well and bring up the leather bag he would find in a hole in the wall just above the water level. The bag, of course, contained the father's capital.

Now and again a farmer did not confide in his wife. When such a man died, and his money could not be found, it was only natural that yet another treasure legend should be born. In the Malmesbury district of the Cape there is a farm where the great-grandfather of the present owner was believed to have hidden ten thousand pounds in gold. Three generations have searched in vain for the sovereigns that would be worth so much more nowadays. Gold diviners have been called in. The farm is becoming pockmarked, like a diamond diggings, with past excavations. And not a glimmer of gold has been seen.

*

Many of the treasures I have described bear a strong family relationship, especially those hidden in time of war. Now here are a few queer episodes that stand alone.

Klerksdorp has a legend both sinister and unusual. It was there that the murderer Frederick Bailey Deeming worked as mine manager; and there, four miles outside the town, he is believed to have buried ten thousand gold sovereigns.

Deeming murdered four men in Johannesburg and escaped to England. He murdered his wife and two children in England and fled to Australia. They convicted him in Australia for the murder of his second wife, and towards the end of last century he was hanged at Swanston.

On the day of his execution, Deeming is supposed to have told the gaol superintendent of his treasure. And every year on the day of Deeming's death (so they say in Klerksdorp) his ghost appears under the tree outside the house where he lived as mine manager.

Natal offers an ivory treasure, the famous Fynn's ivory. Henry Francis Fynn was the son of a Cape Town hotel proprietor. He and other adventurers founded Port Natal, and Fynn's diary gives the earliest detailed, authentic description of life there and among the Zulus.

It was ivory that lured Fynn to Natal. He was a great trader, and Dingaan once gave him fifty beautiful tusks in return for various presents. However, there came a time when Fynn decided that he and his followers would be massacred if they remained any longer in the domains of the cruel Zulu king. He set off to the south with many wagons loaded with ivory; and when he was hard pressed he buried the great hoard of ivory on the bank of a river.

That was in 1834, and Fynn left Natal. He returned after a quarter of a century; but he could not remember the place of the ivory. Those who have studied his diary (which he kept wrapped for safety in the skin of an elephant's ear) have failed to locate the spot. Fynn's ivory seems to have vanished for ever.

*

You find historical treasure in Cape Town rather than great wealth, and some of it looks grim. I remember hearing of the pennies they collected when the prison was built in Portswood Road on the old cemetery site. They were mainly the large British pennies which became known at the Cape as *dubbeltjies* because they were worth two of the local *stuiwers*. Perhaps you remember the saying: "He would steal the pennies from a dead man's eyes". Well, that is why those pennies were found in the cemetery.

Hopes of finding treasure ran high at the Castle a few years ago when a secret vault was opened up accidentally. Workmen cleaning out a store knocked a hole in the wall and then the unsuspected room, forty feet long, was revealed. But all they found there were the remains of a feast of long ago, hand-blown wine bottles and meat bones, and an old-fashioned candle holder on a ledge.

Five hundred skulls are stored in the South African Museum, many of them dug up along the former waterfront. Indeed, drainage gangs and others who excavate the old streets must think of Cape Town as a city of skeletons. It seems that the smallpox epidemic of

1767 was responsible for mass burials. This date was fixed by the fragments of china and pottery found among the skeletons – Delft, English and Chinese blue and white.

Post office stones and other inscribed stones have come to light in recent years. Five engraved stones recording visits to Table Valley before the Van Riebeeck settlement were found in 1946 on the old General Post Office site.

More than a century ago a post office stone was found with a complete Dutch inscription, engraved by *Schipper Jacob Lodesteyn, gearriveert met schip van Amsterdam.* A date was fixed early in the seventeenth century. It was a valuable historical relic, for all the other Dutch stones were fragmentary.

But where is this stone now? It was found when the Heerengracht canal wall was demolished, and the *Cape Monitor* gave an account of it. Someone named G.T., who said that he appreciated the value of such relics, rescued it from the debris. Unfortunately it has never reached the museum.

Treasure, that scintillating word, comes from the old French *tresor* and the Latin *thesaurus.* On shore it is usually the wealth in the shape of precious metal or precious stones, which someone has hidden in a place supposed to be safe; wealth without a living owner. One old English jurist defined treasure trove as "any money or coin, gold, silver, plate or bullion found hidden in the earth or any other private place, the owner thereof being unknown."

That seems to be the crux of the matter – the absence of a claimant. The law in South Africa is clear enough. If you find anything valuable (and forgotten) on your own land you will probably be allowed to retain the lot. When someone else finds the treasure, he is required to give you half.

I have slept on treasure and (naturally enough) known nothing of it. That was in a small hotel in Keetmanshoop, South West Africa, a place built in the German colonial days very early this century. I always stayed overnight at that hotel during my journeys through the territory.

They pulled the hotel down in 1957. Under the wooden floor of a room I had often occupied, the contractor found hundreds of gold German coins. Wrapped in waxpaper, perfectly preserved, they bore dates between 1872 and 1910. Kaiser Wilhelm II and other monarchs adorned these ten mark and twenty mark pieces.

Who left them there? I can only imagine that they belonged to some German soldier who retreated from Keetmanshoop during World War I and was killed in action. But I may easily be wrong. I wish that I knew the story of those coins under the floor.

SOMETHING RICH AND STRANGE

The Cullinan Mystery

1962

Famous diamonds have a way of appearing and vanishing, only to shine again in all sorts of dramas, all too often of the tragic sort. I am thinking now of the Cullinan, the greatest diamond of all (or rather the lost half of the Cullinan), and the last words of a murderer in the Kimberley prison condemned cell.

All the great diamonds of the world seem to have carried a curse during some parts of their careers. One owner of the Hope diamond went to the guillotine, another was torn to pieces by dogs. The slave who slashed his thigh to hide a huge diamond he had stolen, known later as the Regent, was thrown to the sharks. For six hundred years the story of the Koh-i-Noor has been recorded, and there was a time when it left a trail of blood across the East.

Perhaps the Cullinan has lost its sting. The man who was bold enought to split this giant collapsed and spent three months in a sanitorium. Since then, however, the nine stones cut from this largest of all diamonds have gleamed serenely as the brightest gems in the British crown jewels.

But what of the lost half? Nearly everyone knows that the stone was found in the Premier Mine near Pretoria by Captain Fred Wells, surface manager, nearly sixty years ago. Wells had to climb a vertical face in the open mine to investigate the dazzling sparkle of a huge object reflecting the rays of the setting sun. He levered the blue-white monster out of the soil with his pocket knife and fell, almost breaking his neck in the excitement, with by far the largest diamond ever found.

Yet it was obviously only half the diamond, possibly less than half. One side was formed by a fracture. There was a "cleavage face", and experts declared immediately that this mighty diamond was only a part of a larger octohedral stone. Yet the part measured four inches by two by two. It weighed one pound six ounces; more than three thousand English carats. This meant that the diamond (named Cullinan after the discoverer of the mine) was three times the size of any other diamond known at that period.

Were the experts right in searching feverishly for the lost half of the Cullinan? The theory was supported by some of the leading authorities on the diamond. Among them were Dr G.A.F. Molengraaf, former state geologist in the Transvaal Republic, and Sir William Crookes, president of the Royal Society.

This is not a romantic legend, but something very close to a geological fact. The missing portion may have been stolen; or broken up unnoticed in the crushing machinery; or it may still rest in the blue clay pipe leading to unknown depths in the bowels of the earth.

In an evil moment the mine manager, McHardy, showed the Cullinan with innocent pride to one Johannes Faurie, a poor farmer living near the Premier Mine. By this time the rumour had gone round that the missing half had been stolen by a mine labourer. Faurie became obsessed with the idea of finding it.

Faurie was really a dangerous criminal, with convictions for robbery and other crimes. He spread a report in the Pretoria underworld that he was willing to pay one thousand gold sovereigns for a very large diamond. There was no immediate response, but in 1907 the offer brought him into touch with a native named Paulus, who had worked on the mine.

At this stage Faurie entered into an agreement with a Dr D.J. van Wyk, who financed the venture. Dr van Wyk, it should be mentioned, intended to return the missing half to the mine authorities and claim a substantial reward. The queer arrangement read as follows:

"We the undersigned Johannes Hendrik Hermanus Faurie and Dr Daniel Jacobus van Wyk hereby guarantee and bind ourselves, persons and property to Johannes Paulus that he will not get into any trouble, and that he will not be prosecuted by law in any way whatsoever if he secure and hand over to us certain two parcels of diamonds of which one is a special big one, the whereabouts of which is known to him, and to pay to him his share of cash as agreed by us for his services in this business, on receipt of such cash by us."

It seems that the agreement was drawn up to reassure Paulus, who feared prosecution. A meeting was arranged, and Dr van Wyk insisted on a detective being present. Detective Hill, who had been stationed at the Premier Mine, accompanied Dr van Wyk and Faurie to the meeting place on the veld near Pretoria at night.

Faurie, far from sane and crooked to the marrow, hoped to hand Paulus a bag containing metal washers, with a top layer of genuine sovereigns, in exchange for the great diamond. Paulus appears to have discovered the trick, for he fled into the darkness. The three white men never saw him again, though Detective Hill heard in 1927 that Paulus was still alive.

Hill declared that he never saw the diamond. He was some distance from the others, probably hidden. Van Wyk and Faurie caught a glimpse of something which looked like an enormous diamond. It was a momentary flash, revealed in the light of the lamp which Faurie had lit to show Paulus the sovereigns.

Faurie was now more determined than ever to carry on the search. He questioned hundreds of natives, until information came to him that the missing half was in the possession of Chief Mathibe in a tribal area near Pretoria. Faurie played a leading part in the intrigues of the tribe – always with the diamond at the back of his mind – and finally he gave the chief a glass of poisoned brandy. As the chief was dying, one of the tribesmen asked Faurie to sign his name. The crazy Faurie did so.

Detective Hill secured the evidence that sent Faurie to the gallows. Faurie's last words in the condemned cell were: "I alone know who the man is who has the other half of the great diamond. He is a man in Mathibe's tribe. If it was not for the diamond I would not be here. And now that I must die, I know where the diamond is."

Faurie was hanged, but the search for the lost half of the Cullinan went on. Several of South Africa's most experienced diamond detectives were involved in a number of episodes – Major S.R. Brink, his brother S.J.H. Brink and Captain MacIntosh.

Again and again the detectives went out at night with bags of gold to meet natives who were supposed to have the diamond. Major Brink made one appointment at Moselikatse's Nek, above

Hartbeespoort dam. He had a leather handbag filled with sovereigns, and a revolver in each trouser pocket. So dense were the trees at the spot that he took other precautions against attack. Another detective was hidden in the neighbourhood, ready to rush out if he heard a shot.

Andries Molife, the native Brink had come to meet, appeared and examined the sovereigns. Molife then pointed to a farm in the valley. "It is buried there – I will fetch it," he said.

"How big is this diamond?" inquired Brink.

Molife clenched his fist. "As big as that," he said. Then he went away. And like Paulus, he never returned.

It is difficult to explain these episodes. The native must have known that they would never have received any money unless they had something to offer. Perhaps they distrusted the police and feared arrest.

When the Jonker diamond was found in 1934, described as the world's fourth largest diamond, many people said that this pure white, flawless gem was the missing half. The diggings where the seven hundred carat Jonker stone appeared are only three miles from the Premier Mine. Experts did not agree with the theory. The missing half should be much larger than the Jonker.

Strange to say, the owners of the Premier were not altogether enthusiastic about the large diamonds which came out of that mine. No one knew what to do with the magnificent Cullinan until General Louis Botha thought of presenting it to King Edward VII. After all, how many people could afford half a million pounds sterling for one diamond?

Exquisite sky-blue diamonds also come out of the Premier, diamonds of a colour seen in no other mine. Others have a peculiar double colour, yellow and blue or brown and blue, with an oily appearance.

But the Cullinan was regarded as almost a miracle. The blue white stone of over four hundred carats, and valued at one hundred thousand pounds, which was found at the Premier in 1954, was only a midget compared with the Cullinan.

Perhaps there will be a miracle one day, when the lost half of the Cullinan is found in the mine – or in an African witch doctor's bag of tricks.   SOMETHING RICH AND STRANGE

Over the years the name of Lawrence Green has become inextricably linked with Africa, and his works are collected by bibliophiles the world over. He has preserved, for all time, a unique collection of stories of a vast and mysterious continent; stories which delight the historian as much as the lover of a good yarn.

Maureen Barnes

Lawrence Green titles published by Timmins Publishers,
P.O. Box 94, Cape Town 8000.

1933	*The Coast of Treasure*
1935	*Great African Mysteries*
1936	*Secret Africa*
1937	*The Coast of Diamonds*
1938	*Strange Africa*
1940	*Old Africa Untamed*
1945	*Where Men Still Dream*
1946	*So Few Are Free*
1947	*Tavern of the Seas*
1948	*To the River's End*
1949	*In the Land of Afternoon*
1950	*At Daybreak for the Isles*
1951	*Grow Lovely Growing Old*
1953	*Lords of the Last Frontier*
1954	*Under A Sky Like Flame*
1955	*Karoo*
1956	*There's A Secret Hid Away*
1957	*Beyond the City Lights*
1958	*S.A. Beachcomber*
1959	*These Wonders to Behold*
1960	*Eight Bells at Salamander*
1961	*Great North Road*
1962	*Something Rich and Strange*
1963	*A Decent Fellow Doesn't Work*
1964	*I Heard the Old Men Say*
1965	*Almost Forgotten Never Told*
1966	*Thunder On the Blaauwberg*
1967	*On Wings of Fire*
1968	*Full Many A Glorious Morning*
1969	*Harbours of Memory*
1970	*A Giant in Hiding*
1971	*A Taste of South Easter*
1972	*When the Journey's Over*

Grootfontein •

KAOKOVELD

SOUTH WEST
AFRICA

Rietfontein

Gobabis •

Swakopmund

Walvis Bay

KALAHARI
DESERT

Meob
Sylvia Hill

Hollam's Bird
Island

Schloss Duwisib
Maltahöhe

Mercury Island
Ichaboe Island

Keetmanshoop

Possession Island

Lüderitz

FISH RIVER
CANYON

•Ai-Ais

•Warmbad

```
0      50     100    150    200 miles
0       100        200      300 km
```

CAPE PROVINCE